The Church and Its Functions

Introductory Theology, Volume 3

By Grace Communion International

With articles written by Joseph Tkach, Paul Kroll, Michael D. Morrison, J. Michael Feazell, John Halford, and others

April 2016
Minor edits June 2018 and Sept. 2020

CONTENTS

Part 11: Church history

1. WHAT IS THE CHURCH?

The Bible says that people who have faith in Christ become part of the "church." What is the church? How is it organized? What is its purpose?

Jesus is building his church

Jesus said, "I will build my church" (Matthew 16:18). The church is important to him—he loved it so much that he gave his life for it (Ephesians 5:25). If we have the mind of Christ, we will love the church, too, and give ourselves to it.

The Greek word for "church" is *ekklesia,* which means an assembly. In Acts 19:39, 41, it is used for a large group of townspeople. But among Christians, the word *ekklesia* came to have a special meaning: all who believe in Jesus Christ.

For example, the first time that Luke uses the word, he writes, "great fear seized the whole church" (Acts 5:11). He does not have to explain what the word meant, for his readers were already familiar with it. "The church" means the disciples of Christ. It refers to people, not to a building.

Each local group of believers is a church. Paul wrote to "the church of God in Corinth" (1 Corinthians 1:2); he referred to "all the churches of Christ" (Romans 16:16) and the "church of the Laodiceans" (Colossians 4:16). But he could also use the word *church* to refer to all believers everywhere: "Christ loved the church and gave himself up for her" (Ephesians 5:25).

The church exists in several levels. At one level is the universal church, which includes everyone worldwide who accepts Jesus Christ as Lord and Savior. Local churches are a different level, including people who regularly meet together. Denominations are an intermediate level, containing groups of congregations that work more closely together because of shared history and beliefs.

Local congregations sometimes include unbelievers — family members who have not accepted Jesus as Savior, yet nevertheless meet regularly with believers. Local congregations sometimes include people who consider themselves to be Christians, but may not be. Experience shows that some of these will later acknowledge that they were not really Christians.

Why we need the church

Some people claim to believe in Jesus Christ but do not want to attend any of his churches. The New Testament shows that the normal pattern is for believers to meet together (Hebrews 10:25). Paul repeatedly exhorts Christians to do different things to "one another" (Romans 12:10; 15:7; 1 Corinthians 12:25; Galatians 5:13; Ephesians 4:32; Philippians 2:3; Colossians 3:13; 1 Thessalonians 5:13). It is difficult for people to obey these commands if they do not meet with other believers.

A local congregation can give us a sense of belonging, of being involved with other believers. It can give us some spiritual safety, so that we are not blown around by strange ideas. A congregation can give us friendship, fellowship and encouragement. It can teach us things we would never learn on our own. A congregation can help train our children, help us work together for more effective ministry and give us opportunities to serve that help us grow in ways we did not expect. In general, the value that we get out of a local congregation is in proportion to the amount of involvement we give to it.

But perhaps the most important reason for each believer to participate in a local congregation is that members need each other. God has given different abilities to different believers, and he wants us to work together "for the common good" (1 Corinthians 12:4-7). If only part of the work force shows up, it is no surprise that the congregation is not able to do as much as we would like, or to be as healthy as we would like. Unfortunately, some people find it easier to criticize than to help.

Our time, our abilities, and our resources are needed to fulfill the work and mission of the church. The commitment of mission-focused people is essential in order for the church to effectively reflect Jesus and his love to the world. Jesus said to pray for laborers (Matthew 9:38). He wants each of us to be working, not sitting on the sidelines.

Individuals who try to be Christian without the church fail to use their strengths to help the people the Bible says we should be helping. The church is a mutual-aid society, and we help each other, knowing that the day may come (and in fact is already here) that we will need to be helped.

Descriptions of the church

The church is described in several ways: the people of God, the family of God, the bride of Christ. We are a building, a temple and a body. Jesus described us as sheep, a field of grain and a vineyard. Each analogy describes a different aspect of the church.

Many of Jesus' parables of the kingdom describe the church, too. Like a mustard seed, the church started small and yet has grown large (Matthew 13:31-32). The church is like a field in which weeds are scattered among the wheat (verses 24-30). It is like a fishnet that catches bad fish as well as good (verses 47-50). The church is like a vineyard in which some people work a long time and others only a short time (Matthew 20:1-16). The church is like servants who were given money to invest for the master, and some produce more fruit than others (Matthew 25:14-30).

Jesus described himself as a shepherd, and his disciples as sheep (Matthew 26:31); his mission was to seek lost sheep (Matthew 18:11-14). He described his people as sheep that must be fed and cared for (John 21:15-17). Paul and Peter used the same analogy, saying that church leaders should be shepherds of the flock (Acts 20:28; 1 Peter 5:2).

"You are…God's building," Paul says (1 Corinthians 3:9). The foundation is Jesus Christ (verse 11), and people are the structure built on it. Peter said that we are all "living stones…being built into a spiritual house" (1 Peter 2:5). As we are built together, we "become a dwelling in which God lives by his Spirit" (Ephesians 2:22). We are the temple of God, the temple of the Holy Spirit (1 Corinthians 3:17; 6:19). Although God may be worshiped in any place, the church has worship as one of its purposes.

We are "the people of God," 1 Peter 2:10 tells us. We are what the people of Israel were supposed to be: "a chosen people, a royal priesthood, a holy nation, a people belonging to God" (verse 9; see Exodus 19:6). We belong to God, because Christ purchased us with his blood (Revelation 5:9). We are his children, and his family (Ephesians 3:15). As his people, we are given a great inheritance, and in response we are to try to please him and bring praise to his name.

Scripture also calls us the bride of Christ—a phrase that suggests his love for us, and a tremendous change within ourselves, that we might have such a close relationship with the Son of God. In some of his parables, people are invited to attend the wedding banquet, but in this analogy, we are invited to be the bride.

"Let us rejoice and be glad and give him glory! For the wedding of the

Lamb has come, and his bride has made herself ready" (Revelation 19:7). How do we become ready for this? It is a gift: "Fine linen, bright and clean, was given her to wear" (verse 8). Christ cleanses us "by the washing with water through the word" (Ephesians 5:26). He presents the church to himself, having made her radiant, spotless, holy and righteous (verse 27). He is working in us.

Working together

The picture of the church that best illustrates the way that members relate to one another is that of the body. "You are the body of Christ," Paul says, "and each one of you is a part of it" (1 Corinthians 12:27). Jesus Christ "is the head of the body, the church" (Colossians 1:18), and we are all members of the body. If we are united to Christ, we are united to one another, too, and we have responsibilities to one another.

No one can say, "I don't need you" (1 Corinthians 12:21), and no one can say, "I don't belong in the church" (verse 18). God distributes our abilities so that we work together for the common good, helping one another and being *helped* by working together. "There should be no division in the body" (verse 25). Paul frequently warned against the sin of divisiveness, even saying that a person who causes division should be put out of the church (Romans 16:17; Titus 3:10). Christ causes the church to grow "as each part does its work"— as the various members cooperate (Ephesians 4:16).

Unfortunately, the Christian world is divided into denominations that sometimes squabble with one another. The church is not yet perfect, since none of its members is perfect. Nevertheless, Christ wants the church to be united (John 17:21). This does not require a merger of organizations, but it does suggest a common purpose.

True unity can be found only as we draw closer to Christ, preach his gospel, and live as he would. The goal is to promote him, not ourselves. The existence of different denominations has a side benefit, however: Through diverse approaches, more people are reached with the message of Christ in a way they understand.

Organization

The Christian world has three basic approaches to church organization and leadership: hierarchy, democracy and representative. These are called episcopal, congregational and presbyterian. Variations exist within each type, but in general, the episcopal model means that a denominational officer has the power to set policy and ordain pastors. In the congregational model, church members choose their policies and their pastors. In a presbyterian system, power is divided between the denomination and the congregations. Elders are elected and given power to govern.

The New Testament does not require any particular church structure. It talks about overseers (bishops), elders and shepherds (pastors) as if these were different words for the same type of church leader. Peter told the elders to be shepherds and overseers (1 Peter 5:1-2). Similarly, Paul told a group of elders that they were overseers and shepherds (Acts 20:17, 28).

The Jerusalem church was led by a group of elders; the church in Philippi was led by several overseers (Acts 15:2-6; Philippians 1:1). When Paul told Titus to ordain elders, he wrote one verse about elders and then several about overseers, as if these were synonymous terms for church leaders (Titus 1:5-9). In the book of Hebrews, the leaders are simply called "leaders" (Hebrews 13:7).

Some church leaders were also called "teachers" (1 Corinthians 12:29; James 3:1). The grammar of Ephesians 4:11implies that pastors and teachers were in the same category. One of the primary functions of a church leader is teaching—one of the qualifications for leadership is that the person must be "able to teach" (1 Timothy 3:2).

One thing is consistent in this: Certain people were designated as leaders. The local churches had some organization, though the exact title didn't seem to matter much. Believers were exhorted to respect and obey these leaders (1 Thessalonians 5:12; 1 Timothy 5:17; Hebrews 13:17). If the leader commands something wrong, people should not obey, but for the most part, members are to support their leaders.

What do leaders do? They "direct the affairs of the church" (1 Timothy 5:17). They shepherd the flock, leading by example and by teaching. They watch over the church (Acts 20:28). They should not lord it over others, but serve them (1 Peter 5:2-3). They are to "prepare God's people for works of service, so that the body of Christ may be built up" (Ephesians 4:12).

How are leaders chosen? We are told in only a few cases: Paul appointed elders (Acts 14:23), implied that Timothy would choose overseers (1 Timothy 3:1-7), and authorized Titus to appoint elders (Titus 1:5). At least in these cases, there was a hierarchy. We do not find any examples of church members choosing their own elders.

Deacons

However, in Acts 6:1-6 we see members choosing some leaders to help distribute food to the needy, and the apostles then appointed them for this work. In that way the apostles could concentrate on spiritual matters, and the physical needs could also be taken care of (verse 2). This distinction between spiritual leadership and physical leadership is also seen in 1 Peter 4:11-12.

Leaders who serve in manual work are often called deacons, from the Greek word *diakoneo,* which means to serve. Although all members and leaders are to serve, some are specifically appointed for service roles. At least one woman is called a deacon (Romans 16:1). Paul gave Timothy a list of traits needed in a deacon (1 Timothy 3:8-12), but he did not specify what they did. Consequently different denominations assign them different roles, ranging from custodial work to financial management.

The important thing in leadership is not what people are called, how they are structured or how they are appointed. The important thing is the purpose of leadership: to help God's people grow in maturity so that we become more like Christ (Ephesians 4:13).

Purposes of the church

Christ has built his church, given his people gifts and leadership, and he has given us work to do. What are the purposes of the church?

A major purpose of the church is worship. God has called us that we "may declare the praises of him" who called us "out of darkness into his wonderful light" (1 Peter 2:9). God seeks people who will worship him (John 4:23), who will love him above everything else (Matthew 4:10). Everything we do, whether as individuals or as a congregation, should be for his glory (1 Corinthians 10:31). We are called to "continually offer to God a sacrifice of praise" (Hebrews 13:15). We are commanded, "Speak to one another with psalms, hymns and spiritual songs" (Ephesians 5:19). When we gather, we sing praises to God, we pray to him and we listen to his word. These are forms of worship. So is the Lord's Supper, baptism and obedience.

Teaching is another purpose of the church. It is at the heart of the Great Commission: "teaching them to obey everything I have commanded you" (Matthew 28:20). Church leaders should teach, and members should teach one another (Colossians 3:16). We should encourage one another (1 Corinthians 14:31; 1 Thessalonians 5:11; Hebrews 10:25). Small groups provide an excellent setting for this mutual ministry.

If we want to be spiritual, Paul says, we should want to "build up the church" (1 Corinthians 14:12). The goal is to edify, strengthen, encourage and comfort (verse 3). The entire meeting should "be done for the strengthening of the church" (verse 26). We are to be disciples, people who learn and apply the word of God. The early church was praised because they "devoted themselves to the apostles' teaching and to the fellowship, to the breaking of bread and to prayer" (Acts 2:42).

Ministry is a third major purpose of the church. Paul writes, "As we have opportunity, let us do good to all people, especially to those who belong to the family of believers" (Galatians 6:10). Our first duty is to our family, and then to the church and then to the world around us. The second-greatest commandment is to love our neighbors (Matthew 22:39).

This world has many physical needs, and we should not ignore them. But the greatest need is the gospel, and we should not ignore that, either. As part of our ministry to the world, the church is to preach the good news of salvation through Jesus Christ. No other organization will do this work—it is the mission of the church. Every worker is needed—some on the front lines, and some in support. Some will plant, some will nurture and some will harvest, and as we work together, Christ will cause the church to grow (Ephesians 4:16).

Michael Morrison

2. SIX FUNCTIONS OF THE CHURCH

Why do we meet together each week for worship and instruction? With a lot less bother, couldn't we worship at home, read the Bible and listen to a sermon on the radio or the internet?

In the first century, people gathered weekly to hear the Scriptures — but today we have our own copies of the Bible to read. Then why not stay at home to read the Bible on our own? It would be easier — cheaper, too. Through modern technology, everyone in the world could listen to the best preachers in the world, every week! We could have a menu of options, and listen only to the sermons that apply to us, or only to subjects we like. Wouldn't it be lovely?

Well, not really. I believe that stay-at-home Christians are missing out on many important aspects of Christianity. I hope to address these in this article, both to encourage faithful attendees to get more out of our meetings, and to encourage others to return to weekly attendance.

To understand why we gather each week, it is helpful to ask, Why did God create the church? What purposes does it have? By learning the functions of the church, we can then see how our weekly meetings serve various purposes in God's desire for his children.

God's commands are not arbitrary things just to see if we will jump when he says *jump*. No, his commands are given for our own good. When we are young Christians, we may not understand *why* he commands certain things, and we need to obey even before we know all the reasons why. We simply trust God, that he knows best, and we do what he says. A young Christian may attend church simply because that's what Christians are expected to do. A young Christian may attend simply because Hebrews 10:25 says, "Let us not give up meeting together."

So far, so good. But as we mature in the faith, we should come to a deeper understanding of *why* God tells his people to meet together.

Many commands

Let's begin exploring this subject by noting that Hebrews is not the only book that commands Christians to assemble with one another. "Love one another," Jesus tells his disciples (John 13:34). When Jesus says "one another," he is not referring to our duty to love all human beings. Rather, he is referring to the need for disciples to love other disciples — it must be a mutual love. This love is an identifying characteristic of Jesus' disciples (verse 35).

Mutual love does not express itself in accidental meetings at the grocery store and sporting events. Jesus' command assumes that his disciples are meeting with one another on a regular basis. Christians should have regular fellowship with other Christians. "Do good to all people, especially to those who belong to the family of believers," Paul wrote (Galatians 6:10). To obey this command, it is essential that we know who the family of believers is. We need to see them, and we need to see their needs.

"Serve one another," Paul wrote to the church in Galatia (Galatians 5:13). Although we should serve unbelievers in certain ways, Paul is not using this verse to tell us that. He is not commanding us to serve the world. Rather, he is commanding *mutual service among those who follow Jesus Christ.* "Carry each other's burdens, and in this way you will fulfill the law of Christ" (Galatians 6:2). But how can we carry each other's burdens unless we know what those burdens are — and how can we know unless we meet each other regularly?

"If we walk in the light…we have fellowship with one another," John wrote (1 John 1:7). John is talking about spiritual fellowship, not casual acquaintances with unbelievers. If we walk in the light, we seek out other believers with whom to have fellowship. Similarly, Paul wrote, "Accept one another" (Romans 15:7). "Be kind and compassionate to one another, forgiving each other" (Ephesians 4:32). Christians have special responsibilities *toward one another.*

Throughout the New Testament, the early Christians met with one another to worship together, to learn together, to share their lives with one another (for example, Acts 2:41-47). Everywhere Paul went, he raised up churches, rather than leaving scattered believers. They were eager to share their faith and zeal with one another. This is the biblical pattern.

But some people today complain that they don't get anything out of the sermons. That may be true, but it's not an excuse to stop attending the meetings. Such people need to change their perspective from "get" to "give." We attend worship services not just to get, but also to *give* — to give worship to God with our whole heart and to give service to other members of the congregation.

How can we serve others at church services? By teaching children, helping clean the building, singing hymns and special music, arranging chairs, greeting people, etc. We provide an atmosphere in which others can get something out of the sermons. We talk with others, and find out needs to pray about and things to do to help others during the week. If you aren't getting anything out of the sermons, then at least attend in order to give to others.

Paul wrote, "Encourage one another and build each other up" (1

Thessalonians 4:18). "Spur one another on toward love and good deeds" (Hebrews 10:24). This is the reason given in the context of the Hebrews 10:25 command for regular assemblies. We are to encourage others, to be a source of positive words, whatsoever things are true and lovely and of good report.

Consider Jesus as an example. He regularly attended synagogue and regularly heard readings of Scripture that didn't add anything to his understanding, but he went anyway, to worship. Maybe it was boring to an educated man like Paul, but he didn't let that stop him, either.

Duty and desire

People who believe that Jesus has saved them from eternal death ought to be excited about it. They enjoy getting together with others to praise their Savior. Sometimes we have bad days and don't feel like attending. But even if it is not our desire at the moment, it is still our duty. We can't go through life doing only the things we *feel* like doing — not if we follow Jesus Christ as our Lord. He did not seek to do his own will, but the Father's. Sometimes that's what it boils down to for us. When all else fails, the old saying goes, read the instructions — and the instructions tell us to attend.

But why? What is the church for? The church has many functions. To help bring out different aspects of the church's work, some Christians have used a four- or five-fold scheme. For this article, I will use six categories.

1) Worship

Our relationship with God is both private and public, and we need both. Let's begin with our public interaction with God — worship. It is possible to worship God when we are all alone, but the term *worship* usually suggests something we do in public. The English word *worship* is related to the word *worth*. We declare God's worth when we worship him.

This declaration of worth is made both privately, in our prayers, and publicly, in words and songs of praise. 1 Peter 2:9 says that we are called to declare God's praises. The implication is that this a *public* declaration. Both Old and New Testaments show God's people worshiping *together,* as a community.

The biblical model, in both Old and New Testaments, is that songs are often a part of worship. Songs express some of the emotion we have with God. Songs can express fear, faith, love, joy, confidence, awe and a wide range of other emotions we have in our relationship with God. Not everyone in the congregation has the same emotion at the same time, but we nevertheless sing together. Some members would express the same emotion in different ways, with different songs and different styles. Nevertheless, we still sing together. "Speak to one another with psalms, hymns and spiritual songs" (Ephesians 5:19). We have to meet together to do this!

Music should be an expression of unity — yet often it is a cause for disagreement. Different cultures and different age groups express praise for God in different ways. Most churches have several cultures represented. Some members want to learn new songs; some want to use old songs. It seems that God likes both. He enjoys the psalms that are thousands of years old; he also enjoys new songs. It is helpful to note that some of the old songs — the psalms — command new songs:

> Sing joyfully to the Lord, you righteous; it is fitting for the upright to praise him. Praise the Lord with the harp; make music to him on the ten-stringed lyre. Sing to him *a new song;* play skillfully, and shout for joy. (Psalm 33:1-3)

In our music, we need to consider the needs of people who may be attending our services for the first time. We need music that they will find meaningful, music that expresses joy in a way that they comprehend as joyful. If we sing only the songs that we like, it sends the message that we care about our own comfort more than we care about other people. We cannot wait until new people start attending before we start learning some contemporary-style songs. We need to learn them so we can sing them meaningfully.

Music is only one aspect of our worship services. Worship includes more than expressing emotion. Our relationship with God also involves our minds, our thought processes. Some of our interaction with God comes in the form of prayer. As a gathered people of God, we speak to God. We praise him not only in poetry and song, but also in ordinary words and normal speech. And the Scriptural example is that we pray together, as well as individually.

God is not only love, but also truth. There is an emotional component and a factual component. So we need truth in our worship services, and we find truth in the Word of God. The Bible is our ultimate authority, the basis for all that we do. Sermons must be based in that authority, and our songs should be truthful.

But truth is not some vague idea that we can discuss without emotion. God's truth affects our lives and hearts. It demands a response from us. It requires all our heart, mind, soul and strength. That is why sermons need to be relevant to life. Sermons should convey concepts that affect how we live and how we think throughout the week, in the home and on the job.

Sermons need to be true, based on Scripture. Sermons need to be practical, directed to real life. Sermons need to be emotive, calling for a heart-felt response. Our worship includes listening to God's Word, and responding to it with repentance and with joy for the salvation he gives.

We can listen to sermons at home. There are many good sermons available. But this is not the full church experience. As a form of worship, it is only partial involvement. It is missing the community aspect of worship, in which we sing praises together, in which we respond together to the Word of God, in which we exhort one another to put the truth into practice in our lives.

Some believers cannot attend services because of ill health. They are missing out — as most of them know quite well. We pray for them, and we also know that it is our duty to visit them to make mutual ministry possible for them (James 1:27). Although shut-in Christians may need to be served in physical ways, they are often able to serve others in emotional or spiritual ways. Even so, stay-at-home Christianity is an exception based on necessity. It is not what Jesus wants his able-bodied disciples to do.

2) Spiritual disciplines

Worship services are only *part* of our worship. The Word of God must enter our hearts and minds to affect what we do throughout the week. Worship can change its format, but it should never stop. Part of our worship response to God involves personal prayer and Bible study. People who are becoming more spiritually mature hunger to learn from God in his Word. They are eager to give him their requests, praise him, share their lives with him, and be aware of his constant presence in their lives.

Our dedication to God involves our heart, mind, soul and strength. Prayer and study should be our desire, but if they are not yet our desire, we need to do them anyway. This is the advice John Wesley was once given. At that time in his life, he said, he had an intellectual grasp of Christianity, but he did not *feel* faith in his heart. So he was advised: Preach faith until you have faith — and once you have it, you will certainly preach it! He knew he had a duty to preach faith, so he did his duty. And in time, God gave him what he lacked: heart-felt faith. What he had formerly done out of duty, he now did out of desire. God had given him the desire that he needed. God will do the same for us.

Prayer and study are sometimes called spiritual disciplines. "Discipline" may sound like a punishment, perhaps an unpleasant thing we have to force ourselves to do. But the real meaning of the term *discipline* is something that "disciples" us, that is, teaches us or helps us learn. Spiritual leaders throughout the ages have found that certain activities help us learn about God, love him and become more like him.

There are many practices that help us walk with God. We are familiar with prayer, study, meditation and fasting. There are other disciplines we can also learn from, such as simplicity, generosity, celebration or visiting widows. Church attendance is also a spiritual discipline, giving benefits for the individual relationship with God. We may also learn more about prayer, study and other spiritual habits by attending small groups in which we see how other Christians worship.

Real faith leads to obedience — even when that obedience is not comfortable, even when it is boring, even when it requires us to change our behavior. We worship him in spirit and in truth, at church meetings, at home, on the job and everywhere we go. The church is composed of God's people, and God's people have private worship as well as public worship. Both are necessary functions of the church.

3) Discipleship

Throughout the New Testament, we see spiritual leaders teaching others. This is part of the Christian lifestyle; it is part of the great commission. "Go and make disciples of all nations…*teaching* them to obey everything I have commanded you" (Matthew 28:19-20). Everybody must be either a learner or a teacher, and we are usually both at the same time. "Teach and admonish one another with all wisdom" (Colossians 3:16). We must be learning from one another, from other Christians. The church is an educational institution as well as a place of worship and transformation.

Paul told Timothy, "The things you have heard me say in the presence of many witnesses entrust to reliable people who will also be qualified to teach others" (2 Timothy 2:2). Every Christian should be able to teach the basics of the faith, to give an answer concerning our hope in Jesus Christ.

What about people who have already learned? They should become teachers, to pass the truth along to new generations. Teaching is often done by pastors. But Paul commands *every* Christian to teach. Small groups provide one way in which this is done. Mature Christians can teach both in word and in example. They can tell others how Christ has helped them. When their faith is weak, they can seek the encouragement of others. When their faith is strong, they can help the weak.

It is not good for a Christian to be alone. "Two are better than one, because they have a good return for their work: If one falls down, his friend can help him up. But pity the man who falls and has no one to help him up!… Though one may be overpowered, two can defend themselves. A cord of three strands is not quickly broken" (Ecclesiastes 4:9-12).

By working together, we help one another grow. Discipleship is often a mutual process, one member helping another member. But some discipleship flows more purposefully, with more direction given to it. God has appointed some people in his church for that very reason:

> It was he who gave some to be apostles, some to be prophets, some to be evangelists, and some to be pastors and teachers, to prepare God's people for works of service, so that the body of Christ may be built up until we all reach unity in the faith and in the knowledge of the Son of God and become mature, attaining to the whole measure of the fullness of Christ. (Ephesians 4:11-13)

God provides leaders who have the role of preparing others for their roles. The result is growth, maturity and unity, if we allow the process to work as God intended. Some Christian growth and learning comes from peers; some comes from people in the church who have the specific assignment of teaching and modeling the Christian life. People who isolate themselves are missing out on this aspect of the faith.

We have much to learn — and much to apply. Local congregations need to offer Bible studies, classes for new believers, training in evangelism, etc. We need to encourage lay ministry by giving permission, giving training, giving tools, giving control and getting out of the way!

4) Fellowship

The church is sometimes called a fellowship; it is a network of relationships. We all need to give and to receive fellowship. We all need to give and receive love. Fellowship means a lot more than talking to each other about sports, gossip and news. It means sharing lives, sharing emotions, bearing one another's burdens, encouraging one another and helping those who have need.

Most people put a mask on to hide their needs from others. If we are really going to help one another, we need to get close enough to one another to see behind the masks. It means that we have to let our own mask fall down a bit so others can see our needs. Small groups are a good place in which to do this. We get to know people a little better and feel a little safer with them. Often, they are strong in the area in which we are weak, and we are strong where they are weak. So by supporting one another, we both become stronger. Even the apostle Paul, although he was a giant in the faith, felt that he could be strengthened in faith by other Christians (Romans 1:12).

In ancient times, people didn't move very often. Communities would develop in which people knew each other. But in industrialized societies today, people often do not know their neighbors. People are often cut off from families and friends. People wear masks all the time, never feeling safe enough to let people know who they really are inside.

Ancient churches did not need to emphasize small groups — they formed them naturally. The reason we find it necessary to emphasize them today is that society has changed so much. To form the interpersonal connections that ought to be part of Christian churches, we need to go out of our way to establish Christian friendship/study/prayer circles.

This will take time. It takes time to fulfill our Christian responsibilities. It takes time to serve others. It even takes time to find out what kinds of service they need. But if we have accepted Jesus as our Lord, our time is not our own. Jesus Christ makes demands on our lives. He demands total commitment, not a pretend-Christianity.

5) Service

When I list "service" as a separate category here, I am emphasizing physical service, not the service of teaching or the service of encouraging others. A teacher is also a washer of feet, a person who illustrates the meaning of Christianity by *doing* what Jesus would do. Jesus took care of physical needs such as food and health. In a physical way, he gave his body and his life for us. The early church gave physical help, sharing their possessions with needy people, collecting offerings for the hungry.

Service should be done both inside and outside the church: "As we have opportunity, let us do good to all people, especially to those who belong to the family of believers" (Galatians 6:10). Folks who isolate themselves from other believers are falling short in this aspect of Christianity. The concept of spiritual gifts is important here. God has placed each of us in the body "for the common good" (1 Corinthians 12:7). Each of us has abilities that can help others.

Which spiritual gifts do you have? You can take a questionnaire to find out, but much of the questionnaire is based on your experience. What have you done in the past that turned out well? What do other people say you are good at? How have you helped others in the past? The best test of spiritual gifts is serving within the Christian community. Try a variety of roles in the church, and ask others what you do best. Volunteer. Every member should have at least one role in the church. Small groups provide many opportunities for involvement, and many opportunities for feedback on what you do well and what you enjoy doing.

The Christian community also serves the world around us, not only in word, but also in deeds that go with those words. God did not just speak —

he also took action. Actions can demonstrate the love of God working in our hearts, as we help the poor, as we offer comfort to the discouraged, as we help victims make sense of their lives. It is those who need practical help who are often the most responsive to the gospel message.

Physical service may be seen as supporting the gospel. It is a method of supporting evangelism. But service should be done with no strings attached, no attempt to get something in return. We serve simply because God has given us some resources and has opened our eyes to see a need. Jesus fed and healed many people without any immediate appeal for them to become his disciples. He did it simply because it needed to be done, and he saw a need that he could fill.

6) Evangelism

"Go into all the world and preach the gospel," Jesus commands us. Frankly, we need a lot of improvement in this area. We have been too conditioned to keep our faith to ourselves. People cannot be converted unless the Father is calling them, but that does not mean that we shouldn't preach the gospel! Jesus told us that we should.

To be effective stewards of the gospel message, we cannot just let other people do it. We cannot be content to hire other people to do it. Those forms of evangelism are not wrong, but they are not enough. Evangelism needs a personal face. When God wanted to send a message to people, he used people to do it. He sent his own Son, God in the flesh, to preach. Today he sends his children, humans in whom the Spirit is living, to preach the message and give it appropriate shape in each culture.

We need to be active, willing and *eager* to share the faith. We need enthusiasm about the gospel, an enthusiasm that communicates *at least something* about Christianity to our neighbors. (Do they know that we *are* Christians? Does it look like we are *happy* to be Christians?) We are growing and improving in this, but we need more growth.

I encourage all of us to give thought to how we might be Christian witnesses to those around us. I encourage every member to obey the command to be prepared to give an answer. I encourage every member to read about evangelism, and to apply what they read. We can all learn together and spur one another on to good works. Small groups can provide some training for evangelism, and small groups can often become places of evangelism.

In some cases, members may learn faster than their pastors. That's OK. The pastor can then learn from the member. God has given them different spiritual gifts. To some of our members, he has given a gift for evangelism that needs to be awakened and directed. If the pastor cannot equip this person for this form of ministry, the pastor at least ought to encourage the person to learn, and implement, and provide examples for others, so that the whole church might grow.

Conclusion

I have commented at length on the purposes of the church, and I have highlighted areas in which we need growth. I hope that people find it helpful to see the bigger picture of what we are doing.

Most people who read this article are faithful and supportive. However, I would like to add a few words for people who don't attend anymore. I cannot know your heart. I do not know all your hurts and questions. But I do know that you are missing out on a significant percentage of the Christian life. The biblical picture throughout is that Christians meet together regularly. If you are not, please consider attending again. There is so much God wants to do in your life. Christianity works best when we work together.

Joseph Tkach

3. UPWARD, INWARD AND OUTWARD IN WORDS AND DEEDS

People sometimes use the phrase "upward, inward, and outward" to describe our Christian lives. "Upward" refers to our relationship with God. "Inward" refers to our relationship with fellow believers. "Outward" refers to our relationship with nonbelievers. Let's look at some of the ways these three areas can be expressed in words and in actions.

Our *upward* relationship is the most important, and I will say more about it shortly. But I'd like to begin with our *inward* responsibilities – the relationships Christians have with one another.

Inward in words

There are two major ways in which we relate to fellow Christians. One is through fellowship, and the other is through ministry, or service. That is, our relationships are expressed in words and in deeds. Sometimes our words are simply "small talk" – chatting about the weather, sports, jobs, and other facts. Other times, as relationships develop, our conversations go beyond that, so that we are also discussing opinions, feelings and matters of the heart.

Christian fellowship includes spiritual matters, too – not just doctrinal facts, but the practical issues of the spiritual life. Small group fellowship is designed to bring out discussions on such a level, because sharing such things as the people of God helps us grow spiritually. That's why I encourage church members to find or form a small group in their congregation.

"Encourage one another daily," Hebrews 3:13 tells us. Such encouragement as this is a two-way process. It involves both the *giving* and the *receiving* of encouragement from one another. I find that sometimes I am up and can encourage others, while other times I am down and need to be encouraged by others. Frequent fellowship with other believers gives us an opportunity to help and to be helped in this way. God designed the church to be like this, with people helping, strengthening and lifting up one another.

"Encourage" is a translation of the Greek word *parakaleo,* which comes from roots meaning to be called alongside, or to stand with. God has called us to stand *together,* so that we might continually give hope, courage and support to one another. That is a major reason that we should meet together: "Let us consider how we may spur one another on toward love and good deeds. Let us not give up meeting together, as some are in the habit of doing, but let us encourage one another" (Hebrews 10:24-25).

How can we "spur one another on" in attitudes and in actions? In a variety of words and ways, all of which require that we meet together regularly. Otherwise, we will drift away (Hebrews 2:1), slowly and unconsciously getting further from Christ to the degree that we neglect Christian fellowship.

Inward in deeds

Our relationships need to involve more than words. We are exhorted to have brotherly love for one another, and that means more than lip-service. It means action. It means helping people who need help. The earliest disciples held their goods in common (Acts 2:44). Later, collections were taken to help the poor (Acts 11:29). Believers often ate together and helped one another in practical ways.

Service can be person-to-person, or it can be toward a group or even toward the entire congregation. Setting up chairs for a meeting is one example. It serves the whole church and fills an important practical need. It is a type of ministry.

Each member is most "at home" in the body of Christ when he or she is involved in some type of ministry or service to others. Some serve by giving encouraging words. Some encourage by giving physical helps. Some minister to individual needs, and some minister to the congregation as a whole. God takes joy in the wonderful variety of ways that we interact with one another.

Outward in words

Just as ministry applies to our relationships within the church, it also applies to our *outward* relationships. We minister to our neighbors, to our relatives and to the people we work with. On our jobs, we work not just for the money, but also to be able to help others. In our families and neighborhoods, we do not just do the minimum, but we try to make a positive contribution. Because we are God's children in the world, we want every place we live, and every place we go, to be better because we have been there. This is not because we are so great, but because God has given us his love and called us to do the kinds of things he would do if he were one of us.

We do this as individuals, and sometimes we do it as congregations. Working together, we can make a positive difference in our neighborhoods.

Our *outward* relationship also includes words. Words can be a powerful force – not in a magical sense, but in their potential to influence people. Words can give strength, or they can destroy. They can honor, or they can debase. "The tongue has the power of life and death" (Proverbs 18:21).

As God's people in the world, as ambassadors of Jesus Christ, our words should be wisely chosen to build up the people around us. Our words need to be truthful, filled with things of good report (Ephesians 5:4). We are to be good stewards of our tongues.

One way to be a good steward of words is through evangelism. The gospel is a powerful message that we have been given and told to share. This is the pearl of great price that we are to keep and give at the same time. This is the word of truth, the message of good report, the word of life we can give others. Paul says we have been *"entrusted* with the secret things of God" (1 Corinthians 4:1), the message of salvation.

Outward in deeds

By talking about words and deeds, I do not want to imply that everything we do can be neatly categorized. Our words and our actions work *together.* As we seek to encourage other Christians with our words, we also need to give them practical help when needed.

The same is true for the words we say to non-Christians. If we are living like unbelievers, it is unlikely that the gospel will have any impact on their lives. If we lie and cheat, gossip and gripe, people won't tend to *believe* us when we share the gospel, no matter how convincingly we say the words. If we ignore their practical needs, they will be skeptical that we care about them.

There is also an overlapping of *inward* and *outward* activities. Small groups are not only inwardly nourishing, but they are also an excellent entry point for people interested in Christianity. Certain kinds of inward service can also open doors for evangelism. For example, children's ministry volunteers serve children by sharing the gospel, serve them physically in their needs, and at the same time, give *parents* a practical service so that the parents can take part in the worship service. Several types of ministry are being accomplished at once!

Children's ministry serves those within the church – but *just by being there,* it provides an avenue for evangelism, too. Children can invite their friends to join them for church, which in turn creates a relationship between the church and the friends' parents. Members can also feel free to invite friends and neighbors to church, knowing their children will be cared for, given good teaching and have fun during the service.

Upward in words

Our *upward* relationship may also be divided into words and actions. Our words with God may be further divided into two kinds: God's words to us, and our words to him.

How does God speak to us? Primarily through Scripture. These are the words he has inspired to be written and preserved for us today. These writings tell us how God has spoken in the past, and how he has been perfectly revealed in his Son, Jesus Christ. As we read these words again and again with spiritual openness, God speaks to us afresh, helping us apply the words to situations in our lives. Bible study is part of our worship response to God, who has revealed himself and his Word to us in the Scriptures.

God speaks to us in sermons, too. Anyone who speaks to the church should seek to speak "the very words of God" (1 Peter 4:11). It is appropriate for us to listen, then, with the expectation that words of God will be spoken. Not every sermon is a "thus saith the Lord," but we still need to listen attentively, for this is one of the ways God has chosen to speak to us. We evaluate the sermon by Scripture, our ultimate authority, but we still listen for what God may be saying through the imperfect speaker. "The others should weigh carefully what is said" (1 Corinthians 14:29).

Elders have the responsibility to speak "the very words of God." That is a formidable challenge! It underscores the need we all have to pray constantly, and to prepare thoroughly. Speakers want their messages to be words that Jesus himself would approve. Teachers will be called into stricter judgment (James 3:1). That is another reason that we encourage exegetical sermons: messages that explain the written word of God. A message that conveys the sense of the text will be speaking the words of God.

God speaks through sermons; he may also speak through *any* member of the church. As we are called to exhort one another to good works, we are called to speak God's words of encouragement to one another. We often learn from one another what God wants us to do. Through fellowship, through small group discussions, we can come to know his will better.

These words from God to us are part of our upward relationship: our worship. When we listen attentively, willing to respond, we are worshipping God. The sermon is part of our worship service. Our worship does not stop when the "worship leader" sits down – rather, our worship changes from singing to listening. Our discipleship, our willingness to learn, is part of our worship.

Our worship includes the words we speak to God, too. In prayer and in song, we speak to God. This is part of our upward relationship. We are telling him what we think about him, about ourselves, and about others. Praise is a form of worship, but even our *requests* are a form of worship when we recognize that God is the one who has the power to grant all our requests (and the wisdom and the love to not grant them all!). "In everything, by prayer and petition, with thanksgiving, present your requests to God" (Philippians 4:6).

The Psalms give us examples of worship songs filled with great emotion – fear, frustration, anxiety, even anger, as well as joy, hope, peace and love. In our relationship with God, we do not hide our true thoughts (it does no good, since he knows them, anyway).

Upward in deeds

Last, I want to comment on *actions* that we do in our upward relationship. The Old Testament religion stressed actions of worship: sacrifices, rituals, times and places. The New Testament has little of this. Our rituals include baptism and the Lord's Supper. Some Christian traditions have more rituals – they may follow a liturgical calendar, recite creeds and prayers in their weekly liturgies, have a more prominent place for communion, etc. Such rituals are not wrong, but neither are they commanded. Christian traditions vary, and each of them can be respected for the particular strength it brings to the fabric of the body of Christ.

What other actions form part of our worship? We offer our "bodies as living sacrifices" – that is a "spiritual act of worship" (Romans 12:1). Everything we do is part of our worship, our service toward God. God doesn't *need* anything from us, but we serve him by obeying him and by seeking to make a difference in this world for his kingdom. In our words and in our actions with other people, we want our lifestyle to be one of submission to the One who is all-wise, all-powerful and all-loving.

When our actions are done in obedience to God (at home, at work, in the marketplace, etc.), they are an expression of our worship of him. When we use our time for his glory, to advance his glory instead of ourselves, we have actions of worship, actions that strengthen our upward relationship. When we use money for his glory instead of for ourselves, we have actions of worship. In our words, in our time, in our finances, in our spiritual gifts, we want to use what God has given to serve him. Stewardship in all these areas is a life-style of worship.

As a denomination, we want to be good stewards of what God has given. We want to be good stewards of the gospel in our local churches. We want to encourage and edify our brothers and sisters in Christ. We want to be good stewards in our physical and financial assets, too.

"So, as the Holy Spirit says: 'Today, if you hear his voice, do not harden your hearts'" (Hebrews 3:7). Let us look to Jesus, our apostle, our high priest, the author and perfecter of our faith. Let us strengthen our arms and knees, and run with endurance the race set before us. For we have come to a kingdom that cannot be shaken, a kingdom of incomparable glory. Therefore, "let us be thankful, and so worship God acceptably with reverence and awe" (Hebrews 12:28).

Joseph Tkach

4. CHURCH: SOME ASSEMBLY REQUIRED

Just across the road from our home is a beautiful country church. Many of our neighbors go there on Sunday morning to worship.

My wife's parents were married in that church, and her great grandfather donated the land on which it is built. I like the service. It is dignified and meaningful, and the congregation shares my preference for traditional hymns and music. The pastor is a good friend, and from time to time he has asked me to stand in for him. The people good-naturedly appreciate my clumsy attempts to handle the unfamiliar liturgy, and some have told me they wish I would come more often.

So why, most Sundays, do we make a round trip of about 100 miles to attend "our" church in the big city? That is the closest congregation of the denomination in which I have membership and am ordained. But it is not just a matter of brand loyalty. I feel more or less at home in most Christian churches, and I believe they are valid places to worship. The styles might be different, but I suspect that we are more concerned about styles than God is. Wherever and whenever Christians gather together in his name, Jesus said he would be there too. Then why do I drive to my relatively distant congregation instead of just ambling across the road?

Does it matter?

I think about this sometimes as I make the Sunday morning drive. Does it matter where we go? Are we at liberty to just pick a church out of convenience? Or even to go nowhere? Surveys show that many people feel it is quite acceptable to watch a church service on television, never committing themselves to regular assembly. Others say that just talking about God and religion with friends at work or at an informal gathering from time to time is all the "church" they need.

But the Bible places a high importance on belonging to a congregation — and not just belonging, but supporting and participating in its life and work. One reason is that a congregation provides the opportunity for fellowship and joining in worship and communion.

Another reason is that a congregation also requires *accountability,* something that, ironically, is often put forward as an excuse for *withdrawing* from regular congregational worship, and even leaving a church. We don't like accountability. It implies restriction, discipline, correction and demands on our time and money — things we resist in life and certainly don't want from a church.

There are often some disagreeable aspects of congregational life. We tend to get ourselves bogged down in distracting details and stir them into the church mix. But the primary thing God is concerned about is our relationships. Jesus taught that lasting, productive relationships, based on mutual love and respect, are the substance of Christian life. Human societies and organizations rarely put the highest priority on this; they have different agendas. But a congregation of fellow believers should be a safe place to nurture, maintain and, if necessary, repair relationships. To deny ourselves this environment is to miss out on a key aspect of the central dimension of our Christian lives.

I am not suggesting that regular church attendance makes us more righteous, or that to stay away is unforgivable. My long commute to worship does not make me more acceptable to God. Nevertheless, I think he does want me to have a strong commitment to my not-so-local congregation, and I do not take it lightly. The extra effort is definitely more worth than it is trouble.

The early church

People tend to interpret the scriptures about congregational worship in terms of our modern situation. But those instructions were not written against a backdrop of what has become the world's largest religion with over two billion adherents and a bewildering variety of sects, groups and denominations. We need to see what was written in the context of the first-century church.

After the initial surge, the church settled down to a slower growth pattern. The typical congregation in New Testament times seems to have been a relatively small number of people meeting in homes or public places. Some congregations were in contact with one another, and there is evidence of some rudimentary organization and central authority. But most of the time the churches were on their own.

Paul himself seems to have been the linking factor in the churches he founded. Most of his letters have the flavor of a personal, intimate communication to people he knew rather than that of a large, general audience. He never dreamed that his words would be endlessly dissected and analyzed 2,000 years later in churches on continents he did not even know existed. He wrote to people he knew, gathered in little groups around the Mediterranean Sea.

Unlike today, where we have many choices, the early believers were a small minority, struggling to exist in what was often a hostile environment. With enemies, physical and spiritual, waiting to pounce, unity and harmony within the group were vitally important. That is why Paul and the other founding fathers focused their letters so much on *koinonia*, or community.

God's building

One of Paul's favorite analogies was to see the congregation as a building (1 Corinthians 3:9) that was a work in progress. "God is building a home," he reminded the church at Ephesus.

> He's using us all—irrespective of how we got here—in what he is building. He used the apostles and prophets for the foundation. Now he's using you, fitting you in brick by brick, stone by stone, with Christ Jesus as the cornerstone that holds all the parts together. We see it taking shape day after day — a holy temple built by God, all of us built into it, a temple in which God is quite at home. (Ephesians 2:19-22, *Message Bible*)

In such a building, every part was needed. "From him the whole body, joined and held together by every supporting ligament, grows and builds itself up in love, as each part does its work" (Ephesians 4:16, NIV). This does not imply an easy-going "come when you feel like it" approach, does it?

These first Christians were, like us, frail and flawed human beings. Like us, they had their politics and quarrels. So how to handle such problems is often discussed. For example, when two long-standing members of the congregation at Philippi fell out, Paul urged them publicly to settle their differences:

> I urge Euodia and Syntyche to iron out their differences and make up. God doesn't want his children holding grudges. And, oh, yes, Syzygus, since you're right there to help them work things out, do your best with them. These women worked for the Message hand in hand with Clement and me, and with the other veterans — worked as hard as any of us. Remember, their names are also in the book of life. (Philippians 4:2-3, *Message Bible*)

Was Syzygus successful? Let's hope so. Paul valued both Euodia and Syntyche, and did not want to lose either of them. So Paul urged them to reconcile quickly, for the good of the whole group.

The early church was taught to see membership in a congregation as a privilege and a responsibility. It was not a "useful option" or an "added benefit" to take advantage of if and when one felt like it. The instructions have the feeling of "this means you, so listen up" rather than "here are some general principles that you might want to think about in your planning meetings." Hebrews 10:25 was an urgent warning to "not giving up meeting together" because of a trend that needed to be nipped in the bud.

Breaking up is hard to do

Members who persisted in unacceptable or disruptive conduct might eventually have to be denied fellowship — but only as a last resort, after all other efforts to reconcile had failed. Even then, it was not done out of revenge or punishment, but as a last-ditch effort to bring the erring member to their senses. To be barred from fellowship was a serious matter. You couldn't just shrug your shoulders and find another church that would have you. There was nowhere else to go.

Does this mean there is never a reason to leave a congregation? No. A church that is controlling and abusive does not deserve your membership, and you are better off out of it. But most congregations are not like that. They are just a group of imperfect believers struggling with the trials of life. Membership in a group like that should not be taken lightly. In our modern world, nearly every relationship is fraying—marriage, family, neighbors, friends. What should be strong committed relationships have become casual and negotiable. Sadly, that includes membership in a congregation.

Here I go

Reasons for leaving a congregation often sound righteous—a disagreement over a doctrine or a change of worship style. But often, the *real* reason is hurt feelings and wounded pride. We draw ourselves up, puff out our feathers and say, "Here I stand, I can do no other." But what we mean is, "Here I go, I can't stand the others." The result is that people who were once friends now cross the road rather than pass the time of day.

If we are having difficulty with relationships in our church, it is all the more reason to stay and try to work things out. Jesus and his apostles urged their people to solve problems quickly. They knew that, if left to fester, hurts and grudges could spread to others and eventually destroy the *koinonia,* the fellowship. How much stronger, more robust and more influential would the Body of Christ be today if we would commit ourselves to working out differences rather than endlessly splitting and dividing?

A lesson from persecution

Some years ago I met a man in one of the old Soviet satellite countries who published a small Christian magazine on an underground press in his basement. The ruling regime ruthlessly suppressed Christianity, and this man had endured years of prison and persecution. As he drove me around his city, he showed me a dramatic account of what life was like under Communism.

We stopped in front of a pile of rubble. "We built a church here, but they bulldozed it," he told me. We drove on, and after a few minutes, he stopped again and said, "We started a new church here, but they knocked this one down too." He drove us to another site, and another and another, each time repeating the story.

"Finally," he said, "once the authorities realized that European Communism was collapsing, they began to relax the restrictions a little." They summoned the Christian leaders and told them they had permission to meet. There were two conditions. One was that they had to all meet together at a time and a place that the government chose. Second, the government would appoint the pastor.

The man selected was not the best speaker, nor the most educated. But it did not matter. Catholics, Baptists, Orthodox, Pentecostals and even Jehovah's Witnesses would share a common service. "We were so happy to be able to meet that our differences did not matter."

Then, when the Communist government finally fell apart, Western evangelists rushed in. Soon the group broke up into the various sects and denominations again. That brief moment of harmony has been replaced with competitive congregations glaring at each other over their "distinctives."

"We appreciate the freedom, and we do have our different religious traditions," explained my friend as he showed me yet another demolished building. "But you know, in some ways we were never happier than when we had no choice but to get along together."

No one wants persecution. But today, where we have freedom of worship, many of us use that freedom *to reduce our commitment*. And then we wonder why our witness is not as effective as it could be.

A place of safety

A church should be a safe place where there is genuine interaction—sharing the fun, pain, hope, joy, forgiveness and reconciliation of life. You can't experience that as a lone wolf, any more than you can really experience baseball, basketball or soccer by chasing balls all by yourself. Real living must be experienced in community and fellowship.

Bryan Leech's popular hymn, "We are God's People" puts it nicely:

We are a temple, the Spirit's dwelling place,
Formed in great weakness, a cup to hold God's grace;
We die alone, for on its own

Each ember loses fire:
Yet joined in one the flame burns on
To give warmth and light, and to inspire.

When it's all said and done, I suppose that's why on most Sunday mornings my wife and I drive out of our little country town and head up Highway 50 to Cincinnati. I'm sure we could find rich and meaningful fellowship with any group of believers, but we find that our long-term friendships and shared history outweigh the convenience of proximity. We've been through good times and hard times with our church. We've shared hopes, joys, pains and sorrows, disappointments and successes. We feel a commitment there, and despite the long miles and significant tread wear, we would not have it any other way.

John Halford

5. MINISTRY MEANS SERVICE

When the Bible talks about "ministry," what is it talking about? When it says that Christians are to be involved in "works of ministry," what does it mean? This article examines the concept of ministry by seeing how the biblical writers were inspired to use the words for ministry. This can help us understand a little better what we are to be doing in the church and in the world. It also gives us a context in which we can examine other topics about ministry.

Some of the words, although Greek, are not completely foreign to us. For example, our English word "deacon" is related to the Greek word *diakonia,* which is sometimes translated "ministry." The English word "liturgy" comes from *leitourgia,* which can also be translated "ministry."

The word *diakonia* is used to describe the "ministry of the word" (Acts 6:4), the "ministry of the Spirit" (2 Corinthians 3:8) and the "ministry of reconciliation" (2 Corinthians 5:18). *Leitourgia* is used to describe the ministry that Jesus has received as our High Priest (Hebrews 8:6). Similar Greek words can also be used for ministry, ministers and ministering. The Corinthian Christians were a result of Paul's ministry (*diakoneo*), and Paul considered himself a "minister [*leitourgos*] of Christ Jesus" (2 Corinthians 3:3; Romans 15:16).

We can learn much about ministry by seeing how the New Testament uses these words and other words with similar meaning. These give us the tone or flavor of New Testament ministry. We will see that every Christian has a ministry.

Diakonos service

Diakonos is a noun meaning "a person who serves." We get the English word "deacon" from it.

In Philippians 1:1 and 1 Timothy 3:8-13 it denotes an office in the church. But almost everywhere else, the word is used in a more general sense. It refers to apostles, preachers and lay members more often than it does to deacons. The general sense of the word is "assistant." It indicates not just work in general, but work that benefits someone else. Paul used the word *diakonos* to describe himself as a servant of the Lord (1 Corinthians 3:5), a servant of God (2 Corinthians 6:4), a servant of the new covenant (2 Corinthians 3:6), a servant of the gospel (Ephesians 3:7; Colossians 1:23) and a servant of the church (verse 25).

Paul said that many of his co-workers were also servants: the woman

Phoebe (Romans 16:1) and the men Tychicus (Ephesians 6:21; Colossians 4:7), Timothy (1 Timothy 4:6) and Epaphras (Colossians 1:7). Jesus said that his followers should be servants (Matthew 20:26; 23:11; John 12:26). All Christians must do the work of a deacon. We are all deacons of Christ, deacons of his message and deacons of one another.

Diakoneo is the verb form of *diakonos;* it means "serve." The most specific meaning of *diakoneo* is to work with food to serve other people. Martha "served" at a dinner (John 12:2; Luke 10:40). Jesus told parables about servants who were expected to prepare food and serve their masters (Luke 17:8; 22:27). In the early church, seven men were chosen "to wait on tables" (Acts 6:2-3).

Diakoneo can refer to more general types of service, too. Jesus served his disciples (Matthew 20:28; Mark 10:45). Jesus' disciples should also serve (Luke 22:27; John 12:26). When we serve others, we are showing love to God (Hebrews 6:10) — a point also made in the parable of sheep and goats. This parable shows that serving can include not only supplying food and drink, but also clothing and other needs (Matthew 25:44).

Some people served Paul in prison (Philemon 13; 2 Timothy 1:18). Serving can include financial assistance: Several women served Jesus from their own possessions (Luke 8:3). Paul collected an offering to serve the saints in Jerusalem (Romans 15:25).

Diakoneo often means manual labor, but service to others can also be done through speaking. When Jesus said that he served his disciples, he included his teaching. The gospel is included when Paul says that the Corinthian church was a result of his serving (2 Corinthians 3:3).

1 Peter 4:10-11 uses the word in both a general sense and then in a more specific sense: "Each one should use whatever gift he has received to *serve* others, faithfully administering God's grace in its various forms. If anyone speaks, he should do it as one speaking the very words of God. If anyone *serves,* he should do it with the strength God provides."

Everyone should serve (in a general sense), but each serves in a different way — some serve by speaking and some serve by manual labor. It is this latter type of service that forms the core of the office of deacon (1 Timothy 3:10, 13). No matter what type of serving is done, it should be done with the strength God provides, so that he gets the praise and glory (1 Peter 4:11).

Diakonia is another word in the *diakonos* family. It denotes the result of serving — "service" or "ministry." It is translated in a variety of ways. Martha was busy with dinner "preparation" (Luke 10:40). In the early church, there was a daily "distribution" of food for widows (Acts 6:1). Famine relief was also called a ministry (Acts 11:29; 12:25; Romans 15:31; 2 Corinthians 8:4; 9:1, 12-13). When Macedonian believers supported Paul, it was a ministry to him (2 Corinthians 11:8).

Diakonia is often used to refer to a spiritual ministry. The apostles had a "ministry of the word" (Acts 6:4). Paul said that his ministry was "the task of testifying to the gospel of God's grace" (Acts 20:24). Paul's message of reconciliation was his ministry (2 Corinthians 5:18). The new covenant is a "ministry that brings righteousness" (2 Corinthians 3:8-9).

All members are encouraged to have a ministry. Church leaders exist "to prepare God's people for works of *service*" (Ephesians 4:12) — "to equip the saints for the work of ministry" (NRSV). There are different kinds of ministry (1 Corinthians 12:5), but they should all be used "for the common good" (verse 7). Those who have been given a gift of (manual) ministry should use that gift (Romans 12:7). Those who have other gifts should likewise use them to serve others (1 Peter 4:10).

Doulos service

Paul frequently called himself a *doulos* — a slave or servant of Jesus Christ. In Jewish society, a *doulos* was usually a servant. In Greek society, he was usually a slave. However, this type of service is not restricted to slaves and apostles — it is commanded for all Christians. This is another description of our ministry.

Christ himself took on the nature of a servant (Philippians 2:7), and he quoted the proverb, "No servant is greater than his master" (Matthew 10:24-25; John 15:20-21). Since our Master served as a servant, shouldn't we also be servants? In Christianity, greatness is measured by service. "Whoever wants to be first must be slave of all" (Matthew 20:27; Mark 10:44).

Numerous people were called slave-servants of God: Moses, Simeon, Mary, Paul, Timothy, Silas, Luke, Epaphras, Tychicus, Peter, John, James and Jude. All of God's people are commanded to be servants (1 Peter 2:16). Service is part of what it means to be a Christian. Many of Jesus' parables included servants; these parables have extra meaning for Christians, the servants of Christ.

Doulos also has metaphorical uses — sinners are slaves of whatever has power over them (2 Peter 2:19). Christ frees us from the slavery of the fear of death (Hebrews 2:15). He frees us from the slavery of sin (John 8:34; Romans 6:16-20) by redeeming us, purchasing us with his own blood. He frees us from "the yoke of slavery" (Galatians 5:1) so that we may serve him in the new way of the Spirit (Romans 7:6). We become slaves to obedience, slaves to righteousness (Romans 6:16-22).

Christians are "slaves of Christ" (1 Corinthians 7:22; Ephesians 6:6). We are all admonished to serve the Lord (Romans 12:11; 14:18; 1 Thessalonians 1:9), and one of the primary responsibilities our Lord and Master gives us is to serve one another in love (Galatians 5:13). As slaves of Christ and slaves of one another, we serve one another by using the gifts God gives us (see appendix below).

Paul calls us slaves, but he also says that we are not slaves (Galatians 4:7). In some ways we are like slaves, but in other ways we are not. With respect to obedience, our obligation to Christ is like that of a slave — we are to obey. But with respect to reward, we are much better than slaves. "As long as the heir is a child, he is no different from a slave…. You are no longer a slave, but a son; and since you are a son, God has made you also an heir" (Galatians 4:1, 7).

"A slave has no permanent place in the family, but a son belongs to it forever" (John 8:35). "I no longer call you servants…. Instead, I have called you friends" (John 15:15).

Worship service

Some Greek words for service also mean worship. *Latreia* and *latreuo* denote religious service or worship. (We see the root word *latr-* in the English word *idolatry*.) The NIV uses "serve" and "worship" almost interchangeably for these words. Worship was done at the temple (Luke 2:37; Acts 7:7; Romans 9:4; Hebrews 8:5; 9:1, 6, 9; 10:2; 13:10). In Revelation, the saints "serve" God in his heavenly temple (Revelation 7:15) and will "serve" him always (Revelation 22:3).

Christ has cleansed us so that we may "serve" God (Hebrews 9:14). We are exhorted to "worship" God (Hebrews 12:28). Christians "worship" by the Spirit of God (Philippians 3:3). Paul exhorts us to be living sacrifices, which is our "reasonable service" (KJV), a "spiritual act of worship" (Romans 12:1, NIV). Our service to God is not centered on a temple, but is done wherever we are.

Leitourg- words come from the Greek words *laos* (people) and *ergon* (work). They originally referred to a public service, but they eventually came to refer specifically to religious service and worship. We get the English word *liturgy* from these Greek words.

This was the type of service Jewish priests performed (Luke 1:23; Hebrews 10:11; 9:21). This religious service is now done by Jesus, our High Priest (Hebrews 8:2, 6). In the context of priests and sacrifices, Paul said that he was a "minister" of Jesus Christ (Romans 15:16).

A practical service such as famine relief could be called a *leitourgia*

(Romans 15:27; 2 Corinthians 9:12). By using a *leitourg-* word, Paul was reminding his readers that this seemingly ordinary service to the saints was actually an act of worship, a religious activity. All Christians can perform religious service (Acts 13:2; Philippians 2:17).

Ministry of all believers

There is a progression in the way worship words are used. In the old covenant, God required the Israelites to serve him through a priesthood, a sacrificial system and a temple. In the new covenant, *all* Christians worship God through spiritual sacrifices, and we all serve God in the Spirit. The ministry of worship has been given to all the people.

This is one reason the 16th-century Reformers taught "the priesthood of all believers." Jesus Christ is the High Priest, and all Christians are priests (1 Peter 2:5, 9; Revelation 1:6). Every Christian can enter the heavenly Holy of holies because of the once-for-all sacrifice of Jesus Christ (Hebrews 10:19). Christians offer spiritual sacrifices (1 Peter 2:5; Romans 12:1). We also have the priestly duty of interceding for one another in prayers and in practical action.

The Reformers also noted that Christians serve God through their secular work — their vocation or "calling" — as well as through their involvement in the church. A person who grows food is providing a service to society; a person who works in a factory or teaches school does, too. Christian homemakers and government employees are also serving others.

"Whatever you do, do it all for the glory of God" (1 Corinthians 10:31). All work — in the home, in the store, in the car and in the office — is an act of worship to God. We are his slaves — full-time ministers in his service.

Summary

The New Testament says the same thing in many different ways: Christians are commanded to serve one another. None of the words for service or ministry is restricted to the ordained clergy. All members are enslaved to one another. We all have obligations to one another. Whether our service is in word or in deed, it is a religious duty for all Christians. Whether we are ordained or not, we are all called to serve the Lord by serving one another.

As slave-servants, we are ministering to one another, to the church, to the gospel and to the Lord. God has given each of us a ministry. We should minister to one another's needs. God has given us abilities so that we will use them to serve others. All Christians — whether men, women, deacons or elders — are called to be ministers.

Appendix A: *Allelon*

The Greek word *allelon* gives us a helpful introduction to the ways in which Christians should serve each other, because this Greek word means "one another" or "each other." It is often used to describe our mutual obligations — the responsibility that all members have toward one another.

Perhaps the most comprehensive command Jesus gave was the well-known "Love one another" (John 13:34). "As I have loved you, so you must love one another. By this everyone will know that you are my disciples, if you love one another" (verses 34-35). This command is such a fundamental statement of our Christian duty that it is given again in John 15:12, 17; Romans 13:8; 1 Thessalonians 4:9; 1 Peter 1:22; 1 John 3:11, 23; 4:7, 11-12; and 2 John 5. This is the attitude in which we should always interact with one another.

Paul developed the command a little further: "Be devoted to one another in brotherly love. Honor one another above yourselves" (Romans 12:10). "Serve one another in love" (Galatians 5:13). He prayed that the Lord would help the Thessalonians' love to increase not only for each other, but that their love would also increase for everyone else (1 Thessalonians 3:12). "Always try to be kind to each other *and* to everyone else" (1 Thessalonians 5:15). In his second letter to the Thessalonians, he thanked God that their mutual love was indeed increasing (2 Thessalonians 1:3).

In Christ, we belong to each other and form one body (Romans 12:5). We are members of one another (Ephesians 4:25). "We have fellowship with one another" (1 John 1:7). Paul prayed that the Roman Christians would have "a spirit of unity among yourselves as you follow Christ Jesus" (Romans 15:5). To avoid division in the body, Paul wanted members to "have equal concern for each other" (1 Corinthians 12:25). "Offer hospitality to one another" (1 Peter 4:9).

We see further development of the command in the words of Jesus: "Be at peace with each other" (Mark 9:50). Paul put it this way: "Live in peace with each other" (1 Thessalonians 5:13*). [An asterisk indicates that the pronoun is *heautou* instead of *allelon;* the meaning is often the same.] "Live in harmony with one another" (Romans 12:16). Paul shows how this is done: "Do not be conceited" (same verse). "Be completely humble and gentle; be patient, bearing with one another in love" (Ephesians 4:2). "Do nothing out of selfish ambition or vain conceit, but in humility consider [each other] better than yourselves" (Philippians 2:3). "Clothe yourselves with humility toward one another" (1 Peter 5:5.)

"Stop passing judgment on one another," Paul writes (Romans 14:13). "Accept one another, then, just as Christ accepted you" (Romans 15:7). "Bear with each other and forgive whatever grievances you may have against one another. Forgive as the Lord forgave you" (Colossians 3:13). "Be kind and compassionate to one another, forgiving each other, just as in Christ God forgave you" (Ephesians 4:32). "Confess your sins to each other and pray for each other" (James 5:16).

"Serve one another," Paul wrote (Galatians 5:13). Peter gives the same point: "Each one should use whatever gift he has received to serve others" (1 Peter 4:10*). Jesus had given the same lesson when he told his disciples to "wash one another's feet" (John 13:14). "Submit to one another out of reverence for Christ" (Ephesians 5:21). "Carry each other's burdens, and in this way you will fulfill the law of Christ" (Galatians 6:2).

Paul wanted the Roman Christians and himself to be "mutually encouraged by each other's faith" (Romans 1:12). One purpose of our weekly meetings is to "spur one another on toward love and good deeds…encourage one another" (Hebrews 10:24-25). "Encourage one another daily" (Hebrews 3:13*). "Encourage one another and build each other up" (1 Thessalonians 4:18; 5:11). "Build yourselves up in your most holy faith" (Jude 20*).

Paul wanted "mutual edification" (Romans 14:19). "Teach and admonish one another with all wisdom, and as you sing psalms, hymns and spiritual songs" (Colossians 3:16*; Ephesians 5:19*). Paul was confident that the Romans could "instruct one another" (Romans 15:14).

These are some of the ways in which Christians, as servants of Jesus Christ, minister to one another. None of these types of service or ministry is restricted to ordained elders or pastors.

Appendix B: Gifts of the Holy Spirit

The "gifts" of the Spirit are God-given abilities distributed as God knows is best for different aspects of Christian service. There are different kinds of spiritual gifts, Paul tells us, even though they are all inspired by the same Spirit (1 Corinthians 12:4). God gives these special abilities "for the common good" — so Christians can help one another (verse 7).

But not everyone has the same spiritual gift or ability, just as not every part of the human body performs the function of seeing, hearing or walking. Feet, hands, eyes and other parts serve different functions. By contributing to the body as a whole, the various parts serve one another. So it is in the church, the body of Christ (verses 14-27).

God distributes the gifts: one power to one person, another gift to the next person, a third ability to another, just as God determines (verses 8-11). God appoints people with various spiritual functions: apostles, prophets, teachers, miracle-workers, healers, helpers, administrators and speaking in different kinds of tongues (verse 28). By dividing the gifts in this way, God encourages members to work with and help one another. Through a division of labor, God encourages us to work with one another to be more efficient. As we work together, Christ gives his church growth (Ephesians 4:15-16).

What are the gifts? Paul lists some in 1 Corinthians 12:28-30: church leadership positions such as apostle, prophet and teacher, or gifts of miracles, healings and tongues, or less spectacular but equally necessary abilities such as helping others and administration. Another list is in verses 7-10: messages of wisdom and knowledge, faith and healing and miracles, inspired messages of prophecy, tongues or interpretations, or a special gift for distinguishing between spirits. The precise difference between wisdom and knowledge, or faith and healing and miracles may not be important in this list; Paul is simply making the point that spiritual gifts come in many varieties, although they are all "for the common good."

Romans 12:6-8 gives another list of gifts (none of the lists is complete): prophesying, serving, teaching, encouraging, giving to others, leading others or showing mercy. Some of these service gifts should be found in all Christians, but some people are distinctly better at certain activities than other people are. As God gives us these abilities, we should apply them as best we can for the common good of the body of Christ.

The gifts in these lists come in three major categories: church leadership, speaking, and serving others. Peter summarizes "gifts" under the categories of speaking and serving (1 Peter 4:11). "Each one should use whatever gift he has received to serve others, faithfully administering God's grace in its various forms" (verse 10).

Paul said that God had given (the Greek verb is similar to the noun used for "gift") the Philippian Christians the ability to believe in Christ and also the opportunity to suffer for him (Philippians 1:29-30). Suffering patiently and faithfully can be a useful spiritual gift. Paul says he was given a "thorn in the flesh" (2 Corinthians 12:7), which emphasized Paul's weaknesses, therefore showing that the power of his message came not from himself but from God (verses 8-10).

Paul referred to marital status, whether married or not, as a gift (1 Corinthians 7:7). Any of life's circumstances can be considered a gift of God if we are able to use it to glorify Christ and serve others. It does not matter how spectacular or seemingly ordinary the gift is – what matters is how it is used (1 Corinthians 13:1-4). Love, a fruit of the Spirit that all Christians must have, is the test of whether an ability or gift is good.

All gifts should be used to glorify Christ and to benefit others.

Michael Morrison

6. LEADERSHIP IN THE CHURCH – AN EXAMINATION OF EIGHT WORDS

The New Testament mentions a wide variety of leaders in the church: apostles, prophets, evangelists, pastors, teachers, bishops, elders and deacons. What are these offices? Are they commanded for the church today? Let's examine the evidence, starting with the titles given in Ephesians 4:11: "Christ himself gave the apostles, the prophets, the evangelists, the pastors and teachers."

Apostles

The word "apostle" is often used for the highest rank of church leadership. However, the word had a different meaning before the church existed. It originally meant "one who has been sent" — an ambassador or representative. This general meaning is seen in some New Testament uses.

Jesus used the word in a general sense when he said that a "messenger" is not greater than the one who sends him (John 13:16). Similarly, Paul referred to some apostles whose names were not given; the NIV calls them "representatives" (2 Corinthians 8:23). That was the general function of an *apostolos.* When Paul called Epaphroditus an *apostolos,* he may have meant that Epaphroditus was a messenger of the church at Philippi (Philippians 2:25).

Jesus, who was sent by the Father, was an apostle (Hebrews 3:1). The 12 disciples, who were sent by Jesus, were also apostles (Mark 3:14, etc.). The disciples are not in the same category of authority as Jesus, but the same Greek word is used. The focus is on the function, not the rank. Barnabas and Paul were also sent out, and they were called apostles (Acts 14:4, 14).

The disciples and Paul used the term *apostolos* as the name of their leadership office in the church (Acts 15:23; Romans 11:13; Galatians 1:1; etc.). Authority came with the sending — a messenger sent by Jesus Christ had an authoritative understanding of that message.

James may have been an apostle, too — in one verse he is distinguished from the apostles, and in another he is included (1 Corinthians 15:7; Galatians 1:19). Similarly, Timothy is excluded sometimes (2 Corinthians 1:1; Colossians 1:1) and included once (1 Thessalonians 2:6) — but in this latter verse Paul may have been using the term in a general sense of messenger or representative.

The reference in Romans 16:7 is debated. Some say that Andronicus and Junia were apostles; others say that the verse simply means they were esteemed highly by the apostles. Even if they were apostles, however, it is likely that they were messengers rather than having a permanent position of authority in the church. (If they were apostles in the same sense that Paul was, it is odd that we know almost nothing about them, either from the Bible or from church history.)

Some people falsely claimed to be apostles (2 Corinthians 11:13; Revelation 2:2). Paul facetiously called them "super-apostles" (2 Corinthians 11:5; 12:11). Although he was the least of the apostles, he was not inferior to the self-proclaimed apostles (1 Corinthians 15:9). God appointed some people to be apostles (1 Corinthians 12:28; Ephesians 4:11). This was part of the foundation of the church (Ephesians 2:20; 3:5).

What role did apostles have in the church? The Twelve and Paul were instrumental in beginning the church. Soon after Jesus ascended to heaven, the disciples said that a requirement for their "apostolic ministry" was to have been with Jesus during his ministry (Acts 1:21-25). These apostles not only preached, but also exercised some administrative leadership. They laid hands on deacons whom the people had chosen (Acts 6:6) and they made decisions with the elders (Acts 15:22).

Paul mentioned some of his qualifications to be considered an apostle: seeing the Lord and raising up churches (1 Corinthians 9:1). His converts were the "seal" of his apostleship — evidence that he had been sent, at least to them (verse 2). He noted characteristics that marked an apostle: "signs, wonders and miracles" (2 Corinthians 12:12). An apostle preaches the gospel as a faithful messenger of the Lord. He is an official representative of Jesus Christ, more exclusive and authoritative than elders.

Prophets

Isn't a prophet somebody who predicts the future? That may be one meaning of the word, but that's not the only way the word is used. When the Samaritan woman perceived that Jesus was a prophet (John 4:19), it was not because of a prediction about the future, but because of a revelation about the past and present. When the guards told Jesus to prophesy (Matthew 26:68), they were asking for a revelation about the present, not the future.

On the Mount of Olives, Jesus made some predictions about the future. But even before that, the people considered him a prophet (Matthew 21:11). It was because of his teaching and his miracles (Luke 7:16; 24:19; John 6:14; 7:40; 9:17). Moses had predicted such a prophet — "a prophet like me" (Acts 3:22-23) — and Moses was known much more for teaching than for prediction. Jesus was a prophet like Moses, speaking the words of God. The role of a prophet might include predicting the future, but it didn't necessarily require predictions.

God appoints prophets in the church (1 Corinthians 12:28; Ephesians 4:11). In the early church, some prophets made predictions (Acts 11:27; 21:10). Others served in encouraging and strengthening (Acts 15:32). In Antioch, they worked with teachers (Acts 13:1). Philip's four daughters prophesied (Acts 21:9). Paul referred to a prophetic message that accompanied Timothy's ordination (1 Timothy 1:18; 4:14).

On the Day of Pentecost, when people spoke in tongues, Peter said it fulfilled a scripture about men and women prophesying (Acts 2:17-18; cf. Acts 19:6). God was causing them to speak.

Paul listed prophecy as one of the gifts of the Holy Spirit (1 Corinthians 11:5). A prophet is "spiritually gifted" (1 Corinthians 14:37). Paul urged the Corinthians to desire the gift of prophecy (verses 1, 39) — but, judging by the way that Paul used the word, this rarely means predicting the future. "Everyone who prophesies speaks to people for their strengthening, encouragement and comfort…. The one who prophesies edifies the church" (1 Corinthians 14:3-4). Prophecy is also for instruction (verse 31). God inspires prophetic messages to build and help the church.

Prophecy, although a very helpful gift, has limitations. "We know in part and we prophesy in part" (1 Corinthians 13:9). Prophecies will cease (verse 8). Love is much more important (verse 2). Every Christian should love, but not every Christian has the gift of prophecy. "We have different gifts, according to the grace given us" (Romans 12:6).

Paul gave some instructions about how prophetic speaking should be done decently and in order. In keeping with social custom, women were told to cover their heads when prophesying, and men were told they should not (1 Corinthians 11:4-5). Instead of everyone speaking at once, people should take turns (1 Corinthians 14:29-31). If God inspires a second person to speak, the first person should stop (verse 30). The result of such prophecies would then be "that everyone may be instructed and encouraged" (verse 31).

In summary, prophets help the church by comforting, edifying, encouraging, instructing, strengthening and sometimes by predicting.

Evangelists

Some people use "evangelist" as an administrative rank, but Paul was probably not describing a church-government hierarchy in Ephesians 4:11. Although the apostles had more authority than prophets did, Paul does not use this verse to say that. He does not say that prophets had authority over evangelists, or that evangelists had authority over pastors and teachers. He is not prescribing a hierarchy.

Paul seems to be concerned with the order only in 1 Corinthians 12:28, where he numbers the first three gifts: "first of all apostles, second prophets, third teachers." However, we do not have any evidence that prophets exercised any administrative authority over anyone — and the category of evangelist is not even mentioned in this verse.

In most of Paul's lists of spiritual gifts (Romans 12:6-8; 1 Corinthians 12:8-10), he does not seem to be concerned about which gift is most important. Even in verse 28, after the first three gifts are numbered, Paul does not attempt to rank the gifts. Indeed, he argues against that idea, saying that a person's gift doesn't make anyone more important than others. Every gift is given for the common good; every person should use his or her gift to serve others. In Ephesians 4:11, Paul is saying that Christ puts all types of leaders in his church for the same reason: to equip the saints for the work of ministry.

What is an evangelist? The New Testament uses the word only three times, which in itself suggests that the word is not a formal title in the church. Philip was called an evangelist (Acts 21:8). That means he did evangelism — he preached the *euangelion,* the gospel (e.g., Acts 8:5-40). But there is no evidence that he had any administrative authority.

Paul exhorted Timothy to "keep your head in all situations, endure hardship, do the work of an evangelist, discharge all the duties of your ministry" (2 Timothy 4:5). Paul was not conferring a formal title on Timothy — nor is there evidence that Timothy ever had a formal title like that. Paul was simply listing things for him to do. "The work of an evangelist" was evangelism — preaching the gospel. A deacon such as Philip could do the work of an evangelist; so could an apostle, such as Paul, or a pastor, such as Timothy. Paul said "do the work of an evangelist" as a way of exhorting Timothy to do evangelism.

In Ephesians 4:11, Paul says that God gives evangelists to the church. God gives us people who can preach the gospel with extra effectiveness. People gifted at evangelism do not have to be ordained or be given any administrative authority. Ordination and administration involve other gifts, which may or may not be present in someone with the gift of evangelizing. If administrative duties are assigned to people who do not have a gift for handling them, then those duties would decrease their ability to use their true gifts.

Pastors

The word *pastor* appears only once in the NIV (Ephesians 4:11). The Greek word is usually translated "shepherd." Luke 2:8 uses the word in its literal meaning: "There were shepherds living out in the fields nearby, keeping watch over their flocks at night." Shepherds take care of sheep.

"Shepherd" is often used metaphorically for spiritual leadership. Jesus considered himself a good shepherd (John 10:11-14). The people were "like sheep without a shepherd" (Matthew 9:36). His own disciples were "sheep of the flock" (Matthew 26:31; Luke 12:32) — but Jesus had other sheep, too (John 10:16). He is the great shepherd, and we are the sheep of his pasture (Hebrews 13:20; 1 Peter 2:25).

Jesus, using the verb for shepherding, told Peter to "take care of" his sheep (John 21:16). Paul told the Ephesian elders that the Holy Spirit had made them overseers of a flock; he exhorted them to shepherd the church (Acts 20:28). Peter also told elders to shepherd the flock, serving as overseers (1 Peter 5:2).

How should pastors "shepherd" their flocks? The verb has a range of meanings. On one end of the spectrum, it can mean to rule with great power, as Christ will when he returns (Revelation 2:27; 12:5; 19:15). Christ "will separate the people one from another as a shepherd separates the sheep from the goats" (Matthew 25:32).

However, Christ will also be a shepherd of great gentleness: "The Lamb at the center of the throne will be their shepherd [note the irony of a lamb being the shepherd]; he will lead them to springs of living water. And God will wipe away every tear from their eyes."

Church pastors are told to imitate Jesus' gentle style: Serve willingly, Peter admonishes, "not greedy for money, but eager to serve; not lording it over those entrusted to you, but being examples to the flock" (1 Peter 5:2-3). This is the kind of leaders Christ wants in his church. "The good shepherd lays down his life for the sheep" (John 10:11).

We will say more about pastors below.

Teachers

Jesus is the perfect example of every category of church leader. He is an apostle, a prophet, an evangelist, a shepherd, an overseer, a servant and a teacher. He called himself a teacher, his disciples called him teacher, the crowds called him teacher, even his enemies called him teacher. "Teacher" is the Greek equivalent of "Rabbi" (John 1:38; 20:16).

One of Jesus' chief activities was teaching. He taught not only his disciples, but also the crowds — in the temple, in synagogues, in towns and villages, on mountains and at the lakeside. "I have spoken openly to the world," Jesus said. "I always taught in synagogues or at the temple" (John 18:20).

Jesus commanded his disciples to teach (Matthew 28:20), and they did.

41

"Day after day, in the temple courts and from house to house, they never stopped teaching and proclaiming the good news that Jesus is the Christ" (Acts 5:42). Paul taught in Ephesus "publicly and from house to house" (Acts 20:20). He called himself a teacher, and he told Timothy to teach (1 Timothy 2:7; 4:11-13; 2 Timothy 1:11; 4:2).

Paul told the Colossians to teach one another (Colossians 3:16). People who have been in the church a long time should be able to teach (Hebrews 5:12). If they have a gift for teaching, they should teach (Romans 12:7). Although every member may teach, not everyone has the position of "teacher" (1 Corinthians 12:29). James warns us, "Not many of you should presume to be teachers… because you know that we who teach will be judged more strictly" (James 3:1). God appoints teachers in the church (1 Corinthians 12:28); he gives teachers to equip the saints (Ephesians 4:11).[1]

The Holy Spirit teaches (Luke 12:12; John 14:26; 1 Corinthians 2:13; 1 John 2:27). Scripture teaches (Romans 15:4; 2 Timothy 3:16). Overseers should be able to teach (1 Timothy 3:2). Paul warned Timothy, "Watch your life and doctrine [teaching] closely" (1 Timothy 4:16).

We are frequently warned about false teachers and false teachings. Jesus warned about the teachings of the Pharisees; later, some of them taught that Gentiles had to be circumcised (Acts 15:1). John warned about idolatrous and immoral teachings (Revelation 2:14-15; 2:20-24). Keep away from false teachers, Paul warned (Romans 16:17). "If anyone comes to you and does not bring this teaching, do not take him into your house or welcome him" (2 John 10).

Using the word for "teaching," Paul warned about "every wind of doctrine," "human commands and teachings," and "things taught by demons" (Ephesians 4:14; Colossians 2:22; 1 Timothy 4:1). "The time will come when people will not put up with sound doctrine. Instead, to suit their own desires, they will gather around them a great number of teachers to say what their itching ears want to hear" (2 Timothy 4:3). "Do not be carried away by all kinds of strange teachings" (Hebrews 13:9).

What should be taught? The way of God (Matthew 22:16). Obedience to Jesus' commands (Matthew 28:20). The word of God (Acts 18:11). The Lord Jesus Christ (Acts 13:12; 18:25; 28:31). A way of life in Christ Jesus (1 Corinthians 4:17). The teachings given by Paul (2 Thessalonians 2:15; 2 Timothy 2:2). The elementary truths of God's word (Hebrews 5:12). Specific doctrines (Hebrews 6:2). The true faith (1 Timothy 2:7). The truths of the faith (1 Timothy 4:6). The gospel (2 Timothy 1:11). "You must teach what is in accord with sound doctrine" (Titus 2:1).

Teachers play an important role in the church. As a simplification, evangelists bring people into the church, and teachers build on that foundation to enable members in the church to minister according to their spiritual gifts. Of course, the categories overlap — evangelism frequently includes teaching (as seen in the ministry of Jesus and the sermons in Acts), and teaching must include the gospel — but in general, evangelism is targeted at nonmembers, and teaching is targeted at members.

That concludes our survey of the terms found in Ephesians 4:11. We will now look at bishops, elders and deacons.

Bishops

In many denominations, a bishop is a person who supervises all the churches in a region. The bishop often leads the largest congregation in the largest city in the region. Hierarchical churches (Eastern Orthodox, Roman Catholic, Anglican, Methodist, etc.) assign a bishop to each region to have authority over the pastors and churches in that region. Each city or region has only one bishop.

However, the New Testament does not reveal this particular structure. There was more than one bishop (NIV: overseer) in Ephesus, and more than one in Philippi (Acts 20:28; Philippians 1:1). Near Ephesus, Paul sent for the elders, called them all bishops, and told them to be pastors of the church (Acts 20:28). In Philippi, Paul greeted the bishops and deacons without mentioning pastors or elders (Philippians 1:1). This suggests that bishop, pastor and elder are overlapping terms.

When Paul wrote to Timothy, he listed qualifications for a bishop (1 Timothy 3:2) but not for an elder, even though Ephesus had elders (1 Timothy 5:17), and presumably Timothy would ordain elders. Paul left Titus on Crete to ordain elders (Titus 1:5). The qualifications for elders are brief (verse 6) and blend right into qualifications for bishops (verses 7-9). It seems that, although Paul used a different term in verse 7, he was talking about the same type of church leader as in verse 6. Why would Paul tell Titus about the qualifications of a bishop if Titus' only commission was to ordain elders? This again suggests that bishop is another name for an elder.

Although the terms bishop, elder and pastor may have suggested slightly different leadership functions, there was a great deal of overlap in these titles. The difference, if any, between such functions was never spelled out. Paul does not seem to be concerned about what the leaders were called, and he does not detail what they did.

In the original hierarchy, Paul was over Titus and Timothy, and they had authority over the elders, who had some authority over other members. A similar hierarchy exists in some denominations today, with denominational leaders providing supervision over pastors, and pastors supervising elders in the churches. This provides accountability at all levels.

Just as pastor is a functional title, describing the shepherding role that church leaders have, bishop is also a functional title. The Greek word is *episkopos,*[2] which comes from the words *epi* (over) and *skopeo* (see). A bishop is an overseer, a supervisor, someone who watches over others (Acts 20:28). This implies both care and authority. A shepherd watches over the sheep. Jesus Christ is both "Shepherd and Overseer of your souls" (1 Peter 2:25). Peter told elders to be shepherds, "serving as overseers" (1 Peter 5:1-2). Again, we see that the three titles overlap.

What do overseers do? Judging by the qualifications, they must set a good example, both inside the church (1 Peter 5:2-3) and in society (1 Timothy 3:7). Since they must be able to teach (verse 2), teaching must be one of their functions. They must take care of the church in much the same way that they manage a family (1 Timothy 3:4-5). They are "entrusted with God's work" (Titus 1:7). They should "encourage others by sound doctrine and refute those who oppose it" (verse 9). They must teach, rule, encourage and refute (cf. 2 Timothy 4:2). "Whoever aspires to be an overseer desires a noble task" (1 Timothy 3:1).

Elders

"Elder" is the most common translation of *presbyteros,* which means "older one." The prodigal son's older brother was a *presbyteros,* "the older one" (Luke 15:25). Patriarchs and prophets were *presbyteroi,* which the NIV translates as "ancients" (Hebrews 11:2). The 24 elders in heaven are also *presbyteroi* (Revelation 4:4, etc.). Jewish religious leaders were often called elders. The word was used within the Christian community, too (Acts 11:30; 15:2, etc.). Peter and John called themselves elders (1 Peter 5:1; 2 John 1; 3 John 1).

Since *presbyteros* can refer to an older man or to a church leader, we have to look at the context to see which is meant. Since 1 Timothy 5:1-2 deals with younger men, older women and younger women, it appears that *presbyteroi* in verse 1 refers to older men, not to church leaders. Titus 2:2-3 also seems to be about older men and older women. They need to be taught basic things that church leaders should already know. Verses 4-6 then address younger women and younger men, so the context shows that Paul is dealing with older men as an age group, not church leaders.

Paul and Barnabas appointed elders in each of the churches they founded (Acts 14:23). Paul told Titus to appoint elders in every town in Crete (Titus 1:5). In both cases, the churches were young and probably small.

Nevertheless, more than one elder was appointed in each church.

In Jerusalem, the elders seem to have had a ruling function in conjunction with the apostles (Acts 15:6, 22-23; 16:4; 21:18), just as the Jewish elders had a ruling function when they met as the Sanhedrin. Paul referred to "the elders who direct the affairs of the church" (1 Timothy 5:17).

What does it mean to "direct" the church? The Greek word is *proistemi*, which comes from root words meaning "to stand before." This word is used to say that elders and deacons should "manage" their own households (1 Timothy 3:4-5, 12), which should be done with self-sacrificial love. The NIV translates this word "leadership" in Romans 12:8. 1 Timothy 5:17 tells us that elders helped direct the church, but only some of the elders were preachers and teachers. All preachers[3] were elders, but not all elders were preachers.

The extent and limits of elders' authority is not spelled out in the New Testament, but they do have authority. Members are told, "Have confidence in your leaders and submit to their authority, because they keep watch over you as those who must give an account. Do this so that their work will be a joy, not a burden" (Hebrews 13:17). "Respect those...who are over you in the Lord and who admonish you. Hold them in the highest regard in love because of their work" (1 Thessalonians 5:12). "The elders who direct the affairs of the church well are worthy of double honor" (1 Timothy 5:17).

Because elders have a leadership position, they sometimes become the object of a disgruntled person's anger. For that reason, Paul told Timothy, "Do not entertain an accusation against an elder unless it is brought by two or three witnesses" (1 Timothy 5:19). But if the accusation is true, it must be dealt with publicly: "Those who sin are to be rebuked publicly, so that the others may take warning" (verse 20).

Although elders have authority that should be obeyed, they should not use their authority for self-service. Peter told them to serve "as overseers — not because you must, but because you are willing, as God wants you to be not greedy for money, but eager to serve; not lording it over those entrusted to you, but being examples to the flock" (1 Peter 5:2-3). Like overseers and pastors, they are to take care of the flock (1 Timothy 3:5). They anoint the sick and pray for healing (James 5:14). They "watch out for your souls, as those who must give account" (Hebrews 13:17, NKJV).

However, many of the functions of elders are not restricted to elders. The New Testament tells members to serve one another, teach other another, instruct one another, edify one another, admonish one another and submit to one another. The elders serve in all these areas to build others up, teach right doctrines, promote spiritual maturity and equip the saints for works of ministry. Elders preach and direct the church with concern for the spiritual well-being of the members; they work to bring out the most in the other members.

Deacons

The word *diakonos* means "assistant" — someone who works to help others. The word is used in a general sense to describe apostles, preachers, servants and other workers. It is apparently used in a more specialized meaning in Philippians 1:1 and 1 Timothy 3:8-13 to denote an office in the church.

The word *diakonos* and the verb *diakoneo* often mean manual labor. 1 Peter 4:11-12 makes a contrast between those who serve by speaking and those who serve (*diakoneo*). Those who have been given a gift of (manual) ministry (*diakonia*) should use that gift (Romans 12:7). The seven men of Acts 6:3 have often been understood as deacons, because they served by *diakoneo* — waiting on tables (verse 2). Physical service has traditionally formed the core of the duties of a deacon.

We are given a list of qualifications for deacons, but not a list of their duties. The qualifications suggest that deacons *may* have had some teaching and ruling functions. "They must keep hold of the deep truths of the faith" (1 Timothy 3:9). This concern for doctrinal accuracy may have simply been part of the concern for a good example (verse 8), but it may also suggest that deacons helped teach.

Deacons must manage their children and households well (verse 12). The same qualification was given for bishops in verse 4, with the explanation given that bishops must manage the church (verse 5). If the same rationale applies to deacons, it implies that deacons helped direct the church. However, the New Testament does not mandate the specific duties of deacons. The church today is free to assign duties based on current needs.

Summary

The New Testament church had various leaders, who served members through the word and through physical services. Speaking ministries include preaching, teaching, instructing, edifying and admonishing. Physical ministries included food distribution and other internal needs of the church. Leaders also had a role in directing or managing the church, and they were to be obeyed and respected.

All service, whether in speaking, serving or decision-making, should be done for the benefit of those being served. God puts people in the body as he wishes, all for the common good. He has given leadership roles to help the church function in its upward, outward and inward responsibilities.

Ephesians 4:11-16 gives an overview:

"It was he who gave some to be apostles, some to be prophets, some to be evangelists, and some to be pastors and teachers" — God has given various leaders to the church.

"To prepare God's people for works of service" — leaders exist to prepare God's people for helping others. Leaders inform, encourage, train and organize to bring out the most in others.

"So that the body of Christ may be built up" — the result of this is that the church becomes stronger. Works of service help build and unify the church.

"Until we all reach unity in the faith and in the knowledge of the Son of God and become mature, attaining to the whole measure of the fullness of Christ" — this process continues until the church reaches maturity, which means unity in faith and the knowledge of Christ, as measured by the standard of Christ himself. Although the goal is never attained in this life, it is still the goal the church is working toward.

"Then we will no longer be infants, tossed back and forth by the waves, and blown here and there by every wind of teaching and by the cunning and craftiness of people in their deceitful scheming" — maturity in Christ gives us doctrinal stability.

"Instead, speaking the truth in love, we will in all things grow up into him who is the Head, that is, Christ" — maturity in Christ comes from combining doctrinal accuracy with love.

"From him the whole body, joined and held together by every supporting ligament, grows and builds itself up in love, as each part does its work" — it is from Christ that the church grows, and the church is held together by its members, who work together in love to build the church.

Church growth comes as each member does his or her work of service, everyone according to 1) the needs of the church, 2) the place in the body God has given them, and 3) the spiritual gifts he has given them. In short, leaders and laity work together for the same purpose: maturity in Christ.

Lifetime or temporary?

Christians sometimes view the pastoral ministry as a lifetime calling. This is not necessarily true; there is no verse that requires it. God calls every member to serve, but the way in which he wants us to serve may change through the years. God may call a person to serve as a pastor for several years, to serve as a professor for a few more years and then to serve as a business manager for a while. The person might serve as a pastoral supervisor, and then as an assistant pastor a few years later, depending on the needs of the church and changes in the person's family, health or other personal circumstances. The person might serve as a full-time employee or as a self-employed or retired elder.

Due to changing circumstances in their lives, pastors may sometimes need to resign from the pastoral role entirely, depending on what they understand God to be calling them to do. They may need to minister (serve) as laypersons rather than as elders. People who see leadership solely in terms of authority might view this as a demotion, but when ministry is seen in terms of service, a resignation might be seen as a spiritually mature response to God's call to serve in a new way. On the other hand, a resignation could also be a refusal to serve in the way that God wants. Ministers must make their own decisions, without peer pressure or fear of criticism.

Endnotes

1. The Greek construction in Ephesians 4:11 implies that *pastors* and *teachers* are two descriptors of the same people. There is one article for apostles, one for prophets, one for evangelists, and only one for "pastors and teachers." One of the primary functions of a pastor is teaching. We see in Acts 20:28 and 1 Peter 5:2 that pastors are overseers, and we see from 1 Timothy 3:2 that overseers must be "able to teach." The titles overlap.

2. As the word moved from Greek to Latin to English, it was changed to *episcopus,* then *biscopus,* then *biscop* and then *bishop.*

3. Paul here seems to equate preachers and teachers. In Ephesians 4:11, he seems to equate pastors and teachers. He also seems to equate pastors with bishops. Although different gifts may be involved, the gifts often overlap. Paul does not seem to use any one title consistently.

Michael Morrison

7. LEADERSHIP IN THE CHURCH

Since every Christian has the Holy Spirit, and the Holy Spirit teaches each of us, is there any need for leadership within the church? Wouldn't it be better to view ourselves as a group of equals, as every person capable of every role?

Various verses in the Bible, such as 1 John 2:27, may seem to support this idea—but only if they are taken out of context. For example, when John wrote that Christians did not need anyone to teach them, did he mean they didn't need to be taught by him? Did he say, don't pay any attention to what I write, because you don't need me or anyone else to teach you? This is not what he meant.

John wrote the letter because those people *did* need to be taught. He was warning his readers against the idea that salvation is found in secret teachings. He was saying that the truths of Christianity were already known in the church. Believers did not need any secret "knowledge" beyond what the Holy Spirit had already given the community. John was not saying that Christians do not need leaders and teachers.

Each Christian has individual responsibilities. Each person must decide what to believe and make decisions about how to live. But the New Testament is clear that we are not merely individuals—we are part of a body. The church is optional in the same sense that responsibility is optional—God lets us choose what to do, but that does not mean that all choices are equally helpful for us, or that all are equally within God's desire.

Do Christians need teachers? The entire New Testament is evidence that we do. The church at Antioch had "teachers" as one of their leadership roles (Acts 13:1). Teachers are one of the gifts the Holy Spirit gives to the church (1 Corinthians 12:28; Ephesians 4:11). Paul called himself a teacher (1 Timothy 2:7; Titus 1:11). Even after many years in the faith, believers needed teachers (Hebrews 5:12). James warned against the idea that everybody is a teacher (James 3:1), but his comments still indicate that the church normally had people who taught.

Christians need sound teaching in the truths of the faith. God knows that we grow at different speeds and have strengths in different areas. He knows, because he is the one who gives us those strengths in the first place, and he does not give the same gifts to everyone (1 Corinthians 12). Rather, he distributes them so that we will work together for the common good, helping each other, rather than each going off and doing our own thing (verse 7).

Some Christians are gifted with more ability for compassion, some for discernment, some for physical service, some for exhortation, some for

49

coordination and some for teaching. All Christians are equal in value, but equality does not mean being identical or interchangeable. We are given different abilities, and although all are important, all are not the same. As children of God, as heirs of salvation, we are equal, but we do not all have the same role in the church. God puts people and distributes his gifts as he sees fit, not according to human expectations.

God puts teachers into the church—people who are able to help others learn. As a human organization, we do not always select the most gifted people, and teachers sometimes make mistakes. But this does not invalidate the clear witness of the New Testament that God's church does have teachers, that this is a role that we should expect to see in communities of believers.

Although we do not have a specific office named "teacher," we do expect teachers to exist within the church, and we expect our pastors to be able to teach (1 Timothy 3:2; 2 Timothy 2:2). In Ephesians 4:11, Paul groups pastors and teachers together, structuring them grammatically as if this role were a dual responsibility, to shepherd and to teach.

A hierarchy?

The New Testament does not prescribe any particular hierarchy for the church. The Jerusalem church had apostles and elders. The church in Antioch had prophets and teachers (Acts 15:1; 13:1). Some New Testament passages call the leaders elders; others call them overseers or bishops; some just call them leaders (Acts 14:23; Titus 1:6-7; Philippians 1:1; 1 Timothy 3:2; Hebrews 13:17). These seem to be different words for the same role.

The New Testament does not describe an elaborate hierarchy of apostles over prophets over evangelists over pastors over elders over deacons over lay members. "Over" may not be the best word to use, anyway, for all of these are service roles, designed to help the church. But the New Testament does tell people to obey the leaders in the church, to cooperate with their leadership (Hebrews 13:17). Blind obedience is not appropriate, nor is consistent skepticism or resistance.

Paul describes a simple hierarchy when he tells Timothy to appoint elders in churches. As apostle, church planter and mentor, Paul had authority over Timothy, and Timothy had authority to decide who would be elders and deacons. But this is a description of Ephesus, not a prescription for all future organization of the church. We do not see any attempt to tie every church to Jerusalem, or to Antioch, or to Rome. That would not have been practical in the first century, anyway.

So what can we say for the church today? We can say that God expects the church to have leaders, but he does not specify what those leaders are to be called or how they are to be structured. He has left those details to be worked out in the changing circumstances that the church will find itself in. We should have leaders in local churches, but it does not matter so much what they are called: Pastor Jones, Elder Kim, Minister Lawson or Servant Chris might be equally acceptable.

We use what might be called an episcopal model (the word episcopal is based on the Greek word for overseer—*episkopos,* sometimes translated as bishop) because of the circumstances we are in. We believe this is the best way for our churches to have doctrinal soundness and stability. Our episcopal model has its problems, but so do other models, for they all involve fallible humans. We believe that in our historical and geographical circumstances, our style of organization can serve our members better than a congregational or a presbyterian model can.

(Keep in mind that all models of church government, whether congregational, presbyterian or episcopal, can take a variety of forms. Our form of the episcopal model is radically different from that of the Eastern Orthodox, Anglican, Episcopal, Roman Catholic or Lutheran churches.)

The head of the church is Jesus Christ, and all leaders within the church should seek his will in all things, in their own lives as well as in the functioning of the congregations. The leaders are to be Christlike in their leadership, which means that they must seek to help others, not to benefit themselves. The local church is not a work crew to help the pastor get his work done. Rather, the pastor is a facilitator, to help the members get *their* work done— the work of the gospel, the work Jesus Christ wants them to do.

Elders and ministry leaders

Paul compares the church to a body with many different parts. Its unity is not in uniformity, but in working together for a common Lord and for a common purpose. Different members have different strengths, and we are to use these for the common good (1 Corinthians 12:7).

Grace Communion International appoints through *ordination* elders to serve as pastoral leaders. It also appoints through *commissioning* ministry leaders (who may also be referred to as deacons or deaconesses). What is the difference between "ordination" and "commissioning"? In general, ordination is more public and more permanent; whereas commissioning may be done privately as well as in public, and may be revoked easily. Commissioning is less formal, and is not automatically renewable or transferable. An ordination may be revoked also, but this is done only in exceptional circumstances.

In Grace Communion International we do not have detailed descriptions of each church leadership role. Elders often serve in congregations as pastors (senior, associate or assistant pastors). Most preach and teach, though not all. Some specialize in administration. Each serves according to ability, under the supervision of the senior pastor (the overseer, or *episkopos* of the congregation).

Ministry leaders come in even greater diversity, each serving (we hope) according to ability, each according to the needs of the congregation. The senior pastor may commission them for temporary assignments, or for indefinite periods. The roles of these leaders and the councils and committees that advise them are described in our Church Administration Manual. The policies in that manual allow for flexibility in organizing congregational leadership because our congregations exist in a variety of circumstances, having diverse gifts.

Senior pastors serve somewhat like orchestra conductors. They cannot force anyone to play on cue, but they can provide guidance and coordination, and the group as a whole will work much better when the players take the cues they are given. In our denomination, members cannot fire their senior pastor. Instead, senior pastors are chosen and dismissed at the regional level, which in the United States includes Church Administration & Development, in coordination with local leaders.

What if a member believes a pastor is incompetent, or is leading the sheep astray? That's where our episcopal structure comes in. Problems of doctrine or leadership style should be discussed with the pastor first, and then with a pastoral leader (the overseer of the pastors in the area).

Just as congregations need local leaders and teachers, pastors also need leaders and teachers. That is why we believe that our denominational home office has an important role in serving our congregations. We strive to be a source of training, of ideas, of encouragement, of supervision, of cooperation. We are not perfect, but that is the calling we see set before us, and that is what we will strive to do.

Our eyes need to be focused on Jesus. He has work for us to do, and much work is already being done. Praise him for his patience, for his gifts, and for the work that helps us grow.

Joseph Tkach

8. CODE OF ETHICS FOR GCI ELDERS

Preamble

The Code of Ethics for Elders is designed to edify the body of Christ. We pray it will be embraced by all elders of the church serving in any and all congregational or administrative responsibilities. The code is intended to be a living document that helps shape our character as we constantly seek to make it better reflect Christ's will for us as elders in his church.

Ethics provides a framework for how people make decisions and judgments and how we act on them. Decision-making for the Christian is ethical when it is firmly grounded in the Word of God and led by the Holy Spirit, for it is only in these that we find a basis for understanding the will of God.

As church leaders, we must submit ourselves to the Word of God and allow the Holy Spirit to guide us in the application of ethical principles of Scripture. Our Christian conduct must be based on the life and teachings of Jesus, the teachings of biblical writers and the guidance of the Holy Spirit. The New Testament calls for the highest standard of reputation, ethics and conduct for us as elders.

As Christian leaders, we recognize that Jesus Christ lives in us through the Holy Spirit. We ask him to change us so that the reality of his resurrected life is evident in our thoughts and actions. The ethical guidelines and principles in this Code of Ethics for Elders are set forth to tie in the realities of our ministerial activities with this transcendent reality of our Christian lives.

Therefore, as elders in the body of Christ, we must endeavor to conduct our lives according to the spirit of the ethical guidelines and principles set forth in this Code of Ethics for Elders.

Responsibility to God

Knowing that Jesus Christ is the living Head of the church, I will strive to conduct myself in a manner that brings glory to him. This means I will strive to:

be a responsible servant of God.

exercise faithful stewardship in my devotional life through the use of spiritual disciplines, the gifts of the Spirit and acts of service.

exercise faithful stewardship of financial, physical and intellectual resources.

accept accountability for all my actions and avoid situations that could reflect negatively on the name of Jesus Christ.

maintain sexual purity.

exercise Christ's servant-leadership.

Responsibility of denominational leadership to elders

In the spirit of Christian brotherhood, denominational supervisors are responsible to provide support as well as just and fair treatment for elders. This means if I am in a supervisory position, I will strive to:

be accessible and promptly respond to requests from elders.

provide sound and clear spiritual, ecclesiastical and administrative leadership.

openly and respectfully communicate to elders any serious complaints brought against them.

provide reasonable time for feedback to requests for information from elders.

handle sensitive and confidential information about an elder in a responsible manner.

be sensitive to the personal and family needs of elders.

Responsibility to the denomination

As an elder of Grace Communion International, I have a responsibility of loyalty to ecclesiastical supervisors. This means I will strive to:

patiently and prayerfully study all doctrinal materials presented by the denomination.

support and carry out all administrative decisions and policies of ecclesiastical supervisors. If I cannot in good conscience do this, I will immediately notify my supervisors.

cooperate with, and seek assistance from ecclesiastical supervisors, peers and members of my congregation(s) in order to acquire information and to receive training that is relevant to my assignment as an elder.

respect my denomination and be responsible and respectful in discussions about fellow leaders—past and present.

support and promote the global mission of the church.

Responsibility to family

I will place my family responsibilities at the highest level of my priorities, second only to my relationship to God. This means I will strive to:

spiritually, emotionally and physically support my family.

be faithful to my spouse.

be a responsible and dedicated parent to my children.

Relationship with the congregation

I will lead with justice and mercy, striving to express proper balance between strength and gentleness in all situations. This means I will strive to:

provide sound and clear pastoral, spiritual leadership.

help members develop spiritual gifts and mentor spiritual leaders in the congregation.

give sermons that are biblically based, in theological agreement with the church and relevant to the life of the church.

be committed to prompt reconciliation of interpersonal conflicts. I recognize that I must have personal courage, exercised with appropriate tact in facing opposition. I will encourage members of my congregation to seek help from my peers and/or ecclesiastical supervisors if necessary.

be trustworthy in all areas of confidentiality, except as I am legally bound to disclose. I will not betray the trust of a member by disclosing personal information about that person to others without that person's knowledge and consent.

be fair and consistent in my dealings with parishioners.

honor and respect other cultures, genders and races.

Responsibility to fellow elders

As an elder of Grace Communion International, I have a responsibility to respect and honor my colleagues. I will strive to cooperate with and support my fellow elders as we work together to further the work of Christ in the church. This means I will strive to:

respect my fellow elders and will not speak against them publicly or privately, considering them partners in the work of God.

respect the administrative boundaries of another elder's area of responsibility.

treat the office of an elder in a manner so as not to be competitive or enhance my own status or position.

serve my colleagues with counsel, support and personal assistance.

Responsibility to the greater body of Christ

Elders and members of Grace Communion International are a part of the greater Christian community. This means I will:

avoid recruiting members out of other churches.

seek to work in harmony with other Christian leaders and programs to strengthen the body of Christ and advance the kingdom of God.

uphold the theology and doctrine of Grace Communion International without slandering Christians who hold other views.

Responsibility to the local community

The local church is an integral part of the society in which it resides. An active, appropriate role in the community serves as a Christian example of love and is a witness to the gospel of Jesus Christ. This means I will strive to:

be a responsible member of my community.

accept reasonable responsibilities for community service, recognizing this is a function of my public ministry.

encourage the involvement of the congregation in appropriate community events.

comply with the laws of my government as long as they do not conflict with the teachings of Jesus.

take care not to allow political issues to create polarization within the congregation, or to be a focus in sermons, Bible studies, or other church meetings.

9. TEAMWORK IN THE CHURCH

Sometimes Christians assume that full-time pastors serve the Lord more than other members do. Although that may be true in some cases, it is not true in all cases. Paul tells us, "Whatever you do, do it all for the glory of God" (1 Corinthians 10:31). Whenever a Christian works in a bank, he or she does it for the glory of God. A Christian who teaches school does it to glorify God. A Christian who takes care of children at home glorifies God in changing diapers and cleaning floors. They are all serving the Lord—full-time, perhaps 100 hours a week!

Every member lives to the glory and honor of Jesus Christ (2 Corinthians 5:15). Every member serves him as circumstances and abilities allow. Every member is a witness of Jesus Christ working in this world—and that includes secular occupations as well as religious jobs. Jesus served God by working as a carpenter for many years. Even today, Christian carpenters serve God in the work they do.

Members have a mission

The church is not a building, social club or a self-benefit society. The church is the people of God. That means both ministers and lay members. The church has a mission to the world. The people of God have a mission to the world. Ministers and members have a mission to the world.

Lay members have a prominent role in the church's mission—partly because there are many more lay members than there are ordained ministers. Another reason for the importance of lay members is that lay members are more often "in the world." Due to the nature of their job, ministers often interact mostly with people who are already Christians. It is the lay members who are mixing with non-Christians on a daily basis—on the job, in the neighborhoods, in hobbies and sports. They set examples of Christ-like life, hopefully a life that evidences hope and joy despite the troubles of this world. Non-Christians need that kind of example.

The church meets for worship and fellowship a few hours each week. What is the church doing during the rest of the week? Much of our time is spent mixing with the world, in our jobs, in our neighborhoods, even in our families. Most of the time, the church is *dispersed,* setting an example in the world. This is part of our Christian calling, part of our mission, even part of our worship as we seek to make God look good in all that we do.

Our weekly worship services should fill us with the joy of salvation and strengthen and instruct us in living in Christ throughout the week. They remind us of what life is for. They also give us opportunity to come together into the presence of God and express thanks to him for what he has done in our lives the preceding week. They give us opportunity to join the angelic choir in praising him in collective song and prayer. They help us seek guidance from his Word regarding how we serve him in the coming week.

Likewise, our small group meetings give us opportunity to reflect on the Word of God and share with one another the work God is doing in our lives, so that we might encourage one another, and pray for one another that our service might be all the more effective.

All members are ministers of Jesus Christ. We all serve him. Some serve him primarily in prayer, some in helping the poor, some in their family and neighborhood responsibilities, etc.—each according to our circumstances, each according to our abilities. Pastors serve him in pastoring his flock; members serve him in contributing to the spiritual health and unity of the flock, and we all serve him throughout the week in our ordinary activities, too.

When Christ said "take up your cross and follow me," he was not referring to pastors only! We cannot hire someone to do our Christian service for us. Pastors are to lead, to teach, to equip members for service. But each of us must do our own duty, as we have been called and gifted by the Holy Spirit. All Christians follow Christ in denying the self and in serving others. The Lord served others, and service is not beneath the dignity of anyone who accepts Jesus' death as being payment for his or her sins. He served us, and calls on us to serve others, to do good to all.

The question is not *whether* we serve Christ throughout the week—it is *how* we serve him. Whether we want to or not, we represent Jesus Christ in the office, on the highway, in our homes. What we do throughout the week is important—this is where doctrine comes to life to illustrate the fact that we are being transformed into the likeness of Jesus Christ. He is living in us, Paul says, and the effect he can have in our lives is limited only by the vitality of our faith in him.

Most of us are responsive to the will of our Lord. But many of us are not used to thinking of ourselves as ministers of Jesus Christ. Every member is ministering, being led by Christ to work and serve in the world. This fact magnifies the importance of what we do in the name of Jesus throughout the week—not just in the work we do, but also in our relationships with the people we work with.

The fact that our work is a ministry magnifies the importance of community service. Works of service are of value in themselves, but they are also opportunities to witness to what Christ is doing in our lives. Some people are better at sharing the gospel in words; some are better at sharing it through their work. When Christians work together, they can often be more effective than either one would be alone.

Mutual support

Throughout the week, members are at the "front line" of the church's work. We can support each other in prayer in this work. We need to be *aware* of how we are serving, and how others are serving, so that we might better encourage them. We can share our experiences and opportunities whenever we meet. Worship services can also strengthen and equip us for this work. Our success as a church is measured in large part by what we do *during the week*. When members are doing good in Jesus' name throughout the week, and when they are being energized and encouraged by what they do and hear at worship services and in their small group meetings, then the gospel is being spread.

When members realize that they are ministers of Jesus Christ, they have a realistic view of who they are, what they have been called for, and how to live. Their identity is in Christ. They come to worship services not only to give worship, but also to receive instruction that will help them serve even better during the week. Perhaps that also generates fewer complaints of "I'm not getting fed" and more thoughts of "How can I glorify God in my life?"

Pastors are to provide vision and leadership as they equip members for their ministries. For one thing, this means helping people connect to God, from whom all ministry should originate. This means inspiring, encouraging, comforting, exhorting and challenging. It includes preaching and administration, and it also includes training leaders for small groups and developing and mentoring leaders for other ministries.

The church, from the pulpit and in small groups, can provide moral support for the work that is being done, helping remind one another that our activities are serving Jesus Christ, and that he gives us the power and courage to carry out his will. In small groups and other activities, the church also provides practical opportunities for skills to be developed and spiritual gifts to be discovered and ministries to be encouraged.

How to help pastors

Pastors have a difficult job. How can members help their pastors? For one thing, pray for them. The pastors' job cannot be done without supernatural help. For another thing, ask pastors what to do to help. Be a volunteer—don't wait for an assignment. Third, help create an environment of love in the congregation. This will give "weak" members comfort and time to work through some of their needs. Strong members need to assist in the ministry of reconciliation, of soothing hurts within the body of Christ, of encouraging, comforting and edifying one another.

Fourth, many members have some pastoral skills. They can even help equip other members for works of ministry. They can invite other members to join them in their ministries during the week. They can mentor and set examples of service. In small groups and one-on-one, they can share their faith in Christ with other members, to strengthen their faith. They can pray for other members. In all these ways, members can assist the pastor.

Every member is a minister.

Joseph Tkach

10. LAY MEMBERS' ROLE
IN THE EARLY CHURCH

Acts 2 describes the setting: God-fearing Jews from various nations had gathered in Jerusalem for the Day of Pentecost. The Holy Spirit filled the apostles and other disciples, and they spoke in tongues. Although the pilgrims came from 15 territories — north, south, east and west — each traveler heard his or her own native language. After Peter spoke, 3,000 baptisms took place that day (Acts 2:41). The church continued to grow rapidly (verse 47).

What happened to these people? Where did they go? What is their legacy? We know of Peter, John and Paul. Stephen's strength in martyrdom inspires us; Philip's faith encourages us. What of the other members?

Every great work finds support in a group of people with a shared vision. The church is no different. Thousands of members supported Peter, John, Paul and other leaders. The mission of all these dedicated people was to preach redemption through Jesus Christ beginning in Jerusalem and extending to the whole world.

Heroic literature seldom mentions the commoner standing side-by-side with the hero. However, God's Word records the faith, courage, dedication and work of many members of the early church. Their lives are inspiring examples of personal evangelism. They helped spread the gospel.

These faithful members of 19 centuries ago inspire us in our work today. There were no fanfares, booklets or articles. But there was faith, the Holy Spirit, love for others and a vision of a new life. The ordinary members made a difference in their society for the kingdom of God. Let's look at what some of them did.

Examples of the earliest Christians

On the Day of Pentecost, people from many different lands became disciples of Jesus Christ. As the church grew, some of the Jewish leaders caused a persecution. After Stephen's martyrdom, members fled, but they did not remain silent. "Those who had been scattered preached the word wherever they went" (Acts 8:4). They were fruitful. In Acts 11:19-21, we see the result of their faithfulness:

> Those who had been scattered by the persecution in connection with Stephen traveled as far as Phoenicia, Cyprus and Antioch, telling the message only to Jews. Some of them, however, men from Cyprus and Cyrene, went to Antioch and began to speak to Greeks also, telling them the good news about the Lord Jesus.

The Lord's hand was with them, and a great number of people believed and turned to the Lord.

Despite persecution, these believers — probably thousands of them — bravely and faithfully taught the word given them. In the deep conviction of their faith and inspired by the Holy Spirit, they preached the gospel (the Greek word in verse 20 is *euangelizomai*). Many people responded to their teaching and believed in Jesus Christ. Some of these believers may have been the 70 or 72 that Christ had commissioned earlier (Luke 10:1), but most were probably lay members. That's why the Jerusalem church needed to send Barnabas to minister to the new believers (Acts 11:22-23).

One man in the Decapolis

In at least one instance, Jesus instructed someone other than the apostles to tell people what Jesus had done. After casting a legion of demons out of a man who lived on the southeast side of the Sea of Galilee (Luke 8:26-37), the man asked for permission to travel with Jesus (verse 38). Jesus replied, "Return home and tell how much God has done for you."

The man did more than Jesus had asked: "The man went away and told all over town how much Jesus had done for him" (verse 39). "And all the people were amazed" (Mark 5:20). Later, Christ toured the area of the Decapolis. People brought a man to him for healing (Mark 7:31-32). Perhaps the witness of the healed demoniac helped the people respond to Jesus.

Similarly, the Samaritan woman told her people about Jesus (John 4:28-29). "Many of the Samaritans from that town believed in him because of the woman's testimony" (verse 39).

Other early converts

Paul refers to the staying power of some early converts in Romans 16:7. He says Andronicus and Junia "were in Christ before I was." They were probably some of the Roman Jews converted on the Day of Pentecost. Paul also mentions Epenetus, "who was the first convert to Christ in the province of Asia" (verse 5). Acts 2:9 mentions people from Asia in Jerusalem for Pentecost.

Philip

As we follow the church's growth after Pentecost, many members of the earliest era of the church leave a remarkable legacy. Philip, a leader of the Greek-speaking Christians in Jerusalem (Acts 6:5-6), went to Samaria (Acts 8:5-8), perhaps fleeing Saul's persecutions (verses 3-4). There he preached the gospel, as other scattered members did elsewhere. The intensity of his speaking and the power of the Holy Spirit were followed by miracles. "When they believed Philip as he preached the good news of the kingdom of God and the name of Jesus Christ, they were baptized, both men and women" (verse 12).

Later, Philip was led by the Holy Spirit to witness to an Ethiopian (verses 26-40). He explained "the good news about Jesus" (verse 35), and he baptized the Ethiopian. Was Philip ordained? The book of Acts doesn't say. Luke didn't think it important to indicate whether he was or not. Many years later, Philip was an evangelist in Caesarea, and his four daughters had the gift of prophecy (Acts 21:8).

Called to baptize an apostle

Acts 9 records the important role of another member, Ananias. All Judea and the surrounding regions knew of Saul's severe persecutions of the church. While on the way to Damascus, Saul lost his eyesight during a miraculous intervention. In response to a vision (Acts 9:10), Ananias sought out and baptized the chief persecutor, Saul of Tarsus.

We know little of Ananias except that he "was a devout observer of the law and highly respected by all the Jews" (Acts 22:12). Consider the faith and courage required of Ananias. So terrible was Paul's reputation that even the Jerusalem disciples, veterans of many persecutions, feared to meet Paul when he later attempted to join them (Acts 9:26). Knowing Paul's reputation and authority to inflict terror, Ananias asked the Lord if this was the right man (verses 13-14). Assured by Jesus in vision that Paul was indeed the chosen individual, Ananias went into the house.

> Placing his hands on Saul, he said, "Brother Saul, the Lord — Jesus, who appeared to you on the road as you were coming here — has sent me so that you may see again and be filled with the Holy Spirit." Immediately, something like scales fell from Saul's eyes, and he could see again. He got up and was baptized. (verses 17-18)

In Damascus, in a little-known Christian community, Ananias, a member of whom we know little, baptized the New Testament figure of whom we know much, the apostle Paul. In spite of Saul's persecutions, Ananias acted, and God recorded his faith as an example for us. Faith and courage aren't confined to ministers; they are found in lay members, too.

Women

God also records the courage and faithful witness of many women. They bravely withstood not only religious persecution, but also risked social ostracism.

Cenchrea was a city east of Corinth. From there, Phoebe helped Paul minister to the Roman church. While Paul prepared for his journey to Jerusalem, Phoebe had business in Rome. Paul commends her to the church (Romans 16:1-2) as one who showed generosity and hospitality to many. F.C. Conybeare postulates her as a widow (*The Life and Epistles of St. Paul,* page 497). Greek manners and customs would not normally allow a married or single woman to be so prominent. An ancient subscription to the book of Romans states that Phoebe carried the epistle by hand.

Philippi was a city of Macedonia north of Greece. Since no synagogue existed in this city (Conybeare, page 226), devout Jews would seek a "place of prayer" (Acts 16:13). Usually this was outside the city near running water, perhaps because it was peaceful. The group at Philippi was composed primarily of women.

Among these women was Lydia, a businesswoman from Thyatira. God moved in her life, opening her heart (verse 14). Paul baptized not only her, but also her whole household (verse 15); she seems to have been the dominant individual in her home. Her first work after baptism was an act of hospitality. She opened her home to Paul and his companions. Later, after his release from prison, Paul returned to her home to encourage the members before leaving the area (verse 40). The letter to the Philippians expresses thanks and joy for continued support by the believers in Philippi. Lydia, a founding member, set an excellent example for that church. She was a spiritual leader.

Families

Paul mentions Lois and Eunice (2 Timothy 1:5), Timothy's grandmother and mother. Timothy, who had a non-Jewish father, lived in Lystra when he first met Paul (Acts 16:1). Paul referred to the sincere faith of the women (2 Timothy 1:5). They were spiritual leaders in their family.

Paul had first-hand knowledge of their faith. He came to Lystra, in Galatia, on his first journey. There, after a miraculous healing (Acts 14:8-10), the residents declared Paul and Barnabas to be gods. But Paul was eventually stoned and left for dead. "After the disciples had gathered around him, he got up and went back into the city" (verses 19-20). The disciples probably included Timothy and his family (2 Timothy 3:10-11). Living in an area of intense persecution demands sincere faith. Lois and Eunice had that faith and instilled it in Timothy.

In Philippians 4:2-3, Paul acknowledges Euodia and Syntyche. Paul recalls "these women have contended at my side in the cause of the gospel, along with Clement and the rest of my fellow workers." Though Paul was greater in authority, he treated his spiritual brothers and sisters respectfully, as equals. They worked together to spread the gospel.

Priscilla and Aquila

One of the most significant couples mentioned is "a Jew named Aquila…with his wife Priscilla" (Acts 18:2). They lived in Corinth after being expelled from Rome by the Emperor Claudius. Paul went to see them and stayed and worked with them in Corinth. There is no mention of conversion; they were probably already Christians when Paul met them.

Their contribution to the New Testament church is important. Not only were they in Corinth, but they were also in Ephesus (Acts 18:24-26; 2 Timothy 4:19) and in Rome (Romans 16:3). They were probably wealthy. The church in Corinth met in their house (1 Corinthians 16:19). So did a church in Rome (Romans 16:5).

Paul remarks that Priscilla and Aquila were his fellow-workers. "They risked their lives for me" (Romans 16:3-4). They went with Paul on his journey from Corinth to Ephesus (Acts 18:18-19). They helped Paul with physical and spiritual support. In Corinth, Priscilla and Aquila worked with Apollos, an eloquent and zealous man, and "they invited him to their home and explained to him the way of God more adequately" (Acts 18:26). Were they ordained, or were they lay members? Luke doesn't tell us. Service like this can be done by members whether or not they are ordained.

The work continues

Many other faithful members are mentioned in the New Testament. Throughout the centuries, many have dedicated their lives and wealth to proclaiming the name of Jesus Christ.

It is the same Jesus Christ and the same Holy Spirit guiding the church today. It is the same message: salvation through Jesus Christ. It is the same zeal. It is the same God who will not forget the sacrifices we may make. "God is not unjust; he will not forget your work and the love you have shown him as you have helped his people and continue to help them" (Hebrews 6:10).

The book of Acts shows us that various members were instrumental in spreading the gospel of salvation through Jesus Christ. Some of the people mentioned in this article may have been ordained ministers, but others were probably not. *All* members can help spread the gospel. Lay members, as led by the Holy Spirit, continue to be a vital part of Christ's commission to the disciples.

Donald L. Jackson

11. WORKING TOGETHER FOR THE GOSPEL

The Great Commission (Matthew 28:19-20) states the purpose of the church. It involves *going* in order to make disciples, whom we are to baptize and teach. This Commission isn't a stay-at-home project. We won't catch fish unless we go to the water, and it doesn't do any good to catch them if we just throw them back in. We need to go, and we need to make disciples.

Eager to share

Every Christian should be "ready to give an answer." Being ready implies not just having an answer, but being on alert to actually give it. When we believe the gospel, we become eager to do what Jesus Christ wants us to do. Faith make us eager to look for opportunities, even create opportunities, because we want to give this answer that God has given us.

We do not share the gospel to chalk up points or get an obligation out of the way. We share the gospel because Christ, who died and rose again, lives in us. Just as Christ did not come to be served, but to serve, so the church cannot rightly be his body in the world by keeping its faith to itself.

The church exists not for its own sake, but for the sake of the world, just as Jesus came not to do his own will, but the will of the Father who sent him. Christian faith changes how we interact with the world. As Christians, we are still part of the world around us, but we are now, since Christ lives in us, part of the world in an entirely new way—a way that makes a positive impact in the name of our God who loves the world so much that he sent his Son for its salvation.

People need to know that God loves them, that their lives have meaning and purpose, that there is hope even when physical life seems pointless. God has given us good news for them, and the Holy Spirit in us makes us eager to give it to them.

They may not be eager to hear it, to be sure. Many people think they are doing just fine without God. But eventually the things they trust in—money, health, friends, intelligence, etc.—will disappoint them, and they will be ready to hear about a hope that is secure. That's when we need to be ready, and in order to be ready, we need to be alert, and in order to be alert, we need to be eager and looking for opportunities.

It is deeply satisfying to be used by God to help someone else. Evangelism gives us a tremendous sense of significance, because we are taking part in eternal work, sharing by grace in the work of God himself, his work of redeeming from sin and saving from death our fellow human beings.

Working together

Each of us needs other people. None of us are self-sufficient, though we may think we are. God spreads his gifts around so we have to work together for the common good (1 Corinthians 12:7, 11). God wants his people to gather for regular fellowship, worship, discipleship and ministry. That's why evangelism is only the first step in the Great Commission. Infant believers need a family to teach, encourage, protect and help them.

"Independent Christians" who avoid worship meetings rarely share the gospel and rarely live out the biblical commands to love, encourage and help one another. They live as though they are self-sufficient, and they tend to avoid any public acknowledgement that they trust in Jesus Christ. We cannot be ready to express the hope that lies within us when we routinely avoid opportunities to do so. We can hardly "bear one another's burdens" (Galatians 6:2) by avoiding fellowship. No Christian can say to other Christians, "I have no need of you" (1 Corinthians 12:21).

Different people are differently gifted. Some think that evangelism is the main thing; others think that discipleship is the priority; and still others think that fellowship is all that's needed for a healthy church. Some focus on music, some on youths, some on grace, and some on guidance. Some are physically unable to leave their homes, and prayer is their labor of love.

All such people need to learn to work together. Being together is a learning experience in itself—we learn to love not by being surrounded by people easy to love, but by sometimes being with people who are hard to love—people who are different from us. God puts us together for our own good, and we do his work better when we work together.

The church grows "as each part does its work" (Ephesians 4:16). Have you found a meaningful way to support the Great Commission? If not, ask God to help you. It's something worth praying about.

Joseph Tkach

12. THE PASTOR'S CALLING

Many people have no idea what pastors do, and it's not unusual for pastors to feel inadequate in their role. I've felt that way, as Paul apparently did in asking, "who is equal to such a task?" He then noted (speaking of the human body): "we have this treasure in jars of clay to show that this all-surpassing power is from God and not from us" (2 Corinthians 2:16; 4:7). Despite the times of doubt that pastors sometimes face, they find reassurance in remembering that God has called them and that they have his anointing to serve him in this way—an anointing confirmed by their ordination.

I am pleased that our elders approach their calling to pastoral ministry with humility and faith. Paul tells us that pastors, along with other ordained ministers, are called "to equip God's people for works of service, so that the body of Christ may be built up until we all reach unity in the faith and in the knowledge of the Son of God and become mature, attaining to the whole measure of the fullness of Christ" (Ephesians 4:11-13, TNIV).

All Christians are called to share in the ministry of Jesus, through what Paul refers to here as "works of service." Ordained ministers, including pastors, are called to serve by equipping and then leading God's people in these works.

To be called by God to serve as a pastor is a privilege, blessing and responsibility. It's a calling that comes to different people in different ways—sometimes quietly, over a long period of time; at other times dramatically and suddenly—like Paul on the road to Damascus (Acts 26:12-14).

I have been asked, "How do I know 'for sure' that I am called to be a pastor?" The hard answer is that you will know "for sure" only in your spirit and through the confirmation of those you serve. We walk by faith, not by sight, and the opportunity to serve God is unlike any other life endeavor. The center of that service involves feeding others through sharing with them the living and written Word of God. The aim of that service flows out of a desire that others come to know God through Jesus Christ and put their trust in him alone for life now and eternally.

Signs that point to such a calling are love for studying and communicating the Word of God, desire to pray with and for people, desire to enable people to come to God in worship, and desire to help people become a fellowship of those gathered in the Holy Spirit around the Word of God both written and living.

Pastoral service brings with it the power of God moving through us in humility. Though that brings us joy, it can also bring disappointment. None of us are perfect, and neither are the ones we interact with in ministry. Sometimes God's leading is mysterious, beyond our comprehension.

Whether we are rich or poor, learned or uneducated, or anywhere in between, God has a job for us and he calls us to it. We must not confuse the form of that call with the substance of it. He usually calls people by dropping hints. Many have told me that they eventually realized that God was dropping such hints in their life for years, though they did not notice them right away. We humans can be dense at times. But when we look back on our lives and pray about God's will, the little hints he has placed in our lives are recognized as our call to pastoral ministry. It simply takes some time for us to hear, and it comes when we are ready to respond.

There are numerous ways we experience such affirmation. You might feel that you have fallen into this role because no one else was stepping up. But this may be a sign that God wants you to join others in his service. Some of us have been serving in pastoral ministry for years without perhaps even recognizing it ourselves. But others have seen the fruits of your service, and this could be God's affirmation. If you have been asked by others to serve in a pastoral leadership role, then this may also be a call on you to serve.

Pastoral ministry, regardless of the specific area of service, is extremely challenging. The stress level can be significant, rated by some to be second only to medical doctors. To function properly as a pastor requires that we resist the pull of our fallen human nature and maintain humility before God. We are all called to be his servant, using the gifts he has given us to direct others to him. As we let our Lord serve us, we must then grow in our ability to shepherd and serve others.

For that reason, we require our U.S. senior pastors to participate in a Continuing Education Program. Some pastors fulfill the requirement by taking classes at Grace Communion Seminary. Earning a degree takes considerable time, finances and other resources. If you are able to pursue a degree at GCS, or simply want to take a few classes there, I urge you to do so. GCS also offers several non-credit lectures that are available online at no cost. You'll find them at www.gcs.edu/course/view.php?id=32.

Because many of our pastors cannot pursue a GCS degree, we offer other continuing education options, including classes at Ambassador College of Christian Ministry (http://www.ambascol.org/).

Joseph Tkach

13. A CHALLENGING ROLE

Peter Drucker, who spent much of his life studying leadership, said that the four hardest jobs in America are the U.S. President, a university president, a hospital CEO, and a church pastor. Though some might disagree with Drucker's assessment, I doubt that many of our pastors would. Being a pastor is a high calling, but it is often a great challenge—one that is sometimes made even greater by unrealistic expectations placed upon them.

According to the Barna organization, about 85% of the churches in the U.S. have less than 200 people, 60% have less than 100, and the average size is 89. Even in small congregations, the demands placed on pastors are experienced throughout the day, throughout the week. Pastors are expected to be theologians, Bible teachers, accountants, vision-setters, counselors, public speakers, worship directors, prayer warriors, leadership developers and fundraisers. Given these expectations, I'm sure that those serving as pastors closely identify with what Paul wrote to the church at Corinth:

> Remember, our Message is not about ourselves; we're proclaiming Jesus Christ, the Master. All we are is messengers, errand runners from Jesus for you. It started when God said, "Light up the darkness!" and our lives filled up with light as we saw and understood God in the face of Christ, all bright and beautiful. If you only look at us, you might well miss the brightness. We carry this precious Message around in the unadorned clay pots of our ordinary lives. That's to prevent anyone from confusing God's incomparable power with us. As it is, there's not much chance of that. You know for yourselves that we're not much to look at. We've been surrounded and battered by troubles, but we're not demoralized; we're not sure what to do, but we know that God knows what to do; we've been spiritually terrorized, but God hasn't left our side; we've been thrown down, but we haven't broken…While we're going through the worst, you're getting in on the best!… So we're not giving up. How could we! Even though on the outside it often looks like things are falling apart on us, on the inside, where God is making new life, not a day goes by without his unfolding grace. These hard times are small potatoes compared to the coming good times, the lavish celebration prepared for us (2 Corinthians 4:5-17, *The Message Bible*).

I want to express my deep appreciation and thanks to all our pastors for all that they do in service to our Lord and his children. My feelings about our pastors are expressed eloquently by Paul in his letter to his coworkers in the church in Philippi:

> Every time I think of you, I give thanks to my God. Whenever I pray, I make my requests for all of you with joy, for you have been my partners in spreading the Good News about Christ from the time you first heard it until now (Philippians 1:3-5, NLT).

Joseph Tkach

14. SHEPHERDS OF GOD'S FLOCK

We should view church leaders as faithful *shepherds of God's flock*. This imagery is common in Scripture. In the ancient middle-east, raising sheep and goats was an important part of the economy (it still is today). Sheep, goats and chickens were some of the first animals to be domesticated. Fairly low maintenance ("easy keepers," we'd say), they yielded a high return for nomads and people with a more settled agricultural lifestyle. As noted in the *Baker Encyclopedia of the Bible,* the term *shepherd* was used historically (including in the Bible) to refer to leaders:

> Because of the fundamental role of shepherding in the ancient world, the word "shepherd" became a common term for a ruler. The kings of Assyria, Babylon, and Egypt were often referred to as shepherds who protected their people. This imagery formed the background for the Old Testament, where the same usage is found. God is pictured as the shepherd of Israel, concerned for every aspect of his people's welfare. Rulers and leaders of the people are often referred to as shepherds (cf., e.g., Numbers 27:17; 1 Kings 22:17; Jeremiah 10:21;12:10; 22:22; 23:1-2).

Though in our day it's popular to think of sheep as dull or silly, studies show that they are actually intelligent. The Bible talks about sheep as hearing the master's voice—able to distinguish their shepherd from all others. The Bible uses sheep and shepherds as metaphors to portray two truths: the helplessness of humanity to save itself, and the goodness of God, who lovingly cares for his sheep—especially those that are lost. The New Testament refers to Jesus as "the good shepherd" (John 10:11), "the great Shepherd" (Hebrews 13:20) and "the Chief Shepherd" (1 Peter 5:4). To serve his flock, Jesus calls some people to serve as under-shepherds (called *pastors*)—joining with him in leading, protecting, feeding and caring for his sheep, including seeking after those that have gone astray.

Serving with Jesus as an under-shepherd is not always easy. When I travel and meet our pastors around the world, I'm reminded of the struggles they face daily. In some cases we can offer them material assistance, and in all cases I try to give them encouragement by reminding them that they are constantly in our thoughts and prayers. They are not alone.

Like us, Jesus had many struggles, including conflict among his first disciples. Yet he shepherded them sacrificially: "I am the good shepherd; I know my sheep and my sheep know me—just as the Father knows me and I know the Father—and I lay down my life for the sheep" (John 10:14-5). He also said, "My sheep listen to my voice; I know them, and they follow me. I give them eternal life, and they shall never perish; no one will snatch them out of my hand" (John 10:27-28). He then spoke of them as the Father's gift to him (John 10:29). Such statements reveal the heart and the commitment of our Chief Shepherd—the heart and commitment shared by his faithful under-shepherds.

The Christian life is not only knowing about our union with Christ. It's also about living into that union, in communion with the Father, Son and Holy Spirit. As pastors, we're called to lead people in the way of communion—joining with Jesus, the Chief Shepherd, in caring for his flock. I'm thankful for the shepherd-leaders that our triune God has provided for us. I ask that you join with me in not only in praising God for these pastoral leaders, but also in praying for them.

Joseph Tkach

15. GIVING HONOR AND LOVE TO PASTORS

Paul told the Thessalonians, "Now we ask you, brothers, to respect those who work hard among you, and are over you in the Lord and who admonish you. Hold them in the highest regard in love because of their work. Live in peace with each other" (1 Thessalonians 5:12-13). Eugene Peterson puts it this way in *The Message* paraphrase:

> We ask you to honor those leaders who work so hard for you, who have been given the responsibility of urging and guiding you along in your obedience. Overwhelm them with appreciation and love! Get along among yourselves, each of you doing your part.

Please give me a few moments to share some insights about three key thoughts Paul expressed: 1) honor, 2) overwhelm with appreciation and 3) get along.

Honor

Many congregations have seen spiritual pain, hurt and wounds. Pastors and wives are often caught in the middle of "hand-to-hand" combat. They are unable to leave the field of battle, for it follows them everywhere. Families have broken up over doctrines. Friendships have ended because of grace. There have been ugly scenes of hostility and animosity, with emotions fractured and nerves frayed. Walking in the warfare have been pastors and their spouses, attempting to comfort, soothe, encourage, uplift, direct and gently admonish.

Many pastors have realized that they had to "go back to school." I have sometimes joked that we should contribute to writing a book, *Everything We Knew Was Wrong*. The title would be an exaggeration, as everything was not wrong. But we do need to grow in what we know. Pastors have had to face members and acknowledge that some of what they had taught was in error.

It is not an easy thing to face this. Some of us, like Jonah, initially tried to run from what God was showing us. Each of us has our own story. It has not been easy to face the fact that we all have many things to learn.

Meanwhile, pastors have to stand before congregations and teach. We thank God that so many men and women yielded to the Holy Spirit and did not allow pride, vanity and ego to cloud their judgment. I thank God for faithful people who have taken care not to inflict their own uncertainties and difficulties on the flock.

Pastors, elders and their families have taken a stand for truth. And in some cases lay members took a stand for truth when the former pastor did not. I think of the symbolism of that old hymn, "Faith of our Fathers." In many cases we have all continued to stand up for Jesus "in spite of dungeon, fire and sword."

It is not easy to be ridiculed, or to be shamed because you believe in and accept Jesus Christ. It is not a pleasant experience to be the object of rumors and slanders simply because you believe that grace makes us free from legalism and human traditions. It is not easy to be characterized as a permissive liberal. It is not easy to be blamed for problems, dysfunctions and unbiblical practice and teaching, especially when you were not directly responsible. Peter reminds us that such suffering is Christ-like, part of the Christian calling:

> It is commendable if a man bears up under the pain of unjust suffering because he is conscious of God. But how is it to your credit if you receive a beating for doing wrong and endure it? But if you suffer for doing good and you endure it, this is commendable before God. To this end were you called, because Christ suffered for you, leaving an example, that you should follow in his steps. (1 Peter 2:19-21)

It is fitting that we honor Christian soldiers who displayed courage under fire. A big "Thank you" to all of our members, men and women of God, and especially our pastors and spouses who have endured criticism because of the cross of Christ. We salute the bravery, humility, love and dedication of the men and women who stand for Jesus Christ in the face of opposition. We honor you.

Overwhelm with appreciation and love

The work of pastors is often compared to that of shepherds. Shepherds lead, prod, take care of, watch out for, nurture, rescue and direct the sheep. As shepherds, we work under the Shepherd and Overseer of our souls (1 Peter 2:25). A shepherd's work can be hazardous and grueling. The powerful story of rescue and salvation in Luke 15, of leaving the 99 to find the one who is lost, motivates all men and women of God. But we must always remember to give thanks and appreciation to those who sacrificially give of their lives so that others might be saved.

"Pits" are an oft-used metaphor in the Bible. Salvation is often pictured, in both the Old and New Testaments, as rescue from a pit. The land of the Bible was filled with natural and man-made pits, some of which were used as cisterns to capture rainwater. Joseph was thrown into a pit by his jealous brothers. Daniel was placed in a pit with a den of lions. Jeremiah found himself in a cistern and narrowly escaped death in a muddy mire.

There are many present-day pits into which the people of God may fall. There are the pits of drunkenness and drug addiction. There are pits of unemployment, illness and disease. There are pits of immorality, of anger and hatred, of lying, deception and greed. There are pits of self-pity and victimhood. There are pits of depression, despair and discouragement. When we are asked how we are doing, many of us have described our condition as being "in the pits."

God lifts us out of those pits. God saves us. Jesus walks among us, as our Shepherd, to lift us and carry us away from the pits into which we fall. Pastors and ministers constantly find themselves ministering around the edges of pits into which the people of God have fallen. We need to thank those who courageously and self-sacrificially give of themselves that we might be pointed to the One who can lift us out of the pit.

You may remember the words to a song that was popular many years ago:

> Love lifts us up where we belong,
> on a mountain high,
> where the eagles fly.
> Love lifts us up where we belong,
> from the world we know,
> up where the clear wind blows.

When some say, "what's all this love-stuff you are preaching?", we should remember that it is God who first loved us. And his love should flow through us. We need to express our appreciation to those who express this love toward us, which they can do only because they know that Jesus has saved them. As Bill Leisner expressed, "Most pastors are not looking for rewards here on this earth, but they need to know we are behind them in what they are doing. A little help from you can go a long way in telling your pastor that you are grateful for all he has done for you."

We want pastors to know that we appreciate and love them. At our denominational office, we hold up our pastors in prayer constantly. We appreciate them and pray that God will richly bless them and their families. Dedicated pastors who are in love with Jesus are valuable resources to any denomination, and God has seen to it that we have our share. Thanks to each and every one of you. We love you and admire you.

Beyond getting along

We get along with each other fairly well. But we all need occasional reminders so that we can continue the good work, and even improve in the areas in which we sometimes fall short.

We are all members in ministry. God has given us all gifts, and we are a priesthood of all believers. That is why we are instructed: "Do nothing out of selfish ambition or vain conceit, but in humility consider others better than yourselves. Each of you should look not only to your own interests, but also to the interests of others" (Philippians 2:3-4).

We are given gifts in order to minister and to serve. That means it is not appropriate to "inflict" our gift on someone else. We should not think ourselves superior or better than someone else because that person doesn't have our gift (at least in our estimation). We should honor and look up to one another. Treat every believer as the child of God that he or she is.

Our fellowship had a history of falling into pits. In addition to the personal problems that beset us all, we have fallen into many spiritual pits of unbiblical practice and teaching. We have seen what legalism can do and how it traps and enslaves. We have experienced the fruits of despair and bewilderment of prediction addiction. We know about the arrogance and vanity that results from exclusivism, thinking that we are the "only true church." We have seen what false doctrinal understanding does. We have experienced the disillusionment of being taught a false view of history, majoring in conspiracy theories and fables.

We have also seen members fall into the pit of experiences, feelings and manifestations. We do not condemn these brothers and sisters, but we must point out that many of these manifestations do not edify. Instead, many of these "gifts" can become a new legalism. Some members are told that they are inferior, they are not as deeply converted, they are not walking as closely with God as they could, simply because they have not had a particular experience. Such teaching is not biblical.

The Bible tells us to get along. We are not in the business of exalting ourselves or our own gifts. We exalt Jesus Christ. He is the one who lifts us up out of the pit into which we have fallen. In order for us all to "get along," the pastoral ministry must point out the "pit-falls" of erroneous teachings and all that goes with them. We do this not because we wish to criticize or condemn, but in order that we all get along.

Pastors should not be territorial. It is hard for a pastor when someone decides to attend another congregation, whether that be of our denomination or another. We usually take this as a loss, and we might take it personally. But we must understand that individuals can have appropriate reasons for moving to another congregation. Sometimes individuals move for good reasons — and sometimes not-so-good reasons.

If members are moving to an unhealthy church that does not preach Jesus as central to the gospel, then we as pastors should be rightly alarmed. If individuals are moving away from a church that preaches from the Bible and are moving *to* one that (for example) discourages prayer in order to emphasize manifestation and experience, then we as pastors are obviously concerned.

As Christians we all need to be reminded that there have always been many different forces at work against the church. In whatever era or age that Christians have lived, there have been plenty of controversies competing with the gospel. Worship music is a hot button for some. Spiritual gifts is controversial for others. Some like to debate the Hebrew calendar, as if it is relevant for today. Others feel that it doesn't matter which day you worship on (as long as the worship service is held during the daylight portion of Saturday). There are many reasons that can cause us not to get along.

We could all contribute to what would be an endless list of reasons that we should not get along. But Jesus has called us to peace. He has called us to get along. We are no longer foreigners and aliens, but fellow citizens (Ephesians 2:19). "One in Christ" is an apt description of the church of God in the world.

Our most singular distinctive as the church of God is that we do not stand for secondary distinctives. We stand for the plain and main teachings of Scripture. One of the major identifiers that Christ gave for authentic Christians is love — "by this shall all people know that you are my disciples."

As we get along, let's remember to honor our pastors, ministers and families, and to overwhelm them with love and appreciation. Let's remember our brothers and sisters in other denominations. Let's also pray for those whose growth is restricted by erroneous teachings.

We love you all, and we pray without ceasing for you. We are here to serve you and want to hear from you about how we can do that more effectively.

Thank all of you for the love and appreciation that you send to us. We are all one in Christ, and we thank God for what he has done in our lives collectively and individually. We hope that you are growing closer to our Lord and Savior as the days and weeks go by. Let's be diligent about being the men and women of God that he has called us to be. Let's labor to make our fellowship a healthy and dynamic church, one that is filled with the love and excitement that Jesus Christ gives to his body.

Joseph Tkach

16. DEVELOPING LEADERS

How do you feel about being evaluated or evaluating someone else? I imagine many of us are uncomfortable with both. Maybe we've had a painful evaluation at work or in the church. Perhaps a little humor will help—here are quotes from actual employee evaluations (the employees probably failed to see the humor!):

- Works well when under constant supervision and cornered like a rat in a trap.
- Slipped into the gene pool when the lifeguard wasn't watching.
- She brings a lot of joy when she leaves the room.
- Some drink from the fountain of knowledge—he only gargled.
- If brains were taxed, he'd get a rebate.
- Gates are down; lights are flashing; but the train isn't coming.

Though evaluations within the church might seem at odds with respecting and loving our brothers and sisters in Christ, it's our responsibility as leaders to appropriately evaluate those we are called to lead. Why? Because through processes of discernment, which include evaluation, we respond to what the Spirit is doing in the lives of those we lead. We acknowledge how they have been gifted (and not gifted), and observe their level of maturity (the presence in their lives of the fruit of the Spirit and wisdom—see Galatians 5:22-25 and 1 Timothy 3:6). With this understanding, we then work to provide clear and accessible "pathways" into opportunities where they are enabled to use their gifts to share in Jesus' mission, through the church, to the world.

A lack of evaluation has, at times, led to appointing people to the wrong ministry roles. It also has contributed to a lack of intentionality in developing new leaders. Perhaps worse, failure to evaluate has led to a lack of discerning the rich variety of the Spirit's gifting, evidenced by "yellow-pencil," assembly-line approaches to developing leaders.

By pointing out these deficits, I'm not suggesting that all we did in the past was of the "yellow-pencil," cloning-ourselves variety. I was blessed to work under leaders who recognized that my gifts and skills were different than theirs. One pastor saw that I was a better speaker than he was and gave me more preaching assignments than he gave himself. Another saw that I had more administrative talent than he did and helped me get more involved in that area. I recall him saying to me, "Nobody likes paperwork, but you know how to get it done!" I have fond memories of all the people who supervised me as a ministerial trainee, assistant pastor and associate pastor.

It delights me that we're now taking a more comprehensive approach to leader selection and development. In the U.S. we're now using a comprehensive system that includes assessments to help employed pastor and church planter candidates confirm that their calling, gifting and experience is a good fit for their prospective ministry role. These assessments are conducted by leaders who have been appropriately trained.

I encourage our pastors to have in place within their congregations a process for identifying and developing new leaders (assistant pastors, ministry leaders, etc.). There often is pressure to recruit people to fill ministry slots, but it's usually best to leave slots unfilled than to force-fit the proverbial "square peg into a round hole." Developing leaders takes time and focused care that includes appropriate evaluation.

In one church I attended, a musically-challenged elder was appointed to lead the choir. It wasn't a matter of not having gifted and qualified people to serve in that role, it was just a bad discernment-appointment process. The results were disastrous.

As one author put it, "What the Lord anoints, the church appoints." I like that, because it reminds us that raising up new leaders is about spiritual discernment (Who has the Lord anointed, and how?), and about investing time and other resources to develop those individuals, leading to appointing them to roles within the church that are consistent with their divine calling. I'm grateful to see that many of our established leaders are investing time and other resources in this way.

As we follow the Holy Spirit's lead in developing leaders, it's important to remember that leadership within the church is not limited to a special, professional class. Christ's ministry, including roles of leadership, is to be shared by all of his followers in accordance with the way the Spirit fosters in them both gifts and fruits. My deep thanks to all who serve, and special thanks to those called to lead who understand that a big part of that calling is to identify, equip, mentor and then release other leaders. That is the way of Jesus, and I'm delighted it's becoming our way more and more.

It's vital to the joy and health of each congregation that its members participate in mission with Jesus—most as ministry workers, some as ministry leaders. Every member and thus every congregation is like the vine on the branch, organically connected to and dependent upon Christ for its life (see John 15). As a living organism, the church's concern should not be, "What do we want to do?" but rather, "What is Christ doing and how may we get involved?" The difference may seem subtle, but it's critical.

I pray that we all work together to follow where Jesus leads, doing what Jesus does, and bringing with us others whom the Spirit is calling to active participation.

Joseph Tkach

17. LEADERSHIP SUCCESSION

We're in a time when the aging Boomer generation is leaving the workforce, making leadership succession a pressing reality in all sorts of places, our church included. In GCI, we have an increasing number of denominational and congregational leaders reaching the stage in life when they are retiring from active pastoral leadership. I'm not implying that our older leaders need to step aside at a particular age. However, as we get older (and I include myself), we must give careful thought to the issue of leadership succession.

As we age, it's natural that our energy level and overall health become limiting factors, and those in leadership roles need to step aside to be replaced by those who are younger. With this in mind, we have increased our efforts to prepare younger members for church leadership. In the U.S., we have the GCI Intern Program, Generations Ministries leadership development programs, and other initiatives. I'm grateful that many of our congregations are actively addressing this issue by creating "open lanes" for younger adult members to participate in leadership. In these ways and more, I see God answering a prayer I have prayed for a long time—that he would raise up in GCI a new generation to take up the mantle of church leadership.

Good planning helps minimize the times we might stumble in "passing the leadership baton." Pastoral transitions are particularly delicate, yet they can be accomplished in a healthy way when we work together. Our U.S. Church Administration and Development (CAD) staff have established a process for pastor succession, and we have similar processes in place outside the U.S.

Please cooperate with those processes, including planning well in advance for leadership transitions. Why? Because the unexpected often occurs, as reflected in the well-known Murphy's Law: *If anything can go wrong, it will* (and Murphy was an optimist!). I'm also reminded of some corollary laws:

- *Nothing is as easy as it looks.*
- *Everything takes longer than you think.*
- *If there is a possibility of several things going wrong, the one that will cause the most damage will be the one to go wrong.*
- *If you perceive that there are four possible ways in which a procedure can go wrong, and circumvent these, then a fifth way will promptly develop.*
- *Left to themselves, things tend to go from bad to worse.*
- *Whenever you set out to do something, something else must be done first.*

81

- *Every solution breeds new problems.*
- *It is impossible to make anything foolproof because fools are so ingenious.*
- *Nature always sides with the hidden flaw.*

I firmly believe that God calls ministers to particular leadership roles. But I also believe that leaders have a responsibility to prepare for the future care of their congregations and ministries. Think of it this way: *What God anoints, we appoint.* We have an important calling to shepherd leadership succession processes within our areas of responsibility. In doing so, it's vital to proactively seek God's direction and take other steps to prepare well in advance for leadership transitions. When we do, great joy results—a joy that often "passes understanding," because it can mean that we decrease in order that others might increase. "Passing the baton" is not always easy. When it appears to have been easy, it's because God's grace prevailed.

With all this in mind, I urge our established leaders to take positive steps toward preparing for leadership succession within their congregation or ministry. Let's work with our teams to prepare for the transitions that are coming. Such transitions are inevitable—the only question is whether they will be done well.

Successful succession processes minimize the drama involved. One factor that heightens drama is when established leaders are unwilling to step aside so that others can step up (are they struggling to let go of the honor and esteem that go with their office?). Another factor is existing leadership teams failing to adapt to new leadership (including not letting incoming leaders re-fashion the team).

To avoid such drama, we have succession processes in place. I call on our established leaders to actively engage those processes, approaching them with a selfless, cooperative spirit, trusting God to lead us in identifying and appointing new leaders. In the U.S., our regional pastors are there to assist in lead pastor succession—please enlist their involvement early on. Our policy is that when lead pastors reach age 62, they are to have a discussion with their regional pastor concerning plans for eventual leader succession. Outside the U.S., lead pastors should contact their regional director or mission developer. This advance planning helps avoid all sorts of problems. Remember Booker's Law: "An ounce of application is worth a ton of abstraction."

Let's be reminded that leader transitions are not just about the established leaders—they are also about the congregations and the ministries they have been called to serve. None of us has our "own" ministries—there is only one ministry, and it belongs to Jesus, the Great Shepherd. We are his "under-shepherds," called to protect and care for our Lord's ministry and his people.

We must not be possessive of what was never really "ours." Leader transitions call for careful shepherding of God's flock so it is "strengthened" instead of "scattered" (Ezekiel 34:1-6). Leader transitions need to be handled with great care and in a timely way so that a congregation has time to adjust, say their goodbyes, and process through the grief that inevitably occurs. Thank you, my brothers and sisters, for your cooperation in this important matter.

Joseph Tkach

18. A NEW GENERATION OF LEADERS

As we get older, the questions we ask about the future begin not just with "what," but "who"? This is not a new problem. The first Christians expected Jesus to return almost immediately, and certainly in their lifetime. "Succession planning" was not a high priority. They were not thinking two thousand years in the future!

However, as the years went by, they had to consider how the work would continue after they had gone. They had to consider the welfare of the church after their contribution had been made. For example, in Acts 20, we have the account of Paul's farewell to the elders at Ephesus. Knowing that it was unlikely that he would ever see them again, he said:

> What matters most to me is to finish what God started: the job the Master Jesus gave me of letting everyone I meet know all about this incredibly extravagant generosity of God. And so this is good-bye. You're not going to see me again, nor I you, you whom I have gone among for so long proclaiming the news of God's inaugurated kingdom. I've done my best for you, given you my all, held back nothing of God's will for you.
>
> Now it's up to you. Be on your toes—both for yourselves and your congregation of sheep. The Holy Spirit has put you in charge of these people—God's people they are—to guard and protect them. God himself thought they were worth dying for. (Acts 20:24-28, *The Message*)

Paul had learned that it is not easy to replace pastors and elders who would put the welfare of their congregations ahead of their own interests. He wrote to the congregation at Philippi, "I have no one quite like Timothy. He is loyal, and genuinely concerned for you. Most people around here are looking out for themselves, with little concern for the things of Jesus" (Philippians 2:20-21, *The Message*).

Timothy had proven to be reliable. But there was only one of him. So Paul advised him to "throw yourself into this work for Christ. Pass on what you heard from me—the whole congregation saying Amen!— to reliable leaders who are competent to teach others" (2 Timothy 2:1-2, *The Message*).

I see some similarities with our situation today. Thankfully, our ministry involves those who are loyal, hard-working and faithful. But we are aging, as are our people. Perhaps if you are the pastor of a small congregation of older people, you might wonder about the future—not just what, but who will come after you?

That is why we should all be encouraged by the conferences attended by many of our young people. Not only that, some of our middle-aged leaders have "passed the baton" on to another generation of young leaders, and have moved into mentoring roles. In this way, their experience is not lost, while a new generation of leaders has the opportunity to build their own experience. This is vitally important for our future.

Our GenMin programs (camps, mission trips and young-leader development programs like Journey with the Master) serve as "incubators" to develop the next generation of pastors and other church leaders. We will invite those who show promise for pastoral ministry into our pastoral internship program. We can help them receive a quality theological education through ACCM (undergraduate level diploma) and/or GCS (graduate degree).

Maybe you do not have many, or any, young leaders. However, think beyond your congregation. The GenMin conference shows that our denomination does have an up-and-coming generation of leadership, and we do have a future.

It would be foolish in this ever-changing world to be too specific about what that future will be like. New challenges, new conflicts and new technologies will continue to change the world, as they have in our lifetime. But whatever the situation, I know there will always be a need for men and women who hear and obey God's call to pastoral ministry.

Joseph Tkach

19. THE INTERNS

Grace Communion International is looking for men and women, either married or single, who have a strong sense of calling to pastoral ministry and a willingness to be immersed into a "hands-on" learning experience that will last 12-24 months.

Interested? Ask us for more detailed information and an application. The application and selection process is carefully designed to help prospective candidates really know whether they are being called to serve in this way.

To see this church reach the next generation for Christ, we need to invest in future leaders.

The coordinator of the GCI Pastoral Internship Program processes the applications and matches the interns with qualified pastors, and then assists the pastor and intern in creating a development plan specific to their needs. The goal for interns who successfully complete the training is to place them as GCI Associate Pastors, planters of new churches, or Senior Pastors.

The Paid Intern positions are handled as a partnership between the GCI home office and the host congregation. Paid intern positions are limited, but volunteer internships are readily available for qualified candidates, including college and seminary students needing internships for class credit.

GCI is keenly interested in welcoming more and more intern applicants, and encourages congregations and church districts to budget for this program.

As the GCI Pastoral Internship Program entered its second year, we asked three of the interns in the program to tell us about their experience.

Jason was assigned to the Cincinnati West, Ohio, congregation, working with Pastor Rick Shallenberger.

Hillary was assigned to the Greensboro, North Carolina, congregation, working with Pastor Joel Trusta (her dad, which makes cross-gender mentoring much easier).

Skyeler was assigned to the Eugene, Oregon, congregation, working with Pastor Tim Sitterly.

Question: What made you decide to become a pastoral intern?

Hillary: I never, ever imagined I would be in pastoral ministry. In fact, when GCI decided to ordain women, I flat out told God not to even think about it. But I think a part of me knew then that I would end up right here.

I chose to study Bible and Religion in college. I planned on volunteering in church youth ministry while pursuing an education and career in counseling. However, professors and advisors began encouraging me towards further theological/pastoral education and pastoral ministry. Eventually I began to listen.

Skyeler: I was actually a pastoral intern three times prior to this. But I was frustrated. Many churches wanted me to work for free, or be a member of their congregation for a year or greater before providing me an opportunity. I was at a point where I was burned out of trying, and another internship was not what I was looking for. Then an opportunity presented itself at Living Grace Fellowship Church [a GCI congregation] and I decided to give it another go.

Q: How did you get into the program?

Jason: My wife found out about the program on the GCI website and, knowing that our desire was to one day be in full time ministry as a pastoral family, we filled out the application and contacted the appropriate individuals to discuss the next step in the process. And now here we are.

Hillary: During the summer of 2010, my father, a senior pastor with GCI, asked me if I would like to apply. I spent some time in serious prayer about this, and sought spiritual direction with mentors and professors who knew me well. Then I turned in an application, spent a couple months discussing details, and officially began as a GCI intern in January 2011.

Skyeler: I transferred my job from Eugene to Winston-Salem, North Carolina, and was laid off the day my wife Tracy and I arrived. So we moved to Reno, NV. My wife needed to be on campus to finish her Masters. I also wanted to be closer to my dad, who was dying of liver failure. I had reconnected with Tim Sitterley (Pastor of LGCF) and he made the commitment to me that if I returned to Oregon, he would make an internship program happen.

Q: Describe your life as an intern. What do you do?

Hillary: My two main "projects" right now are to develop and lead a youth ministry and to help the congregation become more active in outreach in the community. I also preach every five weeks. I read a lot! I attend adult discipleship classes and a mid-week small group so that I can learn from the pastor. I attend staff meetings, not only to participate, but to learn how to lead them. I am mentored in ministry by the pastor (which is made easier since he's my father). I attend district pastoral meetings and conferences.

Jason: Life as an intern is exciting and difficult, challenging and rewarding. I spend my time working on my ACCM classes, organizing and facilitating the small group that I have started. I am the worship director for our congregation. I spend several hours a week working with the pastor in pastoral ministry. And I preach once a month.

Skyeler: I have started a small group and have oversight in another that recently started. Our community group ministry is growing, and it is my job to facilitate that growth. I develop videos and video content for our website and sermons. I speak on occasion and attend most church functions. I help plan activities for our camp, I get to shadow my pastor to various congregations, and I also get to help with the regional conference.

Q: What advice would you offer someone considering joining the program?

Jason: If God has placed it on your heart to "feed his sheep," then jump on board. GCI is a wonderful denomination, with its grace-filled and humble servant leaders and its passion to participate in God's work and a deep desire to share the life and love of Jesus Christ.

Hillary: Pray, pray, pray! Talk to fellow Christians and Christian leaders who know you well—parents, spouses, mentors, teachers, pastors, significant others, and friends. Listen to them, but also listen for the Holy Spirit speaking through them. Don't worry if it takes a while to really be certain. Reflect on your passions, on what fulfills you, and on why you want to do this. Pastoral ministry is not glamorous, but if you are called to it, it will be one of the most fulfilling things you will ever commit to.

Skyeler: Be patient and realize you are needed. This denomination has good leadership, and those leaders want to mentor you and provide you an opportunity to succeed and make a difference for Jesus Christ.

Q: How do you see the future?

Jason: I see myself as a future full-time pastor of an existing GCI congregation.

Hillary: I'll be attending Wake Forest University School of Divinity beginning in the fall of 2011. I hope this internship will last two years. After that, I would like to serve as an associate or assistant pastor for another year or two—I'm a firm believer in pastors needing thorough training, education, and experience before becoming a senior pastor. After that, I will consider pastoral openings in GCI, but at this point I feel more apt to pursue planting a daughter church with the support of GCI and the congregation I am interning in.

Skyeler: I don't know exactly. I know I will be involved, but where and in what role is still up in the air. I want to get a doctorate in philosophy and help transform people's minds. I will probably sit tight at LGCF, as there are some loose ends to tie up, and my Youth for Christ job and schooling require some time beyond October. I look forward to what opportunities God puts in my way, and will gladly follow where he leads.

Q: How do you support yourself while training? Are you paid?

Jason: It has been a blessing that the congregation and the denomination have been able to pay me as a part-time intern. To supplement the difference, my wife works as a part-time police and fire dispatcher for the city we live in, and I am a licensed massage therapist and give several massages a month to help out.

Hillary: I am paid a part-time, hourly salary as a GCI Pastoral Intern. I tried to find a second part-time job to help cover some expenses, but that was pretty impossible in my area. I am a recent college graduate, so I am blessed to be able to live at home with my family for now. Financial aid is helping me attend divinity school. Besides that… it's a step of faith.

Skyeler: The internship provides me with some money for rent, food, and some basic needs. I am also bi-vocational with another ministry. My wife works as a teacher and for my other job, I work at raising funds.

Q: Anything else you would like to say?

Jason: I am very excited for what this program holds for the future of GCI and for the kingdom of God. God is preparing the hearts of the younger generations to step up and be strong, committed and humble servants who will partner with all generations to participate in the work he is doing.

Hillary: Yes! For any young women out there considering pastoral ministry with GCI, God knows you and accepts you; if he has called you to this, he knows what he's doing. Don't be intimidated by what is still very much a male-dominated field. If God is sending you, go! We need young men and women with passion, who are not considering pastoral ministry to fulfill their own needs.

Skyeler: Not everyone can be an intern, but everyone can have a part. If we want to see this denomination reach the next generation for Christ, we need to invest in future leaders. One way to do this is to donate to the internship fund.

We are very thankful for this wave of new pastoral leaders in our fellowship. We pray for their growth and eventual placement in ministry, and we ask the Lord of the harvest to bring more laborers to join in this movement!

20. THE POWER OF MINISTERING IN PAIRS

I have always appreciated the opportunities to share in ministry with partners. One of my favorite memories is the time when I was on the road with a district pastor. We made a wide, sweeping tour, and our first appointment was lunch with one of our newer pastors. This new pastor also happened to be one of our female pastors, and she simply needed to have a chance to be heard. Two sets of ears made the lunch conversation twice as encouraging. We then moved northward to meet with a church leadership team that was searching for another ministry leader to join them. We had a lovely meal and a spirited conversation about their needs. The high point of the meeting was when one of the local leaders told us they sensed our heartfelt desire to help them and how they were amazed that we kept track of their individual names and the issues that weighed them down. They were deeply grateful, and together we experienced the reality of Jesus being present and powerful among us. We were pastors ministering to other pastoral leaders, and there was no doubt that working in tandem had a much greater impact than if we had been flying solo.

That experience made me stop and think of Jesus' example. We know he gave the original followers the promise that as they spread the gospel and made new followers he would be with them, even to the end of the age. He wanted them to know that ministry was a participation in what he is already doing. But have you ever noticed when he sent disciples out to minister he sent them in twos (Mark 6:7)?

Twice as many villages and people could have been reached if Jesus had sent his protégés out individually. So why did Jesus send them out as ministry partners? I think there are several good reasons.

The first reason comes from the Old Testament tradition of "two witnesses." No person could be convicted of a crime in the Old Testament by the testimony of just one witness: the law stipulated that at least two witnesses were needed in order to convict someone (Deuteronomy 19:15). (See the New Testament application in 1 Corinthians 14:29.)

The disciples were called to be Jesus' students and companions, but also to be his witnesses. They were called and chosen to give first-person testimonies about Jesus—his ministry, teachings, and miracles. The disciples were certainly more likely to be heard because they came in teams of two— both witnessing about Jesus from their own perspectives.

A second reason is because of the power of shared ministry, the added impact when two or more people work together toward a shared goal. This co-laboring is not only effective, but also reflective of the collegiality that would become the hallmark of the Spirit-filled, New Testament church.

A third reason Jesus sent the disciples out in pairs was simply for encouragement and endurance in ministry. There is a high attrition rate among missionaries in the mission field, and the most common problems are discouragement and loneliness. Jesus was no stranger to loneliness—think of the 40 days of temptation in the wilderness and then think of his arrest, trial and crucifixion. Sending out the future church leaders in groups of two displayed the deep concern that Jesus had for his friends. He didn't see these 12 men as tools to carry out his mission, but rather as dear brothers who were joining him in the joy of broadcasting the good news and ushering in the kingdom of God.

As a rule of thumb, I encourage ministry leaders to not engage in ministry alone, but rather always take another person with them; the witness will be more powerful, the ministry will be more impactful and the reward of relationship will be richer!

Working in pairs: the common practice of the early church

Jesus often sent his disciples in pairs. Two disciples were sent to find the donkey for Palm Sunday (Luke 19:29). He sent Peter and John together to prepare for the Passover (Luke 22:8). Prior to becoming disciples Peter and John had worked as pairs with their brothers Andrew and James. Jesus put special effort into teaching them to function as a pair. They went up the mount of transfiguration together (Matthew 17:1). Jesus left them to pray together at Gethsemane (Matthew 26:37). Peter and John continued to work together as a pair after Jesus died (John 20:2-3; Acts 3:1, 4:1,13). The book of Acts continues with the team of Barnabas and Paul, who soon split into Barnabas and John Mark, and Paul and Silas.

Greg Williams

21. MANAGING THE POSTMODERN CHURCH

A conversation with Dr. Karl Moore, Associate Professor at the Faculty of Management, McGill University in Montreal, Canada. He also taught at Oxford University from 1995-2000. He has worked as a consultant on the area of study called "Change" to several denominations and this year gives a LW Anderson Lecture at Presbyterian College, on Leading Change in Churches.

Question: Some people think the traditional congregational style of church within a denomination is doomed. Do you agree with that?

Karl Moore: Not at all. Quite the opposite.

I think there are few things as useful to a Christian life as a good congregation. I grew up in a couple of different ones and when moving between three countries found them a great source of strength, encouragement and friendships. This summer my family and I spent six weeks in another part of the world, and what a delight it was for us to meet other Christians in our denomination and begin to develop friendships and a sense of "oneness." We believe that the congregation is a great institution. But like many other great institutions it needs to "morph" into something a bit different from time to time.

To be successful in the postmodern culture, many institutions are finding it necessary to "reinvent themselves." To what extent do you think this is true for churches?

KM: Reinvention seems to be the order of the day for our society. Whether it be the way in which families are much more diverse, universities are no longer just for the elite or the voice of the BBC is no longer *the* voice of Britain.

When we think about the auto industry, we realize that GM and Ford are struggling, Chrysler was owned by Germans, Rover is dead all over, BMW makes "British" brands like the Mini, Jaguar is a Ford and Rolls is German. Stunning changes, yet we largely still drive internal-combustion engine-driven vehicles.

The tension is how do we keep what is the core of the institution — the most continuously valuable bits — and what do we see as something that can flex with the times. I believe Christianity is going through this type of process of discarding the Western/European culture parts to rethink what is at the heart.

The growth of the church in Africa and Asia is particularly helpful in this matter. As the center of Christianity, if not in power at least in numbers, shifts south and east, our brothers and sisters in these countries will bring extremely helpful views on what being "Christ-like" in today's world really means. Humility and profound willingness to listen and learn will be paramount in this process, which will undoubtedly take a decade or two to fully unfold.

What current management trends are particularly helpful for church leaders?

KM: What we are experiencing in management is the early days of what might be called "postmodern management." Operating in a turbulent, rapidly evolving environment, leaders must spend less time relying on their own experience from years ago and spend more time listening to the front-line troops.

These front-line employees are often our youngest and least experienced, but their experiences can help us more rapidly realize when key changes are taking place. Strategy-making still lies with those at the top, but input must be gathered from a more diverse set of people.

Humility and listening strike me as Christian values! Though Christians still hold to eternal verities, the fact is that we are generally much less dogmatic than 20 years ago. We simply "know" less than we thought in the past.

We are also making more room for emotion in the workplace. The "baby-boomers" were overly focused on work, ambition, careers and their high need for achievement. At the same time the MBA-ization of business occurred with its concurrent focus on analysis, spreadsheets and the numbers. This excessively crowded out the human side of management.

Getting this balance is a very considerable challenge for business leaders, perhaps doubly so for church leaders. I believe that the leadership style of churches should evolve over time in concert with the changes in how members are led at work. Otherwise we will simply appear to be horrifically out of date and "fuddy-duddyish." Not that we should follow every fad, but we should change over time to be within the broad direction of management in our particular country. However, the core ideal of "servant leadership" should remain always at the heart of Christian leadership.

The members of the younger adult generation — what some call "Generation X" — are leaving the traditional denominations, although they are not necessarily abandoning Christianity. Do you see this as a problem, or just a trend?

KM: This is a troubling trend. As an active member of a congregation, I certainly feel the loss of too many of the younger generation. We would love to have them around. On the other hand, this action is often not done out of a malicious attitude or even out of a particularly bad experience, but rather as simply a much better fit with their lives. They feel that it is a better way of living out their Christian lives.

Perhaps we may question their wisdom and judgment, but I don't think we should question their sincerity or desire to do the Christian thing. I wish it was different, nevertheless undoubtedly Jesus is involved and will—and has—turned this to his ends and glory.

How do you define "success" in terms of church leadership in the postmodern world?

KM: Success for me in the church is about changed lives, people brought into a life-changing relationship with Christ, the Father, the Spirit and a Christian community. Many times this is a qualitative rather than a quantitative thing and thus difficult to measure. This can make Christian leadership more trying at times, but when we are part of the process of Christian growth it is wonderfully rewarding.

So if there was just one aspect of leadership that you wish you could get across to church leaders, what would it be?

KM: Recently I did a summer leadership series for the *Globe and Mail*, a Canadian broadsheet, where I interviewed one CEO a week. After eight weeks of this I wanted to hear from younger leaders. So I gathered three young university leaders (20, 22 and 30 years old), whom I knew fairly well, to talk about their view of leadership. They were very critical of the "boomers" — my generation. Subsequent interviews with other young leaders have only reinforced this rather sad thought.

What they did stress at some length was that leaders need to listen more, much more. Not to be so quick to rush to giving the solution, getting it done and dusted.

Of course, younger people often have silly ideas. We did at their age, and to be honest, we still do from time to time. An acquaintance of mine who taught executive courses with me at Oxford worked for the Strategic Planning unit in the Pentagon. It is interesting what the military — or at least parts of the military — do in "after action reviews." Rather than starting with the General, they start with the newest buck private and let her give her comments. She will have some truly off-the-mark ideas, but she also doesn't know whose sacred cow she is goring, so she presses ahead to say some quite insightful things as well. From there they work their way up the ranks. Better listening is my "number one request" to church leaders.

When you have church conferences, what percentage of time is given over to listening to those from denomination headquarters? Hopefully less and less. If you want new ideas and things that work, make time — plenty of time — for those in the field and their experiences.

22. TIME FOR NEW TREES

It is an interesting time in the life of the Williams family apple orchard. Our modest 35 acres of trees in the rolling hills of western North Carolina are going through two major transitions. The orchard has been leased to the Henderson family for the past 25 years. The arrangement has worked well, and it is now time for a younger generation to take over. The second major transition is the uprooting of old trees and the planting of new ones.

Transitioning to a new generation can be a nightmare. Whereas in the past a man's word and a handshake were good enough for an agreement, today it is often much more complicated. A younger generation is concerned about fair market prices, risk of liability and a multitude of other legalities. Thankfully, in our case, our two families had a heart-level discussion about all of the concerns, and the handshake won out over the multi-page document produced by a high-priced lawyer.

The younger Henderson caretaker has decided that the best long-range strategy is to re-invest in the orchard. There are nearly 2500 varieties of apples grown in the U.S., but for our North Carolina market, the Golden Delicious, Red Delicious, Rome Beauty, Gala, Mutsu, and Jonagold are the varieties that are consistently in demand. So the young Mr. Henderson is faced with a challenge on two fronts. There are some varieties in the orchard that are not profitable, and then there are also five acres of Golden Delicious trees that are too old to produce quality apples. So Mr. Henderson took drastic action. He brought in the backhoe, dug out the five acres of trees, pushed them together into a huge brush pile and ignited a major bonfire.

As I watch my friend work with the challenges of the family orchard, I find some interesting parallels with my other job. I am employed by my denomination to help coordinate our plans to prepare for the future.

Like an orchard, a church goes through various seasons as it bears fruit.

Like farming, this is a multi-layered process requiring wisdom, patience and faith. In his first letter to the Corinthians, the apostle Paul likened the church to a field that had to be tended by workers through the stages of preparing the soil, planting, weeding and eventually harvesting. My apple-farming experience has taught me some useful lessons that I can apply to the ever-changing seasons of our church.

Like an orchard, a church goes through various seasons as it bears fruit. And like trees, individuals and congregations go through various phases in their lives. There are those that are newly planted, needing extra care and attention in the first stages of growth. Then there are the years when they are mature and bear much fruit. But, let's face it, there are also times when even the most vigorous tree or the most robust of people begin to get old and less productive. Pastors who could once pastor two or three congregations and seemed to be a never-failing source of energy and ideas begin to slow down. The spirit may still be willing, but the flesh becomes weak. This is part of the natural cycle of life.

However, my orchard and churches analogy can only go so far. Pastors and congregations are not trees and orchards, to be used until the time comes to dispose of them. We cannot administer a church with a backhoe and a bonfire. There are feelings and emotions to be considered. None of us likes to be reminded that we may be past our prime. So although the process of aging and renewal in church life is inevitable, it must be done with sensitivity, love and due caution.

This is not just my challenge. It concerns all of us who are joined in fellowship. None of us are plants that "flourish and are cast into the fire." We are members one of another, and we owe each other a duty of care. The old must serve the young, and vice versa.

Let me then share the challenge with you, and ask for your prayers and concern. On the one hand, we are looking for young people who display leadership qualities, and most of all a desire to go deeper in ministry. This is why we have begun the Pastoral Internship program. It is gaining momentum with a slow, steady stream of applicants, and it holds great promise for developing a "young orchard" of future pastors. However, just as young trees require special attention in their early years of growth if they are to grow straight and strong, these young leaders require good care from skilled and patient mentors who can help them grow into the best pastors the Lord desires them to be. Part of my job is to assist in the process of matching approved intern applicants with the best-qualified mentoring pastors available.

Apple trees have to be strategically placed within an orchard, with self-pollinating trees close enough to non-pollinating trees so that apples will be produced by all varieties. And we need to place our interns with congregations who are alive and active, so that the intern can grow in a positive atmosphere among experienced and motivated Christians.

Another challenge we face is the growing number of veteran pastors who are nearing retirement age. This reality can easily sneak up on you. No one likes to admit they are getting old, and the transition to a less prominent role can be especially hard for men and women who have given many years in dedicated service and commitment. And, unlike old trees, elderly Christians are not "taking up valuable space." Those years of experience are still useful, even though the physical frame may need a change of pace.

Several of our older pastors have already made this transition. We are learning from them, and one of our challenges is to harness their experience to help the rest of us as we reach retirement age.

Like an orchard, a church cannot just be left to itself if it is to continue to bear fruit. It looks like our family orchard is in safe hands for the next few years. I pray that we can work together so we can say the same about our church that we are all privileged to belong to.

Greg Williams

23. TIME FOR NEW METHODS

No sooner had I written the article "Time for New Trees" than it seemed the Lord had another series of lessons for me to learn from my family orchard.

You may have noticed that McDonald's has added sliced apples to its menu for side items. This has helped increase the demand for apples, which is good news for those who grow them, including the Williams orchard.

In the earlier article you will recall that our current tenant, whose family had managed the orchard for 26 years, had agreed to continue the arrangement. That arrangement was based on trust and a handshake. So now I had the challenging task of meeting with him, to discuss some new terms related to the orchard. What I was afraid would be a difficult conversation with our longstanding renters turned into a pleasant conversation. Our tenant realized that he was overextended in his present operation, and it made sense to release our orchard. So I was free to explore a new direction for the orchard.

There were several growers interested, and several ideas were offered. One grower wanted us to consider planting berries instead of apples. Another proposed turning the orchard into a completely organic operation—an interesting concept, but impossible due to neighboring farms. A third candidate, Mr. Nix, wanted to grow packing apples instead of the current strategy of growing processing apples. (Packing apples are the shiny, perfectly shaped apples you buy at the supermarket; processing apples are turned into juice, applesauce and baby food.)

The Williams family met to consider all of the possibilities and unanimously agreed that we wanted to return the orchard to the days when our father and grandfather grew packing apples. Arrangements were made to meet with Mr. Nix and his orchard manager.

I, along with my two brothers, walked the orchard with the new potential renter. Together we examined the varieties of trees and their present condition. Mr. Nix pointed out that many of the trees had become misshapen, due to faulty pruning. He demonstrated how they would repair the trees by making some major cuts high up in the trees to allow much needed sunlight to get in. He showed how they would redirect limbs by cutting out a small slice of wood at the base of the limb, stretching them out, and tautly tying them to the trunk of the tree. These better practices may have seemed drastic, but they would lead to a more productive orchard that would grow a better quality fruit.

As our new tenant talked, I began to see parallels with my other job—a minister of the gospel, asked by my denomination to coordinate plans for our future. I remembered the words of the apostle Paul in 1 Corinthians 3:11-13:

"For no one can lay any foundation other than the one already laid, which is Jesus Christ. If anyone builds on this foundation using gold, silver, costly stones, wood, hay or straw, their work will be shown for what it is, because the Day will bring it to light. It will be revealed with fire, and the fire will test the quality of each person's work."

Paul indicates that there are different qualities of work even as it relates to ministry. As I reflect and look inward, I ask myself if I am building with straw or precious stones. Or, using my orchard as an analogy, does my ministry produce processing apples or packing apples? The good news is that the foundation of my ministry, like my trees, is strong and will endure anything. But what am I building on that structure? Quality and attention to good practices matter.

My brothers and I were impressed with Mr. Nix's knowledge and experience. He explained what varieties of apples he would plant in the open spaces. He pointed out the need to plant a cover crop that would properly prepare the soil for the future planting of trees. He said he would plant the new trees in the opposite direction from where we had them in the past. His logic was to allow better air circulation to lessen the effect of frost forming on the blooms and young fruit. I'd never thought of that.

This new caretaker is a highly educated apple grower who continues to discover better methods. He doesn't settle for the status quo. He has traveled to the other apple-growing areas of the country to observe how other successful growers operate. Mr. Nix is a life-long learner in the art and science of growing quality apples.

This positive step forward gives me great hope for an improved orchard that will become one of the top apple-growing operations in Western North Carolina. I see a close parallel with our denomination and our desire to move past the status quo. I have taken many educational trips outside, which allowed me to work with a huge cross-section of evangelical churches, and see various ways of doing effective ministry as believers serve under the leadership of the Spirit. I have also been challenged to learn how to relate to various groups in the community where I serve and move well beyond the confines of the land-locked church world.

Most recently my journey back into seminary has helped me to see how other Christian leaders are at work to grow spiritual fruit within the people they serve. I am part of a group of 11 students studying the specific area of

Congregational Growth and Development. Out of 11 students, five different denominations with their particular styles and distinctives are represented. We are a mixed group—including four women, seven African-Americans, four Caucasians, and one man who is a pastor from Haiti. Our discussions go deep into the difficulties of doing ministry in the 21st century, and we thoroughly evaluate the material from our stack of textbooks. We are all seeking better methods and practices for making more followers of Jesus.

We in GCI can learn from and with our brothers and sisters within the Body of Christ as we prepare for the future. It is vital that we are open to learning from others and being courageous enough to try new things.

I am deeply thankful for my heritage and ongoing involvement in the life of the apple orchard. I thank God for Mr. Nix and the future work he will do for my family's farm. And I thank him also for the rich lesson he has shown me as it relates to my call to ministry. Jesus often used the natural world to teach his servants what they needed to know as his disciples. Seems like he still does.

Greg Williams

24. WHY DON'T MORE PEOPLE GO TO CHURCH?

What can we do to help the unchurched find their way home to the Father?

The most precious gift God has given us is our personal relationship with him. God knows us personally, and we know him. By God's grace we are calmed by his presence in the midst of our difficulties. When everything and everyone else fail, we rest confidently in his loving care. During less troubled times, we soar like eagles on the updrafts of joy. There is nothing more important than this intimate relationship given us through Jesus Christ.

According to George Barna, many Americans want a personal relationship with God. God created us to have this relationship with him, so it would seem that evangelism would be easy. Since people are hungry for a personal relationship with God, let's open the church doors wide and let them pour in.

But this isn't happening. People who have given exit surveys after visiting a church say they found the people to be friendly but they didn't perceive God's presence. They complain that the church doesn't seem relevant to their need. We could point out that God is always present, so if they didn't experience him, they must be spiritually deficient. While this would be true for some, we need to consider our part in this.

The importance of worship

Jesus said, "God is spirit, and those who worship him must worship in spirit and truth, for the Father seeks such as these to worship him." Jesus didn't say God is seeking teachers, evangelists or preachers. While he gives some of us these spiritual gifts, Jesus said that God seeks worshipers.

Our loving response to his love for us is *worship*. Gratitude follows grace. Like the forgiven woman washing Jesus' feet with tears of joy, or the apostle Paul remembering what he did when he was Saul of Tarsus, we also bow and worship, thanking him for his grace. God draws us to Jesus; Jesus saves us from sin; the Holy Spirit gives us life and gifts. Worshiping God is our individual and corporate response in this intimate relationship.

George Barna, Henri Nouwen, Sally Morgenthaler, Robert Webber, Jack Hayford and others believe that the missing dimension in today's churches in the United States is worship. Too many churches are looking at the unchurched as consumers who are seeking products rather than children seeking their Father. Our local churches can serve the unchurched week in and week out by helping them find God by following our lead as we worship him.

Our personal daily worship is the power behind relational evangelism, and corporate worship is the power that makes our church services real or relevant. Everything that distracts people from experiencing Jesus' presence must be removed from our lives and our worship services. Hungry souls need Jesus. We need to focus on how we can share the Bread of Life with hungry souls.

This is a challenging goal. Worship teams and pastoral teams need to plan and pray together to ensure that Jesus Christ is front and center in our congregations. We seek to create an environment that is grace-based, Christ-centered, Spirit-led, Word-directed, fellowship-building, and disciple-making. We can, by God's grace, express our gratitude in worship from start to finish in our weekly services. The unchurched can then follow our lead in worship and come home to our Father in heaven.

Ken Williams

25. GIVE ME ONE GOOD REASON
I OUGHT TO GO TO CHURCH

"Why do I need to belong to a church? Why shouldn't I just believe in Jesus and live a good life? Church can be a real pain, you know."

Yes, church can be a real pain. All human relationships can be. Jesus' command that we "love one another" (John 13:34-35) would not be much of a command if there were no good reasons *not* to love another. When we love one another in spite of how unlovable we are at times, we are loving others the way Jesus loves us. He loves us even though we are sinners, even though we betray his love.

We want the church to be close to perfect, even though the church is made up of people just like ourselves—quite imperfect. No church is exactly the way "it ought to be." Every church has problems. Despite that, there are good reasons to belong to a church, and we will look at some of them.

Participation in Christ

Jesus said that his followers would be known by their love for one another. We demonstrate our love for one another in the context of a committed fellowship. If we avoid such a commitment, we are shunning our personal participation in the very love Jesus wants us to experience.

We are called into the fellowship of the saints. Paul wrote, "God...has called you into fellowship with his Son Jesus Christ our Lord" (1 Corinthians 1:9). In what way has God called us into fellowship with his Son? One way is into a personal and direct friendship with Christ.

But there is also another way. In Romans 12:5, Paul wrote, "In Christ we who are many form one body, and each member belongs to all the others." All Christians are called into the one "body of Christ," and therefore we all have fellowship with one another because we are all in union with Christ.

Paul puts it this way in Ephesians 4:16: "From him [Christ] the whole body, joined and held together by every supporting ligament, grows and builds itself up in love, as each part does its work." Jesus expects each of us to do our part to build up his body in love. It is meaningless to say that Jesus is our friend, or that we love him, if we refuse to have anything to do with the others he calls his friends.

Individualism

Americans tend to be individualistic. We think we can do things on our own, and we don't like to feel dependent on others. But the body of Christ, the church, is far bigger than any one of us. To be part of Christ's body is to belong to the fellowship of the saints. And the fellowship of the saints is the fellowship we all share with Jesus Christ, in whom we are made one with God as God's own children.

My, or your, local church is probably not ideal, but at some level it is a collection of believers—each with his or her unique set of baggage, problems, quirks and sins. Despite our inadequacies, however, because we are believers, each of our local churches forms a visible sign in the world of the invisible reality of the kingdom of God. In its weakness, every local Christian church is a declaration that God has sent his Son to save sinners—like you and me.

Freedom for action

Although we are sometimes a sorry sight, because of what God has done through Jesus Christ, we have been delivered from the slavery of sin to the freedom of God's children. That means we are free to be more than we are—more because we are never alone. We stand together in Christ in the power of the Holy Spirit.

We are free together, as one family, one body in Christ, to take active part in the life of the kingdom of God, a life that no longer has to remain in bondage to destructive patterns of thought and behavior. The church is where we can practice our new life, learning to forgive others as we have been forgiven, and learning to love others as Christ loved us and gave himself for us (Ephesians 4:32).

Working together, each local church can make a strong, positive difference in its community, in the lives of hurting men, women and children. It is often a ministry (a group of concerned and motivated members) of a local church that feeds hungry people, provides clothing for those who are poor, offers after-school homework help for underprivileged neighborhood kids, organizes addiction-recovery groups or provides training in finding and keeping a job. Churches become the arms and hands of Jesus in the world in countless ways, as he gives them opportunity, occasion and the love to do it.

Despite our weaknesses and sins, God has given us a new heart of love, a heart motivated not only to trust him for forgiveness, not only to work on overcoming our destructive habits, but also to extend ourselves for the good of others. "We love because he first loved us" (1 John 4:19). Armed with his love, we are equipped to love him in the ways he said his followers would—when we meet him in the poor, the disenfranchised and the sick (Matthew 25:37-40).

New creation

Yes, church can be a pain. But church is also where we participate in Communion, the body and blood of our Savior. In Communion, we take part in the unity of the household of faith, the unity we have with the Father, the Son, and the Holy Spirit. In the letter to the Hebrews, we read about the invisible spiritual assembly to which each Christian has been called:

> You have come to Mount Zion, to the heavenly Jerusalem, the city of the living God. You have come to thousands upon thousands of angels in joyful assembly, to the church of the firstborn, whose names are written in heaven. You have come to God, the judge of all, to the spirits of righteous people made perfect, to Jesus the mediator of a new covenant, and to the sprinkled blood that speaks a better word than the blood of Abel. (Hebrews 12:22-24)

In the church, something greater is going on than meets the eye. When the church gathers, it is more than a collection of sweet old ladies, Sunday school teachers, men's groups, grumps, watchdogs, gossips, kids and hypocrites. It is a group of redeemed people, made new in the death and resurrection of the Son of God, and the whole creation is resounding in joyful celebration of the amazing revelation of God's redeeming power and grace displayed in this otherwise motley crew. To us, it may seem like just another boring day at church. To the cosmos, it is a pulsating symphony of God's creative and redemptive glory.

Variety in unity

There are small churches, midsize churches and big churches. There are Bible study groups, Sunday school groups and prayer groups. There are big denominations, little denominations and independent churches. There are mainline churches, evangelical churches and fundamentalist churches. There are Calvinists and Arminians. There are Pentecostals, charismatics, semi-charismatics and cessationists. There are premillenialists, postmillenialists and amillenialists.

The list of permutations goes on and on. *The unity of the body of Christ does not lie in such things. Rather, the unity of the body of Christ lies in Christ himself.* Only in Christ are we brought into the fellowship of the saints.

When we take part in an assembly of believers in Christ for the purpose of offering praise, thanksgiving and worship to God, we are, in Christ, participating as redeemed members of the fellowship of all saints. Regardless of the puniness of our local church, our often off-key songs are made one, in perfect harmony, with the joyful assembly of "thousands upon thousands of angels" and the "church of the firstborn, whose names are written in heaven."

Whether you are looking for a church or whether you have found one, your church attendance is always more than meets the eye. It may feel like mere duty, a chore or a burden. But it is one of those otherwise mundane activities that our merciful Savior has chosen to enlist into his service so that we might, as individual members of his own Body, learn to experience the richness of vital union, renewal, peace and power with him in the midst of our mutual trials, challenges, pains, fears and joys.

So why not give church, and yourself, another chance? Maybe this time you could expect things *not* to be perfect. Maybe this time you could feel the freedom just to take your rightful place in our mutual journey of grace.

J. Michael Feazell

26. THE QUEST FOR THE IDEAL CHURCH

Are you on a quest to find The Ideal Church?

Perhaps you know the one I mean. It is the church where no errors of doctrine or practice ever occur. In the Ideal Church, grace, obedience and legalism are always clearly understood and distinguished. The pastor never gives a boring, irrelevant or inaccurate sermon; and the congregation only sings the songs that you like and think are worshipful. In the Ideal Church, all members love one another all the time. No one ever sins or gives offense. There are no disagreements about how the church should be run, or how money should be spent.

Is this Ideal Church what you are looking for? If so, I've got bad news for you: you won't find it. Why not? Because it doesn't exist!

To create a perfect church, you need perfect people, and all Jesus' churches are made up of imperfect people. Since the Real Church is made up of flawed people, it is inevitably a flawed body. The mixture of good and bad, success and failure cannot be escaped by changing denominations or congregations.

Russian author Alexander Solzhenitsyn points out that the separation between good and evil does not fall conveniently between groups of people, or between those in our church and those outside it. It runs through the middle of every human heart.

Many years ago, I went through the most traumatic two years of my life when I was confronted with the flawed nature of our church. It happened when I first grasped what it meant to be saved by the grace of Christ. While it was the most wonderful discovery of my life, it was also the most traumatic. It was a shock to realize how far our church had fallen short of the gospel of grace. I realized that the gospel we—I—had preached had been a confused mixture of legalism and grace that had burdened people instead of freeing them from their burdens.

I thought: Surely I have to leave, and find a church that is free from legalism, free from error, free from these kinds of flaws. I prayed for guidance, and began to read everything I could find on grace.

Two books helped me decide what to do. One was written by a Lutheran, the other by another Protestant pastor. The Lutheran, a seminary professor, described how his own church, though founded on the principle of salvation by grace through faith apart from works, in practice emphasized performance at the expense of grace. The illustrations of legalism he gave, from his experience in congregations and in college, were startlingly similar to attitudes and practices in our own church and its college.

The second writer pointed out that humanity's most persistent heresy is legalism, a person's determination to justify himself before God by works or performance. This problem was not limited to our church! There was nowhere for me to go to where the battle for the gospel would not have to be fought. It has to be fought in every human heart. It will never be finally won until the Lord returns.

Our churches are as much in need of grace as we, their members are. When Jesus looks at us, he sees our flaws, our sins, our errors and omissions; and his grace is sufficient to cover these things. As much as we need him to forgive us, our churches need us to forgive them. Can we learn to extend grace toward our churches as Jesus Christ extends it to us? We know we are to forgive one another as he forgives us. Can we learn to forgive our churches as he forgives them?

Our quest is not to find the Ideal Church; it is to help improve the Real Church. Jesus wants us to commit ourselves to the Real Church, his church, in one of its real, flawed denominations or congregations. He will give us strength to persevere in the quest to improve it.

Flawed as it is, that church is the form Jesus has chosen to take in this world. If you have been looking for the Ideal Church, give up your futile quest. Commit yourself instead to the Real Church and to the daily work of improving it.

Don Mears

27. TURN-KEY OR MAKEOVER?

If you are thinking about finding a new church home, you might want to consider doing your shopping with a real-estate tip in mind. The "perfect" church might not be the best spiritual investment.

In the real estate market, a house that is in tip-top shape is often referred to as a "turn-key" house. If you buy the home, it is in nearly perfect condition. Someone else has done all the work and the only work you need to do is "turn the key" and move in. Such properties are popular, and they usually sell for a premium. Unfortunately, when it comes time to sell, you stand to make little profit unless the market has appreciated considerably.

My wife and I, on the other hand, have purchased fixer-upper properties. In the last 15 years we have bought seven and lived in three of them. These properties were "cosmetic" fixers, rather than fixers that needed highly qualified, skilled work. The types of improvements our properties have needed were new paint, flooring and fixtures. The most "construction" we have done was to tear out and replace kitchen and bathroom counters and sinks. When more difficult repairs needed to be done, we always hired skilled professionals.

We've put hundreds if not thousands of hours of labor into our properties. We have spent quite a bit of money on tools and supplies. Some people think we are a bit crazy and want to know why we do it. Let me share with you some of the benefits of getting involved in a fixer.

The more work you put into a place, the more it feels like a home.

You might wonder at times if all the work is worth it, but when the job is complete you realize it was worth every bit of effort you put into it.

By doing most of the work yourself instead of paying others to do it, you discover and develop skills and talents you might not have realized you had.

By choosing your own colors and decorating schemes, you can create an atmosphere that meets your particular needs.

You have more pride in your property. You are more likely to take better care of it and want to share it with others.

And the financial rewards can be substantial.

I've found that it's much the same with a church. (I'm speaking of a congregation, not a building.)

The more work you put into church, the more it feels like home.

You might wonder at times if all the work is worth it, but when you see how your work has touched people's lives, you realize it was worth every bit of effort you put into it.

By doing some work yourself instead of paying others to do it, you discover and develop skills and talents you might not have realized God has given you.

By choosing your own name, styles of worship, children's church program, women's and men's ministry programs, etc. you can create an atmosphere that meets your particular needs.

You have more pride in your church. You are more likely to pray for it and take better care of it and want to share it with others.

And the spiritual rewards can be substantial.

If you are interested in "fixing-up" your church, make sure you aren't doing it alone. Otherwise you will soon become overworked and burned out. Find a handful of others who see the potential and sit down together to assess the areas that need to be improved, figure out who has the skills and tools to do the job, and even consider whether you need to hire outside laborers to help.

As long as your church has the solid foundation of Jesus Christ and the leaders are supportive of the makeover project, it will be well worth it to roll up your sleeves and start making your church the glorious spiritual home it is meant to be.

Shane Bazer

28. WHY YOU NEED THE CHURCH

Here's what every Christian needs to know about the church.

The second chapter of the book of Acts tells the story of the birth of the New Testament church. It was born in a dynamic display of power that was a dramatic witness to its divine origin. The community of believers multiplied as the power of God was evidenced by the outpouring of the Holy Spirit. The disciples of Jesus Christ were filled with zeal. The sermons of the apostles proclaimed Christ and his resurrection from the grave. Jesus Christ and the power of his resurrection ignited the church.

On that first New Testament Pentecost, the apostle Peter bridged the gap between the old and the new by proclaiming this outpouring of the Holy Spirit to be the fulfillment of the words of the prophet Joel: "In the last days, God says, I will pour out my Spirit on all people. Your sons and daughters will prophesy, your young men will see visions, your old men will dream dreams" (Acts 2:17).

Nearly 2,000 years later, Christians still band together as a community of believers. The Holy Spirit still bonds and unites Christians as in the first century. In common with our New Testament family, we are conscious of our link with the past. Just as Peter declared that the New Testament church had its roots in Old Testament Israel, so Christians today must be established and founded in the faith of our first-century forefathers. Paul wrote:

> You are no longer foreigners and aliens, but fellow citizens with God's people and members of God's household, built on the foundation of the apostles and prophets, with Christ Jesus himself as the chief cornerstone. In him the whole building is joined together and rises to become a holy temple in the Lord. And in him you too are being built together to become a dwelling in which God lives by his Spirit. (Ephesians 2:19-22)

Paul gives us a clear historical foundation for the church. He traces the Christian heritage, the roots to which every believer is connected, to the New Testament community of believers.

The identifying sign

The primary sign that identifies Christians is found in John 13:35. After washing his disciples' feet, Jesus said, "By this everyone will know that you are my disciples, if you love one another." Love, concern for others, doing good to our brothers and sisters, sharing and caring for those who need us, is central to Christianity. We are enabled to love one another through Jesus Christ (1 John 4:7-9). Christians are different because Christ lives in them. Their lives bear the fruit of the Holy Spirit — "love, joy, peace, patience, kindness, goodness, faithfulness, gentleness and self-control" (Galatians 5:22-23). The difference is inward, not outward.

As Christians, we need to ask ourselves about particular beliefs and distinctive practices that make us unique. For many people, their nationality, race and professions are key signs of identification. But Christians, children of God, do not establish their primary identity through nationality, race or profession. For Christians, the primary key must always be love.

A parable of identification

Parables are a literary and teaching device usually designed to emphasize one or two major themes. Generally, parables are not predictive, nor does every element have a specific or literal meaning.

The parable of the sheep and goats teaches us how Christians can be known by their selfless acts of giving and service. This parable identifies love as an attitude that reveals itself in the actions we take to serve and care for others. Jesus' parable of the sheep and the goats can be understood as a parable of identification. The principal difference between the sheep, who inherit the fullness of the kingdom, and of the goats, who do not, is expressed in the loving actions of service by the sheep. The goats failed to feed, clothe and visit the "least of these" (Matthew 25:31-46).

In addition to being identified by their love, believers accept the supremacy and sovereignty of Jesus as Lord. Believers no longer live for themselves, but, they live to do the will of God. Paul said: "I have been crucified with Christ and I no longer live, but Christ lives in me. The life I live in the body, I live by faith in the Son of God, who loved me and gave himself for me" (Galatians 2:20). By believing in, accepting and receiving Jesus Christ, the Christian submits to his Lordship. Christ is our ruler. We submit to him and follow him.

Believers are identified by our acceptance of and identification with Jesus Christ. The fact that we are called Christians draws attention to our desire to find our fundamental identity in him. As a result of our identification with Christ (or rather, Christ identifying himself with us), we are:

Reconciled to God. We are told in 2 Corinthians 5:18, "All this is from God, who reconciled us to himself through Christ and gave us the ministry of reconciliation."

Forgiven and cleansed. "We were therefore buried with him through baptism into death in order that, just as Christ *was* raised from the dead through the glory of the Father, we too may live a new life" (Romans 6:4). "But if we walk in the light, as he is in the light, we have fellowship with one another, and. the blood of Jesus, his Son, purifies us from all sin" (1 John 1:7).

Born again, from above. Jesus declared, "No one can see the kingdom of God unless he is born again" (John 3:3).

Sharing our faith

Being an active part of the church is vital to the spiritual health and growth of each Christian. Paul tells us that Christ

> gave some to be apostles, some to be prophets, some to be evangelists, and some to be pastors and teachers, to prepare God's people for works of service, so that the body of Christ may be built up until we all reach unity in the faith and in the knowledge of the Son of God and become mature, attaining to the whole measure of the fullness of Christ. (Ephesians 4:11-13)

The church provides a necessary framework and structure for each member of the Body of Christ. The church has been given the responsibility of making disciples and of teaching them (Matthew 28:18-20). Together, as the Body of Christ, we can accomplish this mission.

Jesus had instructed his disciples, "You will receive power when the Holy Spirit comes on you; and you will be my witnesses in Jerusalem, and in all Judea and Samaria, and to the ends of the earth" (Acts 1:8). Jesus expects his disciples to share their belief. As Jesus said in the Sermon on the Mount, Christians must not hide their light (Matthew 5:14-16). Jesus said, "No one lights a lamp and puts it in a place where it will be hidden, or under a bowl. Instead he puts it on its stand, so that those who come in may see the light" (Luke 11:33).

The challenge

Christians must share the love that dwells within them. Jesus Christ's commission to the church in Matthew 28:19-20 identifies the Christian responsibility to proclaim the gospel: "Therefore go and make disciples of all nations, baptizing them in the name of the Father and of the Son and of the Holy Spirit, and teaching them to obey everything I have commanded you."

The challenge to adhere to New Testament teaching and the responsibility to make disciples apply to all whom God calls. Jesus promises to be with us and live in us, strengthening and empowering us: "Surely I am with you always, to the very end of the age" (verse 20).

On that first New Testament Pentecost, when Jesus Christ founded the church, the apostle Peter preached a sermon that personally confronted each of his listeners. He challenged observant Jews, gathered at Jerusalem from all over the Roman world, to believe in and accept Jesus Christ. He told them that Jesus is the Messiah. "Therefore let all Israel be assured of this: God has made this Jesus, whom you crucified, both Lord and Christ" (Acts 2:36).

Peter also told the assembly that the risen Jesus Christ could change their lives. After the people had heard Peter's appeal, they wanted to know how they should respond. "Peter replied, 'Repent and be baptized, every one of you, in the name of Jesus Christ for the forgiveness of your sins. And you will receive the gift of the Holy Spirit. The promise is for you and your children and for all who are far off — for all whom the Lord our God will call'" (verses 38-39).

Three thousand people were baptized after Peter's sermon in Acts 2. The church began when the believers came together to be taught, to fellowship and to share their lives. They were able to mature as disciples of Jesus Christ as a result of being joined to the community of believers.Jesus Christ gave another promise to Christians of every generation since: "I will build my church, and the gates of Hades will not overcome it" (Matthew 16:18). The church has survived, and will continue to survive, any and all attempts to overcome it. Christ, the head of the church, promises us that.

We have committed ourselves to faithfully understanding and practicing the Christianity of the New Testament. We want to extend our help to you as you seek to worship and follow Christ. As the Holy Spirit leads you, we are committed to serving your spiritual needs. May God bless and guide you as you seek him and his Son. Christ founded the church, and as we follow him, we should seek to find how we can more perfectly understand his will, and how we can "grow in the grace and knowledge of our Lord and Savior Jesus Christ" (2 Peter 3:18).

G. Albrecht

Members of one body

Paul provides a significant metaphor that explains the church and its functions. He tells us that the church is the Body of Christ. "The body is a unit, though it is made up of many parts; and though all its parts are many, they form one body. So it is with Christ" (1 Corinthians 12:12). He explains further, "Now you are the body of Christ, and each one of you is a part of it" (verse 27).

This is a metaphor rich with meaning for Christians. It allows for and demands both unity and diversity, cooperation and individuality. No matter how we or others may perceive our function, our individual role is vital to the functioning of the whole. Paul emphasizes the worth of every Christian with the metaphor of the Body of Christ.

In their book, *Fearfully and Wonderfully Made,* Paul Brand and Philip Yancey comment on this relationship:

> In our Western societies the worth of persons is determined by how much society is willing to pay for their services. Airplane pilots, for example, must endure rigorous education and testing procedures before they can fly for commercial airlines. They are then rewarded with luxurious life-styles and societal respect. Within the corporate world, visible symbols such as office furnishings, bonuses, and salaries announce the worth of any given employee. As a person climbs, he or she will collect a sequence of important sounding titles (the U.S. government issues a book cataloging ten thousand of them).

Brand and Yancey continue:

> Living in such a society, my vision gets clouded. I begin viewing janitors as having less human worth than jet pilots. When that happens, I must turn back to the lesson from the body, which Paul draws against just such a background of incurable competition and value ranking. In human society, a janitor has little status because he is so replaceable. Thus, we pay the janitor less and tend to look down on him. But the body's division of labor is not based on status; status is, in fact, immaterial to the task being performed. The body's janitors are indispensable. If you doubt that, talk with someone who must go in for kidney dialysis twice a week. (pages 38-39)

It should be encouraging to realize that we have a contribution to make, that we are members of the Body of Christ and that Christ needs us as part of the good news of the gospel message.

The people of God

Perhaps the most fundamental term that is applied to the church is that of the people of God. The church is composed of those who are God's own people.

> You are a chosen people, a royal priesthood, a holy nation, a people belonging to God, that you may declare the praises of him who called you out of darkness into his wonderful light. Once you were not a people, but now you are the people of God; once you had not received mercy, but now you have received mercy. (1 Peter 2:9-10)

At the beginning of the church, the majority of its members were Jews. Their race, culture, heritage and former religion was Jewish. The term Jew had, and continues to have, the dual connotation of ethnicity and religion. However, Paul later wrote to the Galatians that the New Testament people of God, the church, should remember that "there is neither Jew nor Greek, slave nor free, male nor female, for you are all one in Christ Jesus" (Galatians 3:28).

The ethnic origin of church members has no bearing on their relationship with God. The people of God are called and chosen by grace, not by heritage or right. The church becomes the children of Abraham through the righteousness given to Christians because of the saving work of Jesus Christ (Romans 4:6; 2 Corinthians 5:21; Galatians 3:29). Paul called Christians "the Israel of God" (Galatians 6:16).

Just as God was present with the nation of Israel in the pillar of cloud and the pillar of fire, so he was with his called-together and chosen New Testament church (2 Corinthians 6:16; Ezekiel 37:27).

The transition from children of Abraham to followers of Jesus Christ involved trauma and turmoil in the New Testament church. A change in focus from race to grace formed the background for most of Paul's epistles. Many people found it difficult to accept a change from righteousness through heritage to salvation by grace.

The watershed event in the conversion of Gentiles, those who were not Jewish, was the calling of Cornelius. He was a Roman officer, a centurion, a Gentile. The story of how God revealed his plan to include Gentiles in the household of faith is recorded in the 10th chapter of Acts. God provided supernatural guidance for Peter, leading him to understand that Cornelius was to be accepted as a child of God.

Paul further explained, "As he says in Hosea: 'I will call them "my people" who are not my people; and I will call her "my loved one" who is not my loved one,' and, 'it will happen that in the very place where it was said to them, "You are not my people," they will be called "sons of the living God"'"

(Romans 9:25-26).

The church is a people, not a corporate body. The church is not a building or a structure. The church is not a multinational institutional conglomerate. The church is people—all who believe in Jesus. This does not mean that the people of God should not be organized, or that no formal structure should exist. The New Testament gives a basic structure and coherency to the people of God. But the church should never forget that it is composed of people, special people, the people of God. Unfortunately, the history of Christianity demonstrates that the people of God have often been overlooked, forgotten and even abused by the corporate institution of the church.

The *ekklesia*

Jesus' disciples used the Greek word *ekklesia* to refer to the church of God. The fact that God inspired the writers of the New Testament to use this word is instructive. Until the New Testament writers applied *ekklesia* to the church, the Greek word was used in a political context and meant an assembly. It did not refer to a religious body. In Christianity, the word referred to the people of God, whether they were assembled or not.

Many have broken the word *ekklesia* into its two constituent parts and have defined it by the etymology, the origin of the word. The word comes from roots meaning "out of" and "call." Some have then explained that the church consists of those "called out of the world." Although Christians are "called out," the word *ekklesia* does not have this exact meaning. The word might be better translated "called together."

Members of the New Testament church saw themselves as a people called together, a chosen people, the people of God. They were the people of God at all times, and not just when they were assembled for worship services.

The kingdom of God

Jesus Christ has saved us sin and its consequences (Ephesians 2:5, 8). We have received the Holy Spirit, the seal and guarantee that we will one day inherit eternal life in the kingdom of God (2 Corinthians 5:5; Ephesians 1:13-14; Titus 3:5-7).

Jesus brought the gospel of the kingdom of God. He preached, taught and started that kingdom. It started as small as a mustard seed and began to grow (Matthew 13:31-32). He called his church together "from the dominion of darkness" of this world and brought us into his kingdom (Colossians 1:13-14). The kingdom is a present reality for those who believe and accept Jesus Christ and his gospel.

Christians become part of the kingdom of God on earth. However, we experience the kingdom in only a partial sense. The fullness of the kingdom is our destination and our goal. Yet, a foretaste of the kingdom is present now in the Body of Christ. It is this present reality that enables and empowers us to be Christian pilgrims (2 Peter 1:3-4).

Christian ecology

We have confidence and trust that our leader is the eternal Son of God. He is our Savior, the One who gave his life for us on the cross and rose from the grave to be the living head of the church.

Humans whom Jesus Christ may use to serve his Body are just that: human. Christians can, and should, always look beyond the humanity that composes the Body of Christ. They should look to the divine love and mercy of the One who leads the church, Jesus Christ.

We can apply the concept of ecology to the church. Ecology refers to the way created things interact with one another and with their created environment. The church is the Body of Christ, a living organism that is mutually interdependent. We all need one another, and especially, we need the head, Jesus Christ. Christian life and growth is primarily focused on the community, because the part always contributes to the well-being of the whole.

Christians grow as a result of being nourished and taught. The role of the church is to provide the nourishment and direction that will enhance spiritual growth for individual members. Christ told his disciples to teach what he had taught them. "Go and make disciples of all nations, baptizing them in the name of the Father and of the Son and of the Holy Spirit, and teaching them to obey everything I have commanded you" (Matthew 28:19-20).

Individual Christians should not shirk their responsibilities to help others by casually assuming that the church will do all of the teaching and nurturing. Every Christian has a responsibility to be a spiritual environmentalist. We must bear one another's burdens. We must nurture, care and assist rather than use, abuse and throw away. Our brothers and sisters are precious resources we should treat and handle with care. We must practice Christian recycling. Each of us contributes to the health of the church, our spiritual life-support system.

29. YOUR CHURCH NEEDS YOU

During World War II, some posters displayed a stern Uncle Sam pointing and saying, "Your country needs you!" Many people responded to that challenge, going to work or to fight for the country even though they knew it would mean personal sacrifice and change of priorities. They responded because they believed in the cause they were fighting for.

Chances are, somewhere along the way many of these people realized that not every decision being made by their own side was perfect. But they knew that it was better to keep on helping the right side, for all its faults, than to quit and sit it out on the sidelines, or even worse, to fight against the right side.

Rediscovering our commitment

The idealism and self-sacrificing commitment of that wartime generation are harder to find in our society today. But as Christians, we are challenged to rediscover that commitment. Jesus is saying to his people today the same sort of thing Uncle Sam said in those posters. Jesus is saying to us, "Your church—my church—needs you!"

Remember your promises

Do you remember the promises we made to Jesus when we were baptized? We promised to love, honor, obey and serve him. He called us, and we promised to offer our lives in his service. We heard him say it would not be easy.

He has been faithful to his word, hasn't he? We have gone through difficult times. We have experienced growth in our understanding, and this has challenged us. It has not always been easy. Sometimes it has hurt so much that we have felt discouraged and depressed and abandoned.

But Jesus has not abandoned us. The fact that these things have come upon us is not a sign of his displeasure; it is instead a sign of his relentless love, working always to build his likeness in us. Now is not the time to lose courage. He who began to do this work in and through us does not intend to abandon it, nor does he want us to abandon it. The church has experience and special qualities and gifts that Jesus has given to us.

Blessings

We have something special in our fellowship, a blessing most churches don't have. We have ties of fellowship that make us a worldwide family. Many of us know members around the world. How many of our friends in other fellowships have that kind of worldwide family? They have congregations in many nations—but many do not have the personal ties with such congregations that we are blessed to have.

Let yourself be encouraged by what Jesus Christ is doing in your church. Let yourself believe that he wants to and will do such things in this country. We are a smaller church than we were. But we are a living miracle. Cheer up, little flock; it is your Father's plan and delight to give you the kingdom!

Ask what you can do for your church

In 1961, U.S. President John F. Kennedy spoke some challenging words at his inauguration: "Ask not what your country can do for you," he said, "ask what you can do for your country." The motto of our culture is almost a reversal of John Kennedy's words: "Ask not what you can do for your country or neighbor or family or friend; ask what they can do for you!"

Sadly, those ethics have infected Christians and their churches. Too many Christians approach church with the question: "What's in it for me?" These are not God's ethics. They are not the ethics on which a church is built. We are not called so that the church can do things for us. We are called to be the church in order that we may do things for others.

The life of Christianity, the life of the church, is the quest to become a better and better servant. I am deeply grateful and appreciative of so many of you who commit your time, talents and treasure to the work of the church—the local work and the worldwide work. If you have been sitting on the sidelines, I urge you to rejoin us, help us and support us—and let us support you—as we continue to do the work of Jesus Christ together.

Don Mears

30. BUILDING UNITY:
THE STORY OF EUODIA AND SYNTYCHE

Let me tell you about two people who worked side-by-side in the church. But something happened. They fell into a trap—a disagreement arose between them. Perhaps it began as a small argument, but it mushroomed into a rift that not only affected them but began to hurt the entire congregation.

You may know of similar circumstances. The people I'm referring to, however, lived almost 2,000 years ago. Their story is told by the apostle Paul in Philippians. He doesn't provide much detail, but we get the picture if we read carefully: "I plead with Euodia and I plead with Syntyche to agree with each other" (Philippians 4:2).

Here in the midst of his letter to the church in Philippi, Paul exhorts Euodia (yoo-OH-dih-uh) and Syntyche (SIN-tih-kee), to end their disagreement. This short exhortation packs a powerful lesson for us today— a lesson about addressing division and producing unity in the church.

Euodia and Syntyche

Contention had arisen between these women, and it concerned Paul enough to address it in this public letter. Why? Paul knew that contention between members spreads. If unchecked, it leads to a lack of unity in the congregation. Paul was concerned. He wrote the book of Philippians, in part, to address the subject of church unity.

Paul describes Euodia and Syntyche as "women who contended at my side in the cause of the gospel" (4:3). From this we infer that they were leaders, making the contention between them all the more harmful. Paul addresses both women. Both needed to change, as is the case in most disagreements.

Paul tells them that the solution to the problem is to "agree with each other"—but not just any kind of agreement, rather "in the Lord" (4:2). They are to solve their disagreement, not their own way, but in and through Christ.

Paul not only urges the women to seek reconciliation between themselves, he also enlists the help of others: "I ask you, loyal yokefellow, help these women" (4:3). We don't know who the "loyal yokefellow" was—it may have been Luke, or perhaps Epaphroditus. In any case, Paul calls on others to reach out to Euodia and Syntyche and help them reconcile.

If you had the opportunity to help two believers settle a dispute, how would you go about it? Paul gives us some valuable advice: "If you have any encouragement from being united with Christ, if any comfort from his love, if any fellowship with the Spirit, if any tenderness and compassion, then make my joy complete by being like-minded, having the same love, being one in spirit and purpose" (Philippians 2:1-2).

Encouragement toward unity is available in four ways. Paul gives four tools for building unity.

1. The encouragement of Christ's example

Paul begins by pointing to the "encouragement in Christ" (New Revised Standard Version). He is apparently focusing on the example of Christ himself. Jesus models for us an attitude that produces reconciliation.

2. The incentive of God's love

Paul describes the second tool as "any comfort from his love." "Comfort" can be translated "incentive" with the added element of tenderness. God tenderly gives us the incentive to display the love he showers on us. As believers love each other with the love of God, divisions begin to cease and unity unfolds.

Paul echoes the same thought in Colossians 3:14, "Above all, clothe yourselves with love, which binds everything together in perfect harmony" (NRSV). Love is the glue that binds us together.

3. The unifying indwelling of the Holy Spirit

Next Paul mentions "fellowship with the Spirit." This refers to the work and presence of the Holy Spirit in us. God dwelling in us through the Holy Spirit enables us to live in unity with each other. Paul exhorted the Ephesians "to keep the unity of the Spirit through the bond of peace" (Ephesians 4:3).

God's people are a diverse group. We come from varied backgrounds, races and economic and educational levels. We have different tastes, preferences and needs. How can such a diverse group have unity? By God's Spirit that binds us together.

4. The unifying qualities of tenderness and compassion

Tenderness and compassion involve the way we treat one another. We have received tenderness and compassion from God—and that should inspire us to treat others the same way. When believers are tenderhearted with each other, progress can often be made toward unity.

Paul goes on: "Make my joy complete by being like-minded, having the same love, being one in spirit and purpose. Do nothing out of selfish ambition or vain conceit but in humility consider others better than yourselves. Each of you should look not only to your own interests, but also to the interests of others" (Philippians 2:2-4).

Paul says to get rid of the rivalries and the selfishness that separate us. We are brothers and sisters of one body—therefore let every member feel and labor for the welfare of all.

Christ's example

Having made this plea for unity, Paul returns to the first tool, the encouragement of Christ's example. In Philippians 2:5-8 he exhorts us to be Christlike in the way we treat one another: "Your attitude should be the same as that of Christ Jesus" (2:5).

What was Christ's attitude? One of willingness to give up personal privilege in order to serve others: "Who, being in very nature God, did not consider equality with God something to be grasped, but made himself nothing, taking the very nature of a servant, being made in human likeness" (2:6-7).

Christ is God, and he set aside many of the privileges of being God to become human. As God in the flesh, he humbled himself to the point of the excruciating pain of crucifixion (2:8). Christ set aside his own interests for the sake of others. So should we.

Unity required

Unity in the church is vital to the success of the mission God has called us to. That is why Paul says: "Whatever happens, conduct yourselves in a manner worthy of the gospel of Christ. Then, whether I come and see you or only hear about you in my absence I will know that you stand firm in one spirit, contending as one person for the faith of the gospel" (Philippians 1:27).

We must stand firm in unity to advance the work of the gospel. As individual members, we advance this work by creating unity, and we set it back when we cause division.

Paul commends Euodia and Syntyche for their past labors, but warns them of the danger of hindering the work of God by destroying the unity of the congregation. It takes work to reverse this dangerous trend. It takes "standing firm" and "contending as one person." It takes effort and positive action.

The rest of the story?

Reading the few words in Philippians about Euodia and Syntyche leaves us hungry for more detail. Did they resolve their disagreement? To do so they would have needed to see unity as more important than what separated them. They would have had to swallow human pride and take positive steps to reconcile. How? By following Christ's example of humility and selflessness. By allowing Christ to live that same selfless life in them through the indwelling Spirit.

We have some indirect historical evidence that, perhaps, they did reconcile. Early in the second century, the church in Philippi wrote to the church leader Polycarp. They asked about another minister who was arrested and taken to Rome. We don't have their letter, but Polycarp's reply was preserved.

Polycarp commends the congregation in Philippi, writing that they "have followed the example of true love and have helped on their way, as opportunity offered, those who were bound in chains." Then he adds, "I rejoice also that your firmly rooted faith, renowned since early days, endures to the present and produces fruit for our Lord Jesus Christ."

These words could only be spoken about a congregation that had developed and maintained godly unity. Can we conclude that Euodia and Syntyche resolved their differences? The answer is lost in history, but perhaps Polycarp's letter gives us some indirect reassurance that they did.

I wonder what will be written about our congregations years down the line? Will they bear the fruit of unity? They will, if we follow Paul's admonition and put to use these four tools that build unity. If we work together, the fruit of unity will grow and remain for many years to come.

Ted Johnston

31. WHATEVER HAPPENED
TO CHURCH GROWTH?

A discussion with Dr. Eddie Gibbs

Question: Church growth was a popular idea 15 or 20 years ago. It promised to halt the decline in congregations and turn things around. Why hasn't it worked?

Dr. Eddie Gibbs: It depends upon the criteria by which you judge whether something has worked or not. If you have a lot of previously churched people, the insights and techniques of church growth were helpful. In the USA we had a wave of returning baby boomers following Watergate and Vietnam. Many of the boomers resisted traditional Christianity but responded to an approach which was contemporary and which fitted their needs and their cultural context. Some church growth insights were helpful in those contexts.

However, I think that with the wisdom of hindsight, the ideas of Donald McGavran, the founder of the church growth movement, were not really heard in the West. His principles were missionary and outreach principles. In North America particularly, they became marketing principles. In other words, how can I increase my slice of the religious market? The principles were misunderstood—even prostituted.

Outside the US, there was no phenomenon of returning baby boomers. So the standard approach was to remove all the barriers we thought would get in the way of people coming to faith. That was okay when you had folks who were coming in your direction—were in your aisle of the spiritual options supermarket, so to speak. But that is not where they came from.

Has it worked in terms of turning the tide of church going? Clearly no. In North America, if you believe the marketing figures, which I don't, between 39 and 43 percent are supposed to be in church on Sunday. But when you change the research methodology and see who is actually there, it is estimated that only between 18 and 25 percent of the population are actually in church.

Q: Do you think it is a mistake to assume genuine church growth is subject to market forces? There is some brilliant marketing of Christianity. But does it misrepresent the "product"?

EG: It certainly can. If we use marketing techniques to edit the gospel, so that only those aspects which serve our purpose are highlighted, then it is no longer the gospel. There is a tendency to proclaim a gospel that meets people's needs without challenging their priorities or values. We fill our churches with members that are not disciples. There is little evidence of life transformation, particularly amongst those who are simply at the worship service once a week.

It is only when you separate out the 10 percent who are involved beyond the worship service that you see a significant statistical difference in lifestyle. If it is just the general churchgoing population, there is little difference between them and the population at large when you look at their attitudes on racism, truth telling, divorce and lifestyle in general.

Q: What are we doing wrong?

EG: We have not recognized a profound cultural shift. From the conversion of the Emperor Constantine until the First World War in Europe and the 1960s in America, churches have lived in a "Christendom" framework. Most people were at least notionally Christian. They would come to church for weddings and baptisms and funerals.

Under that umbrella the church was a central institution of society and our strategy in communicating good news was "come to us on our terms, to events where we are in the majority and in power." Now we are no longer within a Christendom framework. We are in post-Christendom—some would say a neo-pagan society. In that environment you don't operate in a "come to us" way. But most church leaders are not trained to function in that environment.

Look at the various positions in Ephesians 4:11. This is a pre-Christendom model of leadership that emphasizes the need for missional leadership. It is apostles, prophets, evangelists, pastors and teachers. The pastors and teachers are your settlers—the others are the pioneers. We don't train pioneers; we train settlers. As Leslie Newbiggin said when he returned from India and settled in Birmingham, we are in a missionary situation but we don't train missionaries. So we have a chronic shortage of "APE's"— apostles, prophets and evangelists.

We have to define the church not as a place but as people. Not a gathering but a community. We have got to turn the idea of church inside out.

Q: Is that possible?

EG: Not with the mindset of present leadership. I think we need a recall, just as you have a recall of a defective car model. We need a recall so we can be trained as missionaries.

Q: But you don't downplay the importance of the local congregation and weekly worship service.

EG: No—not at all. The issue is whether worship finds expression in mission. When worship does not show in witness by word and deed, it becomes spiritual self-indulgence. The worship service is the heart of mission. It is the pit stop in the race.

The church is as much the church in dispersion as it is when we are gathered. Where is it when it is in dispersion? Where God has placed it to be strategic. The task then becomes how can we support God's people in the locations where God has already placed them?

You never "dismiss" a congregation—you disperse it—and if possible you go with them. Get out of your office and whenever you possibly can, be with the members of the church where God has placed them and see what is going on there.

Q: Do you have any words of advice for pastors who have a crumbling church building, a shrinking congregation and declining income, who do more funerals than baptisms?

EG: They must remember that they are doing a valuable job loving an aging congregation to see them safely to eternity. That is a valid ministry. So, do the traditional things with those folk and do them well.

Second, be careful of change. Most change they have experienced has been for the worse. But remind them that your concern is also for their children and grandchildren. So ask for permission to do new things apart from what is so meaningful for them. Ask them to be intercessors; old saints are great intercessors. You may be surprised. Some of those older folks are young at heart. They may be ready for their final fling in life. As a 67-year-old professor, I am on the steepest learning curve of my life. As I look at the emerging churches across the Western world, my students have become my teachers.

At the time of the interview, Edmund Gibbs was the Donald A. McGavran Professor of Church Growth in the School of Intercultural Studies at Fuller Seminary in Pasadena, California. In conjunction with Ryan K. Bolger, he has published *Emerging Churches,* a controversial and hard-hitting analysis of the challenges to Christianity in the postmodern cultures of Britain and America.

32. WHAT MAKES A CHURCH GROW?

What creates church growth? Are members responsible for growth of the body of Christ? Jesus used an analogy from farming to explain the manner in which the kingdom of God grows (Mark 4:26-29). Once the farmer plants the seed, it grows by itself. Although fruit comes through the miracle created within the seed, the farmer has to work hard to prepare the ground for productivity.

So it is with church growth. The apostle Paul explained that he had planted churches, Apollos had watered, but it was God who gave the increase (1 Corinthians 3:6). So how do Christians plant and water so God's kingdom can grow?

In his book *Natural Church Development,* Christian A. Schwarz helped answer this question based on research from more than 1,000 churches in 32 countries. He identified eight characteristics that helped a church grow. All eight were needed for a church to have healthy growth.

Here are those church-growth principles:

Empowering leadership provides nurturing for Christians to attain their spiritual potential.

Pastors focus on discipleship, delegation and relationships to empower members to attain their spiritual goals. Lay members are not helpers to simply promote the pastor's goals, but rather they collectively establish goals for the church. Greatness in leadership comes through a genuine heart of service (Matthew 23:11-12).

Gift-oriented ministry enables members to serve where their God-given spiritual gifts can best flourish.

Joy in daily living was found to be closely related to being freed to serve in areas of one's strengths. It is important that pastors provide appropriate training for volunteers to enable their success. In this way members become the priesthood of believers (1 Peter 2:9).

Passionate spirituality ignites from hearts on fire for Jesus Christ.

Enthusiasm sparks their personal commitment to love the Lord their God with all their heart, soul, mind and strength (Mark 12:30). God's grace inspires serving, not the legalism of just doing one's duty. Prayer is an inspiring experience as a life of faith represents a genuine relationship with Jesus.

Functional structures provide order so productivity can thrive.

Adjustments are made as needed so everyone can function effectively to do the right things (1 Corinthians 14:33). Pastors focus on the continuous need to balance tradition with the need for change to enable beneficial growth. Department heads are appointed to coordinate each area of ministry so that groups function well. Each leader develops more leaders.

Inspiring worship services exalt Jesus as Lord and Savior.

Corporate worship nourishes the body of Christ, the church members (Ephesians 4:11-16). Attending church is enjoyable, not laborious or done out of legalistic requirements. An appropriate setting for the service frees members to worship and praise their King. A friendly welcoming team greets members of the body, a competent worship leader facilitates collective praise and prayer, and a meaningful order of service highlights the gospel message.

Holistic small groups meet regularly to apply the Bible to the reality of living in today's society.

Collective prayer and discussion promote communion with God and reflection on his will. As cell groups grow, they split to enable continued effectiveness. As in the example of the early church, members gather in fellowship to praise God (Acts 2:42-47).

Need-oriented evangelism proclaims the gospel message of the kingdom (Acts 1:8).

Christians spread this special message to friends and acquaintances in existing relationships. The focus of evangelism is on the needs of non-Christians, showing them how Jesus fulfills our needs.

Although each member of the body of Christ should share with non-Christians, by example and by sharing their story, only about 10 percent of members appear to have received the gift of evangelism. Pastors assist in identifying those members who have received the gift and empower them to serve God.

Loving relationships come through sharing in thought and action, caring for one another (Matthew 25:37-40).

Friendships are developed and maintained through commitment of time, talents and emotion. True, unfeigned love fills their time together, even during times of hardship. Joyful laughter highlights those churches alive in Jesus.

Christian Schwarz concludes that interplay of all eight characteristics is vital if growth is to occur. When all eight were at least at a 65 percent level, that church grew. This goal, although difficult, is attainable by focusing on qualitative growth within the present membership, leaving quantitative growth to God (1 Corinthians 3:6). Ministers provide leadership to facilitate the growth of each member and the corporate body (Ephesians 4:11-13). But leadership is not limited to the ministry.

What should each member do?

Consider these eight characteristics:

1) Lead by empowering other members to grow.

2) Use your God-given gifts to serve God and your neighbor.

3) Be passionate, on fire, with joy and enthusiasm for the body of Christ.

4) Enable structure in the church to function effectively.

5) Participate as your gifts allow and pray for inspiration in worship services.

6) Join or form a small group to apply weekend worship to daily living.

7) Evangelize by sharing your Christian life by example and story.

8) Practice sincere love by sharing your joy with other members.

Which of the eight characteristics is your weakest? Ask God for strength and allow Jesus to lead you to grow. Which are your strengths? Use them to serve Jesus and his church.

Russell Duke

33. SPIRITUAL GIFTS AND CHURCH GROWTH

Christ gives each of us grace, in the form of spiritual gifts, as he determines to apportion it (Ephesians 4:7). These gracious gifts include various roles within the church — apostles, prophets, evangelists, pastors and teachers (verse 11). And what are these leaders supposed to do? They are to "prepare God's people for works of service" (verse 12). A more literal translation is "a work of ministry." In other words, the leaders of the church are to prepare the members for action in the work of the ministry of the gospel.

But not everyone has been given the gift of preaching, any more than all parts of a body are mouths. Acts 6:2-4 describes two overall types of ministry in the work of the gospel: the ministry of tables, and the ministry of the Word — giving physical nourishment through service and giving spiritual nourishment by preaching and teaching the gospel. Both kinds of ministry are essential to the church.

Gifts to work together

Christ gives different gifts to different members of the Body. Our job is not to compare our gifts and abilities, nor to feel superior or inferior to other members of the Body, but to make use of our respective gifts to serve others. Our works of service are to be used for building up the body of Christ (Ephesians 4:12).

As we work together, each of us serving according to the gifts and opportunities Christ gives us, we will grow into "unity in the faith" (verse 13). Although there is only one faith (verse 5), God's people reach unity of the faith through works of service, ministering to one another's needs in Christ.

Further, it is only through mutual service that we all reach unity "in the faith and in the knowledge of the Son of God" (verse 13). Our faith is in the Son of God, Jesus Christ. Part of knowing him is doing what he said. Two of his most frequent commands are, first, that we believe on him and, second, that we love one another. Belief in Christ makes us Christian, and love for one another demonstrates the validity of our faith. Belief and love are hallmarks of our Christian identity. Indeed, mutual love is the primary means by which the public can know that we are his disciples (John 13:35). Love, of course, is not just a feeling — it is action. It results in works of service.

By living the way of love in Christ, by implementing mutual service in him, the church comes to maturity, "attaining to the whole measure of the fullness of Christ" (Ephesians 4:13). Through mutual love and service, we become mature in the faith, closer to what Christ wants us to be, closer to the example of service he set for us. With that maturity, Paul says, we will not be easily misled by erroneous teachings (verse 14).

But by speaking the truth (in this context, true doctrines) in love, we will grow up — become mature — into Jesus Christ (verse 15). Jesus himself is the goal.

From Christ, the church grows up "as each part does its work" (Ephesians 4:16). Jesus has given a variety of gifts to the members of the Body as it pleases him, so that each of us can use our respective gifts as a vital part of the Body — in service, in the work of the ministry, to help each other. It is in this way that the church "builds itself up in love" (same verse). In the Body of Christ, as in any healthy body, each part contributes in its appropriate way to the overall growth, development, maintenance, and work of the Body as a whole.

For the common good

We find a similar emphasis on mutual service in 1 Corinthians 12, where Paul also discusses spiritual gifts. There is only one Spirit, Paul says, but there are different kinds of gifts (verse 4). There is only one Lord, but there are different kinds of service (verse 5). As members of the Body of Christ, we serve in different ways, each according to the gifts Christ has given us through the Spirit. There is only one God, but he leads and equips each of us to do the kinds of work that please him (verse 6). These spiritual gifts are distributed "for the common good" (verse 7), in other words, for the overall healthy functioning of the Body.

If he had wanted to, God could have given each of us ability to do everything, but he did not. He distributes his gifts differently to each of us, and this means we have to work *together*. Working together is, in a way, just as important as getting the job done — because working together in Christ is an expression of God's love, which itself is part of the work of God. God is love, and he wants us to grow in love for one another.

Some spiritual gifts are spectacular; others are not. That fact can lead to pride, or to feelings either of superiority or inferiority. But Paul's point in this passage is that all gifts are *from God,* and he is the one who distributes them *as it pleases him, as he desires and determines best.* Therefore, none of us has any reason to boast or to think our particular gift is more important than another, or to think our gift shows that *we* are more important than others. And, on the other side of the coin, no one has any reason to feel inferior, or to feel that his or her gift is not so important.

The truth is, Paul explains, each person has at least one gift or ability given by God, and each person has the responsibility to use it for the common good of the Body of Christ. I hope we can begin to see why mutual service, cooperation and love are vital to the health and growth of the church.

Just as a human body has to have a variety of parts, the church of God must have a variety of members, each doing a variety of functions for the common good. Every member can have faith, but some have an unusual gift of faith (verse 9). Every member can be a personal witness to the life-transforming power of the gospel, but some have the gift of evangelizing unbelievers. Every member can teach others, but some have the gift of being an unusually effective teacher (verse 28). Every member can help others (same verse), but some have an unusual ability to help others.

Paul does not list every possible gift here. He could not, because they are too numerous to mention. There could be as many gifts as there are people in the church! God distributes them according to his own purpose and plan.

Use gifts in love

Seek the best gifts, Paul encourages us (verse 31), and then he shows us in the love chapter "the most excellent way." Each member, no matter what gift he or she may have, should seek to express love for others — that is how *every* gift should be used — in loving service to others. Whatever God gives us, whether it is physical or spiritual, should be used for others' benefit.

We are called to serve. We exist to serve. That is Christian maturity. And our works of service should point to Christ. They should give evidence that we are his disciples. They are done for his honor and glory, and in his name. We do not deserve any of the credit ourselves. It is *his* work in us. It is Christ in us that identifies us as his own disciples. We are his slaves, with all being done in service to him in the work of his gospel.

We need to train and mobilize our congregations for the work of the gospel — evangelism. We need to develop positive godly relationships with others through Christian love and service, as individual Christians and as local congregations. This means pure, holy living in Jesus Christ as his ambassadors. It means being ready, when asked, to give an answer about the hope that lies within us, and about living in such a way that we are more likely to be asked. We should remember the first part of 1 Peter 3:15: "In your hearts set apart Christ as Lord."

Evangelism means the whole Body of Christ working together in unity, each one doing his or her part according to the gifts God has given, whether in ministries of physical service or of teaching the Word, supervised and led by the local pastor and supported by headquarters, all to the glory of God in the work of the gospel. It means diligent, prayerful, focused effort, by one and all, in unified cooperation and mutual encouragement and strengthening in love, so that the light of Christ might shine in the darkness through us, as his faithful servants.

Paul, speaking to the elders from Ephesus, said, "However, I consider my life worth nothing to me, if only I may finish the race and complete the task the Lord Jesus has given me — the task of testifying to the gospel of God's grace" (Acts 20:24). The same is true of God's elect today. The Body of Christ lives to do the work of Christ, to proclaim and exemplify the gospel of the grace of God.

Joseph Tkach

34. CHURCH BUILDINGS AND CHURCH GROWTH

Sometimes a congregation that has declined in numbers and morale comes to believe that their situation could be reversed if they build or buy a church building. Some begin to think, with all the best intentions, "If we buy our own building, we could do so many things we cannot do now!" Like the theme of the movie *Field of Dreams,* some may begin to believe: "If you build it, they will come!"

But experienced pastors know that a building program is not a ready solution for a church's attendance problems. In fact, it is frequently a death knell for a congregation, generating conflict, hostility, frustration and morale problems the members never anticipated.

Some churches may indeed be at the right point in their growth and maturity as a congregation where a building is the right and appropriate step for them to take. Before a congregation is prepared for a church building, several important factors need to be carefully considered.

1. A church must realize that owning a building is not an end in itself. The explosive growth of Christianity in the first and second centuries took place without church buildings.

Their focus was on the joy of the gospel, and it was spread by the testimony of believers through personal relationships, not by attracting people to an building. Members met in homes and temporary facilities for worship, prayer, instruction, study and praise.

2. We can't solve non-building problems with a building. Lack of growth in a congregation can be due to many factors, but lack of a permanent building is not one of them.

Sometimes the reason for lack of growth is that God is simply not currently calling people in that area. Most of the time, however, the reason is that the congregation is still working through its own internal problems and is not ready for an influx of new converts.

Evangelism has often been called overflow. Evangelism, or reaching out with the gospel, results from being so filled with the love of God and the joy of his salvation that it simply bubbles out, or overflows from us. This usually can't happen when we are struggling to cope with hurts, relationship problems and a sense of loss. While we are in a grieving process, it is difficult to reach out to others. During such a time, we are still in need of nurture ourselves.

Effective evangelism can't happen if we are not on fire for Jesus Christ in our private lives. When most of the congregation is still lukewarm, the first need is prayer for the spiritual renewal of the congregation. Spiritual renewal won't happen by acquiring a building. It will happen through prayer and proclamation of the Word of God.

3. Despite the best intentions, people will not improve their giving habits just to support a building. Some pastors and churches come to believe that if the church buys or builds a new building, the members will increase their giving to support the added costs of the mortgage, insurance, maintenance and repairs. But that doesn't happen.

The initial spark of good intentions cannot withstand the steady rain of reality. Unless a building is paid off or nearly so before members begin using it, mortgage payments will be a continual albatross around the congregation's neck, creating a constant source of requests for giving until the building is either paid off or sold, which may be decades.

4. Buildings are not the primary reason new people are attracted to a church, nor the primary reason people choose to stay.

People today are attracted to a church by what that church does for them and their children. Where it meets is not nearly as important as how much it cares and how much it provides for the needs of the members. It's true that a building can play a part in meeting needs. But the heart of love and commitment to Christ of the congregation is infinitely more important.

Several large, successful churches today grew into thousands of members before finally investing in permanent facilities. That's because who they were as the people of God was more important than where they met.

Rick Warren wrote: "I'm often asked, 'How big can a church grow without a building?' The answer is, 'I don't know!' Saddleback met for 15 years and grew to 10,000 attenders without their own building, so I know it's possible to grow to at least 10,000!" (*The Purpose-Driven Church,* page 46). A building, or lack of a building, should never be allowed to become a barrier to a wave of growth. People are far more important than property.

5. Consider the following point made by church consultant Lyle Schaller in an article in the Winter 1997 issue of *Leadership* called "You Can't Believe Everything You Hear About Church Growth": "The typical congregational planning process is overloaded with wishes, dreams, and myths, which undermine effective decision-making."

Some common examples illustrate this syndrome:

Myth 1: If we build it, they will come. "We now average about 400 at worship, and we have designed a comprehensive strategy to double our membership over the next six years. The recent and projected population growth in this community suggests that is a realistic goal. Therefore we have launched a capital funds campaign to double the size of our physical facilities. We're convinced if we build it, they will come."

Reality: That slogan was a great story line for a wonderful baseball movie, but for churches, it overlooks two crucial variables: The initial focus on responding to rapid population growth should be on expanding the ministry and raising the quality of what is offered. That usually means that adding staff should come before constructing additional facilities.

A second issue is the assimilation of newcomers. Unless the process for assimilating new people is improved and expanded, a 50 percent increase in membership may produce only a 10 percent increase in worship attendance. Schaller points out that a congregation must be ready to receive and assimilate new members before it can properly bring them in. Otherwise, new converts will become disillusioned and either drop out or move on to another church that is prepared to receive and spiritually nurture new converts.

What does this mean? It means that owning a building should be way down the list of priorities for a congregation. The first order of spiritual business is to begin the discipling process—building effective disciples of Jesus Christ from the members God has already placed in the congregation. Effective disciples become effective disciplers. A congregation of effective disciplers is ready to receive and assimilate new converts.

That's why the development of small groups, leadership training classes, Christian education classes and service goals, all bathed in private and corporate prayer, should be far higher priorities than a new building. Key ingredients of a congregation that is ready to evangelize, receive and assimilate new converts include such basics as these:

Compelling, committed personal and corporate Bible study.

Devoted, faithful personal and corporate prayer.

Meaningful, Spirit-guided personal and corporate service inside and outside the church.

Until these are in place, a congregation is not ready to own a building until it has carefully

    a) studied the demographics and needs of its community,

    b) discovered and developed the spiritual gifts of its members, and

    c) prayerfully developed a plan for

        1) serving that community with the gifts God has provided and

        2) for assimilating new converts into the active life of the church.

In other words, only when a congregation is already successfully fulfilling its reason for existence *without* owning a building, is it ready to evaluate whether ownership of a facility is part of God's will for its future. A building will not make kingdom work happen, and until kingdom work is happening, a building will be a curse, not a blessing.

Owning a building isn't the purpose of the church. But the time may come in a congregation's life when owning a building fits appropriately into the true purpose of the church, not as an end in itself, but as a clear enhancement of what God is already doing in that congregation.

I urge every church leader to read *When Not to Build,* by Ray Bowman (Baker Books, 1992). Ownership of local church buildings will be part of our future as a denomination. But we need to proceed wisely and in accord with God's call, learning from the mistakes of others, so that our buildings can truly be blessings.

Joseph Tkach

35. WHEN WE FALL SHORT

"Some of the pastors in my region are discouraged," a district superintendent said. "They haven't been able to rally their churches to a vision of reaching out to the community. Some of them have general goals, but don't have a specific vision. Others are frustrated because the congregation isn't supporting the vision the pastor has."

Let me offer a few encouraging words for those who are discouraged.

It is good to have goals larger than what we are able to achieve. On an individual level, Christ calls each of us to perfection, or wholeness (Matthew 4:48; Ephesians 4:13). Even though we are unable to achieve complete wholeness in this life, we should still strive toward it — yet without discouragement, for we know that we are clothed with the righteousness of Christ, and there is no condemnation for those who are in Christ Jesus (Romans 8:1). Because of God's faithful grace, we are encouraged to go forward with confidence, knowing that Christ lives in us, even though we haven't yet reached our goal.

Jesus Christ sets before us a job far beyond our abilities: to bring the gospel to the entire world. Christian churches have been working at this for almost 2,000 years, and there are still large segments of the world that have not been reached — and some areas that were once Christian are not Christian any more. Still, we do not lose heart. We continue the work because Christ lives in us. It is his work, and we can be sure that he will bring it to completion. We do not need to worry or be discouraged about that.

Actually, if we were able to achieve all our goals, we would also be tempted to take the credit. We might claim to have the right method, the right formula for success, the right wisdom or even the right level of humility! But because we fall short, we are reminded that the tasks set before us are humanly impossible. The gospel is not humanly received. We cannot take credit for conversions or for individual growth in the gospel. We must rely on Christ.

But what about having a vision and leading our congregations to serve the communities we are in? I am encouraged that people want to reach out to their communities, for congregations to become effective outposts for the kingdom of our Lord and Savior. This is in itself a sign of growth — a symptom of a church being led by the Holy Spirit. But we often encounter some inertia. We are usually slow to change, both individually and collectively.

First-century struggles

Consider for a moment the first-century church, the church with all the apostles, the experiences with Jesus, and the eyewitnesses of his resurrection. These were the people Jesus told, "Go into all the world." Was there a sudden rush for missionary work? Hardly. The apostles stayed in Jerusalem for several years. Miraculous visions had to occur before Peter would even go into a Gentile's house. Even that small step had to be carefully explained to the critics in the Jerusalem church. A major conference had to be held to clarify just what the gospel is, that people are saved by faith, and that Gentiles are to be accepted. The process took many years, and not everyone finally agreed.

In time, the apostles left Jerusalem and carried the gospel to other peoples. But the Jerusalem church itself remained rather conservative, a victim of inertia. They were slow to change their view of the world and their view of how they were to serve God. They limited themselves, but God was not limited. He raised up others to share in the work. Antioch became a center of missionary activity. Antioch became the church that called Paul and sent him out, and the church grew.

Our goal is to be like Antioch, not like Jerusalem. If we do not change, we will end up like Jerusalem, and God will raise up other people to do the work. He has plenty to choose from. The good news is that we are being transformed. Though inertia affects us, it is being overcome! But it does take time.

Our frustration, our discouragement is — ironically — a symptom of our progress! If we were solidly mired in our inertia, we wouldn't care. We wouldn't even be *trying* to change. We would be like a turtle that pulls its legs and head into its shell, protecting itself and not going anywhere.

Whenever there is a change, some people are quicker to adapt than others are. That's just the way people are. Eventually more and more people grasp the idea, but at first only a small number do. Let's suppose that 10 percent of members have a vision for reaching out. (The actual figure would be higher in some congregations and lower in others.) It is easy for them to become discouraged, since it might seem that 90 percent of the people don't "get it." It is natural for them to want more people to share their enthusiasm, and it is natural for them to be discouraged when so many don't join in.

Looking at the positive

But I would like to point out the other side of the coin — that significant progress has already been made. The good leaven has begun to permeate the lump of dough. The mustard seed has sprouted and has begun to grow. Christ is working, and he will complete the work he has begun. But it takes time, and people who are quick to adapt to change are not always gifted with patience!

Let me assure you: I firmly believe that we need to continue to change, to be transformed under Christ's leadership. When I sound a note of patience, I do not want anyone to think it is an opportunity to dig in and resist change. I want us to move forward, but with some realism about how much work it takes for us to move forward. We need to run with patience the race set before us. We must never stop running, but we must run with patience.

Now let me further address the above-mentioned situation. Some pastors are discouraged because they have either not formulated or have not gathered support for an outward-reaching vision. Some have read books about vision that say, in essence, that if a person spends enough time on the "mountaintop" with God, then God will give that person a vision engraved in stone. Some pastors become discouraged when no vision seems to materialize, and they sometimes begin to doubt their relationship with God, or their call to leadership.

Vision isn't always like that. Paul Ford says that only 30 percent of pastors are visionary by gift or style. Some pastors get out front and shout for people to follow; while many others lead by coming alongside the people, comforting and counseling and encouraging members to go forward together. Such pastors exercise leadership more by coordinating efforts of the members than by commanding new efforts. Both approaches are legitimate forms of pastoral leadership, but it is difficult for a person of one style to try to function according to the other style. We all function best when we spend most of our time operating in the way God has gifted us.

Let me return again to the matter of outward vision. In some cases, we need not be too concerned about outward vision right now. God may not yet be giving an outward vision because it is not yet his time for new people to come into the congregation. First, the congregation must mature and become a nurturing fellowship. I say that not to condemn, but to diagnose the situation so that we can deal with it.

Upward, inward, outward

My dad used to talk about "upward, inward, and outward," and he placed them in that order for a reason. Our highest priority is to get our upward relationship right. We are to worship God with all our heart, mind, soul and strength, and we are to love him with all our depth of being. When our relationship with God is strong and growing, we also find ourselves growing in the second priority — "inward." We find ourselves growing in love for one another, in service toward one another, in caring for one another and in encouraging one another.

Our relationships with one another need to be built on the solid ground of faith in Christ — not on the desire for uniformity. There is value in doctrinal unity. But our *relationships* must be based on more than that — they must be based on a loving relationship *with Christ* that leads us to *love one another*. Our belief is in the One who saves us by his grace, and therefore we can allow some variations in behavior without letting those variations divide us from one another.

When our relationships with one another are strained, it is more difficult for us to display the love of Christ to new believers. If we can love only those who agree with us, how can we be a good incubator for people just beginning to come out of the world? Christ leads his people to love another even when we have different ideas, different practices and different ways of worshipping God.

When the upward and inward are healthy, the outward will fall into place. We will see the diverse gifts of our congregation and how those gifts can serve the church and the community — and we will have the desire to do so.

In short, we do not need to feel frustrated or discouraged if an outward vision is not yet developing for our local congregation. It will, in time. Until then, we need to focus most of our attention on the upward and inward (even as we remain alert to and involved in outward opportunities). We do not need special visions in order to worship God and love one another. We do not need a supernatural revelation for us to pray together, to sing spiritual songs and care for one another. We have already been given a supernatural revelation — the Bible — telling us to do those things.

Eager but patient

We will never be perfectly healthy, but we want to improve the health of our worship, our discipleship, our fellowship and our mutual ministry. Rick Warren has described one approach to church health; Christian Schwarz describes another. Both methods are effective in getting churches to take a systematic look at the diverse functions a church should have, and both methods help people identify areas in which they need to improve. Other authors (Elmer Towns, George Barna, Aubrey Malphurs, Ralph Neighbor, Lyle Schaller, etc.) contribute yet other approaches. There is no perfect method, and what works well for one congregation may not work as well for another. But by seeking wise counsel in books, in conversation with pastors and members, and in Scripture, we can be led by God into increasing joyful participation in his plan for us.

Just as we must have a patient eagerness for the return of the Lord, we must also have a patient eagerness for the completion of his work in our fellowship, as he transforms us to be closer to "the whole measure of the fullness of Christ" (Ephesians 4:13). To him we give all praise and honor and glory.

Joseph Tkach

36. GOOD THINGS IN SMALL PACKAGES

Most Christians are in small churches. Though megachurches usually get more attention, small churches are the backbone of Christianity. People are more likely to come to faith in a small church than in a megachurch.

Of all congregations in the world, most are small, averaging less than 100 people in attendance, so it is important to understand how small churches function. They are not miniature imitations of multi-ministry megachurches. Rather, they have a dynamic of their own, often a slower pace and a more friendly face.

Small churches in our denomination will be a little different from small Baptist, Methodist or Presbyterian churches. Our history and our geographical circumstances will make some things different for us. Yet we can learn from other small churches and get some ideas that may help us in our congregations.

Small churches are not confined to small towns—they are found in the biggest cities, too. Some are dying, but others are thriving, and God is working in and through them. We need to see what small churches do best, so we can make the most of our strengths, and not try to be something we are not. If Christ has made us a little toe in his body, we want to be the best little toe we can be.

Strengths

Small churches have several important strengths:

Relationships. People know one another and care about one another. If someone is missing, others notice. When big churches set up small groups, they are trying to imitate something that comes naturally to a small church.

Involvement. Everyone gets actively involved in the church. A high percentage of people have assigned duties: setup, cleanup, ushering, greeting, sound system, music, scripture reading, teaching children and speaking.

Stability. Large churches may lose five percent of their members each year. Small churches retain members better, partly through involvement and largely through relationships.

In general, the larger the church, the more business-like it must function. The senior pastor must be an executive, an administrator. The programs of the church must be well organized, well coordinated, professionally done. There must be a clear organizational structure. Small churches tend to function more informally, more through the relationship networks of the church. Decisions are made more on how they affect people, and less on logic.

Church management textbooks are usually designed for mid-size and larger churches, so their advice doesn't always work in the small church. This is especially true when it comes to programs or ministries. The books say "the more the better. Have something for every age group, every need, every day." This is impossible for the small church. The small church cannot offer the same array of special-interest ministries. It cannot follow the same methods and expect the same results. It cannot have the same kind of children's ministry or the same kind of youth group. But neither does it neglect these parts of the body.

Small churches tend to have activities in which everyone is involved: seniors, teens, singles and marrieds, all involved together. The activity is a success if most of the congregation comes. Small churches don't always have a designated women's ministry—the women are already involved in ministry. They don't have a big teen ministry—they involve their teens in ministry and activities anyway. They may have only a tiny children's class, but they make sure that the children enjoy it and feel welcome at church.

These observations are not intended to be an excuse for small churches to abandon ministries they ought to have, but they point out that a small church doesn't have to have everything. Women, teens, children and men should all be involved in the church. Small churches cannot do everything, but each one can do something, and they need to do it as best they can.

- "Small congregations have more in common with other small churches than they do with larger congregations in the community, or in their denominational communion" (Dudley, p. 16).

- "One half of all Protestant churches in the United States and Canada average fewer than 75 at worship, and a fourth average fewer than 35" (Schaller, p. 58).

- "Too many small-membership churches spend an excessive amount of time lamenting their weaknesses, bemoaning their shortcomings and emphasizing their limitations. A more productive approach is to identify, affirm, and plan to build on strengths" (Schaller, p. 73).

- "God wants us to use what we have, not moan about what we don't have…. God will not hold you accountable to match the deeds and ministries of a larger church. You will be accountable, however, to be the best small church you can possibly be" (Bierly, p. 75).

- "Researcher George Barna has observed that the most effective churches deliberately limit their ministries, focusing on those specific areas for which they have resources and in which they have the ability to serve with excellence. If even large churches have to observe this principle to be effective, how much more do small churches whose resources are even more limited need to follow it?" (*No Little Places*, Klassen and Koessler, p. 90).

Making decisions

The pastor's role in a small church is more relational. Leadership is exercised less by command and more by consensus-building. Members want good sermons, but they want good relationships even more. They want pastors who love them, who care for them. They will reject his ideas (no matter how good they are) if he doesn't love the people.

It takes time for a pastor to build these relationships, to build the trust needed to lead. It usually takes several years. The pastor needs to learn the culture of the church and how to work within that culture. The pastor needs to know how to suggest ideas, whom to suggest them to and how to implement the ideas the members have.

Pastors grow in influence by spending time with members, by visiting the sick, by performing funerals and weddings, by caring about the people. He initiates change more by asking questions, by helping people see the need for change, than by having all the answers.

Churches need leadership, or else they stagnate. Pastors need to be optimistic about what God is doing in the church, and what he may do in the future. Pastors need to help members be excited about the mission, to have a clear idea of what they are doing. This leads to growth.

Healthy small churches grow. Growth can affect the relationship networks within the church, and because of that, some members may resist growth. They do not want new people taking the pastor's time away from them. They do not want new people taking ministry roles away from them.

Growth means change, and some people have a low tolerance for change. Change means conflict. But a refusal to change means slow death. "We may have to choose between the past and the future, between clinging to our old ways and having a vital church for our children and grandchildren" (Klassen and Koessler, p. 61). If we want our church to survive, we must be willing to change.

Growth

How do small churches grow? It is generally through personal relationships, through members inviting friends and relatives to church. People may be invited for special programs, or for a weekly worship service, but the invitation begins with a relationship.

When people visit a small church, they should be warmly welcomed. The greeter or usher does not just shake hands and give a bulletin—the greeter begins a relationship, making the person feel loved, making sure the visitor gives his or her name and address in the guest book.

In many small churches, there is follow-up within the week. A lay member brings cookies, fruit or some gift to say, "We're glad you visited." The church is building on its strength: relationships. The church is saying: "We care. We like you. We want you back." Love is the water that helps the seeds sprout and grow.

The most important ingredient in church growth is the members' attitudes about their church. They make no apologies for their small size. They belong to the church and are involved in the church not because of its music or its building, but because God is working in the church, and they want to be where God is. When people are excited about what God is doing in their lives, and when they see the church as a place in which God works, they find it easier to invite people. "Come and see," they say. "I think you'll like it."

In our impersonal, technological world, many people are looking for greater meaning to life, something spiritual, something that gives them community and friends. Some try to find this in a bar; others find it in small churches. The people who care about them convince them that God cares about them.

Small churches must look toward God. He's the one who has set us in our places, and he wants us to be the best we can be, to bloom even if we are small. As long as we are small, we want to be the best small church that we can be.

Resources for small churches

Steve Bierly, *Help for the Small-Church Pastor*. Zondervan, 1995.
Ron Crandall, *Turnaround Strategies for the Small Church*. Abingdon, 1995.
Carl Dudley, *Making the Small Church Effective*. Abingdon, 1978.
Ron Klassen and John Koessler, *No Little Places*. Baker, 1996.
Lyle Schaller, *The Small Church Is Different!* Abingdon, 1982.

Michael Morrison

"In a big world, the small church has remained intimate. In a fast world, the small church has been steady. In an expensive world, the small church has remained plain. In a complex world, the small church has remained simple. In a rational world, the small church has kept feelings. In a mobile world, the small church has been an anchor. In an anonymous world, the small church calls us by name—by nickname! As a result, small churches have survived where others have failed" (Dudley, p. 176).

37. CHOOSE YOUR FUTURE

a review article

Small churches have numerous options for the future — some more attractive than others, some more viable than others. Some small churches will be able to do things that others cannot, due to their circumstances and personnel. The options are described in Lyle Schaller's 142-page paperback *The Small Membership Church: Scenarios for Tomorrow* (Abingdon, 1994).

Schaller writes, "Most congregations are really confronted with two choices: change or gradually fade away" (page 21). "Small churches have a bright and promising future—if they are willing to adapt to a new role in a changing culture" (page 12). But he warns, "Small churches cannot enjoy substantial numerical growth without making what many will identify as unwelcome or disruptive changes" (page 13). "Change is more difficult in smaller congregations than it is in big churches" (page 20).

First or second commandment?

Schaller describes a major choice that small congregations face — to focus on God, or to focus on each other. He describes it as first-commandment churches (love God with all your being) and second-commandment churches (love your neighbor as yourself). The second group focus on loving each other; the first look more at worship. "The best small churches are organized primarily around the principle of loving your neighbor…. By contrast, the best of the larger churches are organized primarily around the first great commandment" (30-31).

To state it another way, churches that focus on loving each other do not attract as many new members as do churches that focus on relationship with God. Don't people want to be loved? Of course they do. The problem is that small churches love each other so much that a visitor generally feels like an outsider.

"The churches most likely to reach newcomers to the community are the first-commandment congregations that concentrate on identifying and responding to the religious agendas of people" (34). "Congregations that are primarily organized around nurturing interpersonal relationships and/or building a sense of community are less likely to attract strangers" (35). "Most unchurched individuals who do become regular churchgoers are attracted to first-commandment parishes that focus on meeting the religious needs of people" (111).

"In the small congregation, the Sunday morning schedule and program are usually designed with the members as the number-one constituency" (16). "By contrast, most large and rapidly growing churches think in regional, not neighborhood, terms and focus more on people's spiritual and personal needs rather than on established kin or friendship ties" (19).

So the choice set before us is this: "Do we want to be a healthy second-commandment congregation that places at the top of the agenda the quality of the relationships among our people? Or do we want to transform ourselves into primarily a first-commandment church that concentrates first of all on identifying and offering a meaningful response to the religious needs of people we have yet to meet?" (82).

He warns that this change is not easy — it could involve "internal conflict over identity and role" (82). This requires a leader with vision, but "most small congregations have failed to create a congregational culture that is compatible with this leadership style" (85). They function by consensus.

Competition

Large churches "assume that competition is the norm," whereas small congregations tend to "believe that cooperation should be the norm" (62). The choice we make will affect our future. "Intercongregational cooperation in programming [i.e., worship, teaching, youth ministries, etc.] is rarely compatible with numerical growth" (71, 77). "Instead of recognizing the need for change, a cooperative arrangement often promises that yesterday is a viable model for tomorrow" (75).

If the goal is growth, Schaller gives this advice: "Concentrate on matching the local competition in quality; in publicity; in creating additional entry points for newcomers to welcoming places in your fellowship; in identifying and responding to the religious agendas of skeptics, pilgrims, searchers, agnostics, seekers and others on a religious quest; in serious and in-depth Bible study; in the ministry of music; and in the proclamation of the gospel" (74).

Congregations need a mission strategy. Although they are willing to accept anyone, they need to focus their evangelistic efforts. The question is: "Who are the folks your congregation is seeking to reach?... The goalless congregation that is drifting into tomorrow usually answers that question in these terms, 'Everyone'" (81).

No congregation has to save everyone on the planet. "No one congregation...is obligated to be all things to all people.... Therefore, who are the people your church will *seek* to reach, serve, and challenge?" (86). Will we scatter our seed everywhere equally, or will we focus our efforts? "The first-commandment church is far more likely to follow a marketing strategy" (87). They seek to identify needs of the audience, not just what they are already doing (which is based on their own needs). "In marketing the beginning point is on the needs of the customer, not on the product" (102).

Schaller says that churches have a choice; they can create a self-fulfilling prophecy. What do they want to be in five years? The choices we make now will affect our future. "The most productive results probably will come if identifying a future constituency is the beginning point for the discussion" (100).

From other books...

Weaknesses of small churches

"Many small churches do not have any noticeable social ministry. They are concerned only with their own doings..... Congregations who care only for themselves are becoming smaller and smaller. Eventually their place will have no meaning, for they have not shared it with anyone" (Carl Dudley, *Making the Small Church Effective* [Abingdon, 1978], 99, 103).

"The small church cannot grow in membership size without giving up its most precious appeal, its intimacy" (Dudley 49). "They cannot receive new members without losing touch with those whom they already know" (50). "Members of the congregation must want to grow so much that they are willing to give up the satisfactions of knowing, or knowing about, *everyone* else in the congregation" (51).

"A large proportion of the minister's time and energy must be reserved for face-to-face contacts with potential new members and new members. Obviously that reduces the amount of time the minister has [available] to spend with members. This is one of the basic prices of church growth, and one that many members are unwilling to pay.... Some of the oldtimers may begin to feel neglected" (Schaller 1982, 72, 82)

"Even though new people are seen as desirable to help carry the load, there is also the fear that they will take control and change things" (Ron Crandall, *Turn Around Strategies for the Small Church* [Abingdon, 1995], 73).

"Adoption is a serious problem in many congregations where new members are kept on the fringes for several years, or even longer.... Most congregations cannot adopt members until they take pride in their own congregation's 'story of Christian witness'" (Dudley 58, 57).

"For some congregations, memory has been their strength and inspiration. For others, the weight of the past has become a millstone and a source of despair... Some history can be a burden, and some can be oppressive.... What is nostalgia for some people may be nauseous for others" (Dudley 83-84).

"What we 'choose' to remember may be our deepest longings for what will unfold in the future... Our memory tells us more about who we are than who we were, more about our hopes and fears for the future than what really happened in the past" (Dudley 86).

"We can identify five major problems faced by churches and their pastors as they seek to move from a survival mentality to renewed investment in ministry and evangelism. The problems are: (1) low self-esteem and apathy, (2) lack of vision for the future, (3) lack of concern and love for 'outsiders,' (4) finances and stewardship of resources, and (5) issues of power and interpersonal conflict" (Crandall 61).

"Negative self-image is the number one problem facing smaller churches" (Crandall 42). "The lower our self-esteem, the more likely it is that we will concentrate on 'our problems' and on institutional survival rather than on the potentialities for ministry" (Schaller, quoted in Dudley 20). "In most numerically growing churches the members are enthusiastic about (a) their faith as Christians, (b) the congregation of which they are members, and (c) their minister" (Lyle Schaller, *The Small Church Is Different* [Abingdon, 1982], 70).

"Small congregations prove particularly susceptible to social conflict.... [Some congregations] seem to chew up pastors" (Dudley 132-33). "Sinners in your congregation will, at times, reject you and your ideas for no good reason" (Bierly 30). "Wherever two or three are gathered together, problems develop" (Eugene Peterson).

"It is rare to find a small congregation that has experienced substantial numerical growth, and sustained that growth, without the benefit of a long pastorate" Schaller 1982, 71). "Smaller congregations tend to seek to grow by following the attraction model, while the proclamation approach is usually found in larger congregations" (Schaller 1982, 40).

Denominational tensions

"Small church leaders [tend] to see the denominational structure as bureaucratic machinery that squeezes people for money.... They show distrust of and hostility toward the hierarchy.... Small-church pastors and denominational officers often find it convenient to distrust and dislike each other. In many situations, each provides a convenient scapegoat for the other" (Dudley 158, 160).

"Small-church pastors and denominational executives have more in common than they have to divide them. They are both ministers (administrators) caught in the middle between the same irreconcilable expectations.... A first step toward the resolution of the denomination/small church problems lies in the simple admission that each will serve the Lord better when both agree to disagree honestly, openly, and without personal innuendo, in a spirit of Christian love. They have more to offer when they share their differences in perspective and resources. Neither alone can deal with the problems that confront small churches and concern the whole church of Jesus Christ" (Dudley 160-61).

"Denominations can serve congregations in two general ways: by a wider perspective on their ministry, and by specific resources for their mission" (Dudley 161). "Pastors and congregations in smaller denominations benefit even more from the counsel and programs of their denominational leaders than do those serving in larger denominations" (Crandall 164).

"Financial subsidies and high morale rarely go together!" (Schaller 1982, 60). "Denominational subsidies tend to produce dependency, passivity, low morale, and self-centeredness" (159). "The largest number and the heartiest of small churches are in those denominations where funds are simply not available" (Dudley 167).

"A growing portion of small congregations will depend on bivocational pastors and bivocational ministerial teams" (Schaller 1984, 13). "Effective pastoral service in a small church requires a different set of gifts, skills, priorities, and personal characteristics than are required to be the effective senior pastor of a large congregation" (14). "The smaller the congregation, the more influential are the volunteer lay leaders in formulating policies" (14). "The traditional dream of 'having our own pastor' who does not have any outside demands on his or her time is not a realistic goal for at least half of all the Protestant churches on the North American continent" (Schaller 1982, 88).

Twelve Emerging Turnaround Strategies

Listed in order of importance:

Enhance congregational confidence and hope for the future.

Stimulate concern for unreached persons in the community.

Engage in proactive and effective pastoral leadership.

Encourage an open, loving atmosphere in the congregation.

Clarify your own personal vision and be an example.

Help develop a clear, shared, congregational vision.

Work and pray for spiritual renewal among the members.

Provide high quality preaching and inspirational worship.

Lead the effort to reach new people and grow.

Emphasize and practice prayer.

Develop new programs, especially for children and youth.

Plan to take risks and take them. (Crandall 22-23)

Handling conflict

"Some of us, especially the relational types who like small churches because relationships are highly valued, tend to function like turtles, teddy bears, or foxes. We handle conflict by avoidance, submission, or egalitarian compromise. The first approach will never be a leader for change. Change produces conflict. To avoid conflicts is to abdicate leadership. Pastors can function this way and be loved, but they cannot lead a church out of trouble.

"The second approach sounds most 'Christian' to some ears…but teddy bears will always be eaten by sharks. And there is a danger in giving too much away to sharks. Shawchuck and Moeller write: 'When "I must win" individuals are allowed to rule the church, anger builds in others, people feel coerced, and a dangerous dependency on the strong-willed individual develops.' This is true whether the shark is a member or a pastor.

"The compromise suggested by foxes solves all problems in the same way: 'Divide the living boy in two; then give half to the one, and half to the other'…. Such an approach may work well in some situations, but it can also destroy the dynamic and responsive life of the church as Christ's body, which does not exist simply to make everyone happy, but to serve the purposes of the risen Lord.

"The recommended approach is that of the collaborative owl…. First, generate as much useful information as possible about all sides of the issue. Second, help the group see where they agree not just where they don't. And third, bring all who are involved into the decision-making process and motivate them to personally commit themselves to the final agreement. This is indeed hard work" (Crandall 80-81).

Seven characteristics of growing churches

Bible preaching.

Emphasis on evangelism.

A fellowship circle as large or larger than the membership circle.

Opportunities for members to express their commitment through using their gifts.

Leadership emerging from among new first-generation members (not the children of older members).

Specialties in ministry beyond the traditional.

A minister who likes people and is happy as a pastor. (Schaller, quoted in Crandall, 175)

Two approaches to volunteers

"As pastor, I need to ask myself why I want people to be involved in the ministries of the church. The first possible motivation is employment: I want them to help me achieve my ministry goals...

"The second possible motivation is empowerment. In this model, the pastor serves the members of the church. The pastor is motivated by a desire to see them find fulfillment in Christ by helping them discern God's call and develop their full ministry potential. When people know I am more interested in helping them fulfill their potential than in getting them to help me reach my goals, they feel valued, not used.... People should never serve programs; programs should be tools that enable people to better fulfill their calls" (Ron Klassen and John Koessler, *No Little Places: The Untapped Potential of the Small Town Church* [Baker, 1996], 91-92).

"I want to get over using the word volunteer and start using the word disciple" (Barbara Florey, quoted in Crandall, 121).

"The most important decision about children's classes is not the curriculum — it is the teacher. People remember the teacher far better than they remember the lesson material.... To a very substantial degree the teacher *is* the curriculum" (Schaller 1982, 113). "In a growing number of small-membership churches, the Sunday school is perceived as the most important single channel for reaching and attracting the new generation of parents" (118).

"If adults teach by who they are and by what they *do,* an adult class may be the critical element in developing a strong Sunday school in the small congregation.... Perhaps the best beginning point for strengthening the children's division is to have at least one male-dominated adult Sunday school class meeting in a very conspicuous place, so the children can see that participation in Sunday school is appropriate behavior for adults" (120).

Stewardship

"There is no need to tell anyone how much to give, but there is a need to tell why to give and how to make stewardship decisions.... Focus on financial stewardship as a spiritual discipline and not primarily a way to raise money or pay bills" (Crandall 77-78).

"It usually takes four to six years for complete turnaround to come in most churches. Giving is not only linked to spiritual renewal and vision, but to trust. Trust takes time" (Crandall 79). "It takes about five years to lay the groundwork for an effective ministry in the small church" (Klassen and Koessler 35).

Michael Morrison

38. HOPE FOR THE LEFT BEHIND CHURCH – INTERVIEW WITH DR. RUTH A. TUCKER

Is bigger always better? Are numbers the only way to measure success? Not according to Ruth Tucker, author of *Left Behind in a Megachurch World.*

By Sheila Graham

Ruth Tucker grew up in what she refers to as a left-behind church — a little rural church that was the center of activity for her and her friends. "I will carry memories of those spirited times to the grave, whether the free-for-all softball games with the pastor as pitcher or the sultry days of summer Bible camp or the rollicking harvest hayrides or the frigid sledding parties with a bonfire at the top of the hill," she remembers.

Her little church was established by two missionary ladies in the 1930s. Tucker wondered if they could have imagined the outcome of their work. "Did they imagine that their little ripple effect — their humble and often awkward efforts—would nurture sons and daughters whose ministries, vocations and influence have spanned the globe?"

I asked her what she meant by left-behind churches. "The title of the book came out of a class. I realized most of my students would be going out into smaller churches. We hear of wonderful stories of this church and that church doubling in size every four years, but that's not the rule. I felt it's important for these young ministers to see that God works in little churches, even churches losing membership, not just the ones holding their own. It doesn't mean God is not working if the church is not growing or if the church is getting smaller. It also doesn't mean we shouldn't want to grow, but again the growth should be the right kind of growth. So much of the growth in the megachurches, or the mega-wannabes, comes at the expense of another church."

Dr. Tucker says that in the arena dominated by megachurches, the most authentic Christian voices may be heard in small congregations. "When I think of authentic Christian voice I'm often thinking of Paul's reference to 'When I am weak then I am strong,' or Jesus' 'the first shall be last' and 'take up your cross and follow me.' Yes, we do see in Acts numbers of people who came to the Lord, but when it was the church itself, in the first century especially, we're looking at small numbers. We're looking at a rag-tag bunch of disciples living and working in very tenuous times.

"There's real danger when the church of Christ sees great success. Jesus and Paul warned about that, and we ought to see dangers. That's not what Jesus was talking about when he spoke the words, 'follow thou me' and 'come and take up thy cross.'" But can a church become too small to be effective? "There are churches of thousands that are too small, too big, too something, to be effective. But small churches have peculiar problems that other churches do not have. Being able to provide for a minister is always an issue, and so is having a facility or location. But you can have a wonderful group of a dozen or two dozen, three dozen people who are vibrant Christians reaching out to the neighborhood."

Yes, but what about those churches where many of their members don't live in the neighborhood where the church is located? "That's unfortunate," Tucker said, "If you are a little neighborhood church and you have 36 people, you're a lot bigger than the church of 36 spread all over three counties. A church so spread out has to transition into becoming a neighborhood church. Whether it's a rental property or whatever it is, get your base in that community. How good it would be if this church of 36 expanded so some of its members could start a group of eight or so in their towns, with the church still maintaining the 36 people and pulling in people from the neighborhood.

"A wonderful student of mine was involved in a little left-behind church where nothing was happening. Then a woman in their church was called by a neighbor to help out some relatives who lived in a mobile home park. One after another this family and their friends got connected to the church. Within a month or two the church had doubled in size with people with tattoos and bandanas coming on motorcycles and in beat-up trucks. That church was revitalized with everyone so excited because they've got more people coming.

"We've got to put roots down in a neighborhood and do it the way Jesus did. That is 'come follow me.' When we are way too small to get involved in large projects by ourselves, we've got to get people in the neighborhood involved in humanitarian outreach programs. There are people out there who really would like to have opportunities to help and work."

If you're part of a small congregation, or large, whether pastor or member, you'll find *Left Behind in a Megachurch World* well-researched and full of encouraging and inspiring examples of how God works through ordinary churches to accomplish the extraordinary. Dr. Tucker is an author, lecturer, and former associate professor of missiology at Calvin Theological Seminary in Grand Rapids, Michigan.

39. SMALL GROUPS OR CELL GROUPS?

What is the difference between small groups and cell groups?

Good question. The terms "small groups" and "cell groups" are often used interchangeably. So what is the difference?

A quick answer is that all cell groups are small groups but not all small groups are cell groups. Small groups can meet specific needs of group members. Small groups have a history of benefiting the body of Christ especially in time of revival. Most small groups are one of the programs offered by a church congregation.

Cell groups are a specific type of small group that has a specific model of ministry. Cell groups are not a program of the congregation. They are the most basic unit of the congregation. Cell groups are the smallest units of people who have teamed up to do the work of the congregation and the denomination.

In a cell group, Christians come together in a covenant relationship to do the work of the kingdom. Cell members join with one another to accomplish four specific tasks: edification, equipping, evangelism and leadership expansion. Small groups can also have one or more of these tasks, but cell groups intentionally strive to do all four.

Relationships

Edification occurs when church members learn to be in loving relationships with one another. God values relationship. The Trinity is God living in relational community. Our purpose in life is to come into relationship with God and one another. Cell members are committed to growth in Christian intimacy and support.

Cell members are accountable to God and to one another in their Christian walk. Praying together and for one another is a powerful path for bonding, healing and edification. Equipping best occurs in a cell group of people who edify and support one another. Christians who know you are best suited to confirm your spiritual gifts.

They team with you and complement your gifts and talents with their gifts and talents. Christians together do the work of ministry Christ sets before them. Christians learn to disciple in the community of a cell group.

Facilitating evangelism

Relational evangelism works best in the cell model of ministry. Cell members intentionally pray together for unbelievers to come to a relationship with Jesus. Cell members cultivate relationships with unchurched people.

Through cell-group outreach, the cell practices body-life evangelism. When an unbeliever sees the life of Christ manifested in a bonded community of Christians, evangelism is easier and more enjoyable (John 13:34).

Cell groups provide an effective and efficient method of developing leaders. Mentoring future leaders is intentional in a cell-based church. Everyone can develop leadership skills in a cell group. God will grant growth according to the availability of leadership to handle the growth. Coaching and encouraging future leaders is one of the most basic objectives of the cell model of ministry. Cell leaders strive to train cell leaders who train more cell leaders, and the cycle continues.

Charles Calahan

Charles A. Calahan earned a doctorate in family life education and consultation at Kansas State University.

40. EDIFICATION OR BUILDING UP THROUGH CELL GROUPS

Have you ever wanted to have a Christian friend who *really* knew you? This friend would know and understand you at the deepest personal level. He or she would really listen to you. This friend would love you when you were unlovable. This friend could be trusted with your secrets and even your sins. He or she would extend grace to you if you shared your heart, your hopes and your faults. This friend would hold you accountable for habitually making the same mistake. He or she would tell you clearly and honestly when you were wrong or if your attitude was not the best. This friend would accept you as less than a perfect Christian.

Is it possible to have more than one friend who was this close to you? Is it possible to have a small group of friends such as this? These friends would be a lot like Jesus. These friends would be centered on Christ and would share your spiritual journey.

I have just described cell group edification. This spiritual "building up" of a Christian is what Paul describes: "Encourage one another and build each other up, just as in fact you are doing" (1 Thessalonians 5:11).

Edification is one of the four intentional tasks of the cell model of ministry. Cell strategy requires believers to be willing to enter into covenant relationships with one another and to accept responsibility for one another. Spiritual building or edification does not come from social talk about the weather around the coffee pot at the monthly church potluck. This is real spiritual building of Christian life. It requires Christian *commitment to community* centered on Jesus Christ as Lord.

Edification occurs when Christ in me reaches out to connect with Christ in you. It happens when Jesus ministers through me to you, and through you to me. *We* do not do the fixing. Rather, we depend on Jesus to do the helping and the healing. Christ does the edification through Christians in relationships.

This quality of building up does not happen overnight. It takes time. It may require spiritual maturing through resolving conflict. It may require confession and repenting of spiritual strongholds. Cell group members will need to be committed to Jesus and then to one another. Trust and transparency are required. The presence and a relationship with Jesus is required of individuals forming the cell community.

Edification is not always warm, fuzzy and comfortable feelings of encouragement. Sometimes edifying happens when a Christian friend kindly tells you that you are wrong or mistaken.

Spiritual edification is an intentional and primary task of a cell group. It is interdependent ministry. Believers are released to use their spiritual gifts to edify. The priesthood of believers is empowered to build up the body. It requires Christ to be present. He is present with believers living in edifying relationships (Matthew 18:20).

This kind of edification is spiritually mature. It is not nominal Christianity, in name only. It requires commitment and time. A relationship with Jesus and walking with him is vital. A Christian needs to be willing to be vulnerable and correctable. For some, this is not easy.

In the bonded Christian community of a cell group, Jesus makes it easy. The Holy Spirit, the Comforter, reaches out and helps cell members to relate to each other. When Christ is central, trust and transparency can grow and flourish.

Praying together and for one another powerfully promotes edification. When believers pray together, the Holy Spirit bonds them together. It is from this bonded relationship and basic Christian community centered on Christ that spiritual edification springs forth naturally.

Edification is not something we do without Christ. It is not a program of the congregation. It is not a dependent ministry of the local church. It is the ministry of Jesus living in the lives of Christians who share their spiritual journey. Edification is Jesus working in the midst of a small group of believers who are centered on him and who are committed to spiritually sheltering and to building up one another.

Charles A. Calahan

41. CELL-BASED CHURCH:
COMMUNITY, NURTURING, OUTREACH

Some visionaries of church growth believe that the cell-based model of ministry is an important model of the church in the 21st century. It is a strategy of ministry that some congregations are adopting or are considering adopting. The cell-based approach is a shift in the purpose and function of a congregation. The cell church is based on members meeting in small groups and then coming together weekly to praise and worship as a congregation.

The small group or cell group component enables the presence of Christ to be manifested in relationships of caring Christians. In this environment people are edified and equipped to minister. Unbelievers are saved and discipled. Leadership is raised up and mentored. The weekly corporate worship becomes a time of praise and celebration centered on the glory of God.

Under the unity of the larger congregation, the cell groups are mobilized to carry out the ministry vision of the congregation and the denomination. The cell groups nurture a sense of belonging that is difficult to experience in the large weekly worship assembly. In the cell groups, love, community, relationships, discipling and reaching out to unbelievers spring up naturally and powerfully.

The spiritual gifts of members are confirmed and used, worship is expanded, prayer is prominent, and ministry is extended by cell church strategy. It is in the cell group that caring for one another occurs. It is this loving, bonded community of believers, which is the manifested body of Christ, that reaches out to unbelievers and brings Christ to the world (John 13:35). Members and new believers are taught to know, to grow in, to serve and to share Jesus. A cell-based church actively seeks to develop each Christian into the likeness of Christ.

In the human body the basic unit of life is the cell. In a cell church, the basic unit of the body of Christ is the cell group. This basic unit is the means by which Christian community is built and the work of the kingdom is performed.

Below are testimonies from two cell members. Pastor Ron Dick asked for and received their permission to publish their testimonies.

Pat Arthur: To me, the cell-church model has been an awakening into the workings of the body of Christ. In my cell group we have people of all ages. I am a woman in my mid-50s. I have become a grandmother figure for a teenage boy. What a joy this has been for me. We talk about everything. We pray about things in his life as well as mine.

Men and women in our cell are close. We discuss problems openly and help each other see things we might not see otherwise. Together we are working toward God's kingdom using the gifts of the Holy Spirit. Only in a cell group could I have ever hoped to get to know and love these wonderful people I now call my family.

Jenni Heaton: Facilitating a cell has been a wonderful experience. Every week I am amazed to see God working so strongly in the cell. I don't have much natural leadership ability, but I don't need it. Jesus leads the cell. I just take care of some administrative duties, ask questions and make sure we start and stop on time. The Spirit has been more evident to me as I have experienced the cell-church model than ever before in my life. I don't have to make it happen. God is taking care of everything.

I have been able to grow more as a Christian since joining a cell than in the last 10 years. I can once again see God working directly in my life. He is in control, and I feel more joy and peace than ever. I think everyone should have a chance to be equipped for Christianity and evangelism by a living cell. You don't know what you have been missing until you experience Jesus working through you in a cell.

Charles A. Calahan

42. SHOULD YOU PLANT A CHURCH?

An Interview with Ed Stetzer

Randy Bloom, then Director of Church Multiplication Ministries for Grace Communion International, interviewed Ed Stetzer, President of LifeWay Research. An experienced church planter, Ed trains church planters and pastors around the world.

RB: Tell us about your experience as a church planter.

ES: I have a great love for church planting. I planted my first church in Buffalo, New York. I was 21 years old, and God was calling my wife and me to move into the city among the urban poor. We started knocking on doors, and we started our first church there. That was 22 years ago.

Depending on how you count, I've had the privilege of planting five churches. The last church I planted was about three or four years ago. I've written some books on the subject. The newest is *Viral Churches: How Church Planters Can Become Movement Makers.* It is focused on how we can move from church planting by addition to exponential multiplication.

I love your title as "director of church multiplication." I think that's better than just "church planting director." We need churches planting churches. Every church, I think, needs to be involved in church planting in some way. It's just a natural extension of what God is doing in the world through the work of Christ and his church.

RB: What is church planting?

ES: Really, it's not planting a church—it's planting the gospel and making disciples. Then a church flows from that. Any movement that's going to be serious about reaching the lost world is going to be involved in church planting. Just to maintain status quo in terms of membership, a movement needs to plant new churches every year at the rate of three percent, that is, about three new churches for every 100 existing churches. Church planting is essential to the growth of the kingdom, the work of Christ through his church.

RB: What is the first step for a church planter?

ES: To pursue it with wisdom and discernment. Experiencing the prompting of the Holy Spirit and being obedient to the leadership of the Holy Spirit is key. In Grace Communion you have an assessment process. I think it would be essential for people to go through that assessment process. Not everyone can plant a church. You could be a very effective pastor but not have the wiring to be a church planter. That's why you go through an assessment process.

You begin to look into church planting. You go to the website, you read some information there about church planting, you read books on church planting. If you're going to throw your life into the establishment of a new congregation, you really want to have thought through and prayed through this. You'd consult with some people who know and love you and would speak into your life and say, what do you think about me being a church planter?

Assessment, preparation, getting more knowledge and getting more advice are good steps in the process.

RB: What are some of the major pitfalls?

ES: I think a lot of times people start churches for the wrong reasons. If you're starting a church because you're mad at the leadership of your old church or they wouldn't let you preach, or you've got something to prove, I think those are wrong reasons to plant a church. So I'd be really cautious with those.

The other thing is, church planters tend to be self-starters and mavericks, go-getters and entrepreneurs. I would say that a Spirit-filled church planter who is walking in humility before God and before others is a lot more powerful than just the entrepreneurial "I know what I'm doing" church planter. I think one of the common mistakes is not listening to advice and counsel. That's one of the reasons I say, "Read the books and listen to the people who are already doing it." But don't just listen to their success stories. Listen to what they did wrong and learn from their mistakes along the way.

RB: Any parting words of advice?

ES: I would encourage the churches and the leaders not to grow weary, but to be faithful with what God has called them to do and to trust him for the results. It isn't our work—it's his work, and he's called us to join him in it.

GCI Church Multiplication Ministries (CMM) trains and supports individuals and congregations as they start new faith communities in various geographic locations, cultural contexts and social networks. CMM helps pastoral leaders develop and implement plans for church multiplication. For information on CMM training events and resources, visit the CMM website at cmm.gci.org.

43. WHAT IS WORSHIP?
A SURVEY OF SCRIPTURE

Many Christian churches have changed their worship styles. As is often the case with experiences, we have different impressions and reactions to worship styles. In this article, we examine what the Bible says about worship. Let's look at the way God's people worshiped before Moses, after Moses, and after Jesus. Then let's see how that biblical insight can help inform our worship in the modern world.

Definitions

The Bible doesn't give a formal definition of worship. But perhaps we can start by seeing what various words for worship mean. The English word "worship" comes from two Old English words: *weorth,* which means "worth," and *scipe* or *ship,* which means something like shape or "quality." We can see the Old English word -*ship* in modern words like friend*ship* and sportsman*ship* – that's the quality of being a friend, or the quality of being a good sport.

So worth-ship is the quality of having worth or of being worthy. When we worship, we are saying that God has worth, that he is worthy. Worship means to declare worth, to attribute worth. Or to put it in biblical terms, we praise God. We speak, or sing, about how good and powerful God is.

This is a purpose for which we are called: "You are a chosen people, a royal priesthood, a holy nation, a people belonging to God, *that you may declare the praises of him* who called you out of darkness into his wonderful light" (1 Peter 2:9). We were called for the purpose of praising God, worshiping God. That is one of the job descriptions of a Christian. We should declare that God is worthy, more than everything else put together.

Now let's look at the biblical words. In both Hebrew and Greek, there are two major kinds of words for worship. The first kind means to bow down, to kneel, to put one's face down as an act of respect and submission. Our body language is saying, I will do whatever you want me to. I am ready to listen to your instructions and I am willing to obey. The other kind of biblical word means to serve. Roughly half of the time these words are translated as worship, and the other half as serve. It carries the idea of doing something for God — making a sacrifice or carrying out his instructions.

Of course, word meanings don't prove what worship is, but they do illustrate three kinds of worship. There is

1. worship that involves speaking, and
2. worship that involves listening, and
3. a worship that involves doing.

There is a worship that expresses the heart, and worship that involves the mind, and a worship that involves the body. There is a worship that is giving praise upward, a worship that is receiving instructions from above, and a worship that carries out instruction in the world around us.

We need all three types of worship. Some people focus primarily on speaking or singing praise to God. Praise is good, but if all we do is praise God, without ever *listening* to what he says, we have to ask whether we believe the words we are saying. If he is really all wise and all loving, then we need to be attentive to what he is telling us, because he is worth listening to.

Similarly, all talk and no action does not show God the respect he deserves. Actions speak louder than words, and if our behavior isn't changed by God, then our actions are saying that God isn't important — he's a nice idea, but not relevant to our day-to-day lives. When we really believe that God is worthy of every praise, then we will be willing to listen and to change the way we live in response to such a worthy God. We will trust him and *seek* him and want to *please* him as much as we can. Worship should affect our behavior.

Response with all our being

Another preliminary point is that worship is a response to God. We can't know God's worth, much less declare it, unless God reveals himself to us. So God *initiates* worship by revealing himself to us. Then we respond, and the proper response is worship. The more we grasp his greatness, his power, his love, his character, the more we understand his worthiness, the better we can *declare* his worth – the better we can worship.

Our worship is a response to what God has revealed himself to be, not only in who he is, but also in what he has done and is doing and will do in the future. Worship includes *all* our responses to God – including a response with our mind, such as our *belief* in God's worthiness, our emotions, such as *love* and *trust,* and our actions and our *words.* Our heart expresses itself in words and songs; our mind is active when we want to learn what God wants us to do, and our bodies and strength are involved when we obey and when we serve.

Both Old Testament and New Testament tell us that our relationship with God should involve our *heart, mind, soul, and strength.* It involves all that we are. Worship involves heart, mind, soul and strength, too.

The fact that we *believe* God says something about his worthiness. The fact that we trust him and love him declares that he is worthy of love and trust. The fact that we *obey* him also says that he has worth. Our words complete the picture by *saying* that God has worth. In the words we say to one another, in the prayers we say to God, in the songs we sing, we can declare that God is worth more than all other gods, worth more than all other things.

We can worship God all by ourselves. But it is also something we do together. God has revealed himself not just to me, but to *many* people. God puts us in a community, he reveals himself to a community and *through* a community, and the community together responds to him in worship, in declaring that he is worth all honor and praise.

Moreover, God promises that whenever we gather in Jesus' name, he will be there. We gather in his presence, and because of his promise, we *expect* him to be with us. He is the One who calls us together, who reveals himself to us, who initiates the worship and is the object of our worship.

One important method we use to worship God is that of music. In church, we have someone called a worship leader, who leads us in singing hymns and spiritual songs. So a worship leader is a song leader, and because of that some people automatically think of music when they hear the word worship.

Music is important, but worship is not just music – it involves our entire relationship with God, all our heart, mind, soul, and strength – it involves *all* the ways in which we can respond to God, all the ways we can praise him by what we say and do, all the ways we can demonstrate that God is worthy of all praise and honor and allegiance.

Worship before the time of Moses

If we survey the Bible, we will see a wide variety of methods that God's people have used to worship him and express their devotion to him. Some of these methods were done by specific command from God; others seem to have been the choice of the persons involved. We see this pattern throughout the Bible: some things are commanded and some things are optional.

We don't have to read the Bible very far before we encounter a story about worship. Genesis 4 tells us that Cain and Abel brought an offering to the Lord. We aren't told why – we are just told that they did it. A few chapters later, we read that Noah built an altar after the Flood, and he sacrificed some animals.

Later, Abraham made sacrifices. He built an altar at Shechem, another at Bethel, then at Hebron, and at Mount Moriah. As part of his worship, Abraham also prayed, circumcised and tithed. Isaac built an altar at Beersheba and he prayed. Jacob set up a stone pillar at Bethel and poured a drink offering on it, and he poured oil on it as some sort of worship. He built an altar at Shechem, and one at Bethel. He vowed to tithe and he prayed. What conclusions can we draw from this?

- First, no one needed a priest. Everyone built their own altars, sacrificed their own animals and did their own worship. The head of the household acted as the religious leader for the family. We see that in the book of Job, too: Job made sacrifices on behalf of his children. There was no special priesthood. Each person could worship without a priest.

- Second, there aren't many commands about the worship that the patriarchs did. God sometimes told his people where to build an altar and what to offer, but for the most part, the altars and offerings seem to have been initiated by the people. There's no mention of special times or special days or special seasons. There doesn't seem to be any restriction on place, either. The patriarchs stayed away from Baal worship, but other than that, they worshiped the true God wherever and whenever and however they wanted.

- Third, not much is said about method – the people could pour out wine or oil, incinerate an animal, or roast it and eat part of it. Abel, Noah, Abraham, Isaac and Jacob were not limited by time, location or method. The key word is flexibility. The detailed rules that God gave through Moses did not apply to the patriarchs. They were not restricted by rules about special places, people, rituals and days.

One thing was important – probably the greatest commandment about worship, the most important rule about worship no matter who we are or when we live. The first and greatest commandment is this: You shall worship no other gods.

When God dealt with Jacob, he was not concerned about *how* he was worshiped – his primary concern was *that* Jacob worship the true God and no other gods. God demands exclusive worship, 100 percent allegiance. *Only that* can do justice to his worth. There's no room for loving any other gods even 1 percent. We cannot allow *anything* to get in the way of our worship relationship with God. We cannot let money, self-consciousness, busyness or anything else get in the way. Worship is to be our highest priority.

Moses and the tabernacle

In the days of Moses, worship went from very little structure to very specific and very detailed structure. God specified exactly

- *when* sacrifices were to be made,
- *how* they were to be made,
- *where* they were to be made, and
- *who* was supposed to make them.

Worship became much more formal. Under the law of Moses, there were holy places, holy people, holy animals, holy rituals, and holy times. God designated certain things for certain uses in worship.

The tabernacle was a holy place. Wherever it was, it marked off holy space. It was somewhat holy in the outer court, more holy in the inner court, and extremely holy behind the veil. The design of the tabernacle communicated something important about God: that he was holy. You just can't walk up on him every day. You had to be a very holy person on a very holy day in order to walk into the Holy of Holies, and you had to go through special rituals in order to do it. The tabernacle was a symbolic message about God.

The tabernacle pictured God's holiness, but it also pictured that he was not some far-off God. No – he was in the camp of Israel. When the Israelites broke camp and the tabernacle was dismantled, the ark of the covenant could be seen. People knew what it was, but when the tabernacle was set up, it was hidden. Close, but not accessible. Although God was near, he was also holy and off-limits, and people could come to him only by using proper channels.

For worship in ancient Israel, there were holy people. The Levites were holy and assigned to work with the tabernacle. There was a priesthood between the people and God. For many acts of worship, the priests had to perform the actions. There were also holy animals and holy plants. Every firstborn animal was holy, dedicated to the Lord. The first-ripe fruits were holy, set apart for worship. There was a holy incense formula, too, and if anyone made the same formula, they were supposed to be expelled from the nation. It was that special. It was reserved for worship. It was holy.

There were holy times. Every week, one day was holy. Every year, some extra days were holy. Every seven years and every 50 years, a whole year was set apart for special use. These designated times gave structure to the Israelite worship. The who, the what, the when, and the where were all spelled out. Everything was structured, organized, formalized.

Most of those details are obsolete, but the most important principle carries over into today's worship, too. Only God should be worshiped. It's not that he should be worshiped *more* than other gods are. It's that he is the only God *worthy* of worship. He is so great, nothing else is even close. There is no god like our God. Nothing can compare with him, so we give him *exclusive* worship. We do not divide our loyalties between him and Baal, or between him and Mammon, or between him and self. All allegiance and all worship go to him alone.

A matter of the heart

In the Law of Moses, it is easy to be distracted by all the detailed worship regulations, but that is not the real focus. All those details were given in order to serve a larger purpose, and that is God. Our focus should be on God, and the same was true for the ancient Israelites. They were to focus on God.

Worship in ancient Israel was not just at the tabernacle – it was also in the *heart* and in the home. God did not want people to think that they could do the rituals and then live as they please. It was not enough to "do" the worship – a person's honor and respect for God should be genuine, in the heart, which meant that God was to be praised in all of life.

In Deuteronomy 6, Moses told the Israelites to put God's instructions in their hearts, and teach them to their children, to talk about them when they sat, when they walked, and when they lay down. They were to write these instructions on the doorposts, to immerse themselves in God's way of life. All of life is worship.

Some of the later prophets build on this theme. Samuel told Saul that obedience is better than sacrifice. God wants a right attitude more than he wants correct rituals. In Jeremiah 7:22, God says, I didn't bring you out of Egypt because I wanted sacrifices. I just wanted you to obey me, and sacrifices are only a tiny part of what I commanded.

Isaiah is even stronger – saying, in effect, "I'm sick of your sacrifices. I'm sick of your sabbaths and holy days." Here is Isaiah 1:11-17: "I have no pleasure in the blood of bulls and lambs and goats.... Stop bringing meaningless offerings! Your incense is detestable to me. New Moons, Sabbaths and convocations – I cannot bear your evil assemblies. Your New Moon festivals and your appointed feasts my soul hates.... When you spread out your hands in prayer, I will hide my eyes from you; even if you offer many prayers, I will not listen." The people were doing rituals, bringing animals, keeping Sabbaths and festivals, even praying, but despite all that, there was something seriously *lacking* in their worship.

Why didn't God like their worship? He does *not* say they were keeping the wrong days or doing the rituals incorrectly. The problem was that their lives were full of sin. So Isaiah counsels: "Your hands are full of blood; wash and make yourselves clean.... Stop doing wrong, learn to do right! Seek justice, encourage the oppressed. Defend the cause of the fatherless, plead the case of the widow."

Their sacrifices, prayers and praises were not accompanied by performance in their day-to-day lives. They had worship rituals, but they did not obey God's commands for how to treat their neighbors, and the result was unacceptable worship. As Jesus said, quoting Isaiah 29:13, their worship was in vain. It was hypocritical to do the worship if it wasn't changing the other aspects of their lives.

For worship to be acceptable to God, we must have obedient lives. The ritual is not enough – the attitude is what is most important. God does not want hypocritical worship, people who say he is great but do not act like it. Perhaps this is commandment number 2 regarding worship – that it must be sincere. If we are going to say that God is worthy of all worship, then we should believe it in our hearts, and if we believe it, it will show in our actions. Real worship changes everything we do, because it changes who we are. Worship must be in the heart, not just at the place of worship.

Micah tells us this: "With what shall I come before the Lord and bow down before the exalted God? Shall I come before him with burnt offerings, with calves a year old? Will the Lord be pleased with thousands of rams, with ten thousand rivers of oil? Shall I offer my firstborn child?… He has showed you, O man, what is good. And what does the Lord require of you? To act justly and to love mercy and to walk humbly with your God" (Micah 6:6-8).

We do not have to have a perfect life. David did not have a *sinless* life, yet overall, he pleased God. His attitude was right, and that's the kind of worship God wants most. God even used David in two major developments in Israelite worship.

Music at the temple

Many know that David initiated the building of the Temple, a "permanent" place for worship. But David's other contribution has lasted even longer than the Temple did. That is in the area of music. David had a background in music. As a shepherd, he played the lyre, a simple stringed instrument. He composed music and sang about God. He worshiped God while he took care of his sheep – it was worship on the job. David's songs are called *psalms*. That comes from the Greek word *psallo*, which means "to pluck a string." Psalms is a book of songs for stringed instruments. We can worship God with songs and musical instruments.

David didn't write all the psalms. Some were written centuries later. But David got the psalm-book started, and he organized the way that music is used in worship. He assigned some of the Levites to be worship musicians (1 Chronicles 23:5; 25:1-8). Music became a permanent part of worship.

Psalms come in a wide variety. Some are historical, reminding us of God's great works in creation, in the Exodus, in giving the Israelites the land. Some psalms offer praise. Other express thanksgiving, or ask for God's help. Some express adoration, ask questions, or complain to God about suffering. The mood ranges from anguish to hope, fear to joy, anger to pride. These songs may have begun as private prayers, but they became prayers in which all the people could join in. The people became participants in these worship songs.

All the psalms are worship – even the psalms that complain. The fact that our questions and complaints are directed to God shows something about our relationship to him. All of life is in his hands, in his control. The psalms show our dependence on him.

The psalms are often in the form of a prayer, in words spoken to God. He is the audience, and the people are the participants, the worshipers. These songs are memorized prayers, since they are spoken to God. Some people think that Christians shouldn't have memorized prayers. But we actually have several of them during worship services every week. We just have them with a melody, and that is a legitimate form of worship. Even without the melody, a recited prayer can be a legitimate form of worship.

Psalm 150 points out a variety of worship methods: "Praise the Lord. Praise God in his sanctuary; praise him in his mighty heavens. Praise him for his acts of power; praise him for his surpassing greatness. Praise him with the sounding of the trumpet, praise him with the harp and lyre, praise him with tambourine and dancing, praise him with the strings and flute, praise him with the clash of cymbals, praise him with resounding cymbals. Let everything that has breath praise the Lord."

We might find some of these worship methods unusual today, but all these artistic expressions are permissible when they are done to the glory of God. The main principle of worship is that we worship only God, and that we really mean it.

Synagogue worship

After the temple was destroyed and Jews were scattered throughout the Middle East, a new format for worship was developed. In the synagogue, the focus was on <u>Scripture</u>, not on sacrifices. It was a much simpler format.

Synagogue services typically began with praises and prayers. There were standard prayers and benedictions, some of them used every week. The Scriptures would be read, translated when necessary, and explained in some sort of sermon. We can see glimpses of this in the New Testament, but the best description is in Nehemiah 8. Under the leadership of Ezra, some of the Jews had come back to Jerusalem.

"Ezra the scribe stood on a high wooden platform built for the occasion…. [today we might call it a pulpit] Ezra opened the book [the Law of Moses]. All the people could see him because he was standing above them; and as he opened it, the people all stood up. Ezra praised the Lord, the great God; and all the people lifted their hands and responded, 'Amen! Amen!' Then they bowed down and *worshiped* the LORD with their faces to the ground" (verses 4-6).

Have you ever seen that kind of response in a modern church service — people lifting their hands, saying Amen, and bowing down? If it's a genuine response to God, it is a good response. They listened with great respect, with a willingness to obey. "The Levites…instructed the people in the Law while the people were standing there. They read from the Book of the Law of God, making it clear and giving the meaning so that the people could understand what was being read" (verses 7-8). Synagogue worship followed in this pattern, with a focus on Scripture.

Even though the Temple was eventually rebuilt, the public reading of Scripture in synagogues continued to be an important part of Jewish worship. Most Jews could not go to the temple every week. But with a synagogue, they could gather for worship every Sabbath, with prayers, songs, and Scripture.

One result of this was a new focus for the Sabbath. Even in the days of David, most Israelites could not go to Jerusalem every week. The focus of Sabbath-keeping was therefore on rest, as commanded in Scripture. But when synagogues became common, the Sabbath was also seen as a day of participating in worship. Laymen had a greater role in worship – they could do every portion of the synagogue service. People could worship without a temple, without priests, and without sacrifices.

Jesus

Now let's survey the New Testament. What did Jesus do in worship, and what did he *say* about worship? We may begin by noting that he grew up in Galilee. Although he went to Jerusalem for annual festivals, most of his worship was done *away* from the temple. We are told that he went to the synagogue, where he would read and explain Scripture. He prayed, in private and in public, and he sang songs.

Jesus would have been involved in some rituals, such as killing a Passover lamb every year. He taught in the temple and chased moneychangers out of it because he wanted the place to be worshipful, a place of prayer. But Jesus also predicted the destruction of the temple. It was not necessary for worship.

The Gospels' most direct teaching about worship is in John 4. This is set in the context of the centuries-old Jewish-Samaritan squabble about the correct place of worship. The woman said, "Our fathers worshiped on this mountain, but you Jews claim that the place where we must worship is in Jerusalem." Jesus replied, "Believe me, woman, a time is coming when you will worship the Father neither on this mountain nor in Jerusalem" (verses 20-21). In other words, location will not be important. Worship will not be associated with *any* particular spot.

Jesus added, "You Samaritans worship what you do not know; we worship what we do know, for salvation is from the Jews. Yet a time is coming and has now come when the true worshipers will worship the Father in spirit and truth, for *they* are the kind of worshipers the Father seeks. God is spirit, and his worshipers must worship in spirit and in truth" (verses 22-24).

God seeks people who will worship him. Worship is something he wants. He knows it is good for us to worship him. In speaking of "spirit and truth," Jesus is echoing the prophets: worship must be sincere. External things don't matter if the heart isn't right. It doesn't do us any good to worship at the right place or with the right rituals if our attitude isn't right. We can sing the right songs and hold our hands in the right way, but if our heart isn't in it, it isn't really worship.

Jesus criticized the Pharisees, quoting Isaiah, when he said, "These people worship me in vain; they honor me with their lips, but their hearts are far from me." They are hypocrites, he said. (Matthew 15:8). They said the right things, but they didn't believe them. God does not want hypocritical worship — he wants sincere worship. We aren't supposed to fake it. We need to believe the praises we say, and if we really believe them, our lives will show it.

Externals are not primary, but if our hearts are right, then we will have externals. Rituals are not primary, but we do have rituals. Jesus himself gave us some, and it is inevitable that people will also develop some *customs* in their worship. But the focus should be sincere praise for God.

The early church

Acts 2 tells us how worship was done among the people who saw Jesus' example and followed it. "Those who accepted his message were baptized, and about 3,000 were added to their number that day. They devoted themselves to the apostles' teaching and to the fellowship, to the breaking of bread and to prayer" (verses 41-42). This is their response to God, their devotion, their worship: they accepted the message — they believed, they were repentant, they were baptized — and they devoted themselves to

- being taught,
- sharing with one another,
- breaking bread, and
- prayer.

Luke is giving a summary description, not a formula for worship services.

"Every day they continued to meet together in the temple courts. They broke bread in their homes and ate together with glad and sincere hearts, praising God and enjoying the favor of all the people" (verses 46-47). They worshipped in the temple, and they worshipped in their homes. They praised God, they were happy, and they were sincere.

Apparently many of the Jewish Christian in Judea continued to participate in the temple rituals until the temple was destroyed in A.D. 70 (Acts 21:20-26). Christian faith did not require them to abandon the rituals – but neither did the rituals seem to help them in their faith.

When we examine worship customs, we need to distinguish between what is required, what is permissible, and what is helpful. *Few* things are required, and *few* things are forbidden. The *many* things in between are permissible – if they are done for the glory of God. Luke doesn't tell us much more about worship. To learn more about worship, we turn next to the writings of Paul.

Paul's words for worship

Paul is a primary source for what first-century churches did and how they operated. But Paul says very little about worship. Words for worship are found only a few times in Paul's letters. He doesn't tell us how we should worship. Perhaps that is because Paul sees worship as something we are to do all the time. John Piper expressed it in this way: "What we find in the New Testament, perhaps to our amazement, is an utterly stunning degree of indifference to worship as an outward ritual, and an utterly radical intensification of worship as an inward experience of the heart.... The very epistles that are written to help the church be what it ought to be in this age [are] almost totally devoid of...explicit teaching on the specifics of corporate worship" (http://www.soundofgrace.com/ piper97/11-09-97.htm).

Of course, the New Testament clearly tells us that Christians meet together regularly. It gives us commands regarding meeting together regularly. And if we are worshipping in all aspects of life, we will certainly worship when we get together. Paul uses worship-related words in some surprising ways. Romans 12:1 is one of the better-known uses: "I urge you, brothers, in view of God's mercy, to offer your bodies as living *sacrifices*, holy and pleasing to God — this is your spiritual act of worship."

Worship is the giving of our entire self, our thoughts and our emotions, to God's use. All of life is an act of submission, an act of worship. Our service to God is not centered on a time or a temple, but is done whenever and wherever we are, because we *are* the temple of God. The emphasis is taken away from ceremony, seasons, places and rituals, and is shifted to what is happening in the inner person. Worship should invade our entire lives. The test of worship is not only what happens at church, but what happens at home, on the job and wherever we go.

Paul used another word for worship in Romans 1:9: "I serve [*latreuo,* one of the Greek words for worship] God with my whole heart." How? "...in preaching the gospel of his Son." A similar thought is in Romans 15:16: "God gave me the grace to be a minister of Christ Jesus to the Gentiles with *the priestly duty* of proclaiming the gospel of God, so that the Gentiles might become an offering acceptable to God, sanctified by the Holy Spirit."

In these verses, preaching the gospel is an act of worship. Paul was not a Levite, but he had a priestly duty, and that was to worship with all his heart by preaching. In our worship services today, the *sermon* is just as much a part of the worship as the songs are. Whenever the gospel is preached, worship is being done. God's greatness is being proclaimed. Worship is in the listening, too, as people seek to learn what God wants us to be doing. A worshipful attitude toward God is one that respectfully listens to what he may be saying to us.

Every act of obedience is an act of worship. It declares that God has worth. And whenever we share the gospel with someone, we are declaring God's worth. We are engaging in the priestly service of preaching the gospel, the worship of being a witness to God's grace. We tell what a great thing God has done in Jesus Christ, and how that has been good news in our life. We are declaring his worth. We are giving worship in everyday life. We don't have to wait for a church service.

We get our English word "liturgy" from the Greek word *leitourgia.* In the Greek Old Testament and in pagan Greek literature, it refers to public works of worship. But Paul used it in a different context — an offering of money — money to be used in helping other Christians in famine relief, or money to be used in helping spread the gospel of Jesus Christ. Romans 15:27 uses this word: "If the Gentiles have shared in the Jews' spiritual blessings, they owe it to the Jews to minister to them" — literally, to give liturgy to them — "with material blessings." Paul uses this word for worship to describe financial help. This seemingly ordinary service to the saints was actually an act of worship, a religious activity.

We see a similar thing in Philippians 4:18, which Paul wrote after receiving financial help from the Christians in Philippi: "I have received full payment and even more; I am amply supplied, now that I have received from Epaphroditus the gifts you sent. They are a fragrant *offering,* an acceptable *sacrifice,* pleasing to God." And in 2 Corinthians 9:12, he wrote, "This service – this liturgy – that you perform is not only supplying the needs of God's people but is also overflowing in many expressions of thanks to God." The people were worshipping with their money, which we can do with our offerings today, as well.

Hebrews 13 combines two New Testament forms of worship. "Through Jesus, therefore, let us continually offer to God a *sacrifice* of *praise* — the fruit of lips that confess his name. And do not forget to do good and to *share* with others, for with such sacrifices God is pleased" (verses 15-16). Some worship is given in words of praise, and some worship is given to God when we help one another.

In the old covenant, God required the Israelites to serve him through a priesthood, a sacrificial system and a temple. In the new covenant, all believers are priests, all believers offer sacrifices all the time, and we as a body of people *are* the temple of God. Worship is dramatically different. The ministry of worship has been given to all the people.

Devotion

Historically, several types of devotion have been recognized as important in a person's spiritual maturity. The top two are prayer and Bible study. These have demonstrated their value time and time again in the lives of millions of Christians of all denominational affiliations. If we want spiritual health, we need a good spiritual diet, and these disciplines are helpful. They don't *guarantee* spiritual growth, but they do provide an environment in which growth can occur more readily.

If we are in poor spiritual health, we need to check ourselves: Are we doing the things that Christians throughout the centuries have found helpful? We'd like to have quick fixes, like an easy-to-swallow pill that puts us right, but there aren't any shortcuts like that. We may be able to get away with a junk-food diet for a while, but eventually we are going to feel some negative results, and we can't expect one week of good food to restore us to excellent health. It requires a long-term commitment for slow, almost imperceptible improvement, and the same is true for spiritual health. There are no quick fixes, no magic potions. It requires a long-term commitment and some sacrifices.

God doesn't give us rules about prayer and Bible study. He doesn't say 30 minutes a day or 90 minutes a day. We have to make our own decisions, and what's right for you isn't necessarily right for me. But we each have to make spiritual health a *priority* in our lives.

Of course, we do not worship entirely on our own, each going our separate way. The New Testament picture is that we regularly get together – and when we gather, we *will* worship. That's what we do all day long, so how much *more* will we do it when we gather together! But our gatherings are not the only place we worship. True worship is in the heart, and in its outward expression it can take place in the home, on the job, *and* in the church.

Worship services

In our worship services today, where is the worship? It's in the songs, in the sermon, and in the attentiveness that we have in listening to the sermon. But there is also worship in the work that goes on behind the scenes. People who get the building ready may be making sacrifices to God that are pleasing to him. Those who help with refreshments may worship as they work. When we do good and share with others, we are giving the kind of worship that God wants.

People who work with children are worshiping as they help children understand the good news about Jesus Christ. In their actions *and* in their words, they are praising God. They are showing that he changes our lives, and he changes our priorities. We no longer live to please ourselves, but to serve others. This is a form of worship.

During the time of the apostles, what happened in church meetings? We don't know for sure. Neither Luke nor Paul gives us a complete description. However, we have some glimpses. We saw in Acts that prayer, teaching and fellowship are involved. Other verses talk about songs, too. Colossians 3:16 tells us the early church sang in their worship: "Let the word of Christ dwell in you richly as you teach and admonish one another with all wisdom, and as you *sing psalms, hymns and spiritual songs* with gratitude in your hearts to God." Ephesians 5:19 is similar: "Speak to one another with psalms, hymns and spiritual songs. Sing and make music in your heart to the Lord."

Prayer was also part of the worship. It was mentioned in Acts 2, and it's supported by 1 Timothy 2. What kind of prayers were these? Did everyone say the same prayer in unison, like Jews in the synagogues did? Or did they just take turns, each saying a prayer out loud? We do not know. Either way would be possible.

Scripture reading was probably an important part of the church meeting, since it had been an important part of the synagogue service. In addition to this, the New Testament admonishes believers to stick to the apostles' doctrine, to the standard of teaching, to the word of life, to the words of faith, to good doctrine and sound words, to sound teaching and the faith once delivered. These are different ways of saying that doctrine was important to the New Testament church. It was important to teach and learn certain truths.

One of the longest passages about church meetings is in 1 Corinthians 14. Some unusual things were happening in the church at Corinth, and Paul had to give them some guidance about it. Most of the chapter is trying to bring some control to a situation that had gotten out of control. Paul summarized their situation and provided a focus in verse 26: "What then shall we say, brothers? When you come together, everyone has a hymn, or a word of instruction, a revelation, a tongue or an interpretation. All of these must be done for the strengthening of the church."

The church meeting included songs, teaching, and the use of spiritual gifts. Of all the things Paul mentions, what is the most important? Notice what he says in the last part of verse 26: That all "must be done for the *strengthening* of the church." In verse 31 he says the goal is "so that everyone may be instructed and encouraged."

That's the priority: Everything should be done in such a way that the church is instructed, edified, built up, strengthened. It doesn't matter how many songs we sing or what spiritual gifts we have — if we aren't helping anybody, we are missing the point of gathering together. Songs, sermon, and service: All three are forms of worship, and all three are important.

Worship today

Worship involves our entire relationship with God: our words, our attitudes, and our actions. Our words may be normal conversation, songs or prayers. In any style of speaking, we can declare God's praises and express our faith reliance on him.

God wants worship not only on our lips, but also in our hearts. He wants our worship to be sincere — *he* wants to be the most important thing in our lives, that we are truly submissive to him. He wants our worship to affect our behavior, that we make sacrifices, that we put to death the deeds of selfishness, that we seek justice, be merciful and humble, and help others. He wants us not just to obey him, but to serve in ways that go beyond specific commands. We are to worship wherever we go, doing all things to God's glory, praying always, giving thanks always, never ceasing to be a temple of the Holy Spirit. Our worship involves how we work, how we drive, and how we choose what to watch on television.

There are also actions that are more specifically times of worship. We might call these private devotions, or spiritual disciplines. These are habits and actions of worship we do individually, as opposed to worship when we gather as a church.

Worship is not restricted to a specific place and time. The best thing that has ever happened to us is that we have God in our lives. The best thing that's happened to us *this week* is that we have God in our lives. We have reason to celebrate all the time. When we live each day praising God in our hearts, it is natural that we praise God when we gather together, when we speak to one another about the best thing that's ever happened to us. We worship all the time, but we also worship together at specific times at meetings designated for that specific purpose.

What's involved in our worship services?

1. Our first act of worship is <u>gathering together</u>. Simply by gathering, we are showing that God has worth. Where two or three are gathered in his name, he will be present in a special way. When we gather, we gather in the presence of God. As the Old Testament says, we appear *before the Lord*. It's like an ancient throne room, and we are invited to be with him. In our worship services, we *want* God to be present. We specifically *ask* him to be present. He *promises* to be present. And if we are sincere about this, we should *expect* him to be present. And when we sing in God's presence, we are singing *to* him. It's not just a song about God — it is a song *to* God. These are words spoken to him. Like many of the psalms, the hymns we sing are often prayers set to music. He is the audience; we are the participants.

2. Like the psalms, our <u>music</u> comes in a wide variety. Some songs express positive emotions, such as adoration, praise, thanksgiving, confidence, faith, joy or excitement. We should always be happy that God is in our life. Even when we have trials, we are to rejoice. The psalms tell us to come before him and rejoice, to praise the Lord, to sing a new song unto the Lord. Praise him in the heights. Praise him, praise him, praise him. Our joy in him should spill over into praises. Our worship should be dominated by praise. But joy is not the only legitimate emotion we can have with God. The psalms also have prayers of confession and supplication. Some of our hymns are more meditative than celebrative. Some ask questions, some express sorrow, or anguish or fear. All of these are legitimate emotions we can sing about.

3. Our worship services usually contain several <u>prayers</u>, too. They include praise, usually a request, sometimes a confession. When someone near the beginning of services asks God to be in the service, to inspire the service, this is something we all want. We join in the prayer not as an audience, but as *participants*. When we say "amen," we are saying, That's my prayer, too. I want God to be here, too. When we express our dependence on God, when we give all our requests to him, it shows his worth. When we want to be in his presence, it shows that he is good. When we confess our sins to him, it shows his greatness. When we give him thanks and praise, it exalts him and glorifies him. We worship when we participate in the prayers.

4. A fourth major part of our worship service is the sermon. The sermon is a communication of God's word to us. It explains to us what God's will is for our life. We expect God to speak to us through his Word, by inspiring the speaker, and we listen for what God is telling us. God's truth affects our lives and our hearts. It affects real life, and it demands a *heart-felt* response. The sermon should therefore appeal to our mind *and* to our emotions. In the sermon, we are not just an audience — we should also be <u>participants</u>. We should actively *think* about the Scriptures, think about the sermon, think about what it means in *our* lives. This isn't just information about God — it is information about how God wants to change our lives. Part of our worship, part of our respectful response to God, is listening for what he wants to teach us and how he wants to change us. We have to listen with the expectation that the sermon contains something God wants to tell us. It may be different for you than it is for me. The point is that we have to participate in the listening. Just as we participate in the music, and we participate in the prayers, we are all supposed to participate in the sermon, too.

5. As we listen, we should also be ready to *respond* to the message. The response can come in many different forms, depending on the message we have heard. One way to respond is to *do* what God is telling us to do. Some people are doing this by serving in various capacities within the church. Others respond with service outside of the church, and some may respond by *telling* others how good and great God is — worshiping him by doing the priestly duty of sharing the good news of salvation — and hopefully all these responses will be common.

Sometimes the proper response is more in *emotion* than it is in action. The most important response is that of faith – a willingness to believe what God has said. The response may include thankfulness, sometimes expressed as an offering during the worship service. Sometimes the appropriate response is simply joy. Sometimes it is repentance, a change in behavior or a change in attitude toward other people.

Sometimes silence is the best response. Sometimes we are simply dumbfounded at God's greatness, or his mercy, and we just don't have the words to say anything intelligent. So we cover our mouths and sit in awe of God. We are speechless at how utterly different God is from us, how holy, how righteous, how perfect, how powerful, how completely beyond limitations of time and space he is. And we are awe-struck that he has been so humble as to care about persons such as ourselves. Overwhelming awe is one of *many* possible responses to God, depending on how he reveals himself to us.

No matter what, we should expect God to affect both our emotions and our minds. Our relationship with him involves all our heart, mind, soul and strength. God wants all of us, not just part of us, as we worship him.

The real test of worship is not what happens at church, but what happens at home, and on the job, and wherever we go. Is God important enough to make a difference in the way we live, in the way we work, in the way we get along with other people? When the Holy Spirit lives in us, when we are the *temple* of the Holy Spirit, worship is a part of everyday life.

Worship rituals

Last, I will comment briefly on worship rituals. To some people, ritual suggests meaningless actions. Some rituals are like that, but not all rituals are bad. God has commanded us to have some rituals, some repeated actions. We don't want them to become meaningless, and to avoid that, we need to keep reminding ourselves of the meaning.

Some churches have many rituals, a highly structured service, a liturgy with carefully designed prayers, responsive readings, reciting creeds, and other repeated actions. In some respects, this is like what the temple worship was. Other churches are much simpler, more like the synagogue, with a focus on Scripture. Neither approach is commanded or forbidden.

We in Grace Communion International have traditionally been on the simpler side of things. We have a small number of ceremonies, such as weddings, funerals, ordination, blessing of children, anointing the sick, and a few others. But two ceremonies are much more important than the others – baptism and the Lord's Supper. Both of these practices picture in a symbolic way, in physical actions, some spiritual truths about the gospel. They proclaim God's worth not only in what we say, but also by what we do. In different ways, they picture the death and life of Jesus Christ.

I conclude with a simple three-fold test regarding worship practices. This test encapsulates some of the major themes of worship. To analyze a worship practice, we need to ask these questions:

- Does it glorify God? That is one major purpose of worship.
- Does it build up the body of Christ? That is another major purpose.
- And third, does it help us be what God wants us to be in the world? Does it have practical results in our lives?

Michael Morrison

44. RESPONDING TO GOD WITH WORSHIP

We respond to God with worship, because worship is simply giving God what is fitting. He is praiseworthy, not only for his power but also for his gentleness.

God is love, and all that he does is done in love. This is praiseworthy. We praise love even on a human level, don't we? We praise people who give their lives to help others. They did not have enough power to save their own lives, but what power they had, they used to help others—and that is praiseworthy. In contrast, we criticize people who had the power to help but refused to do it. Goodness is more praiseworthy than power is, and God is both good and powerful.

Praise deepens the bond of love between us and God. God's love for us is never diminished, but ours for him often grows weak. In praise, we rehearse his love for us and, in effect, fan the fire of love for him that the Spirit has started within us. It is good for us to remember and rehearse how wonderful God is, for that strengthens us in Christ and increases our motivation to be like him in his goodness, which increases our joy.

We were made for the purpose of praising God (1 Peter 2:9), of giving him glory and honor, and the better we are in harmony with God's purpose for life, the greater joy will be ours. Life is simply more satisfying when we do what we were made to do: to honor God. We do that not only in worship, but also in the way we live.

A way of life

Worship is a way of life. We offer our bodies and minds as living sacrifices (Romans 12:1-2). We worship God when we share the gospel (Romans 15:16). We worship God when we give financial offerings (Philippians 4:18). We worship God when we help other people (Hebrews 13:16). We say that he is worthy, worth our time and attention and allegiance. We praise his glory, and his humility in becoming one of us for our sakes. We praise his righteousness and his mercy. We praise him for the way he really is.

This is what we were made for, to declare his praises. It is simply right that we praise the One who created us, the One who died and rose to save us and give us life eternal, the One who works even now to help us become more like him. We owe him our allegiance, and we owe him our love.

We were made to praise God, and this is what we will do eternally. John was given a vision of our future: "I heard every creature in heaven and on earth and under the earth and on the sea, and all that is in them, singing: 'To him who sits on the throne and to the Lamb be praise and honor and glory and power, for ever and ever!'" (Revelation 5:13). This is the right response: awe at the awesome, honor for the honorable, and allegiance to the trustworthy.

Five basic principles

Psalm 33:1-3 tells us, "Sing joyfully to the Lord, you righteous; it is fitting for the upright to praise him. Praise the Lord with the harp; make music to him on the ten-stringed lyre. Sing to him a new song; play skillfully, and shout for joy." Scripture tells us to sing, shout, to use harps, flutes, tambourines, trumpets, cymbals—even to worship with dancing (Psalms 149-150). The picture is of exuberance, unrestrained joy, and happiness expressed without inhibitions.

The Bible gives us examples of spontaneous worship. It also gives us examples of very formal approaches to worship, with stereotyped routines that stay the same for centuries. Both approaches to worship can be legitimate, and neither one can claim to be the only authentic way to praise God. Let me review some of the broader principles involved in worship.

1. We are called to worship

First, God does want us to worship him. This is a constant we see from one end of Scripture to another (Genesis 4:4; John 4:23; Revelation 22:9). Worship is one of the reasons we are called: to declare his praises (1 Peter 2:9). God's people not only love and obey him, but they also do specific acts of worship. They make sacrifices, they sing praises, they pray.

In Scripture, we see a wide variety in the way that worship can be done. In the law of Moses, many details were specified. Specific people were assigned to do specific actions at specific times in specific places. The who, what, when, where and how were spelled out. In contrast to that, we see in Genesis very few rules about how the patriarchs worshipped. They did not have a designated priesthood, were not restricted to a certain place, and were told little about what to offer or when to offer it.

In the New Testament, we again see very little about the how and the when of worship. Worship activities are not restricted to a certain group of people or a certain place. Christ did away with the Mosaic requirements. All believers are priests and continually offer themselves as living sacrifices.

2. Worship only God

Despite the great variety in worship styles, we see a simple constant throughout Scripture: Only God should be worshipped. Worship, to be acceptable, must be exclusive. God requires all our love—all our allegiance. We cannot serve two Gods. Although we may worship him in different styles, our unity is based on the fact that it is him we worship.

In ancient Israel, the rival God was often Baal, a Canaanite deity. In Jesus' day, it was religious tradition, self-righteousness and hypocrisy. Actually, anything that comes between us and God—anything that might cause us to disobey him—is a false god, an idol. For some today, it is money. For others, it is sex. Some have a bigger problem with pride, or with concerns about what other people may think of us. John mentions some common false gods when he writes,

Do not love the world or anything in the world. If anyone loves the world, the love of the Father is not in him. For everything in the world—the cravings of sinful man, the lust of his eyes and the boasting of what he has and does—comes not from the Father but from the world. The world and its desires pass away, but the man who does the will of God lives forever. (1 John 2:15-17)

No matter what our weakness is, we need to crucify it, to kill it, to put all false gods away. If something distracts us from obeying God, we need to get rid of it. God wants people who worship only him, who have him as the center of all life.

3. Sincerity

The third constant about worship that we see in the Scriptures is that worship must be sincere. It does no good to go through the right motions, sing the right songs, meet on the right days and say the right words, if we don't really love God in our hearts. Jesus criticized those who honored God with their lips, but who worshipped in vain, because their hearts were not close to God. Their traditions (originally designed to express their love and worship) had become obstacles to real love and worship.

Jesus also stresses the need for sincerity when he says that worship must be in spirit and in truth (John 4:24). If we say that we love God when we actually resent his commands, we are hypocrites. If we value our freedom more than we do his authority, we cannot worship him in truth. We cannot take his covenant upon our lips and cast his words behind (Psalm 50:16-17). We cannot call him Lord and ignore what he says.

4. Obedience

Throughout Scripture, we see that true worship includes obedience. This includes God's words concerning the way we treat one another.

We cannot honor God when we dishonor his children. "If anyone says,

'I love God,' yet hates his brother, he is a liar. For anyone who does not love his brother, whom he has seen, cannot love God, whom he has not seen" (1 John 4:20-21). It is similar to Isaiah's scathing criticism of people who perform worship rituals while indulging in social injustices:

Stop bringing meaningless offerings! Your incense is detestable to me. New Moons, Sabbaths and convocations—I cannot bear your evil assemblies. Your New Moon festivals and your appointed feasts my soul hates. They have become a burden to me; I am weary of bearing them. When you spread out your hands in prayer, I will hide my eyes from you; even if you offer many prayers, I will not listen. (Isaiah 1:11-15)

As far as we can tell, there was nothing wrong with the days the people were keeping, or the kind of incense and animals they were bringing. The problem was the way they were living the rest of the time. "Your hands are full of blood," he said—and yet I am sure that the problem was not just with those who had actually committed murder.

He called for a comprehensive solution: "Stop doing wrong, learn to do right! Seek justice, encourage the oppressed. Defend the cause of the fatherless, plead the case of the widow" (verses 16-17). They needed to get their interpersonal relationships in order. They needed to eliminate racial prejudice, social class stereotypes, and unfair economic practices.

Five facts about worship

1. God wants us to worship, to respond to him with praise and thanks.
2. Only God is worthy of our worship and total allegiance.
3. Worship should be sincere, not a performance.
4. If we really respect and love God, we will do what he says.
5. Worship is not just something we do at church — it involves everything we do.

---

5. In all of life

Worship, if genuine, should make a difference in the way we treat one another seven days a week. This is another principle we see throughout Scripture.

How should we worship? Micah asks the question and gives the answer:

With what shall I come before the Lord and bow down before the exalted God? Shall I come before him with burnt offerings, with calves a year old? Will the Lord be pleased with thousands of rams, with ten thousand rivers of oil? Shall I offer my firstborn for my transgression, the fruit of my body for the sin of my soul? He has showed you, O man, what is good. And what does the Lord require of you? To act justly and to love mercy and to walk humbly with your God. (Micah 6:6-8)

Hosea also stressed that interpersonal relationships are more important than the mechanics of worship: "I desire mercy, not sacrifice, and acknowledgment of God rather than burnt offerings" (Hosea 6:6). We are called not only to praise, but also to do good works (Ephesians 2:10).

Our concept of worship must go far beyond music, days and rituals. Those details are not nearly as important as the way we treat our neighbors. It is hypocritical to call Jesus Lord if we do not also seek his sense of justice, mercy, and compassion.

Worship is much more than outward actions—it involves a change of behavior, rooted in a total change of heart, a change produced in us by the Holy Spirit. Instrumental in this change is our willingness to spend time with God in prayer, study and other spiritual disciplines. The transformation does not happen by magic—it happens through time spent in fellowship with God.

Paul's expansive view of worship

Worship involves all of life. We see this especially in the words of Paul. He uses the terminology of sacrifice and worship in this way: "I urge you, brothers, in view of God's mercy, to offer your bodies as living sacrifices, holy and pleasing to God—this is your spiritual act of worship" (Romans 12:1). All of life is to be worship, not just a few hours each week. Of course, if all of our lives are devoted to worship, this will most definitely include some time each week with other Christians!

Paul uses more words for sacrifice and worship in Romans 15:16 when he speaks of the grace God had given him "to be a minister of Christ Jesus to the Gentiles with the priestly duty of proclaiming the gospel of God, so that the Gentiles might become an offering acceptable to God, sanctified by the Holy Spirit." Here we see that preaching the gospel is a form of worship.

Since we are all priests, we all have the priestly duty of proclaiming the praises of the One who called us (1 Peter 2:9)—a worship any believer can do, or at least participate in by helping others preach the gospel.

When Paul thanked the Philippians for sending him financial support, he used words for worship: "I have received from Epaphroditus the gifts you sent. They are a fragrant offering, an acceptable sacrifice, pleasing to God" (Philippians 4:18).

Financial help given to other Christians can be a form of worship.

Hebrews 13 describes worship given both in words and in works: "Let us continually offer to God a sacrifice of praise—the fruit of lips that confess his name. And do not forget to do good and to share with others, for with such sacrifices God is pleased" (verses 15-16).

We are called to worship, celebrate and glorify God. It is our joy to be able to declare his praises, to share the good news of what he has done for us in and through our Lord and Savior Jesus Christ.

Joseph Tkach

45. JOHN 4: TRUE WORSHIP

Jews and Samaritans simply didn't get along. The trouble went way back, five centuries or so, to the days of the Jewish leader Zerubbabel. Some Samaritans offered to help the Jews rebuild their temple, and Zerubbabel rebuffed them. The Samaritans responded by complaining to the king of Persia, and the work stopped (Ezra 4).

Later, when the Jews were rebuilding the walls of Jerusalem, the governor of Samaria threatened to take military action against the Jews. The Samaritans eventually built their own temple on Mt. Gerizim, and in 128 B.C., the Jews destroyed it. Although their religions were both based on the laws of Moses, they were bitter enemies.

Jesus enters Samaria

But Jesus was not shackled by the squabbles of the past. Although most Jews avoided Samaria, Jesus walked right into it, taking his disciples with him. He was tired, so he sat down at a well near the city of Sychar, and sent his disciples into town to buy some groceries (John 4:38). Along came a Samaritan woman, and Jesus talked to her. She was surprised that he would talk to a Samaritan; his disciples were surprised that he would talk to a woman (verses 9, 27).

Jesus shows us a simple way of dealing with people who have different religious beliefs, people who are from a different ethnic group, people who are traditional enemies: just treat them like normal human beings. Don't ignore them, don't avoid them, don't insult them. But Jesus had something much more profound than that to say.

He began in the simplest possible way: He asked the woman for a drink. He was thirsty, but he had nothing to draw water with — but she did. He had a need, she had a means of fulfilling it, so he asked her for help. She was surprised that a Jew would actually drink from a Samaritan water pot — most Jews considered such a vessel ritually unclean. And then Jesus said: I have something a lot better than water, if you want it. I am willing to ask you for a drink of water — are you willing to ask me for something that's better? (verses 7-10).

Jesus was using a play on words — the phrase "living water" usually meant moving water, flowing water. The woman knew quite well that the only water in Sychar was in that well, and there was no flowing water nearby. So she asked Jesus what he was talking about. He said he was talking about something that would lead to eternal life (verses 11-14). He was talking about religious ideas — but would the woman be willing to listen to spiritual truth from a religious enemy? Would she drink Jewish waters?

The woman asked for the living water, and Jesus invited her to get her husband. He already knew that she didn't have one, but he asked anyway — possibly to show that he had spiritual authority. He was the vessel from which she could receive the living water. The woman got the message: "I can see that you are a prophet" (verse 19). If Jesus knew the facts about her unusual marital status, then he probably knew spiritual truths, as well.

True worship

After learning that Jesus was a prophet, the woman brought up the age-old controversy between Samaritans and Jews about the proper place to worship: We worship here, but you Jews say that people have to go to Jerusalem (verse 20). Jesus responded: The day will soon come when that won't be relevant. It won't matter whether people look to Mt. Gerizim or Jerusalem — or any other location. The hour is already here when people will worship God in spirit and truth (verses 2124).

Has Jesus suddenly jumped to a different subject? Maybe not — the Gospel of John gives us some clues about what he meant: "The words I have spoken to you are *spirit* and they are life" (John 6:63). "I am the way and the *truth* and the life" (John 14:16). True worship means listening to the words of Jesus, and coming to God through him. Worship does not depend on place or time or ethnic group — it depends on our attitude to God as shown in our attitude to his Son, Jesus Christ. True worship comes along with the living water.

Jesus was revealing a profound spiritual truth to this stranger — a truth just as profound as what he had discussed with one of Israel's religious leaders (John 3). But the woman was not quite sure what to make of it, and she said, When the Messiah comes, he'll tell us what's right (verse 25).

Jesus responded, I am he — probably his most direct claim to be the Messiah — and yes, what I am telling you is right. The woman left her water jar behind and went back to town to tell everyone about Jesus, and she convinced them to check it out for themselves, and many of them believed. They believed not just because of the woman's testimony, but because they listened to Jesus himself (verses 39-41).

Worship today

Sometimes people today get too opinionated about worship — true worship has to involve a certain day of the week, a certain type of song, a certain posture or some other detail. But I think that Jesus' answer to the

Samaritan woman covers it well: The time will come when you will worship God neither this way nor that, because God is not to be found in earthly places, rotations of the earth, cultural music or human gestures.

God is spirit, and our relationship with him is a spiritual one. We live in time and space, and we use time and space in our worship, but those details are not the meaning of worship. Rather, our worship centers in Jesus, and in our relationship with him. He is the source of living waters that we need for eternal life. We need to admit our thirst, and ask him for a drink. Or to use metaphors from the book of Revelation, we need to admit that we are poor, blind and naked, and ask Jesus for spiritual wealth, sight and clothing. We worship in spirit and truth when we look to him for what we need.

In marriage, different people express love in different ways, and some forms of expression are appropriate in public, and some are not. This is true of worship, too. We express our adoration in different ways, and some ways are more appropriate in private than in public. Certain activities, though they may seem worshipful to one person, may appear disrespectful or distracting to another person. When we worship together, we do not want our activities to put other people off. At the same time, believers who are more formal need to be tolerant of a little diversity. True worship is not defined by external matters, but by our attitude toward Jesus Christ.

When it comes to worship, though there will always be room for improvement and maturity, may we continue to learn from Jesus not only about what worship really is, but also the way we interact with people who think about it differently than we do.

Joseph Tkach

46. PERFECT WORSHIP

There is a serious problem with the way the worship: we don't do it right. We try to be living sacrifices for God, but we don't always do that right. As some have said, the problem with living sacrifices is that they keep crawling off of the altar. Like the people of ancient Israel, our lives are mixed with sin. We do not have the faith that we'd like to have. We do not have as much love as we'd like to have. We do not pray as well as we wish we could. Our songs do not express our emotions as well as we'd like. We would like to present our king with sparkling jewels, but we have only plastic trinkets to give.

How do we face our failure in the area of worship?

We respond in the same way that we respond for other areas of failure: we look to Jesus. He has offered the perfect sacrifice for all of us; he has given his life to God as an act of worship for all humanity. He is our substitute — this is what theologians mean by a *vicarious* sacrifice. What he did counts for us. He had no sins of his own, and yet he gave himself as a sacrifice for sin — our sins.

Many Christians realize that Jesus was our substitute when it comes to sacrifice. "Christ died for us" is part of the New Testament message. He has given the worship that we could not.

But Jesus is our substitute in other ways, too, because our lives are hidden in him (Colossians 3:2), and he lives in us (Galatians 2:20). The prayers that we offer are not perfect, but we pray in Christ's name, and he intercedes for us. He takes our defective prayers, removes the parts where we ask amiss, adds the details that we have neglected, and offers those prayers to God as perfect worship.

Because Jesus Christ is our representative, he offers perfect worship on our behalf, and our role is to join him in what he is already doing for us. Whether it is sacrifice, prayer, study or response, he has already been there and done that for us. The worship he gives to God is a *vicarious* worship, done for us, on our behalf.

We do our best to "get it right," but part of being "right" is admitting that we aren't always right (1 John 1:8). So the last word on worship is that we must look to Jesus as the one who is doing it right for us, and he invites us to join in what he is doing.

47. WORSHIP LOOKS BACK, LOOKS FORWARD

The ancient Israelites recited their history as a reminder of who they were in the world, what their relationship with God was, and how they were supposed to respond to the God of their salvation. Their expressed who they were, and how they were to live. Deuteronomy tells us one of their confessions:

My father was a wandering Aramean, and he went down into Egypt with a few people and lived there and became a great nation, powerful and numerous. But the Egyptians mistreated us and made us suffer, putting us to hard labor. Then we cried out to the Lord, the God of our fathers, and the Lord heard our voice and saw our misery, toil and oppression. So the Lord brought us out of Egypt with a mighty hand and an outstretched arm, with great terror and with miraculous signs and wonders. He brought us to this place and gave us this land, a land flowing with milk and honey; and now I bring the firstfruits of the soil that you, O Lord, have given me. (Deuteronomy 26:5-10)

Remembering our salvation history is part of our worship. It is part of our confession and part of our understanding of who we are before God and how we are to respond to him in the world. That is one reason most Christians celebrate Advent, Easter and other commemorations of our Savior. These say something about who we are, because they rehearse the story that is central to our lives and our identity. Jesus the Christ defines who we are in the world.

We do not know exactly when the story began. The creation story starts simply "in the beginning." We do not know when Adam was created, nor do we know exactly when the Word became flesh. We do not need to know. However, we know that the Incarnation happened at a definite point in history, as recorded by the Gospel writers Matthew and Luke. The story is unparalleled *good news*, and because it is, we celebrate. It is good news for us, and good news for the entire world.

The Christian church has a history, too. In one way, we could say that it began before Moses, with the call of Abraham. In another way, we could say it began with Jesus' birth, or with his calling of his disciples, or with his death and resurrection. From any viewpoint, of course, we could say that the Pentecost recorded in Acts 2 was a significant beginning point for the church. The rest of the book of Acts expands the story, helping us see our connection to the Jesus who died and rose again, and how the church spread from Jerusalem into a worldwide mission. Rehearsing the story, we are reminded of who we are and our call to be about our Father's business.

Church history marches onward, though most of it did not become part of Scripture, as Acts did. The martyrdoms of Polycarp, of Perpetua, and of many others, help us glimpse the faith of the early believers. The rise of Constantine, the council of Nicea, the writings of Augustine, the rivalry between Rome and Constantinople, were major developments that helped shape the future of the church for centuries to come. Sometimes everyone "did what was right in their own eyes." Sometimes there was a powerful leader who ruled well, and sometimes there was a leader who abused the people with excessive power. There were times of sin, of captivity, of exile and of restoration.

A significant moment came in 1517, when Martin Luther challenged the authority of the Roman pontiff on doctrinal grounds, resting his case on the Word of God. There were significant milestones in Geneva, in Holland, in England and in America. People remember these milestones, for they help shape our identity. Though we are not Lutherans, we can identify with the stand of Luther. Though we are not Methodists, we can identify with the Aldersgate experience of John Wesley, when he found his heart strangely warmed as some of Luther's work about the grace of God was read.

We do not want to forget where we have come from, how Christ has led us toward himself, and how grace liberates us from legalism. Many people not in our fellowship have benefitted from our story, just as we benefit from Martin Luther's. Many people can identify with our struggle, with seeing our relationship with God in terms of our works, in terms of what we do. Many well-meaning Christians still need to be liberated with a new and personal reformation.

But we do not need a new holiday on our church calendar. There is something more important to think about than ourselves, and that is Jesus Christ. He is where our salvation begins, where our reformation begins, where our identity is centered and where our response is given. Our identity and our life are based on God made flesh, on God so humble as to freely choose to be born in poverty and oppression as one of us.

What ironies! Jesus, a Jew, was persecuted by Herod, king of the Jews, but Jesus found a safe place among the Gentiles, in Egypt. But he did not remain in safety — he returned to his people, to be rejected by them in his home town and in the capital city. He was killed by religious leaders who prided themselves on their superior ethics, and by political leaders who prided themselves on the administration of justice.

The Holy One died a cursed death, the Righteous One became sin for us. The Author of Life died — all because we humans could not be saved in any other way. We could not save ourselves. Our only hope was that God himself would come to us as one of us, that he would be without sin and be a sin offering for us.

This is where our identity is — in humility, in suffering, in trusting God from birth to death. Jesus set that example and calls us to follow him. Our story begins, as Matthew tells it, with Abraham. Our story includes Gentile ancestors, a prostitute and an adulterer, and a woman who became pregnant before marriage. The glory of God was hidden in Mary's womb in what was, as far as everyone else could see, scandalous circumstances. The glory of God is often hidden today, too, isn't it?

That is our identity — humility and sometimes shame. We don't look like much, even though the glory of God is living within us. Our story begins in shame, in sin, in God seeking us. We have nothing to boast about; we must simply admit our inability and look to God for mercy — mercy he has already shown to us and guaranteed for us in Jesus Christ. Our story becomes merged with his, a story that includes shame and a glory that is hidden until the resurrection.

Jesus is not only our point of identity, he also shapes the response we give to God. The formula "Be holy, for I am holy" is given shape by the saying "Be merciful, for I am merciful" (Luke 6:36). Or, "Forgive, as I have forgiven you" (Colossians 3:13). God's graciousness toward us, shown most tangibly in Jesus Christ, carries with it the power to be gracious toward others. In him, we can do for them what he has done for us. This is how ethics is built in the new covenant; this is how grace teaches us to have godly lives (Titus 2:11-12). As he has loved us, we are freed to love others — tangibly, not just in pious sentiments.

We trust our lives to Jesus and know that our salvation is secure in him. We are freed from the fear of death, freed from the fear of persecution, freed from the fear of ridicule, freed from feelings of insecurity. Because we are secure in Christ, we are free to do good works despite the negative consequences that sometimes come with good works in this fallen world — and we are free not to withhold forgiveness until the other person has been punished enough or is sorry enough. We are free to forgive right away.

We are also free in Christ to worship any time, any place. We are free in Christ to meet when it is most expedient for the *congregation and the mission field,* rather than when it is most comfortable for us personally. In short, we are free to join one another in the stable and make the feed trough our bed, to serve one another in the love of our Savior, to be harmless as doves, wise as owls and always willing to learn.

Time cannot stand still. We can reminisce about and reflect on our journey, but our focus must not stay there. We must move on, for our journey is not yet done. Christ has commanded us, "Go, make disciples, baptize them and teach them to do what I have commanded" (Matthew 28:19-20).

Our understanding is shaped by our history, but our future is in Christ. Our vision is informed by the past, but it exists *for the future*. Any attention we give to our history is pointless unless we also ask how it shapes what we do right now, and how it affects our ultimate destination. So where we were five years ago may not be as important as where we plan to be five years from now. What kind of people do we want to be — rather, what do we believe Christ wants us to be?

Whether we look backward or look forward, let's make sure that we look to Jesus. It is to him that we owe our lives, it is in him and for him that we live and move and have our being. It is his kingdom that we belong to and serve. Christ the King, born in a stable, pleased to dwell with the humble who admit their need for him.

Joseph Tkach

48. WHY OUR WORSHIP STYLE IS CHANGING

God has done marvelous things for us! The love he has shown us in Jesus Christ is beyond our ability to understand (Ephesians 3:19). The joy he gives us in salvation is beyond our ability to express (1 Peter 1:8). The peace he gives is also beyond our comprehension (Philippians 4:7). Words simply fail to describe adequately the experience of salvation we have in Jesus Christ.

How shall we respond to these magnificent blessings? With worship — with praise and thanksgiving, giving glory and honor to God. This is our privilege and our joy. Our relationship with God is characterized by love, joy, peace, praise and worship. All that we do should be for his honor and glory — and we rejoice in being called to proclaim his praises (1 Peter 2:9).

In recent years, many congregations have changed the way they do things in their weekly meetings. Church services are called worship services. Song leaders are called worship leaders. We have more music, and a greater variety of music. The goal, of course, is that we become more conscious that we are gathering to worship our Creator and Savior, and that we express that worship in the words we sing and in the emotions that songs can convey. In a way, the "culture" in the church is changing.

It should be no surprise that some of us find this change uncomfortable. We have grown used to our traditional way of doing things, and we can easily view a change in music as an unnecessary interruption of our comfort levels. With that in mind, I would like to share with you a slightly edited letter I sent a member in response to questions about our changing worship format:

You question whether a revised worship format can bring anyone closer to God. It is true that simply changing terminology and behavior cannot force anyone to change their hearts. However, it can *facilitate* a change of heart. I do not know what songs were done in your church area. I do know that contemporary worship songs have helped many members come to greater awareness of why we gather each week: to worship, to praise God, to rejoice before the Lord.

Salvation is a wonderful gift — better than winning a million dollars in a sweepstakes. Should we treat it as a ho-hum, matter-of-fact experience? I think not. The knowledge of salvation should make us excited, expressive, enthusiastic, anxious to praise our Father and Savior. For many people, this is done with lively songs.

As you note, the way people sing praise to God has varied from culture to culture and century to century. Eighth-century chants were effective worship expressions in the eighth century. Today, they are not. Eighteenth-century hymns were also worshipful in the 18th century. Some still are; others are not. Each type of song began as contemporary music. As time went on, it became traditional and some other style became contemporary. Today, different styles are becoming contemporary, and 18th-century hymns do not invoke worshipful thoughts in large segments of the population.

You suggest that we are changing our worship song styles without scriptural precedent. I believe that Scripture actually gives us precedent for much greater change. Scripture tells us about very expressive worship styles:

- "I will be glad and rejoice in you; I will sing praise to your name, O Most High" (Psalm 9:2).
- "Rejoice in the Lord and be glad, you righteous; sing, all you who are upright in heart!" (Psalm 32:11).
- "Shout with joy to God, all the earth!" (Psalm 66:1).
- "May the righteous be glad and rejoice before God; may they be happy and joyful. Sing to God, sing praise to his name, extol him who rides on the clouds — his name is the Lord — and rejoice before him" (Psalm 68:3-4).
- "Shout for joy, O heavens; rejoice, O earth; burst into song, O mountains!" (Isaiah 49:13).
- "My lips will shout for joy when I sing praise to you — I, whom you have redeemed" (Psalm 71:23).
- "Come, let us sing for joy to the Lord; let us shout aloud to the Rock of our salvation" (Psalm 95:1).
- "Sing, O Daughter of Zion; shout aloud, O Israel! Be glad and rejoice with all your heart, O Daughter of Jerusalem!" (Zephaniah 3:14).
- "Is anyone happy? Let him sing songs of praise" (James 5:13).

Have you ever shouted for joy — in the presence of other believers — at the blessings God has given you? Have you ever exulted in God? Has your heart leaped for joy? Have you clapped hands in worship? There are scriptural precedents for these. We want our worship services to allow people to express their praise and joy in the Lord.

You note that some of our minority members prefer traditional music. That is true. It is also true that some of the majority members enjoy minority music. We want to provide a variety of musical styles that reflects the variety of people that we have in our fellowship. Of course, music preferences change over time, too. After listening to a style of music for a while, it can become more enjoyable.

Another thing that we need to consider is the people who do not attend our services, and yet we want them to. What styles of music will help them worship? What songs will best express to them the joy Christ is giving us? What will magnify the Lord to them? If we want our church to grow, if we want people to stay to hear the gospel message, then we need to consider their preferences, too. Some songs are more beginner-friendly than others. I hope you can take that into consideration, too, because that is another reason we wish to have more variety in our worship music. We want the church to grow, to bring more people to salvation through Jesus Christ.

Joseph Tkach

49. WORSHIP AND CULTURAL DIVERSITY

Worship styles are fundamentally a matter of culture. That means that the outward form of the worship service does not need to be the same everywhere. The key to the worship service is that a suitable environment is created in which people can come into the presence of God in the context of the body of Christ. Worship is a meeting between God and his people.

Robert Logan puts it well when he explains that the worship service should take people through a process of active response to God – helping them recognize who he is, what he is like, who we are and what we are like in relation to him, the change he desires to make in our lives, and our proper response to his will for our lives (*Beyond Church Growth,* page 77). The goal of worship, leading people to meet God, is best attained in the context of their particular cultural expectations.

Why we worship and what happens to us when we do are the *substance* of worship. *How* we worship, or the *form,* is rooted in our culture. If we first understand why we worship God, then we can adapt the form so that it is culturally relevant. This Although it is essential that the substance of worship be the same everywhere, the form of worship will vary from congregation to congregation. Certain forms of expression are more comfortable, expressive or appealing in some areas than others. Resources also vary from place to place.

We do not need an identical worship form in all our congregations. What we need is to provide an environment in every congregation that allows a congregation to express its worship and praise to God in a way that is meaningful to them as they experience and share his forgiving grace and empowering love. Because our congregations come from different cultures, we will naturally gravitate toward varying worship environments.

Joseph Tkach

50. THOUGHTS ABOUT WORSHIP

In the last two decades, our denomination has made major changes in the way we conduct worship. Many of us remember when our worship services began with a song leader and a pianist. They would lead the congregation in two or three hymns as a prelude to the "main event."

We have become more flexible and even adventurous. We have realized that "praise and worship" (as worship in song and prayer is often referred to) is an important component of our services. We have learned to embrace multiple music styles (understanding that people of different backgrounds and cultures express themselves very differently, especially in music). We have learned the importance of skilled worship leaders, musicians and others who facilitate worship. Many of our congregations have praise bands with multiple musicians.

Many of our congregations have learned to use modern technology to enhance worship, but not all congregations have the same resources. Although technology and praise bands can enhance worship, they are not essential to worship.

Worship is an interesting word. It comes from an Old English word, *weorth*, meaning "worth." In its earliest form, *weorthscipe* (worth-ship) meant the appropriate treatment of something or someone of worth. So worth-ship or worship is the act of affirming God's worth. It does not mean we flatter God to boost his self-esteem. Rather, it is a declaration that God is worthy — to be praised, preached about, confessed to and served.

Jesus makes one of the most pointed scriptural statements concerning worship in his encounter with the Samaritan woman. Living in a society polarized over the details of "getting worship right," this woman seized the opportunity to ask Jesus about it. "I can see that you are a prophet," she said. "Our ancestors worshiped on this mountain, but you Jews claim that the place where we must worship is in Jerusalem" (John 4:19-20).

Jesus explained that the practical details of worship were not what was most important. "A time is coming and has now come when the true worshipers will worship the Father in spirit and truth, for they are the kind of worshipers the Father seeks" (John 4:23).

True worship of God is expressed in a number of ways. We see this by noting three basic meanings of the Greek and Hebrew words translated as worship. The first meaning is that of praise and adoration. We express this when we sing and pray (together and individually). The second meaning pertains to public or ceremonial gatherings, like church services, where we sing, pray and fellowship together. The third meaning, which is the broadest, is to serve. In the Old Testament the Hebrew word *abad* is used for both worship and for work. The Greek verbs for this meaning are *latreuo* and the similar word *leiturgeo,* which is the root word for our English word liturgy.

The most important point about worship is found in the New Testament book of Hebrews, where the risen and ascended Jesus is said to be our *leitourgos* ("minister"); our worship leader (8:2). He leads us in worship, conveying all of God's graces to us and taking all our responses to God, sanctifying them and giving them to the Father in the Spirit.

Our worship of God, with and through Jesus, can occur in large groups and small. For the first 300 years of Christianity, church services occurred mostly in homes, and thus in small groups. There is a purity about this original pattern that carries the inherent blessing of simplicity.

The early church did not set up a bank of amplifiers, speakers, soundboards, microphones, projectors and such. These resources are not needed in a very small congregation. It would be ridiculous to set up for a group of 250 people when there is only going to be 10 to 20 in attendance. Sitting in a circle is just as good as sitting in several rows — in fact, it is often better for small congregations, providing an intimate environment where genuine, quality worship can happen.

If you are a small congregation, you need not feel that you are inadequate because your worship service is not a "mega-media-event." Keep it simple — make use of the resources you have, knowing that God will meet you where you are. Instead of becoming preoccupied with the mechanics of doing church (like Martha in the kitchen!), embrace the freedom that Jesus gives you to focus on worship (like Mary at our Lord's feet). Remember what Jesus told us: "For where two or three have gathered together in my name, I am there in their midst" (Matthew 18:20).

Joseph Tkach

51. WHAT EVENTS
ARE WORTH CELEBRATING?

These things are written that you may believe that Jesus is the Christ, the Son of God, and that by believing you may have life in his name. (John 20:31)

Which events of Jesus' life do you think were insignificant? Which of the things he said or did is *not* worth taking notice of, or remembering? The answer is obvious: if God considered any event of Jesus' life worth recording for us, he must consider that event to be important for us.

The life of Jesus has the power to save us. The events that make up his life—what he said and what he did—can be used to lead us to faith in him. As we immerse ourselves in what he did, we can grow in our conviction (Luke 1:4) and become more established in the truth (2 Peter 1:8, 12).

The events of Jesus' life are recorded for us to remember, study, re-enact, commemorate and meditate upon. By regularly doing this—for instance, by an annual cycle that keeps returning us to events in the life of Jesus Christ—we grow in faith, we draw closer to the heart of God and we are increasingly equipped to produce fruit for our Lord.

If events of the past remain nothing more than a written record, they lose part of their power. They exercise their power in our lives only to the degree that we remember them. We are called to do more than just read about them or study them; we are called to experience Jesus' life by celebrating and even re-enacting major events. When we remember those events with ongoing celebrations, lives continue to be transformed.

Ancient Israel's experience teaches us the value of an annual rehearsal of God's acts of salvation. Every year they rehearsed the great salvation events of their history, the events in which God acted to save them. Their weekly Sabbath and annual festivals were designed to remind them how God had freed them from their slavery in Egypt (Deuteronomy 5:12-15; Exodus 12:11-12, 26-27, 42; 13:3, 8-10; Deuteronomy 16:10-12; Leviticus 23:43).

By celebrating this way, they annually remembered what God had done for them, they renewed and deepened their relationship with God, and they remembered their responsibility to God. They were not restricted to worshiping on those days alone. They continued to see the hand of God in their history long after the Exodus, so they created additional days of worship to remember and celebrate his intervention, power and love:

- They instituted fasts in the fourth, fifth, seventh and tenth months to remember the destruction of Jerusalem and the temple by Babylon, and the beginning of their exile (Zechariah 7:5; Jeremiah 52:12; 2 Kings 25:8-25; Zechariah 8:19; 2 Kings 25:1; Jeremiah 39:2).

- When God delivered them from persecution by Haman through Esther in the fifth century B.C., they commemorated his deliverance by creating the Feast of Purim (Esther 9:27-28).

- After God delivered them from the oppression of Antiochus Epiphanes in the second century B.C., they instituted the Feast of Hanukkah, mentioned in John 10:22, as a festival of remembrance and rejoicing.

Like Israel, we Christians have a great salvation-event to remember. Unlike Israel's, ours is not just a salvation event. It is *the* salvation event: the life, death and resurrection of Jesus Christ saved us from sin and death.

The new covenant, which God has made with his church, contains no commanded days of worship. Under the new covenant, the church is free to designate days on which to celebrate and re-enact God's act of salvation in Jesus Christ. Those celebrations can draw upon imagery from some of the festivals of Israel, which, while they looked back to that nation's salvation from Egypt, also can remind us of a greater salvation, which has now come in Jesus Christ. Or they can be Christian celebrations at various times of the year, designed to remember and celebrate events of the life of Jesus.

The church is not commanded to adopt worship celebrations for all the events of the Gospels, but it is permitted to adopt as many worship celebrations as it feels appropriate. The church is also free to reinterpret the festivals of Israel, and to create new festivals to remember major events in our salvation through the life, death and resurrection of Jesus.

Don Mears

52. IS THERE ONLY ONE RIGHT WAY TO WORSHIP GOD?

Liturgy has become a hot topic in the church.

"Excuse me, but what's a liturgy?" you ask.

Liturgy is simply the pattern or program of worship chosen by a church. It includes the gospel-related topics, themes, forms, symbols, styles, seasons and days that help facilitate effective worship for that particular church. In other words, liturgy refers to the whole set of seasons, days, tools and methods we use to worship, celebrate and enjoy God.

We all agree that God doesn't want his people to fight about when to worship him. In fact, all our worship should be a source of unity and joy in the power, love, glory and grace of God. Yet, so often, our choices about when and how to worship our God and Savior become a source of division and controversy.

While some members don't mind attending everything the church offers, and some simply avoid the activities that are not meaningful to them, others get angry just knowing any space is being given to the "other side."

In this article, we'd like to present a few basic principles related to worship that might help us all to lay down our weapons and give each other some space about when we choose to worship our great God who loves us all.

Worship is celebration

The first thing that might help us get some perspective is to understand that worship is a human response to God — who he is, what he has done and what he is doing. It is an active, often spontaneous, celebration of God's work through Christ. In worship Christians are participating in Christ's work of human redemption.

New Testament liturgy is the recurring patterns of worship that developed among the first-century Christians. It developed as the disciples rehearsed and remembered Jesus' death and resurrection by meeting together to participate in the Lord's Supper and to baptize new converts. These events were discussed, read about in the Scriptures, rehearsed and reenacted in an atmosphere of prayer, singing of hymns, thanksgiving and praise.

God likes variety

As we learn to obey Jesus' command to love one another, we also learn to appreciate and respect our cultural diversity. Jesus values human culture and human customs because he values humanity. Our cultural lenses, as it were, are a necessary part of who we are. Consequently, the forms or styles we prefer for worship are necessarily shaped by our particular culture, and rightly so.

As we view life through our particular cultural lenses, we tend to look upon other ways of doing things with suspicion, distrust, ridicule or even fear. Our culture tends to shape our values, and our values govern how we draw our conclusions about what is good and what is bad.

When we come to faith in Christ, God purifies our hearts. He softens our hearts toward others. He gives us a new commandment — that we love one another. This does not require that we must abandon our unique cultural values. It means we must learn to respect the cultural values of others, without feeling threatened ourselves.

Of course, if a particular cultural value is sinful, we must abandon it. But most of our cultural values are not sinful; many are neutral and many are quite compatible with godliness in Christ.

Culture and sin

Culture, of itself, is not evil. Our unity in Christ affirms and purifies culture; it does not do away with it! When Jesus returns, we are told in Revelation, men and women from every tribe and tongue and people and nation will form the kingdom of God. God works with us in the context of our respective cultures. He is the author of human freedom, and he enjoys the rich tapestry of human diversity and cultural variety. God hates sin, but he does not hate culture.

It is sin that corrupts and spoils culture, not culture that causes and produces sin. Because there is sin in every human, there is sin in every culture. As God's people, Christians should turn away from sin in their respective cultures, but they do not need to turn away from their culture to embrace someone else's culture.

At the same time, no particular cultural form is an absolute. In other words, we must not think that just because a cultural form we especially like is not sinful and has a certain value in worship, therefore it must be used in worship at all costs. To make any cultural form essential to worship is to make the opposite mistake from discarding all cultural forms.

We must be free to use cultural forms in worship, while also remaining free not to use a particular cultural form. We must not allow any form or style of worship to become an end in itself. We worship God, freely using forms and styles of worship; we don't, however, allow ourselves to become slaves to those forms and styles.

Communing with God

Silly as it sounds to have to say it, God is just as comfortable communing with Filipinos in a Philippine culture as he is communing with Arabs in an Arab culture, Indians in an Indian culture, Danes in a Danish culture, Mexicans in a Mexican culture or Latinos, Anglos, African Americans or American-born Chinese in a United States culture. And God loves the worship of his people regardless of its cultural flavor and style.

Our congregations do not need to have the same songbooks, the same musical instruments, the same style of body movement or even the same days on which we worship in order to be united in Christ. Our unity comes from our faith in Jesus Christ and our mutual love for one another, not from worshiping in the same way and at the same times in every congregation around the world.

Each culture may have different symbols that are meaningful to them. In many cultures, for example, the cross is a fitting symbol of Christian faith, while in certain other cultures it may not be, because of its widespread use in that culture as a symbol of something else. In many cultures, the Christmas season is a fitting celebration of the birth of Christ, while in certain other cultures it is not, because it has become so entrenched with ungodly rituals.

Liturgy and culture

As a congregation matures, it develops an increasingly deeper participation in the Incarnation of Christ through its worship and liturgy. That means the members of the congregation are growing in love for God and in love for others. And that means they are becoming less and less likely to condemn others for being different and for doing things differently.

It should be obvious that the more we love God, and the more we worship and honor him, the less we would tend to condemn our brothers and sisters in Christ who prefer to worship him on days and in ways different from those we choose.

But it isn't obvious, is it? We tend to condemn it anyway. And Christians always have. Less than 25 years after Jesus' death, Paul addressed this issue in his letter to the Romans: "Who are you to judge someone else's servant? To his own master he stands or falls," Paul writes. "And he will stand, for the Lord is able to make him stand" (Romans 14:4).

Such instructions are necessary for the very reason that Christians do tend to have a spirit of condemnation toward others. Paul continues in verse 10: "You, then, why do you judge your brother? Or why do you look down on your brother? For we will all stand before God's judgment seat."

What does this have to do with liturgy? Just this: We must learn not to condemn one another over the seasons and days on which we decide to worship.

For example, if one of our congregations in the United States decides to adopt an unusual format for worship, then congregations in Europe and South America do not need either to 1) feel they must immediately do the same thing, or 2) get angry and upset that the U.S. congregation has made this decision.

Likewise, if a congregation in South America feels it should not get involved in local Christmas customs, then congregations in the United States and Canada do not have to feel their South American brothers and sisters are being disloyal to Christ.

Freedom not to condemn

We are all free in Christ to worship during whatever seasons and on whatever days we find fitting and appropriate. As Paul wrote to the church in Rome: "He who regards one day as special, does so to the Lord. He who eats meat, eats to the Lord, for he gives thanks to God; and he who abstains, does so to the Lord and gives thanks to God" (Romans 14:6).

Can we let this principle rule our attitudes toward one another? If our brothers and sisters in other congregations are gathering to worship the Lord, then we should not get upset about the particular choice of days on which they do so, or the specific details they incorporate in their worship.

Let's take it one step further. In any given congregation we have fellow believers who want to worship in one way, as well as fellow believers who want to worship in quite a different way.

How do we treat one another? Are we angry and judgmental? Are we considerate and patient? Do we try to understand and appreciate the feelings of those who differ from us? What is the real value of worshiping at all if the fruit of our worship is judgmentalism and condemnation?

Within the essential and central framework of Christian orthodoxy there is much room for diversity. We have unity in the worship of the Lord, the faithful observance of the sacraments (the Lord's Supper and baptism) and the faithful proclamation of the Word.

We have diversity in the styles and forms we use in administering the sacraments, proclaiming the Word and worshiping the Lord. The Holy Spirit makes us one in Christ, and our diversity in how we express that unity is a gift of God.

Responsible choices

Each congregation in its unique setting in the world must take up its own task, with the help of the Holy Spirit, of filling cultural forms with Christian substance. Choices about symbols, order of meeting, styles of music and prayer forms, and choices about seasons and days, must be the responsibility of the local congregation under the pastor's guidance within the broad and general guidelines provided by the denomination and the regional offices.

We allow for flexibility. Congregations are free to gather for worship during those seasons and days that are most fitting for their circumstances and situations. They are not compelled to make the same choices as other congregations (that means there is significant freedom within denominational limitations). At the same time, congregations are expected to respect the choices made by other congregations.

Complications

We realize these issues are complicated. The fact is, some of our members worship in a particular manner for wrong reasons: they believe it is a sin not to observe a particular custom. Many of these members also believe it is a sin to worship in other ways. They feel sullied or dirtied, as some have put it, having to belong to a church in which there are people who worship in a particular way.

Some have defined the old customs as a "better" way to celebrate Christ, and they look down on others as inferior. And they are upset that we no longer forbid or avoid the customs that they view as sinful, and some of them are praying that God will put everything back the way it used to be.

However, there are others who observe the old customs simply because it is their tradition and custom. They associate pleasant memories with those patterns of worship, and they have made them better than they used to be. They are glad they can worship Christ in a new and meaningful way and see their tradition as one means to that end.

But on the extreme, some of them do not want to belong to a church that still observes the old traditions. Many of these have a keen sense of having been freed from the legalism that characterized the way our church understood those customs, and they want to steer completely clear of them. They cannot understand why the church would continue to allow for the old customs when their observance was a major source of our spirit of exclusivity and our misunderstanding of the gospel.

Others don't mind the church observing the old traditions, as long as participation is not mandatory and as long as new forms of worship are used as well.

Our policy

There is no solution that will please everyone. Our goals are 1) faithfulness to God, and 2) denominational unity in the light of his Word.

That is why we provide flexibility within an overall biblical framework. Congregations are free to formulate their own liturgical calendar and practices, taking into account the needs and preferences of all the members.

Whether we can handle such freedom is yet to be seen. Can we have diversity in this way and yet remain united in our faith in Jesus Christ and in the fellowship of the Holy Spirit? Surely we can. Whether we will is a matter of choice. God loves all his children, but his children still struggle with the challenges of working together in love.

May we join together in prayer that as we assemble for worship, God will lead us into a closer walk with him and with one another.

Randal Dick and J. Michael Feazell

53. THOUGHTS ABOUT LITURGY

Churches with a "non-liturgical" worship tradition tend to equate liturgy with formal worship that has lots of ritual (what my friend Professor Eddie Gibbs describes as "bells and smells"), including standardized prayers. Though a "liturgical" approach toward worship might seem contrived and stiff to people used to a less formal style, it is perfectly valid when given to the Father, through Jesus, "in spirit and in truth," as Jesus explained to the Samaritan woman at the well in John 4.

But liturgy is much more than a style of worship practiced by "high churches" like Roman Catholics, Anglicans and Eastern Orthodox. Whether we recognize it or not, liturgy is fundamental to the rhythm of a Christian's daily life before God.

In the Old Testament, the Hebrew word *abad* is used to describe both worship and work. In the New Testament, the equivalent Greek words are *latreuo* and *leitourgia,* from which comes our English word "liturgy." The original meaning of *leitourgia* was not just religious good works, but any public duty or service rendered by a citizen for the benefit of the state.

In Romans 12:1, Paul writes, "I urge you, brothers and sister, in view of God's mercy, to offer your bodies as living sacrifices, holy and pleasing to God—this is your true and proper worship [*latreia*]." He saw a parallel: as citizens of a community accepted their responsibility for public service, so Christians should make themselves available to God for the work of the kingdom. Paul also draws from his own Jewish background of sacrifice in temple worship. The sacrifice here seems to represent an act of total self-giving of one's life for the benefit of and in response to God's mercy.

Notice the radical transformation of the idea of sacrifice. In most religions of the first century, the animal lost its life as it poured out its blood. It died as its life was given over for others. Here Paul proclaims that we are living sacrifices, continually self-giving.

Where did Paul get this striking insight? From the gospel of grace, which he had set forth in the previous eleven chapters! Our sacrifice is a mirror image, reflecting Christ's own self-giving, which passed through death to eternal life, never to die again! We join in and participate in Christ's liturgy of pouring out his life even to the extent of death, but in a way that leads to fullness of life.

Christ's own worship transforms the very notion of sacrifice and worship. Paul goes on to say: "Do not conform to the pattern of this world, but be transformed by the renewing of your mind. Then you will be able to test and approve what God's will is—his good, pleasing and perfect will" (verse 2). Our sacrificial worship demonstrates a whole new pattern of living that comes from sharing daily in the grace of Christ, our crucified, risen and ascended Lord.

Hebrews 8:2 says that Christ is a minister [*leitourgos*] of the true holy place. As one of us, in our place and on our behalf, Jesus is our worship leader in every moment of our lives. In union with him, we daily die to ourselves in repentance and rise with him to newness of life through faith in him.

Liturgy is not just something "religious" we do in church, or when we pray or study the Bible. It is characteristic of the whole rhythm of our daily life. When Paul admonished Christians to "pray without ceasing" (1 Thessalonian 5:17), he was not saying that we continually pray and never stop. The Greek word he chose is used outside the New Testament to describe a hacking cough. When you have a hacking cough, you do not cough all the time, but you feel like you are. That is what it means to pray without ceasing. It means being in an attitude of prayer at all times. So when I say that worship is the rhythm of daily life, it is like saying that we pray without ceasing or breathe without ceasing.

The temple in Jerusalem was a liturgical place that involved more than sacrifice. At its dedication, Solomon prayed, "May your eyes be open toward this temple day and night, this place of which you said you would put your Name there. May you hear the prayer your servant prays toward this place" (2 Chronicles 6:20). We no longer have (nor do we need) a physical temple. God's people are God's temple—built up by the Holy Spirit (1 Peter 2:5), where acts of sacrifice and service continue day and night, "without ceasing" as together we share God's love and life with those around us.

Perhaps we can see how in formal times of worship the same truth and reality are depicted. Baptism and communion in the context of proclaiming the grace of God in Jesus announce in action both the sacrifice of self-giving and the transformation to new life we share with Christ. We die with him in immersion and in the breaking of the bread, and we rise with him as we ascend through the surface the water of his baptism and partake of his life-giving blood by drinking his covenantal wine of life. In both instances we share in what is his, enveloped in his baptism and partaking of his bodily death and resurrection. That's liturgical too!

Joseph Tkach

54. MONEY AND WORSHIP

Are offerings in church an unpleasant mixing of God and Mammon? Perhaps sometimes they have been — but they don't need to be. In fact, an offering *should* be an act of worship to God, motivated by a heart that pleases God.

Paul says very little about worship practices of the early church. In fact, he rarely uses the ordinary Greek words for *worship* in connection with the newly developing Christian communities. But he does take a Greek word for *worship* used throughout the Greek Old Testament, and he uses it for offerings. He was referring to a collection for famine relief (Romans 15:27; 2 Corinthians 9:12). This seemingly ordinary service to the saints was actually an act of worship.

The same is true for offerings gathered for the support of the gospel and the church. These are also a type of worship, and are treated as such by thousands of churches around the world. Most churches include an offering as part of the weekly worship service. As we know, God does not <u>need</u> any of our service — it is <u>we</u> who need to give it. He does not need our money, but <u>we</u> need to be generous. Offerings are one way to express our generosity, to express our devotion to God in an act of worship.

Some ministers have been a bit embarrassed about offerings, and have relegated them to some corner of the room as if they really didn't belong. We believe this is a mistake, perhaps reflecting a lack of understanding of the <u>worship</u> nature of the offerings.

Pastors should emphasize that the offering is an act of worship. It is not the *only* way that we worship God, but it is important. In *every* aspect of our lives, we should be submissive to our Lord and Savior. Offerings are part of the picture.

Offerings may be in the first part of worship services, or after the sermon. Either way, it is appropriate to have a short message explaining that the offering is an opportunity for worship. It is also appropriate to have a prayer about the offering, asking God to accept it and to bless it and guide its use. The prayer sets the offering in its correct context, as part of our relationship with our loving Creator and Savior.

Michael Morrison

55. OFFERINGS EXPRESS LOVE FOR GOD

The church's financial need is less important than the need for each of us, as children of God, to honor him with our substance. God has given us everything. He is our life, our hope, our future. Giving to him is one of the ways his people worship him and express their thanksgiving for his boundless love and grace.

The church has needs, of course, and the need is great. The church depends on these offerings as an important part of the budget. But our giving is not a response to an obligation of the law. By God's grace, our giving is an expression of our love for God, our thankfulness for his grace and love through Jesus Christ.

Our God has transformed us by his grace. And because he is our God, and because he has planted his love in our hearts, our souls long for him. We desire to gather in grateful adoration and worship of the One who has saved us and given us a future and undying hope. Today, we gather to worship him as his children. We gather to praise the name of Jesus with no obligation to the law of Moses.

And we give our offerings not out of obligation to the law, but from worshipful hearts of adoration for our Lord and Savior, and because we are committed to the work of his gospel that we are called and commanded to do.

Friends, God has given us the greatest gift he could have given — his Son. He has blessed us beyond what anyone imagined. The offerings are an opportunity to put our hearts into the work he is doing among us. Let us pray that the offering will not be a disappointing one, and that God will inspire all of us to put our treasure where our hearts are.

J. Michael Feazell

56. POVERTY AND GENEROSITY

In Paul's second letter to the believers in Corinth, he gave an excellent illustration of how the wonderful gift of joy touches the lives of believers in practical ways. "And now, brothers, we want you to know about the grace that God has given the Macedonian churches" (2 Corinthians 8:1).

Paul wasn't just giving a trivial news report—he wanted the Corinthian believers to respond to God's grace in a similar way as the church in Macedonia had. He wanted to describe for them a right and fruitful response to God's generosity.

Paul notes that the Macedonians had a "severe trial" and "extreme poverty"—but they also had "overflowing joy" (verse 2). Their joy did not come from a health and wealth gospel. Their great joy was not in having enough money and goods, but in spite of the fact that they had very little!

Their response shows something "otherworldly," something supernatural, something quite beyond the natural world of selfish humanity, something that cannot be explained by the values of this world: "Out of the most severe trial, their overflowing joy and their extreme poverty welled up in *rich generosity*" (verse 2).

This is astonishing! Combine poverty and joy, and what do you get? Rich generosity! This was not your ordinary percentage-based giving. "For I testify that they gave as much as they were able, *and even beyond their ability*" (verse 3). They gave more than what was "reasonable." They gave sacrificially.

Now, as if that were not enough, "entirely on their own, they *urgently pleaded with us* for the privilege of sharing in this service to the saints" (verses 3-4). They, in their poverty, were begging Paul for an opportunity to give more than what was reasonable!

This is how the grace of God worked in the Macedonian believers. It was a testimony to their great faith in Jesus Christ. It was a testimony to their Spirit-empowered love for other people—a testimony that Paul wanted the Corinthians to know about and to copy. And it is something for us today, too, if we can allow the Holy Spirit to work freely within us.

First to the Lord

Why did the Macedonians do something so "out of this world"? Paul says, "They gave themselves first to the Lord and then to us in keeping with God's will" (verse 5). They did it in service to the Lord. Their sacrifice was to him first and foremost. It was a work of grace, of God working in their lives, and they found themselves *happy* to do it. Responding to the Holy Spirit in them, they knew and believed and *acted* as if life is not measured by the abundance of material things.

As we read further in this chapter, we see that Paul wanted the Corinthians to do the same: "We urged Titus, since he had earlier made a beginning, to bring also to completion this act of grace on your part. But just as you excel in everything—in faith, in speech, in knowledge, in complete earnestness and in your love for us—*see that you also excel in this grace of giving*" (verses 6-7).

The Corinthians had been boasting about their spiritual wealth. They had a lot to give, but they weren't giving it! Paul wanted them to excel in generosity, because that is an expression of godly love, and love is what is most important.

And yet Paul knows that no matter how much a person may give, it doesn't do that person any good if the attitude is resentful instead of generous (1 Corinthians 13:3). So he doesn't want to bully the Corinthians into giving resentfully, but he does want to exert a little pressure, because the Corinthians were falling short in their behavior, and they needed to be *told* that they were falling short. "I am not commanding you, but I want to test the sincerity of your love by comparing it with the earnestness of others" (2 Corinthians 8:8).

Jesus our pacesetter

True spirituality is not found in the things that the Corinthians boasted about—it is measured by the perfect standard of Jesus Christ, who gave his life for all. So Paul presents the attitude of Jesus Christ as theological proof of the generosity he wanted to see in the Corinthian church: "For you know the grace of our Lord Jesus Christ, that though he was rich, yet for your sakes he became poor, so that you through his poverty might become rich" (verse 9).

The riches Paul refers to are not physical riches. Our treasures are infinitely greater than physical riches. They are in heaven, reserved for us. Yet, even now, we can already begin to experience a small foretaste of those eternal riches as we allow the Holy Spirit to work in us.

Right now, God's faithful people have trials, even poverty—and yet, because Jesus lives in us, we can be rich in generosity. We can excel in giving. We can go beyond the minimum because our joy in Christ can even now overflow to help others.

Much could be said about the example of Jesus, who often spoke about the right use of riches. In this passage Paul summarizes it with "poverty." Jesus was willing to be impoverished for us. Following him, we are *also* called to give up the things of this world, to live by different values, to serve him by serving others.

Joy and generosity

Paul continued his appeal to the Corinthians: "And here is my advice about what is best for you in this matter: Last year you were the first not only to give but also to have the desire to do so. Now finish the work, so that your *eager willingness* to do it may be matched by your completion of it, according to your means" (verses 10-11).

"For if the willingness is there"—if the attitude of generosity is present—"the gift is acceptable according to what one has, not according to what he does not have" (verse 12). Paul was not asking the Corinthians to give as much as the Macedonians had. The Macedonians had already given beyond their ability; Paul was only asking the Corinthians to give within their ability—but the main thing is that he wanted generosity to be voluntary.

Paul continues his exhortations in chapter 9: "I know your eagerness to help, and I have been boasting about it to the Macedonians, telling them that since last year you in Achaia were ready to give; and your enthusiasm has stirred most of them to action" (verse 2).

Just as Paul was using the Macedonian example to stir the Corinthians to generosity, he had earlier used the Corinthian example to stir the Macedonians, apparently with huge success. The Macedonians were so generous that Paul realized that the Corinthians could do a lot better than they already had. But he had bragged in Macedonia that the Corinthians were generous. Now he wanted the Corinthians to follow through. Again, he wants to exhort. He wants to exert some pressure, but he wants the offering to be given willingly:

"I am sending the brothers in order that our boasting about you in this matter should not prove hollow, but that you may be ready, as I said you would be. For if any Macedonians come with me and find you unprepared, we—not to say anything about you—would be ashamed of having been so confident. So I thought it *necessary* to urge the brothers to visit you in advance and finish the arrangements for the generous gift you had promised. Then it will be ready as a generous gift, *not as one grudgingly given*" (verses 3-5).

Then comes a verse we have often heard: "Each man should give what he has decided in his heart to give, not reluctantly or under compulsion, for God loves a cheerful giver" (verse 7). This cheerfulness does not mean hilarity or laughter—it means that because Christ is in us, we *enjoy* sharing what we have with others. It makes us feel good to give. Love and grace work in our hearts in such a way that, little by little, a life of giving becomes a greater and greater pleasure for us.

The greater blessing

In this passage, Paul also speaks about rewards. If we give willingly and generously, then God will also give to us. Paul is not afraid to remind the Corinthians of this: "God is able to make all grace abound to you, so that in all things at all times, having all that you need, you will abound in every good work" (verse 8).

Paul is promising that God will be generous to us. Sometimes God gives us material things, but that is *not* what Paul is talking about here. He is speaking of grace—not the grace of forgiveness (we receive that wonderful grace through faith in Christ, not through works of generosity)—Paul is speaking about the many other kinds of grace God can give.

When God gave extra grace to the Macedonian churches, they had less money than before—but more joy! Any sane person, if forced to choose, would rather have poverty with joy, than wealth without joy. Joy is the greater blessing, and God gives us the greater blessing. Some Christians even get both—but they are also given the responsibility to use both to serve others.

Paul then quotes from the Old Testament: "He has scattered abroad his gifts to the poor" (verse 9). What kind of gifts is he talking about? "His righteousness endures forever." The gift of righteousness outweighs them all. The gift of being counted righteous in God's sight—this is the gift that lasts forever. God gives us the best possible gift.

God rewards a generous heart

"Now he who supplies seed to the sower and bread for food will also supply and increase your store of seed and will enlarge the harvest of your righteousness" (verse 10). This last phrase, about the harvest of righteousness, tells us that Paul is speaking metaphorically. He is not promising literal seeds, but he is saying that God rewards generous people. He gives them more to give.

To the person who is using God's gifts to serve, he will give more. Sometimes he gives in kind, grain for grain, money for money, but not always. Sometimes he blesses us with joy immeasurable in return for sacrificial giving. He always gives the best.

Paul did say that the Corinthians would have all that they needed. For what purpose? So that they would "abound in every good work." He says the same thing in verse 12: "You will be made rich in every way so that you can be generous on every occasion." God's gifts come with strings attached, we might say. We need to use them, not hide them in a closet.

Those who are rich are to become rich in good works. "Command those who are rich in this present world not to be arrogant nor to put their hope in wealth, which is so uncertain, but to put their hope in God, who richly provides us with everything for our enjoyment. Command them to do good, *to be rich in good deeds, and to be generous and willing to share"* (1 Timothy 6:17-18).

Real living

What is the reward for such unusual behavior, for the people who do not cling to wealth as a thing to be grasped, but willingly give it away? "In this way they will lay up *treasure* for themselves as *a firm foundation for the coming age,* so that they may take hold of *the life that is truly life"* (verse 19). As we trust God, we are taking hold of the life that is truly life.

Friends, faith is not an easy life. The new covenant does not promise a comfortable life. It offers infinitely more than a million-to-one return on our investments—but it may involve, for this temporary life, some significant sacrifices.

And yet there are great rewards in this life, too. God gives abundant grace in the way he (in his infinite wisdom) knows what is best for us. In our trials and in our blessings, we can trust our lives to him. We can trust all things to him, and when we do it, our lives become a testimony of faith.

God loves us so much that he sent his Son to die for us even when we were sinners and enemies. Since God has already demonstrated such love for us, we can surely trust him to take care of us, for our long-range good, now that we are his children and friends! We do not need to have anxious thoughts about "our" money.

The harvest of praise

Let's go back to 2 Corinthians 9 and notice what Paul tells the Corinthians about their financial and material generosity: "Your generosity will result in *thanksgiving* to God. This service that you perform is not only supplying the needs of God's people but is also *overflowing in many expressions of thanks to God"* (verses 11-12).

Paul is reminding the Corinthians that their generosity is not just a humanitarian effort—it has theological results. People will thank God for it, because they understand that God works through people. God lays it on the hearts of those who have, to give. That is the way his work is done.

"Because of the service by which you have proved yourselves, men will praise God for the obedience that accompanies your confession of the gospel of Christ, and for your generosity in sharing with them and with everyone else" (verse 13). There are several noteworthy points in this verse. First, the Corinthians were able to prove themselves by what they did. They showed in their actions that their faith was genuine. Second, generosity not only causes thanks but also praise to God. It is a form of worship. Third, accepting the gospel of grace also requires a certain obedience, and that obedience includes sharing physical resources.

Giving for the gospel

Paul was writing about generosity in connection with a famine-relief effort. But the same principles apply to the financial collections we have in the church today in support of the gospel and ministry. We are still supporting an important work. It allows workers who preach the gospel to make their living from the gospel, as best as we can distribute the resources.

God still rewards generosity. He still promises treasures in heaven and pleasures forevermore. The gospel still makes demands on our finances. Our attitude toward money still reflects our faith in what God does both now and forever. And people will still thank and praise God for the sacrifices we make today.

We receive benefits from the money we give to the church—the donations help pay for a place to meet, for pastoral support, for publications. But our contributions also help others, to provide literature for others, to provide a place for people to come to know a fellowship of people who love sinners, to pay for the expenses of a body of believers that creates and nourishes a climate in which newcomers can learn about salvation.

These people do not (yet) know you, but they will thank you—or at least thank God and praise him because of your living sacrifices. It is truly a significant work. The most significant thing we can do in this life after accepting Christ as our own Savior is to help the kingdom grow, making a difference as we allow God to work in our lives.

Let me conclude with the words of Paul in verses 14-15: "And in their prayers *for you* their hearts will go out to *you,* because of the surpassing grace God has given you. Thanks be to God for his indescribable gift!"

Joseph Tkach

57. THREE REASONS TO GIVE

God's old covenant people had to give at least 10 percent of their income, plus offerings on other occasions. In contrast, the new covenant does not specify a certain percentage. However, the underlying principle is still valid: Humans ought to honor God by returning some of the blessings he gives them. Here are three reasons: 1) God blesses those who give. 2) God commands his people to give. 3) The church needs money to serve the members.

God could supply all our needs miraculously, if money were the only need we had. Instead, he supplies our needs through the contributions of his people. That's because he is not only working in the church as an organization, he is also working in the hearts of his people. By making the church dependent on the members, he is addressing the most important need we have: that each of us become more closely conformed to the love exemplified by Jesus Christ.

Until Christ returns, the church will always need money. Sometimes the needs will be urgent, sometimes more predictable. There will always be work to do. However, even if the church did not need money, God's people should still give — at the very least, simply because God commands it. And as we know, God's commands are given to us for our own good. Our generosity does not enrich God at all — but it does enrich us (Acts 20:35).

Those who are generous from the heart are becoming more like Christ, putting treasures in heaven for eternity. And God often blesses us in this life, too, for the sacrifices we make in his service (Luke 18:29-30). It takes faith and trust — trust not so much in the people to whom the money is given, but trust in the living Jesus Christ to follow through on the promises he has made. That's where our faith needs to be — and our actions need to be consistent with our faith.

Paul asks for generosity

The apostle Paul encourages us in 2 Corinthians 8. He was encouraging the Corinthian Christians to give an offering. Although this particular offering was not for himself, what he says is relevant to our need to be generous with the church that is teaching us the gospel of salvation.

Paul mentioned the example of the Macedonian churches, who gave even to the point of self-sacrifice (2 Corinthians 8:1-5). Paul is implying that the Corinthians needed to make some sacrifices themselves. But Paul did not command this (verse 8). Instead, he wanted a change of heart — this is the fruit that he wanted most of all. He wanted the Corinthians to give themselves to the Lord first, and then to others. He wanted their gift to be done in love, not grudgingly (verses 5, 8). Paul reminded them that Christ had become poor for their sakes; the implication is that the Corinthians should be willing to make some financial sacrifices of their own.

Of course, the Corinthians could not give more than they had, and they did not have to impoverish themselves to enrich others. But the rich should share with the poor (verses 12-14). Since some of the Corinthian members were wealthy, Paul was confident that they would give generously (verse 14). He asked them to prove their love (verse 24) and to do as well as he had told the Macedonians that they would (2 Corinthians 9:2-5).

Paul again said that the offering should come from the heart (verses 5-7). He reminded them that God rewards generosity (verses 6-11), and that a good example causes people to praise God and puts the gospel in a favorable setting (verses 12-14). These are good reasons to be generous. Christ has made many sacrifices for us, willingly, not grudgingly, so we also ought be to willing to give to benefit others, to share significant portions of our blessings with others.

This collection was for the poor saints in Judea; it was not designed to support Paul. This gave Paul an extra reason to be confident that the Corinthians would be generous. He was not asking for something in addition to ministerial support, but a substitution for it. Paul had not asked for any financial support from Corinth (2 Corinthians 11:7-11; 12:13-16). Instead, he had been supported by Macedonians (11:9).

Paul had a right to financial support

However, Paul had a *right* to be supported by the Corinthians, even though he did not use it (1 Corinthians 9:3-15). This passage in Paul's first letter tells us more about our Christian duty to give financial support to the gospel. Workers should be able to receive benefits of their work (verse 7). Priests, soldiers, vineyard workers, herdsmen, oxen, plowers and threshers all receive pay from their work. Jesus said, "The worker deserves his wages" (Luke 10:7). Paul mentioned these principles again in 1 Timothy 5:17-18. Elders, especially those who preach and teach, should be honored financially as well as with respect.

Jesus also commanded, "Those who preach the gospel should receive their living from the gospel" (1 Corinthians 9:14). This implies that those who believe the gospel must contribute toward the living expenses of those who preach. There is a financial duty, and there is a promised reward.

Jesus had much to say about our use of money. For example: "Sell everything you have and give to the poor, and you will have treasure in heaven. Then come, follow me," said Jesus to a rich man (Luke 18:22). He said the same thing to his disciples (Luke 12:33). He praised a widow who put two coins into the temple treasury, because she gave "all she had" (Luke 21:2). The new covenant makes astonishing demands on us — it demands all that we have. This is fair, since Jesus gave all he had for us, and he paid for our entire lives.

Jesus warns us about the dangers of greed and about the danger of storing up wealth for self without being "rich toward God" (Luke 12:15-21). When we use wealth to help others, however, we gain "treasure in heaven" (verse 33). Generosity helps put our heart in heavenly things instead of earthly, temporary things (verse 34).

Self-examination needed

In summary, Christians have a spiritual need to give, to share their resources and blessings with others. They have a duty to support the preaching of the gospel and give financial support to their leaders.

The old covenant was glorious, but the new has a much greater glory. The old covenant required 10 percent; the new covenant commands us to give as we are able. How shall we respond to the better blessings we are given in the covenant of liberty? Each of us must examine our hearts before the Lamb of God, realizing he gave everything he had for us.

Although the new covenant does not specify a percentage for giving, it does not tell us to give less. Instead, it tells us to give what we can. The new covenant requires more soul-searching, more training for the conscience, more selfless love for others, more faith, more voluntary sacrifice and less compulsion. It tests our values, what we treasure most, and where our hearts really are.

Christians should examine their circumstances and the blessings they have been given in the new covenant — blessings such as the forgiveness of sins, the gift of the Holy Spirit and the promise of eternal life. I believe that when we understand how much has been given to us, we will respond with *greater* generosity to support the church in its collective work of preaching the gospel and for the expenses involved in the congregations and pastors.

The church does have financial needs. Members do have financial responsibilities toward the church. And God does bless the cheerful giver.

Joseph Tkach

58. HOW MUCH IS FREEDOM WORTH?

Jesus once helped a woman who had been held captive 12 years by a health problem that had made her ritually unclean. How important was this problem to her? She had spent all her money seeking a cure (Mark 5:25-29). It was worth everything she had. Women didn't ordinarily touch rabbis, but she reached out and touched Jesus — and Jesus gave her freedom. It cost her nothing, but it was worth <u>everything!</u>

Contrast that for a moment with *the ancient Israelites,* who were in slavery in Egypt. They wanted freedom, too, and they could not buy their way out. They suffered and groaned, and God heard their cry. He delivered them with amazing miracles. It cost them nothing, but how much was it worth to them? Not much, it seems. Although God set them free, they preferred a golden calf. They preferred the unholy fire, murmuring and self-centeredness. They grumbled about the person God was using to lead them. They grumbled about God, their food, and life itself.

Let's go back to the New Testament, where Christ again sets people free — free from spiritual bondage of sin and death (Hebrews 2:14-15). How much did it cost? It was incredibly expensive. It cost God the Son his life, and all of the suffering he endured that we might have eternal life. The benefits of his sacrifice are <u>given</u> to us.

Freedom is given to us without charge, because we are unable to pay. How much is it worth to us? *Our entire lives,* of course. "He died for all, that those who live should no longer live for themselves but for him" (2 Corinthians 5:15). We are to give our entire lives to him in service, as living sacrifices (Romans 12:1).

In the church of God, <u>people are being set free!</u> Free from the fear of "not making it" into the kingdom of God. Free from rules that God does not require us to keep. Free from rules that tempt us to condemn other Christians. Each of us may examine our own hearts to see how much we value this freedom.

It is thrilling to see that many have responded with enthusiastic *worship and support.* But it is sad when it seems that some people are afraid of the wilderness and look for the comforts of Egypt. It is just as sad when some try to enter the promised land on their own, or sit in the desert by themselves.

Christ has given us freedom, and he used humans to bring that about, and people respond to that in different ways. Some rejoice, and some do not. I suppose that there will always be reasons to complain about the imperfections of leaders, the food or the music. But some are *quietly working* to build the kingdom of God.

The old covenant had many obligations. It specified a certain amount of time, a certain amount of money, numerous rules about behavior, and many sacrifices for worship. Those requirements teach us something about God and the relationship we have with him.

As we all know, God no longer requires animal sacrifices — but that does not mean that he no longer requires us to make <u>any</u> sacrifices. The demands are now *more profound than ever*. God no longer requires all the same rules of behavior — but he still gives many commands regarding our behavior, and more importantly, about our *hearts*.

Of course, God no longer has the same rules about money — now, his exhortations are more profound than ever. Do we resent God's claim on "our" money? Some do. Some say that no one is good enough to be given God's money. In a way, that is true, but then that would mean that no one is good enough to keep God's money, either. If we as Christians *keep* all our money, we are not responding to <u>freedom</u> the way the New Testament describes we should.

And what about time? God no longer specifies exactly when people must set aside time for him, but we all need to spend time with the Lord.

God brought the Israelites out of Egypt so that they could serve him. Jesus gives us freedom so that we can serve him. The freedom comes with responsibility.

How much is freedom worth to us?

Thousands of people are rejoicing in the freedom Jesus is bringing to people through the gospel message. You probably know many of them. And yet you probably know quite a few people who still have not accepted that freedom. Please do not abandon them in their time of need. Help us continue to reach out, despite our imperfections, with the message of freedom in Jesus Christ our Lord and Savior.

You may have seen specific people profoundly transformed by God's grace. Perhaps you have experienced sessions in which people begin to grasp the depth and width and height of God's love for them. This experience is one of our greatest joys.

If you cannot see the joy of burdens being lifted, if you cannot see the peace of anxieties released, be assured that freedom is indeed ringing around the world. Ask God to help you see it. Ask him to bless the results of your work and ours. Pray for us so that our priorities might be drawn yet closer to the heart of God. Pray for your brothers and sisters who need to grow in the grace and knowledge of Jesus Christ.

Joseph Tkach

59. STEWARDSHIP:
OUR LIVES ARE NOT OUR OWN

The New Testament, although emphasizing grace, has hundreds of commands. These are not requirements for salvation, but rather describe the *results* of salvation—results of God's grace and his Spirit working within us. The new covenant makes comprehensive demands on us—not just one day a week, but an eternal lifetime. Not just 10 percent, but everything we own. Not just outward conduct, but our hearts and minds.

The apostle Paul explained it like this: "Do you not know that your body is a temple of the Holy Spirit, who is in you, whom you have received from God? You are not your own; you were bought at a price. Therefore honor God with your body" (1 Corinthians 6:19-20).

Here we have a statement of our obligations to God in the new covenant. That price is the crucifixion of Jesus Christ. He is our Redeemer—he has bought us.

In ancient times, this terminology was used in the slave market, where one person could buy another. If a person could not pay a debt, he or she could be sold into slavery to pay the debt. But if a friend or relative could pay the debt, that person could act as a redeemer, to buy the slave back.

Spiritually, this is what Jesus did for us. We were in debt and could not pay our way out. We were in slavery to sin. So Jesus paid our debt, purchased us with his blood (Acts 20:28), so we should no longer be slaves of sin, but be slaves of righteousness (Romans 6:6-18).

Paul says that Christians are to glorify God in everything they do. "Whether you eat or drink or whatever you do, do it all for the glory of God" (1 Corinthians 10:31). This is a comprehensive command. No matter what we do, we are to bring glory and honor to God.

Paul is talking here about eating meats offered in sacrifice to idols. In verse 28, Paul says that "if anyone says to you, 'This has been offered in sacrifice,' then do not eat it, both for the sake of the man who told you and for conscience' sake." He explains: "The other man's conscience, I mean, not yours. For why should my freedom be judged by another's conscience?" (verse 29).

Voluntary limitations

Paul implies that my freedom should not be judged by someone else. But, nevertheless, it is voluntarily limited by someone else. I modify my behavior because of what the other person believes, in this case, about meat sacrificed to idols.

This exact situation may not present itself today, but it illustrates what Paul means when he says all our activities are to be done for God's glory and honor. We serve him by what we do in front of our neighbor. Our decisions about eating and drinking can serve to glorify God in our bodies—but those decisions are shaped in part by the circumstances we are in.

The new covenant does not just give us a list of dos and don'ts—it gives us the responsibility of thinking through a situation to see what brings glory to God, including how we might need to limit our behavior based on the conscience of others.

The gospel does not let us do anything we want. No—far from it. The new covenant limits what we can do not only in our private lives, but even more so in public. The gospel gives us a new perspective toward God and neighbor, a perspective that presses us to do whatever brings honor and glory to God.

Paul says: "I try to please everybody in every way." Does this mean that Paul was a two-faced hypocrite? No, it means he was living out the reality of the new covenant. Notice what he said in chapter 9: "Though I am free and belong to no man, I make myself a slave to everyone, to win as many as possible..... I do all this for the sake of the gospel, that I may share in its blessings" (verses 19, 23).

This is the kind of freedom we have in Christ. We are not our own; we no longer just live as we please. We are slaves of Christ, and to serve him, we make ourselves slaves of others.

Property that belongs to Christ

Our lives are not our own. Our time is not our own. Our minds and hearts are not our own. Our relationships are not our own. Our skills and abilities are not our own. They all belong to Jesus Christ. And yet we still must decide how to use our lives, our time, relationships, skills and abilities.

We have the new covenant gift of managing someone else's property. The biblical term for a person who does this is steward.

In the parable of the faithful and wise steward, we see this concept. "Who then is the faithful and wise manager, whom the master puts in charge of his servants to give them their food allowance at the proper time? It will be good for that servant whom the master finds doing so when he returns. I tell you the truth, he will put him in charge of all his possessions.

"But suppose the servant says to himself, 'My master is taking a long time in coming,' and he then begins to beat the menservants and maidservants and to eat and drink and get drunk. The master of that servant will come on a day when he does not expect him and at an hour he is not aware of. He will cut him to pieces and assign him a place with the unbelievers.

"That servant who knows his master's will and does not get ready or does not do what his master wants will be beaten with many blows. But the one who does not know and does things deserving punishment will be beaten with few blows. From everyone who has been given much, much will be demanded; and from the one who has been entrusted with much, much more will be asked" (Luke 12:42-48).

Everything we have is to be used in the Lord's work. That applies to physical property such as our bodies and homes. It also applies to intangible things such as emotions, relationships and spiritual gifts. Everything we have is the Lord's. Everything we have should be used for his honor and glory.

Michael Morrison

60. WHY BE CONCERNED ABOUT MISSION?

In *Clean Jokes and Inspirational Stories*, Rod Dykstra tells about a successful young executive who was driving through a neighborhood in his new Jaguar. Suddenly a brick smashed into the side of his car. He slammed on his brakes and jumped out to confront a guilty-looking small boy standing nearby.

"Who are you and what is going on here?" yelled the executive. "This is a new car and what you just did is gonna cost you a lot of money. Why did you throw that brick?"

The boy was apologetic and said, "Please mister, I am sorry. I didn't know what else to do. I threw the brick because no one else would stop. With tears streaming down his face, he pointed to a person lying on the ground by the parked car. "It's my brother," he said, "and he rolled off the curb and fell out of his wheelchair and I can't lift him up. He is hurt and is too heavy for me. Would you please help me get him back into his wheelchair?"

Now moved beyond words, the driver lifted the handicapped boy back into the wheelchair. He took out his handkerchief and dabbed gently at the fresh scrapes and cuts. A quick look told him that everything was going to be okay. He never did get the dent in his car repaired. He left it there to remind himself that he should not journey through life without helping others.

In a recent round of conferences, the theme was our participation in mission with Jesus. I was asked a few times, why are we so concerned about mission? If God has already reconciled all people to himself in and through Jesus Christ (2 Corinthians 5:17-19), why are we so concerned with "reaching" them? These questions imply that the mission of reaching people with the gospel is merely one option on a menu that God has given to the church. But mission is not an option for us, and if we think it is, we need to reorient our thinking. That was the over-arching theme of the conferences.

In his presentations, Gary Deddo reminded us that we first must ask the question, *who is God?* The Bible answers that the one God exists as a triune communion of love. In his being (nature) he is love (1 John 4:8), and this explains everything that he does and how he does it. In love, God created the cosmos as a time and place in which to share his triune love and life with his creation. Because his love never ceases or diminishes, he became Redeemer to rescue his creation from its inability to live in communion with him. Before the beginning of time and space, as we experience them, God our Creator and Redeemer has been "on mission." God the Father sent his Son Jesus to accomplish that mission, and Jesus trained others, who in turn trained others. We are part of a long line of those who are called to receive this training.

This is how we should see ourselves. Jesus sends the Holy Spirit to call, form and equip the church to share in his ongoing ministry, which is fulfilling the Father's mission to the world. The church exists because of, and for, God's mission. God has not given us a choice of spiritual "busy work" just to keep us occupied. We are called by God to participate as partners and co-workers in his mission, and that includes sharing the gospel and "the ministry of reconciliation." The Christian life is not a spectator sport. We are following Jesus as he continues by the Holy Spirit to seek true worshipers of his Father.

In her presentations, Cathy Deddo spoke about understanding our participation in God's mission. Since the Ascension and Pentecost, what God is doing in the world in and through the church has principally to do with discipleship—becoming followers of Jesus in daily communion with him. This aspect of God's mission is not so much about "getting people saved," because God has accomplished that already. Rather, the mission is about illumination, education and application, all of which lead to repentance and living trust in our living Lord. Jesus is working in people's lives in all three of these areas through the Holy Spirit.

The church is called to bear witness to Jesus (Acts 1:8) by proclaiming who he is and what he has done for us, sharing as we do in his ongoing acts of healing, mercy and forgiveness. This is why we proclaim the stunning truth of the gospel, and invite others to join us as disciples who are being transformed into his likeness day by day. Many of our members around the world are already doing this.

Do you see the difference between choosing what kinds of things to do as ministry, and participating in the already ongoing ministry of Jesus—letting him choose the ministry? It requires a shift in our thinking, which leads to reordering our priorities. It is not our job to make something happen that is *not* happening. Rather, we are called to discern where and how to "get with the program" that Jesus by the Holy Spirit is actively working out and equipping us to share in. We get to work with God as he directs and enables us. Jesus' feeding of the 5000 with the disciples' few loaves and fish is a great example of how Jesus gets us involved in what he's doing, using what we have.

Participating in mission with Jesus involves being in the world, even though we are also cautioned to be not of it. We cannot remain aloof from the world's problems, and we must be responsive even when the world "heaves a brick at us" to gain our attention. Karl Barth once pointed out, the church cannot say "yes" to the world, if it cannot also say "no." Jesus was a friend of sinners, yet without sin of his own. Today, Jesus is doing this ministry principally through his human presence in the world, in and through his body, the church. We are called to stand with Jesus in solidarity with the world, sharing its plight, proclaiming and demonstrating to our fellow human beings our one and sure hope.

Why should the church be concerned about mission? The answer is simply this: mission is what we are for. So let us be among our Lord's devoted disciples—those who not only hear his voice, but actively join with him as he, in the power of the Holy Spirit, helps people live into the reconciliation with God that forever is theirs in and with him.

I am delighted that most of us do not need a brick thrown at us to awaken us to what we can be doing with Jesus. It is with great thanks that I can say, surely the Spirit of the Lord is graciously and vitally at work among us!

Joseph Tkach

61. LOOKING FORWARD

I think often about what lies ahead, and how our denomination can best prepare to continue to serve God and his people after my time is done and my contribution has been made. I know that many of you, particularly if you are an older member in an aging congregation, are thinking about this too.

I believe that GCI has a future! I don't know all the details, but I see encouraging signs. We are a worldwide church. Some of our congregations are growing rapidly — bursting with youth and energy. In others, growth is harder to come by, but members are growing in love and service. In many congregations, youth are actively and creatively serving. Many are reaching out in mission at home and around the world. Through these activities, grounded in our growing understanding of Trinitarian theology, I believe God is showing us how we are to take the gospel to the world of the 21st century in compelling and powerful ways.

Looking back, especially over the last 15 years during which I have been privileged to serve as GCI's president and pastor general, I realize that I cannot claim credit for what has happened. I feel sometimes that I have been swept along by events that I did not plan, and could not have anticipated. Changing technology has meant we do our work in a totally different way than even ten years ago. Many of the people who report to me hardly ever visit our home office, yet we seem to be in closer contact than ever before.

Our church has grown in parts of the world where we had done nothing to lay the groundwork. We have welcomed dozens of new congregations in the African nation of Mozambique. We had not made a specific effort to reach them—they just "showed up on our doorstep." Our developing understanding of Trinitarian theology has brought us into contact with many leaders and theologians outside of our denomination. Many have become close friends. The world of Christianity is going through some important changes. I pray that we will play a useful role in this exciting journey of discovery.

There are many reasons to be encouraged. Looking back, I can see that the Holy Spirit has been leading us. I am thankful to have been a part of it and look forward to where God will lead us in the years ahead. We should make plans for this journey, though experience tells us that we must be ready for the unexpected. How do we stay ready? Like members of a fire department, we must have in place good equipment, and we must be trained — ready to do what needs to be done. As Paul wrote to Timothy, we must be ready "in season and out of season."

God has much for us to do in his service. I am thankful to have a part along with all of you. Let's continue to work together, submitting in faith to God as we join with Jesus in what he will be doing through the Holy Spirit to take the good news of salvation to a world that desperately needs it.

Joseph Tkach

62. OUR MISSION AND VISION

I am often asked to cast a vision for our denomination's future in the way a CEO might cast a vision for a business. Though, for practical reasons, churches must embrace certain business practices, the biblical model for leading the church is that of a shepherd or farmer rather than a business executive. This does not mean that we are called to sit back and do nothing. However, it explains why my approach is not to *cast a vision* but to *gather a vision*. Let me explain.

In the fifth chapter of Romans, Paul wrote:

> We continue to shout our praise even when we're hemmed in with troubles, because we know how troubles can develop passionate patience in us, and how that patience in turn forges the tempered steel of virtue, keeping us alert for whatever God will do next. In alert expectancy such as this, we're never left feeling shortchanged. Quite the contrary—we can't round up enough containers to hold everything God generously pours into our lives through the Holy Spirit! (Romans 5:3-5, *The Message*)

This passage describes the sense of hope and expectancy that I feel as I receive reports concerning what our congregations around the world are experiencing in Christ's service. We have moved from being a denomination where our congregations existed to support a work that emanated from a central headquarters, to a network of congregations that are working under the overall umbrella of the denomination. Now, each congregation seizes opportunities that God presents to them locally to advance the overall work of the church globally.

I have the privilege of telling the stories of many of these congregations in my presentation at the regional conferences. Like Paul, who couldn't "round up enough containers" to hold everything, I do not have enough time to tell the stories about all the marvelous things the Holy Spirit is doing through our congregations. From these reports, I gather a picture of what God is doing with and through us. That collage, rather than grandiose ideas I might come up with, is what frames my vision for our future as a denomination.

With that in mind, let me share with you some thoughts concerning our mission and vision.

What is our mission?

Grace Communion International is a people called together by God to share in the ministry that Jesus is doing through the Holy Spirit in our world. We are a communion of churches and denominational ministries with a shared mission, which is taking us toward the realization of a shared vision.

We are called to the same mission as all other followers of Jesus—it's often called The Great Commission. There are a number of ways to summarize this mission. We do so in our denominational motto: ***Living and Sharing the Gospel.*** This motto, which appears in our denominational logo, is not just a catchy slogan. It encapsulates our sense of calling to lock arms, sharing together in what Jesus is doing in our world, through the Holy Spirit, to fulfill the Father's mission. We can expand this into a more complete mission statement: *Grace Communion International is committed to living and sharing the good news of what God has done through Jesus Christ.*

We pursue this mission by:

- Building healthy, Christ-centered congregations that are sanctuaries of worship, friendship and nurturing pastoral care.
- Providing sound biblical teaching through our congregations, media and personal outreach in ways that are relevant and meaningful to people of diverse backgrounds and ages.
- Equipping people for Christian service so that the gospel can be known, understood and experienced.
- Sharing in the work of the gospel with the broader Christian community, acknowledging that we can learn from one another and that Christ's love goes beyond denominational boundaries.
- Expressing the love of God to all through the work of the Holy Spirit in our lives.

The result of this mission-focused work is lives transformed by the gospel, one person at a time. This is actually Jesus' mission—and we are called to share in it with him. Through eyes of faith, we are able to see the transforming presence and activity of God that others are not yet seeing. It is not about us "taking God to people," but rather helping people see the God who already is sharing his life and love with them. It's not about helping people "find" Jesus, but of showing them the creative, life-giving Savior who, through the Holy Spirit, is already present and at work in their lives.

What is our vision?

Our vision is a faith- and hope-filled glimpse of what GCI will continue to become as we pursue our mission to live and share the gospel. We summarize our collective vision this way: ***All kinds of churches for all kinds*** *of people in all kinds of places.*

Expanding it, we can say: *Grace Communion International exists to help each congregation of Grace Communion International attain its God-given potential.* Why this emphasis on local congregations? Because it is my belief that God's primary instrument for realizing our collective vision is healthy local churches—here in the U.S. and around the world. As I look ahead, I see us becoming more and more a growing, loving community of congregations that are dynamically living out God's mission in a broken world, and that excites me!

Our core identity (who we are) is founded on our communion with the Father and Jesus, through the power of the Holy Spirit. Who we are drives what we do—our passionate participation in what God is doing in the world. In this way, our mission gives shape to our vision.

Joseph Tkach

63. WELCOMING VISITORS

A strong characteristic of our denomination is that we like each other and enjoy being together. We take our work together seriously, but that does not mean we should not have fun. God created us to be relational beings, and relating to others has always been and still is at the heart of Grace Communion International. Our vision statement is "all kinds of churches for all kinds of people in all kinds of places." I pray that all our congregations reflect that vision.

Many studies have sought to pinpoint what leads visitors to return to a church. A key factor is the friendliness of the people. This is reflected in the experience of a man who visited 18 churches on successive Sundays, seeking to learn what these churches were really like. Here is his report:

> I sat near the front. After the service, I walked slowly to the rear, then returned to the front and went back to the foyer using another aisle. I smiled and was neatly dressed. I asked one person to direct me to a specific place: a fellowship hall, pastor's study, etc. I remained for coffee, if served. I used a scale to rate the reception I received. I awarded points on the following basis:
>
> - 10 for a smile from a worshiper
> - 10 for a greeting from someone sitting nearby
> - 100 for an exchange of names
> - 200 for an invitation to have coffee
> - 200 for an invitation to return
> - 1000 for an introduction to another worshiper
> - 2000 for an invitation to meet the pastor

On this scale, eleven of the eighteen churches earned fewer than 100 points. Five actually received less than 20.

Though all of these churches likely had uplifting music and biblically sound, inspiring preaching, most lacked ways to show visitors that people cared that they were there. As a result, it is unlikely that visitors will return. In contrast, churches that openly reflect the relational aspect of God's nature give visitors great encouragement to return. You could sum it up by saying that people are looking for a place to belong, not just a group with shared beliefs.

Several years ago, I read a story told by a Baptist pastor whose name I cannot recall. It was the story of a surgeon who specializes in reattaching fingers. When he entered the operating room, he knew he faced many hours of squinting into a microscope, sorting out and stitching together the snarl of nerves, tendons and blood vessels—many finer than a human hair. A single mistake and the patient could permanently lose movement or sensation.

On one occasion, the surgeon received an emergency call at three in the morning. He was not looking forward to undertaking an intricate procedure at that early hour. To help him focus, he decided to dedicate that surgery to his father, who had recently died. For the next several hours, he imagined his father standing beside him, encouraging him with a hand on his shoulder.

This technique worked so well that he began dedicating all his surgeries to other people he knew. Then one day he realized that as a Christian, he should offer his life to God in the same way. All the routine things of his day—answering phone calls, dealing with staff, seeing patients, scheduling surgeries—remained the same, but somehow they were different. The task of living a life for God now began to overshadow his days, and he soon began to treat others with more respect and care.

We may not be surgeons, but God calls us to co-minister with Jesus, who is the ultimate surgeon—repairing broken lives. Wouldn't it be marvelous if we could dedicate each day to the Lord, imagining him standing beside us with a hand on our shoulders, watching us, guiding us, counseling us and walking with us? The truth is that it is not just a product of our imagination. God is omnipresent and by his Spirit is personally with us. He has called us to co-minister with him in both simple and profound ways, from offering a smile to performing neurosurgery.

When we live with this perspective, we discover that even the ordinary and routine things in our lives will become saturated with a sense of his holy presence with us. Some of us are naturally more outgoing than others, but never underestimate the importance of showing yourself friendly. When new people visit our congregations, they are probably more nervous about you than you are about them. They don't know what to expect, and when they find that they are welcome and accepted, it is a powerful incentive to return.

Joseph Tkach

64. CHURCH: WHAT'S ON THE MENU?

Even though I am what some would consider a professional nomad, I realized after a recent trip overseas that I needed to plant a few roots somewhere. Anywhere.

When I returned home, I got involved in some local things. I joined the Knitter's Guild and a camera club, plus I started going to a church down the road.

At my first knitting meeting, I nearly poked a bamboo needle in my eye when the president of the club barked at me for "casting on" the wrong way. She used terminology the more skilled grandmas in the room understood, but I was clueless. The ad in the paper said they welcomed knitters with no experience!

I had a similar experience at the camera club. I thought I was in the wrong room; the presenter seemed to be speaking Greek with all his talk about the latest software patch for some photo program I'd never heard of. The camera club's website hailed people of all skill levels, but I felt lost.

I hoped I would fare better when I stepped into church.

It was a non-presumptuous small inner-city church, with simple folding chairs and a food bank. People showed up in jeans and t-shirts. The sign on their door said: "a teaching church." I was drawn to its simplicity.

At my first service, the pastor dove right into a technical, Greek-word-filled background of a passage in Matthew. Eventually I figured out that he had been taking the church through the whole book verse by verse, but he lost me, a newcomer, somewhere in Jerusalem.

Now mind you, I have read that same passage multiple times. And yet, I had no idea what the pastor was driving at. Hoping it was a "once off," I went back to this church several times, but it was always the same—more of an advanced history lesson than a sermon.

It finally dawned on me why all those people in jeans and t-shirts kept coming. It wasn't because the sermons were turning their hearts to Christ. It was because in order to take food from the food bank, they were required to attend the service. The only reason they were coming back was to get free food.

While I applaud the local church's food bank efforts, I wish the messages had had as much relevance for the people as the groceries did.

Sometimes I believe churches are working so hard to get more people in their door that they miss the simplicity of the gospel. We believe if only our ministers were more casual, or if we offered donuts and gourmet coffee before *and* after church, we could keep the numbers high. If only our children's program could have a trendy name and our teens could do an entire service on their own, then we will have "arrived" as a church.

Maybe if the pastor uses a wireless microphone and walks the aisle, or if we stop using songbooks and use projectors, or if we finally get a band instead of playing CDs for worship music, or if people could wear jeans to church, and the guys can lose their ties, or if we do the reverse of any of the above, we will draw in a bigger crowd.

I don't think it works like that. Gimmicks come and go, but the message has never changed. Sermons need to give people the good news. Save the technical stuff for studies or classes at other times. It's the good news that touches hearts and changes lives.

I was excited to see my favorite brand of rice cakes at the church's food bank, but I left feeling hungry for much more than free food.

Brenda Steffen

65. A CONVERSATION ON A PLANE FLIGHT

I spend a lot of time in the air and meet a wide range of people. I met Mat on a recent flight. I'd been settled in my usual aisle seat for a few minutes when Mat showed up at the last minute wearing a large overcoat with a backpack strapped over his shoulder. He reached across me and began unpacking various picnic supplies into his seat. He then scooted into his window seat beside me. As soon as he sat down, he turned to me and said he needed to put his backpack in the overhead. Mat returned to his seat, removed his coat and then decided to place his coat in the overhead. Mat sat down for the third time and turned to me and said he had to go to the restroom.

I chuckled and said, "You're like a big kid." He laughed, and I heard other chuckles and noticed the passengers around us had been amused by the continual up and down activity.

When Mat returned, he asked what kind of work I do, and I shared my story. He then told me that he had just started his career in accounting and was traveling to visit a friend in New York City. The flight took off, and once we climbed to 10,000 feet I opened my laptop and began typing. Mat ate his picnic—summoning the flight attendant at least six times so he could enjoy three cups of hot tea.

Then, when Mat handed the remains of his picnic to the flight attendant, something from his trash left a small stream across the keyboard of my laptop. Mat buried his head in his hands and said, "I am the worst passenger ever." I simply took a napkin and performed damage control on the keyboard and then shut down the laptop so we could talk.

Mat had been raised Catholic and stopped going to church because of the large amounts of money being spent (an accountant would notice such things). I asked him about his view of God and he said he hadn't spent much time thinking about God. We talked about the story of the Prodigal Son and what the heart of the Father is like. I showed him that coming to understand who God is and then who he is in relationship to God are the two big questions in life. I encouraged him to search for a church that focused on building relationship with God and then I gave him was a copy of C. Baxter Kruger's *The Parable of the Dancing God.*

This unique meeting with Mat reminded me of what Peter says in his first letter: "You must worship Christ as Lord of your life. And if someone asks about your Christian hope, always be ready to explain it. But do this in a gentle and respectful way" (1 Peter 3:15-16a, New Living Translation).

I find this instruction from the bold and brash disciple (the one who stepped out of the boat, who rebuffed Jesus when he spoke of his impending death and who pushed John aside to run into the empty tomb) quite interesting. Peter says we must have Jesus as Lord of our lives first and then be prepared to share the good news about Jesus to those who ask. The explanation should be done in a caring and respectful way. What a great guideline for sharing the gospel!

My exchange with Mat was one of those rare encounters when a person asked me to converse about Jesus and his church. I could only tell Mat about the Jesus I know and worship. It wasn't all the seminary training that prepared me to be able to explain the good news about Jesus, but my actual personal relationship and journey with Jesus that allowed me to speak of his redemptive and inclusive love.

I don't necessarily think my comment about Mat being a big kid endeared me to him, but it was honest, and it fit the occasion. Perhaps the Spirit providing me with patience when liquid spilled on my laptop keyboard set the stage for Mat to hear about the hope found in Jesus. I don't try to over-analyze my "plane encounters" like this one. Instead, I celebrate them and pray for more.

Greg Williams

66. EVANGELISM
THROUGH THE LOCAL CHURCH

Evangelism Through the Local Church
by Michael Green
Reviewed by J. Michael Feazell

A few years ago Dr. Billy Graham visited England, and part of the year of preparation was a study entitled "Is Your Church Worth Joining?" It was a tough question, but a very proper one, because many churches, frankly, are not worth joining. "And lots of people must share that view. The shrinking figures for church attendance in much of Western Europe bear testimony to the fact" (page 83).

Shrinking attendance is one of the major questions facing most churches in the U.S. and Canada. Every church has to face the question: Why should someone want to become a member of our congregation?

As we evaluate the question, Michael Green says, our focus has to return to the gospel itself, to Christ himself, and to taking the positive spiritual steps necessary to conform our local fellowship to the image of Christ. Such a process cannot be accomplished by simply continuing down the old, familiar paths. New spiritual vitality must be introduced into the fabric of the church itself if it is to become a fellowship in which new believers can be meaningfully nurtured in the faith and prepared for entering kingdom work themselves.

For most churches, this is a challenge of crisis proportions. Michael Green's work may be one of the most practical guides available to help pastors and concerned members find a meaningful path toward becoming the kind of congregation that actually attracts new believing members.

Evangelism Through the Local Church provides more than 500 pages of interesting, inspiring and immediately practical tools for developing a church-wide self-analysis and casting a vision of what needs to be done. It is no longer in print, but used copies are widely available through online book stores.

Michael Green, *Evangelism Through the Local Church*, Nashville: Thomas Nelson, 1992.

67. THE CHURCH'S LEAKY BASEMENT

If water is coming in through your ceiling, you can put a bucket under the leak, then climb up and patch the roof. Things get more complicated if the leak is in the basement. First, you might not notice it right away. Second, basement leaks are not easily fixed. Analysts tell us that Christian churches in the Western world are leaking badly. Attendance is falling, older members are dying and younger ones are deserting traditional worship in droves. Conservative churches are facing increasing pressure to adjust their policies on once-deplored practices such as couples living together, abortion and same-sex marriages. The roof is leaking, and it is all some churches can do to limit the damage while desperately trying to plug the leaks.

Not surprisingly then, they have not focused on the rising damp in the basement. But seeping in through seams and bubbling up through cracks, new ideas are beginning to make their presence felt. They are ideas that might actually pose a greater challenge to traditional belief than any of the more attention-grabbing problems that currently dominate the agenda. It might be a good idea to take a look down there and see what is happening.

Have we become more concerned with sin than salvation? It would not be the first time in the 2000-year-old history of Christianity that the church has needed to realign its message with the true intent of the gospel.

A recent study showed that the younger generation, on whom the future depends, increasingly holds traditional Christianity in contempt.[1] Many 16-to 29-year-olds use words such as "hypocritical," "insensitive" and "judgmental" to describe the church. And don't be misled by the apparent interest of the younger generation while they are in their teens. As youthful idealism gives way to the realities of adulthood, they become disillusioned. With leadership firmly in the hands of an older generation, who are more interested in maintaining the status quo, the church seems out of touch. So as many as eight out of ten young adults abandon it. Some even become hostile.

Still, although they might abandon formal, institutionalized religion, these young adults do not necessarily lose their interest in Jesus. They are attracted to his message of concern for others, living unselfishly and treating all people with mercy and respect. In him, they see a message that goes to the heart of their world's problems. Jesus is relevant. The church is not. So they would rather be identified as a "follower of Christ" rather than a "Christian." Many also describe themselves as "Generic Christian" rather than identify with a particular denomination.

Losing the plot?

A growing number of writers, preachers and theologians across the whole spectrum of Christianity are telling us we have confused the physical accoutrements of the middle-class dream with spiritual success. They are urging the church to reconsider its priorities if its witness is to be credible. Instead of obsessing over questions that most people do not worry about, they are urging churches to show leadership and a united front in confronting poverty, injustice and oppression and a respect for the physical creation. This, they say, is the appropriate way to present the gospel in the 21st century.

Some of these ideas might sound threatening to conventional believers, but wouldn't we be wise to at least give them some thoughtful consideration? They might well be, as the controversial emergent church leader Brian McLaren has suggested, the "words to a tune that you have been hearing for some time."

A leaky basement is much harder to fix than a leaky roof. You can't just plug the cracks from the inside. Hydrostatic pressure is relentless. The Holy Spirit is even more relentless, and Jesus said the Spirit would lead us into all truth.

Is the Spirit leading the younger generation to tell us something about our direction and priorities? Have we become more concerned with sin than salvation? It would not be the first time in the 2000-year-old history of Christianity that the church has needed to realign its message with the true intent of the gospel.

[1] David Kinnaman and Gabe Lyons, *Unchristian: What a New Generation Really Thinks About Christianity* (Baker Books, 2007).

John Halford

68. GETTING IT BACK TO FRONT

Although I was born in England, I have lived quite contentedly in the USA for many years. But there is something about many Americans' backyards that leave me feeling uncomfortable. They don't have fences.

"Good fences make good neighbors," as the saying goes. But I notice that many American neighbors seem to get along without them. Both my daughters live in Ohio, in beautiful homes on big lots in nice neighborhoods. Out back is an expanse of well-kept lawn that blends seamlessly with the next-door properties. This has its advantages. Children can run free, and there are no awkward "can we have our ball back?" confrontations. But I always feel a bit exposed. I like my backyard to be clearly demarcated with a good solid fence or a hedge, or ideally both. That's how they do it across the pond.

Front yards in America often tell the same story. No walls or fences — just an unbroken stretch of neat lawns with a couple of trees and some individualistic landscaping here and there for variety. I do think that's better. In Britain we like to fence off our front yards too — no matter how small they are. Even if it is just a patch of lawn the size of a small rug, surrounded by narrow flower beds, we will still often add a chest-high wall or hedge and a barred gate to seal it off from the outside world. The Englishman's home is his castle, and any self-respecting castle has to have walls.

Castles maybe — but churches? Churches, like British front and backyards, seem to like to separate themselves with walls. Congregations of different denominations in the same town, or even the same street, often have nothing to do with each other. Often the biggest hurdle to joint projects is just getting the local pastors and priests to sit at the same table, let alone darken each other's doors.

There are exceptions. I belong to our local Ministerial Association, along with ministers from Baptist, Lutheran, Presbyterian, Methodist and Pentecostal congregations. We all get along pretty well, but we do have to respect each other's space.

Perhaps that is the key. Denominations are like families, and they have developed their own ways of doing things. One Christian's tradition may be another's "heresy." I don't just mean major doctrinal and theological differences. It is often minor sociological variations that keep churches apart; things like speaking in tongues, clapping during the hymns or how they "do" baptism and communion.

Those differences need to be respected. Eager evangelists urge Christians to "come out of our comfort zones." And so we should, but not all the time. A church is to some extent a refuge (it is, after all, called a sanctuary), and if those who come there are made to feel continually uncomfortable, they will go somewhere else. Anglicans, Methodists, Catholics, Baptists, Pentecostals and other Christian churches are different, and they need places to be themselves. They need, so to speak, *British-style* backyards.

But what about out front? Here is where we could learn something from our American townscapes. The open lawns and lack of fussy dividing fences turn what would otherwise be a row of houses into an inviting neighborhood.

Why do Christians, who essentially believe the same things and face a common challenge, find it so hard to work together? Why should what others do to worship God pose a threat? Certainly Jesus prayed that the church be "one." But that did not necessarily mean "one size fits all." To work together with other Christians need not mean abandoning the traditions that make *your* church your spiritual home.

So enjoy your spiritual backyard. But surely at this time when the whole idea of Christianity is under threat, we need to blend our front yards into a more inviting neighborhood. Yes, even if those who visit do not end up knocking on *our* door. Is it not time that more of us knocked down some of those silly walls, and gave the hedge a severe pruning? We owe the world a better view of our beautiful Christian neighborhood. Is what those folks across the street do really so awful that you can't work with them?

John Halford

69. WHO STOLE MY CHURCH?

Who Stole My Church? What to Do When the Church You Love Enters the 21st Century
by Gordon MacDonald
Reviewed by Barbara Dahlgren

Do you love your church, but can't stand the new hymns? Do you appreciate your fellow Christians but wish they would dress a bit more formally for services? Do you look forward to the future but find yourself sometimes missing the "old days"? Then this is the book for you.

Gordon MacDonald tackles the difficult topic of churches struggling with change. He wisely uses a fiction genre to make a sensitive subject more readable. Yet, this does not diminish the interesting facts you learn about how churches have made changes through the centuries to remain relevant.

MacDonald presents himself as the pastor of a fictional church in New England. Some of the older members are having difficulty adjusting to newer ways of doing things, such as using contemporary music instead of traditional hymns, using band or CD accompaniment instead of piano or organ, relaxed dress codes, and so on. In frustration, one member asks, "Who stole my church?"

In a bit of desperation, Pastor MacDonald decides to have a weekly meeting of 20 older-generational church members so they can discuss their irritants and concerns. At the meetings these members examine what is happening in their church, compare it to church history, and try not to throw their hands up and say, "What's the use?"

Who Stole My Church is not plot driven, and seems more like a parable than a novel. It doesn't really offer solutions for the problems derived from change, but much can be gleaned from the dialogue form used in these weekly meetings. Having been a pastor for over 40 years, MacDonald offers great insight into local church dynamics. At times I felt as though he had been eavesdropping at some of our leadership meetings.

Toward the end of the book, some of the younger-generational congregants get involved. The result is that both generations end up understanding the other just a little better — not by justifying their feelings but by exploring why they lean toward different styles of worship, don't like each other's music, or see evangelism and discipleship from different perspectives. At the end, not everyone in MacDonald's core group embraces change. Some walk away. Some continue to struggle. Some learn to cope.

Most have a deeper understanding of what church is all about.

I highly recommend *Who Stole My Church*. It is an easy, insightful, and informative read. Personally, I found a certain comfort from realizing I am not the only one trying to adapt, and that churches through the ages have had to continually reinvent the way they "do church" to keep up with changing times. *Who Stole My Church* can also be used as a small-group tool for open dialogue, since there are points to ponder about each chapter at the back the book.

Gordon MacDonald, *Who Stole My Church?: What to Do When the Church You Love Enters the 21st Century,* Thomas Nelson, 272 pages, $21.99.

70. GRANDMA'S OLD CHURCH

When you travel outside of North America, the definition of "old" takes on an entirely different meaning. In my part of Western Canada, if you come across a building that is over 100 years of age, you would say it was old. No so in England, where "old" can refer to structures built more than a thousand years ago.

I was in England recently, and while there I had the opportunity to visit the village of Shurdington near the town of Cheltenham. Shurdington was the home of my grandmother Evelyn, who came to Canada around 1900. It was a thrill for me to walk down the very same road that she walked along as a young girl. In fact, we had the opportunity to see Primrose Cottage, where she was born and raised.

But perhaps the highlight of the visit was to go inside the village church my grandmother attended as a young girl—the very same church my relatives attend today. One can tell that not a lot has changed in St. Paul's, Shurdington, since my grandmother's time. This church was built in the 1200s on the foundation of another church that is dated to about 900. While showing me the interior, my cousin pointed out the plaque near the entrance, which listed all the pastors of the church from its inception until today. I can just imagine someone commenting, "Do you remember old Reverend Smith? His sermons were pretty boring back in 1483!"

It was a moving experience for me to sit in the church pew that my ancestors may have occupied on a given Sunday morning or Evensong. It made me wonder about those who came before me, whose bodies are now buried in the graves around the church.

What kind of life did these people of faith have? What kind of hopes did they have for their families? How many friends did they have? What kind of work did they do? How long did they live? Most importantly, how did they relate to God and their life of faith in him? If only those stone walls could speak. I'm sure they would reveal some very interesting details about my family!

Although we as Christians have a personal relationship with God, we all belong to the community of faith that Jesus has drawn us into. Jesus said, "On that day you will realize that I am in my Father, and you are in me, and I am in you" (John 14:20). None of us is ever alone; we are one with God and one with each other (John 17:22-23). The community of faith we've been made part of is much bigger than the congregation we may attend. It is global. It also spans the sands of time.

Being in my grandmother's church that morning reminded me of the words found in the book of Hebrews, "Therefore, since we are surrounded by such a great cloud of witnesses, let us throw off everything that hinders and the sin that so easily entangles. And let us run with perseverance the race marked out for us, fixing our eyes on Jesus, the pioneer and perfecter of faith. For the joy set before him he endured the cross, scorning its shame, and sat down at the right hand of the throne of God" (Hebrews 12:1-2).

We've been welcomed into the eternal communion of faith created by our great God of love—into a great cloud of witnesses to the joy of life everlasting as the one Body of Christ formed by the Holy Spirit. We stand together in the same faith as all those who have gone before us, who are part of us today, and who will be with us forever into the future.

Bill Hall

71. PARTAKING OF THE PROMISES

The Lord Jesus, on the night he was betrayed, took bread, and when he had given thanks, he broke it and said, "This is my body, which is for you; do this in remembrance of me." In the same way, after supper he took the cup, saying, "This cup is the new covenant in my blood; do this, whenever you drink it, in remembrance of me." For whenever you eat this bread and drink this cup, you proclaim the Lord's death until he comes. (1 Corinthians 11:23-26)

In the bread and in the wine, we remember what our Savior did for us in the historical past. In a unique sacrifice, once for all time, he gave his body and shed his blood for our salvation. In our communion services, we commemorate his sacrifice for us.

But communion also pictures what our risen and living Savior does for us in our own past, present and future. Jesus gave himself for us even when we were sinners, and he continues to give himself for us, serving our needs. Both the bread and the wine point us not only to what Christ did in the past, but also to his loving, ever-present involvement in our lives right now.

The body of Christ

In his letter to the Corinthians, Paul compares the church to the body of Christ. "Is not the bread that we break a participation in the body of Christ?" he asks. "Because there is one loaf, we, who are many, are one body, for we all partake of the one loaf" (1 Corinthians 10:16-17).

The communion bread should remind us that in participating with Christ, we are also participating with one another, because we are all one in him. Although we are different in many respects, we are all nevertheless members of one another (Romans 12:5), for we all partake of Christ, the Bread of Life. Our unity is in him, and this unity is not just a figure of speech—it affects the way we treat one another.

In Corinth, however, the believers were not treating one another the way that they should. There were divisions among them (1 Corinthians 11:18), and instead of commemorating Christ together, they were divided even in the way they ate and drank the memorials of his death. The early arrivals were apparently so inconsiderate that they ate all the food and overindulged in wine, leaving nothing for those who arrived late (verse 21).

Wealthy people could arrive early, but poor people could come only after they had done their work. The result in Corinth was that the hungry people remained hungry, because all the food was gone by the time they arrived, and they felt humiliated (verses 21-22). So Paul scolded the wealthy for their behavior, because it did not reflect the unity in Christ that believers ought to have.

Paul did not require the wealthy to give up their wealth. He simply told everyone to eat at home (verse 34). The bread and wine are not a means of satisfying hunger, but a means of commemorating Christ's death and resurrection, of showing our common faith in our crucified and risen Savior. The believers are to eat at home, and when coming together to eat the Lord's Supper, they are to wait for one another (verse 33), so they will be participating together. Communion is to reflect unity, not discrimination or judgment (verse 34).

So Paul encouraged the Corinthians not only to examine themselves, but also to recognize the body of the Lord (verse 29). He is not talking about the flesh-and-bone body of Jesus (which the Corinthians could not see), but about the body of Christ, the church (which they could see), in which Christ dwells through the Spirit. They were to discern that the believers formed one body, united by their spiritual union with Christ—and this awareness was to make a difference in the way they treated one another.

A symbol of unity

The Lord's Supper is to be an expression of unity in Christ. Since the Corinthians were using their meal to discriminate against the poor, they were not reflecting unity; therefore their meal was not the Lord's Supper (verse 20). It should have been, and in verses 33-34 Paul tells them one way to avoid the problem. He wanted all believers to share equally in "the Lord's table" (1 Corinthians 10:17, 21).

The bread of communion points us not just to Jesus on the cross, but to Jesus very much alive in the church today. The fact that Jesus died and rose for each and every one of us means that we have a spiritual equality. We need to see each other as people for whom Christ died, people Christ loves dearly—and we should love each other dearly, too.

> Christ died and returned to life so that he might be the Lord of both the dead and the living. You, then, why do you judge your brother? Or why do you look down on your brother? For we will all stand before God's judgment seat.... Each of us will give an account of himself to God. Therefore let us stop passing judgment on one another. (Romans 14:9-13)

"Be kind and compassionate to one another, forgiving each other, just as in Christ God forgave you" (Ephesians 4:32).

The new covenant

The communion wine reminds us not just that Jesus shed his blood for us—it reminds us of our new life in Christ right now. Jesus said that the wine is the new covenant in his blood—that is, our ongoing fellowship with God that he makes possible for us. Jesus did not die just for our past—he died so we would have a fellowship with God that extends into eternity.

The new covenant involves several changes:

- First, God writes his laws on our hearts (Hebrews 8:10). This does not mean that we memorize sacrificial regulations or that we have an automatic desire to perform the ritual laws of the Old Testament. What this means is that God works inside us to change us to be more like he is. He puts his love within our hearts.

- Second, the new covenant means that everyone will know God, or have fellowship with him (verse 11). The old covenant, in contrast, was made with a nation containing both faithful and unfaithful people; the new covenant involves a people who are all faithful—made faithful by our faithful Savior.

- Third, the new covenant involves complete forgiveness—God will "remember their sins no more" (verse 12). Although the people had sins, the people are forgiven and will never be condemned.

These are exceedingly great and precious promises, and though in Christ we have entered into them and "tasted them," as it were, they are not yet fully realized as they will be at his appearing, when the resurrection takes place and we "put on immortality."

We already have the down payment of the promises (2 Corinthians 1:22). The Holy Spirit is already at work in our hearts, changing us to be more like Christ. We already know God and have fellowship with him (1 John 1:3), and we are already fully forgiven in Christ (Romans 8:1). The promises are being fulfilled, because the new covenant in the blood of Christ has been established.

When we drink the communion wine, we should remember that we are in covenant with God—an agreement in which he has pledged according to the certainty of his own faithfulness to cleanse our hearts, to renew our minds, and to forgive all our sins. He has promised to complete the work he has begun; we can be confident in what he is doing, because it is all based on what Christ did.

The life of Christ

Blood is not only a symbol of death—in the Old Testament it is also a symbol of life (Leviticus 17:14). Just as the body of Christ (represented by bread) is now visible in the church, the life of Christ (represented by wine) is also visible in his church—through his love in us expressed in good actions.

The church does not perfectly reflect the life of Christ. We have sins and shortcomings. The promises are not yet fully realized—but they are sure and certain promises—guaranteed for us by the death and resurrection of Jesus Christ. The church is where Christ is working not only to preach the gospel, but also to change the hearts of the people who bear witness to his power to forgive, cleanse and transform sinners.

When we take the bread, accepting the bodily sacrifice of Jesus for us, we are also accepting his visible body in the world today—the church. When we take the wine, we accept not only his forgiveness, but also his promise to change our hearts.

The Lord's Supper reminds us not just of Jesus' death—it reminds us that he is raised and lives even now within us, within every member of his body, the church. When we partake of the Bread of Life, and drink the new covenant in Jesus' blood, we are accepting his promises and inviting him to live within us and change us. This coming year, how might he want to change you?

Joseph Tkach

72. THE THREE-FOLD MEANING OF THE LORD'S SUPPER

The Lord's Supper is a reminder of what Jesus did in the past, a symbol of our present relationship with him, and a promise of what he will do in the future. Let's review these three aspects.

Memorials of Jesus' death on the cross

On the evening he was betrayed, while Jesus was eating a meal with his disciples, he took some bread and said, "This is my body given for you; do this in remembrance of me" (Luke 22:19). They each ate a piece of the bread. When we participate in the Lord's Supper, we each eat a piece of bread in remembrance of Jesus.

"In the same way, after the supper he took the cup, saying, 'This cup is the new covenant in my blood, which is poured out for you'" (verse 20). When we drink a small amount of wine (or grape juice) at the Lord's Supper, we remember that Jesus' blood was shed for us, and that his blood inaugurated the new covenant. Just as the old covenant was sealed by the sprinkling of blood, the new covenant was established by Jesus' blood (Hebrews 9:18-28).

As Paul said, "For whenever you eat this bread and drink this cup, you proclaim the Lord's death until he comes" (1 Corinthians 11:26). The Lord's Supper looks back to the death of Jesus Christ on the cross.

Is Jesus' death a good thing, or a bad thing? There are certainly some very sorrowful aspects to his death, but the bigger picture is that his death is wonderful news for all of us. It shows how much God loves us—so much that he sent his Son to die for us, so that our sins would be forgiven and we may live forever with him.

The death of Jesus is a tremendous gift to us. It is precious. When we are given a gift of great value, a gift that involved personal sacrifice for us, how should we receive it? With mourning and regret? No, that is not what the giver wants. Rather, we should receive it with great gratitude, as an expression of great love. If we have tears, they should be tears of joy.

So the Lord's Supper, although a memorial of a death, is not a funeral, as if Jesus were still dead. Quite the contrary—we observe this memorial knowing that death held Jesus only three days—knowing that death will not hold us forever, either. We rejoice that Jesus has conquered death, and has set free all who were enslaved by a fear of death (Hebrews 2:14-15). We can remember Jesus' death with the happy knowledge that he has triumphed over sin and death! As Jesus said, our mourning will turn into joy (John 16:20). Coming to the Lord's table and having communion should be a celebration, not a funeral.

The ancient Israelites looked back to the Passover events as the defining moment in their history, when their identity as a nation began. It was when they escaped death and slavery through the intervention of God and were freed to serve the Lord. In the church, we look back to the events surrounding the crucifixion and resurrection of Jesus as the defining moment in our history. That is how we escape death and the slavery of sin, and that is how we are freed to serve the Lord. The Lord's Supper is a memorial of this defining moment in our history.

Our present relationship with Jesus Christ

The crucifixion of Jesus has a continuing significance to all who have taken up a cross to follow him. We continue to participate in his death and in the new covenant because we participate in his life. Paul wrote, "Is not the cup of thanksgiving for which we give thanks a participation in the blood of Christ? And is not the bread that we break a participation in the body of Christ?" (1 Corinthians 10:16). In the Lord's Supper, we show that we share in Jesus Christ. We commune with him. We are united in him.

The New Testament speaks of our sharing with Jesus in several ways. We share in his crucifixion (Galatians 2:20; Colossians 2:20), death (Romans 6:4), resurrection (Ephesians 2:6; Colossians 2:13; 3:1) and life (Galatians 2:20). Our lives are in him, and he is in us. The Lord's Supper pictures this spiritual reality.

John 6 conveys a similar idea. After Jesus proclaimed himself to be the "bread of life," he said, "Whoever eats my flesh and drinks my blood has eternal life, and I will raise him up at the last day" (verse 54). Our spiritual food is in Jesus Christ. The Lord's Supper pictures this ongoing truth. "Whoever eats my flesh and drinks my blood remains in me, and I in him" (verse 56). We show that we live in Christ, and he lives in us.

So the Lord's Supper helps us look upward, to Christ, and be mindful that true life can only be in him and with him.

But when we are aware that Jesus lives in us, we also pause to think what kind of home we are giving him. Before he came into our lives, we were habitations of sin. Jesus knew that before he even knocked on the door of our lives. He wants to get in so he can start cleaning things up. But when Jesus knocks, many people try to do a quick tidy-up before they open the door. However, we are humanly unable to cleanse our sins—the most we can do is hide them in the closet.

So we hide our sins in the closet, and invite Jesus into the living room. Eventually we let him into the kitchen, and then the hallway, and then a bedroom. It is a gradual process. Eventually Jesus gets to the closet where our worst sins are hidden, and he cleans them, too. Year by year, as we grow in spiritual maturity, we surrender more of our lives to our Savior.

It is a process, and the Lord's Supper plays a role in this process. Paul wrote, "Everyone should take a careful look at themselves before they eat the bread and drink from the cup" (1 Corinthians 11:28). Every time we participate, we should be mindful of the great meaning involved in this ceremony.

When we examine ourselves, we often find sin. This is normal—it is not a reason to avoid the Lord's Supper. It is simply a reminder that we need Jesus in our lives. Only he can take our sins away.

Paul criticized the Corinthian Christians for their manner of observing the Lord's Supper. The wealthy members were coming first, eating a great meal and even getting drunk. The poor members came last, still hungry. The wealthy were not sharing with the poor (vv. 20-22). They were not really sharing in the life of Christ, for they were not doing what he would do. They were not understanding what it means to be members of the body of Christ, and that members have responsibilities toward one another.

So as we examine ourselves, we need to look around to see whether we are treating one another in the way that Jesus commanded. If you are united with Christ and I am united to Christ, then we are united to each other. So the Lord's Supper, by picturing our participation in Christ, also pictures our participation (other translations may say communion or sharing or fellowship) with each other.

As Paul wrote in 1 Corinthians 10:17, "Because there is one loaf, we, who are many, are one body, for we all share the one loaf." By participating together in the Lord's Supper, we picture the fact that we are one body in Christ, one with each other, with responsibilities toward one another.

At Jesus' last meal with his disciples, Jesus pictured the life of God's kingdom by washing the feet of his disciples (John 13:1-15). When Peter protested, Jesus said it was necessary that he wash his feet. The Christian life involves both serving and being served.

Reminds us of Jesus' return

Jesus said he would not drink the fruit of the vine again until he came in the fullness of the kingdom (Matthew 26:29; Luke 22:18; Mark 14:25). Whenever we participate, we are reminded of Jesus' promise. There will be a great messianic "banquet," a "wedding supper" of celebration. The bread and wine are miniature rehearsals of what will be the greatest victory celebration in all history. Paul wrote that "For whenever you eat this bread and drink this cup, you proclaim the Lord's death until he comes" (1 Corinthians 11:26).

The Lord's Supper is rich in meaning. That is why it has been a prominent part of the Christian tradition throughout the centuries. Sometimes it has been allowed to become a lifeless ritual, done more out of habit than with meaning. When a ritual loses meaning, some people overreact by stopping the ritual entirely. The better response is to restore the meaning. That's why it is helpful for us to review the meaning of our custom.

Joseph Tkach

73. THE LORD'S SUPPER
REMINDS US OF GOD'S LOVE

As often as we observe the Lord's Supper, we should let it remind us afresh of God's love for us, a love that will never fail, a love that will never get smaller. Though humans may be unfaithful, God will never leave us or forsake us. Though we may struggle and stumble many times, God never abandons us. He is always ready to welcome us back.

As we commemorate Jesus' death, we are gloriously confident of God's love for us. We do not need to worry that our sins, no matter how many or how serious, have cut us off from him. God always welcomes his children.

We are also mindful that Jesus died *because of sin*. He went to the cross because humans chose to decide for themselves what is right and wrong. We have all done that, and we have all repented of that — many times. We seek to do God's will, not our own. We do not want to participate in self-willed life, for that is the approach to life that sent us away from God, sentenced us to death, and caused our Savior's death. So the Lord's Supper is a reminder to us to humble ourselves (even as Jesus did, even unto death on a cross) and seek to serve others (Philippians 2:4-8).

Each of us is woefully inadequate to the task set before us! It is so hard for us to put aside our own interests and serve others! The good news is that God has provided the way for us to escape this body of death, and it comes through Jesus' life (Romans 5:10). For a balanced understanding of the Christian life, we must remember that our Savior is a living Savior, resurrected from the dead, ascended into glory, seated in a position of honor and power with God the Father. He intercedes for us, and he lives in us, and we in him. Because of his life, we walk in newness of life, living in a state of forgiveness instead of condemnation.

74. IN REMEMBRANCE OF WHAT?

Funny, isn't it, how you can read a scripture many times and still miss something obvious? It even happens to ministers and pastors who have many years of experience.

I belong to our local ministerial association. A regular part of our monthly meeting is a short devotional given by one of the members. At a recent meeting it was the turn of Chuck Clayton, the supervising pastor at one of the local churches.

Chuck said he had been thinking recently about 1 Corinthians 11, starting in verse 23.

"For I received from the Lord what I also passed on to you: The Lord Jesus, on the night he was betrayed, took bread, and when he had given thanks, he broke it and said, 'This is my body, which is for you; do this in remembrance of me.' In the same way, after supper he took the cup, saying, 'This cup is the new covenant in my blood; do this, whenever you drink it, in remembrance of me.' For whenever you eat this bread and drink this cup, you proclaim the Lord's death until he comes."

Well, yes. We all knew those verses. It is pretty much standard fare for a communion service. Our individual churches might have different methods of taking communion, but we all agreed on this basic understanding. "So," Chuck said, "let's read on."

"Therefore, whoever eats the bread or drinks the cup of the Lord in an unworthy manner will be guilty of sinning against the body and blood of the Lord. A man ought to examine himself before he eats of the bread and drinks of the cup. For anyone who eats and drinks without recognizing the body of the Lord eats and drinks judgment on himself."

"How do you explain that?" he asked.

Well, it seems pretty obvious. Before taking the Lord's Supper, you examine yourself, to see if you are worthy. I well remember preaching the importance of doing this in my church's more legalistic past. Surely, such an examination really underlines the seriousness of the ceremony. Or does it? Does this verse, if not explained properly and in context, actually *undermine* the significance of communion?

What kind of examination should it be? Who sets the questions? Who grades it? Who decides what is a passing or failing mark? And are you really in serious danger of damnation if you "fail" but decide to take communion anyway?

I could see by the expressions of my colleagues that I was not the only one with some legalism in my background. "So what does it mean?" asked Chuck, and then explained it in a way I had not thought of before. After the meeting I told him, "I found that really helpful. And I know many people who might need it too. Do you mind if I plagiarize it?"

"Go ahead," he said. So I have.

You see, when we put the emphasis on examining our*selves*, we can shift the focus away from the purpose of what Jesus asked us to do. An examination would inevitably concentrate on your sins and failings — on what *you* have done or not done. As a pastor, I would feel it my duty to remind my flock that they are sinners, that it was because of their personal sins that Jesus came to die, etc.

Always, after such sermons, I would have to reassure some impressionable people who were now convinced that they were "not worthy." Sometimes I would literally have to talk them into accepting the symbols of Christ's broken body and shed blood. They would do so hesitantly, with a, "Well, if you think it is okay. I'll really try harder in the future, I really will." I could imagine them timidly nibbling at the bread and sipping the wine with trepidation, deeply aware of their own unworthiness, knowing from experience that their promises to "do better" were hollow. I have seen ministers hold the microphone so it would amplify the sound of breaking unleavened bread. The congregation was encouraged to imagine the crack of the scourge and the pounding of the nails into Jesus' flesh. We wanted to drive home the point. But actually we were missing it.

Jesus did not say, "Do this in remembrance of what *you* have done." Or even, "Do this in remembrance of what you did to me." He asked us to do it in remembrance of what he did for us. Paul mentions Jesus' request twice — "do this in remembrance of *me*." Our very taking of the bread and wine is our recalling of something about Jesus' love for his body, the church. It is a proclamation until he comes, not about our unworthiness, but about the Lord's death on our behalf, which makes us reconciled to God. That is the proclamation of the Lord's death.

What Jesus did was both pay the penalty for our sins and become our righteousness so that we can enjoy a guilt free, positive and constructive relationship with God. He changed everything. He didn't just die, he was also resurrected. And when we come together to take the symbols of that sacrifice, we do it not in remembrance of our past, but of all that Jesus *is* for all who trust in him.

Without that relationship you are indeed "damned." God does not have to do it—you put yourself in that position. I like the way Eugene Petersen renders these verses in *The Message Bible.*

"What you must solemnly realize is that every time you eat this bread and every time you drink this cup, you reenact in your words and actions the death of the Master. You will be drawn back to this meal again and again until the Master returns. You must never let familiarity breed contempt.

"Anyone who eats the bread or drinks the cup of the Master irreverently is like part of the crowd that jeered and spit on him at his death. Is that the kind of 'remembrance' you want to be part of? Examine your motives, test your heart, come to this meal in holy awe."

Before we take the bread and wine, it is certainly worth pausing for a moment to remind ourselves of the wonderful situation Jesus has made possible. But such an examination is not a "do or die" nail-biting test before cautiously going ahead, hoping you are okay. It is a positive and confident proclamation of your status as a forgiven and blessed believer on the road to immortal life. The purpose of the Lord's death and resurrection was to once and for all open up to us a new and guilt-free relationship with God. Communion is not intended to focus on what you *were* but on *who God has made you to be in Christ.*

John Halford

75. THE JOY OF COMMUNION

The lights dimmed and somber music filled the hall as the ushers solemnly carried the bread and wine forward for communion. The pastor emphasized the broken body and spilled blood of Christ as he talked about Jesus' command to remember him. We sat in silence and prayed as the bread and wine were distributed. It was a time of quiet reflection. And on this occasion it stood in stark contrast to an inspiring sermon the pastor had just given about the joy of being in union with Father, Son and Holy Spirit.

I wanted to stand up and shout Hallelujah at the end of the sermon, not sit in quiet reflection over the broken body. I wanted to celebrate our union with Christ by sharing the joy with others. It was at that point I determined to examine the way I offer communion to my congregation.

I shared with my congregation that communion is not about the crucifixion—it is about our unity with God. The word means "sharing in common." Jesus, the bread of life, shared his life with us. Breaking bread is a symbol of that shared life. Jesus, our redeemer, shared his love for us by laying down his life—this is called the greatest love. The cup represents Jesus sharing his love.

When we take communion, we are actually sharing in Jesus' life and his love. This love and life didn't begin at the Lord's Supper. Communion actually started before the foundation of the earth when you and I were chosen to be in him (Ephesians 1). We were chosen to share in the love and the life shared by the Father, Son and Holy Spirit. Communion is about God's desire to share himself with us by determining to adopt us as his sons and daughters. It's about being one with each other and with the Father as Jesus was one with the Father and is one with us (John 17).

It is certainly appropriate at times to remember the sacrifice Jesus made for us when we participate in communion. But it's also appropriate and right to remember that communion is a reminder that God has invited us to participate in what he is doing in the world. I believe on*e of the reasons Paul called communion a blessing is because it is about our participation with Christ's sharing his life and his love with all.

When Jesus told us to remember him, he wasn't asking us to focus on his suffering, but to focus on his love for us and for the world. I look forward to the time when all of us share in the joy of communion while shouting praises to the One who brought us together.

Rick Shallenberger

76. HOW OFTEN SHOULD WE PARTICIPATE IN THE LORD'S SUPPER?

Shortly before his death, Jesus shared a meal with his disciples. He shared a cup of wine with them, and then some bread. "He took bread, gave thanks and broke it, and gave it to them, saying, 'This is my body given for you; do this in remembrance of me'" (Luke 22:19).

When Jesus told his disciples to do "this" in remembrance of him, what were they to "do"? They were to take bread, give thanks, break it and share it. They were also to share some wine (verse 17; 1 Corinthians 11:25).

Although the Last Supper may have been special due to the festival season, the substances used were ordinary. The disciples were to "do" what they had probably done many times before: share bread and wine. Now, they were to do it in remembrance of the fact that Jesus gave his body and blood on behalf of others so that we could have a new relationship with God.

When two disciples were on the road to Emmaus, the resurrected Jesus walked with them. They recognized him only after "he took bread, gave thanks, broke it and began to give it to them" (Luke 24:30). In the breaking and sharing of the bread, they became aware of who Jesus was.

Jesus' Last Supper became etched into the memory of the disciples. It was a tremendously significant moment. It is therefore likely that they remembered Jesus every time they got together and shared bread. When the disciples came together to break bread and pray (Acts 2:42), whenever they shared an evening meal with other disciples, they would remember their Savior.

An annual observance?

Does Scripture prescribe a correct frequency? Some people say that the Lord's Supper should be taken only once each year. The basic reason is that Jesus did this during a Passover meal, on an annual festival. Further, memorials of momentous occasions are usually observed annually.

However, there is no indication in the Bible that we are required to follow all the details of the original Lord's Supper. For example: The cup was shared after supper (Luke 22:20). We do not know what time that was. We do not know whether the disciples had a quick meal, or a very leisurely one. It might have been as early as 7 p.m. or as late as 10 p.m. If the hour is really important, then we do not have enough guidance to be sure.

We do not have to share the bread during a supper, and we do not have to wait until after a supper to partake of the wine. Nor do we have to go to an upper room or recline at a table. These details are not significant for us.

Second, is the bread and wine a New Testament version of the Passover? Jesus shared the bread and wine at the beginning of the Passover season — that was the date it happened — but Jesus never said that the bread and wine replaced the Passover lamb and meal. The supper Jesus ate was called a Passover meal, but Jesus did not call the bread and wine a Passover. He instituted a new ceremony.

The Passover lamb was a commemoration of the Exodus; it also looked forward to the sacrifice of Jesus Christ. The bread and wine look backward in memory of Jesus Christ. Although they both picture death of Christ, they do so from different perspectives, and they are different ceremonies. The symbolism of the old covenant Passover has been fulfilled, and it does not need to be repeated. The Passover regulations are obsolete, and that would include the requirement that it be done annually.

The Passover is not the only ritual that Jesus fulfilled. He also fulfilled the sin offerings, fellowship offerings, grain offerings, annual offerings, monthly offerings, weekly offerings, and daily offerings. The Passover offering was an annual event, but the others were much more frequent, and the bread and wine commemorate the death of Jesus, which fulfilled daily rituals as well as annual ones.

The Passover lamb commemorates an event in Israelite history. It was part of the law of Moses, and could be observed only by circumcised people. But the early church recognized that Gentile Christians did not have to become circumcised and did not have to observe the law of Moses. What Christians observed in the bread and wine was not a slightly altered version of the Passover lamb. Gentile Christians were not commemorating the Exodus from Egypt. Rather, they were commemorating Jesus Christ. It was a new ceremony. Bread and wine has little in common with lamb and bitter herbs.

Did Jesus observe the Lord's Supper once each year? No. He observed it only once in his lifetime. We cannot determine anything about our frequency from his example. We do not need to be limited by old covenant rules about the Passover when we observe a different ritual under a different covenant. The observance of the Lord's Supper is not mandated or regulated by the old covenant or the Hebrew calendar.

There is no reason to apply rules about the Old Testament Passover to the New Testament Lord's Supper. Although they both symbolize the death of Jesus, they are different ceremonies and have different rules. The old covenant ritualistic rules are obsolete (Hebrews 8:13). Spiritual meaning and reality are much more important. The new covenant does not make rules about when to eat bread and drink wine in commemoration of Jesus' death. The Bible does not require any particular frequency.

If precise timing were important, we should observe this ritual when it is evening in Jerusalem. Shouldn't everyone observe this ritual at the same time, worldwide, no matter where they live? No, the exact time is not important. Jesus did not assign symbolic meaning to the time.

It is not necessary to follow the Jewish calendar. It was designed for old covenant Israel, a people who lived in a specific region and climate. It was not designed for a worldwide church of Christians. Further, the old covenant was not as finicky about calendar dates as some might think. When Hezekiah restored the festivals to Judah, everyone kept the Passover in the second month (2 Chronicles 30:2, 15). Although the law of Moses made provision for keeping the Passover in the second month, the Jews in Hezekiah's day did not qualify for the specific provisions of the second Passover. Hezekiah was doing something that the law of Moses did not allow (verse 18).

Not only did the Israelites observe the Passover in the second month that year, they also observed the Festival of Unleavened Bread in the second month. The law of Moses did not authorize such a thing. And not only did they observe it in the wrong month, they also kept it for 14 days instead of seven! (verse 23). And God was happy with the whole thing (verse 27). An extra festival in the wrong month is perfectly acceptable to God. He looks on the heart more than on the calendar.

The example of Hezekiah shows that it is permissible, even under the old covenant, to observe festivals at different times. It is permissible to add more celebration — even more so in the new covenant!

Third, it is true that many memorials are observed annually. However, some newly married couples commemorate their marriage every month. And we know that the Israelites had a weekly memorial of creation, the Sabbath. So we cannot use cultural customs about commemorations to say anything about how often the Bible requires us to observe the Lord's Supper. The Lord gives us liberty, not detailed rules.

A further examination of the biblical evidence

When we examine the reasons for having an annual commemoration, we find that none of the reasons are conclusive. We might like for the Bible to tell us exactly when and how to do things, but sometimes it doesn't. If we try to force the Bible to answer a question it really doesn't answer, then we will misuse the Scriptures and be dogmatic about things we shouldn't be.

Is it possible that the Bible does not tell us how often we should observe the Lord's Supper? Is it possible that such an important ceremony is left up to the decision of the disciples? Is it possible that different groups of Christians can observe different frequencies, and all be acceptable?

The Bible indicates flexibility in the timing when it tells us that Jesus said, "do this, *whenever* you drink it, in remembrance of me" (1 Corinthians 11:26). "When" might indicate a set time, but "whenever" indicates flexibility.

Paul's letter to the Corinthians also gives evidence that the Lord's Supper was being observed frequently. He corrected them for their behavior at meetings in which they ate and drank, and it sounds like this was done frequently (verses 17, 20, 33). It was done when they came together "as a church" (verse 18). Paul told them that they should satisfy their hunger at home (verse 34) — but they should nevertheless "come together to eat" (verse 33). What were they supposed to eat? Paul was instructing them on their conduct when they ate the bread and wine in commemoration of Jesus' death. This is what the Corinthians had been doing, but in a poor manner. He corrected them on their manner, but said nothing about the frequency.

Paul did not say that the Corinthians should partake of the Lord's Supper every time they met. But he makes no restrictions on frequency, and the words Paul used allow for frequent participation. The Bible simply does not tell us how often to partake of the Lord's Supper. There is no command about how often we should commemorate the Lord's death, just as there is no command about how often we should fast.

Our practice

The Lord's Supper is a new covenant ceremony, and it is not restricted by old covenant rules about the Passover. Since the new covenant does not specify when the Lord's Supper should be observed, we are free to make our own decisions about it. Members may observe communion as often as they wish. This may be done by small groups without any need for prior approval from church leaders. Many of our congregations have a monthly Communion service; some also have an annual service.

Some people think that once a year is often enough. Other people think that it is not often enough. How often should we remember the Lord's death? Very often — even daily. But is it necessary to have bread and wine in order to remember the Lord's death? No, the physical symbols are not necessary.

But are they helpful? For many people, yes. That is why Jesus told us to do these things in his remembrance. Many people understand and remember ideas better when they have not just words, but also actions in which they participate. The lesson is being made in more than one way, and can be communicated to a wider variety of people.

Some people think well in abstract thoughts, in the world of ideas. Others prefer more practical thoughts — they prefer to deal with things they can see, touch, taste, smell or hear. The Old Testament had many rituals that were physical signs and symbols of spiritual truths. God knows that humans often need such physical helps.

Some people will find it helpful to participate in the Lord's Supper more often than others will. Some will find it easy for the bread and wine to remind them of spiritual truths about their Savior; others will find this association more abstract and not so easy.

Some people associate the bread and wine with ritual rather than meaning. In their experience, the focus was on the ritual, not on Christ. This is sad, and it is no surprise that people with such experiences do not want to participate in the Lord's Supper too often. In their experience, frequent Communion is associated with meaningless ritual and perhaps with lifeless churches.

Other Christians have a different background. They had only an annual observance, a funeral-like ceremony, in which people were overly concerned about formality. These members may associate an annual ceremony with a church that didn't understand Jesus' death as well as it should have. They ask, To help us remember what Jesus did for us on the cross, shouldn't we follow his instructions on how to remember him? If we do it more often, then maybe we won't forget.

There is truth on both sides of this issue. We do not want a meaningless ritual — but a ritual can be meaningless no matter how rare or often it is. If it's done too often, it can lose its meaning. But it doesn't have to. Many marriages have daily rituals that continue to be meaningful.

What is most important is not so much the frequency, but a clear understanding and explanation of the meaning. If the meaning is explained once a year and people remember it throughout the year, then once a year might be enough. If the meaning is explained and the action is done throughout the year with that meaning in mind, then the repetitions are not too often. For some members, a more frequent Communion will be helpful. Others may be more bothered by it than helped.

There is no way to please everyone. But people of both persuasions can still do the frequency they want. Those who want to participate only once a year may do so; those who want a greater frequency may do so as often as their groups wish.

Different believers have different fears about frequent or infrequent communion, but the real issue for most people is the meaning of the actions we participate in. For the Lord's Supper, we do not want people to "go through the motions" without remembering the Lord's death. We want to remember the meaning.

Michael Morrison

77. IS EATING THE LAMB OF GOD
ONLY AN ANNUAL EVENT?

"Look," said John the Baptist, "the Lamb of God, who takes away the sin of the world" (John 1:29).

When you think of Jesus as the Lamb of God, which lamb do you identify him with? Perhaps 1 Corinthians 5:7 pops into your mind: "For Christ, our Passover lamb, has been sacrificed." Jesus is our Passover Lamb. Based on that understanding, some people keep the Lord's Supper as an annual event.

Jesus commanded us to "eat his flesh and drink his blood" by taking the bread and wine of Communion. In doing so, we partake of the Lamb of God. Some believers do it annually because they see the Lamb of God as the Passover lamb, and the Passover was an annual observance.

But Jesus is more than just the Passover lamb. As the "lamb of God who takes away the sin of the world" he is the lamb of every burnt offering, sin offering, guilt offering or peace offering of the old covenant. Jesus is the fulfillment of *all* the sacrifices of the old covenant period. We read in Hebrews that the law with its sacrifices and offerings was a shadow of things to come, and the reality or fulfillment of the shadow was Jesus Christ. His one sacrifice achieved everything foreshadowed by the sacrifices of the old covenant (Hebrews 10:1-18).

The Passover lamb was not the only sacrifice eaten by the Israelites. In some offerings — sacrifices that could be offered at any time of year — after a few parts of the sacrificial animal had been burned, the rest of the animal was eaten by those who participated in the sacrificial ceremony. Sometimes it was eaten by the priest and his family (sin offering and guilt or trespass offering), and sometimes the people who brought the offering and their families also ate of the sacrifice (various kinds of fellowship or peace offerings).

This practice is what Paul had in mind when he wrote in 1 Corinthians 10:18, "Consider the people of Israel: Do not those who eat the sacrifices participate in the altar?" Eating part of the sacrifice was an act that displayed participation in the sacrifice, and relationship with the God to whom the sacrifice had been offered. Paul said that just as the people of Israel participated in the altar when they ate of the sacrifices they brought to the altar, so Christians participate in the body and blood of Christ when they eat the bread and wine of Communion (verses 16-17).

How often might an Israelite have partaken of the "lamb of God"? As often as he liked: there was no restriction. As often as he brought a fellowship offering, he would share in the meal. If the Israelite happened to be a priest or the descendant of a priest, he might be eating God's lambs many times a year.

What does this have to do with the Lord's Supper? Just this: the priests of the old covenant freely and frequently ate of the lambs that were brought to the altar. The author of Hebrews points out that we Christians "have an altar from which those who minister at the tabernacle have no right to eat." His implication is that just as they had their altar to eat from, we have our own altar to eat from. As freely as they ate from theirs, we may eat from ours.

Christians, who under the new covenant are a nation of priests (1 Peter 2:9), may eat of the sacrificial Lamb of God as freely and frequently as did those priests of the old covenant. We are not restricted to eating the Lamb of God only once a year, any more than they were.

Jesus is always our sin offering; he is always our guilt offering; he is always our peace and thank offering. When we sin, he invites us to "eat my flesh and drink my blood," and remember that we have forgiveness in him. When we fall prey to guilt, he urges us to "eat my flesh and drink my blood," and remember we are free from condemnation in him.

When we rejoice in his blessings, he calls us to his table to "eat my flesh and drink my blood," and rejoice in him. Thank God our Father for the communion he gives us with himself in his beloved Son!

Don Mears

78. THE NAME OF THE LORD'S SUPPER

Passover, Communion, Lord's Supper, Eucharist: All are traditional names for the observance commemorating Jesus' death. Should we use any (or all) of these to describe our service?

In 1845, in Philadelphia, J.L. Boyd and C.S. Minor led a small sabbatarian church to observe an annual "Passover" with bread and grape juice in commemoration of Jesus' death. "They also washed one another's feet, following Jesus' Passover example. They continued this practice alone for 30 years before they ever found any others who agreed with them."[1]

By the 1880s, those we know today as the Church of God (Seventh-Day) all came to accept this custom. When Herbert Armstrong first learned that the Church of God (Seventh Day) kept an observance called Passover, he disagreed. He agreed that Communion should be kept at the Passover season, but argued that it was wrong to call the service a Passover. In a letter to Katie Gilstrap dated 3 May 1928 he wrote:

> Christ abrogated this Passover entirely, instituting in its stead a new ordinance, called the Lord's Supper.... The Lord's Supper is the true scriptural name and title for the ordinance. Read I Corinthians 11:20-34. The name Passover is not used in the New Testament at any time, as the name of this ordinance under the New Testament, after the crucifixion. It is improper for us, then, to call it the Passover.[2]

By the spring of 1929, Mr. Armstrong had changed his opinion. He began to keep not only the Passover, but all of the other annual Holy Days as well.[3] Two decades after his public ministry began, he published the first version of "How Often Should We Partake of the Lord's Supper?" He thought the name Lord's Supper was a misnomer and the correct name should be Passover. Yet, in print, he did not disparage the phrase Lord's Supper or those who used it. He sometimes used it himself, with quote marks.

Mr. Armstrong also commented on the other common name for this ordinance — Communion. He occasionally applied the term Communion to the bread and wine. Sometimes he put Communion within quotation marks, but not always. Unlike his comments about "the Lord's Supper," he wrote nothing that suggested the word was unbiblical.[4]

As for the term Eucharist, Mr. Armstrong never commented.

1 Corinthians 11:20

Some ministers interpreted 1 Corinthians 11:20 as a command not to call

Passover "the Lord's Supper." When and how this began is not clear. Despite dozens of articles on the Passover, this interpretation appeared in print only three times, and with little explanation.[5] Because 1 Corinthians 11:20 is the key to understanding the correct use of the term Lord's Supper, a detailed explanation of that verse will be given later in this paper.

The term Passover was firmly cemented into WCG tradition. It was the term used in the Gospels for Jesus' last supper.[6] The term Passover reminds us that "Christ, our Passover lamb, has been sacrificed" (1 Corinthians 5:7). Many commentators recognize that early Jewish Christians continued to keep the Passover, but with a new Christian emphasis.

Returning to the questions asked at the start of this article: What about the names Communion, Lord's Supper and Eucharist? Do these names also have a biblical basis, and may we use them as well?

Paul writes about Communion to a divided church

The name Communion is rooted in Paul's first letter to the Corinthian church. Understanding what Paul said about Communion will help us understand what he said about the Lord's Supper.

The church at Corinth was filled with doctrinal, moral and relational problems that were sapping its vitality and threatening its integrity. From the outset of the letter we learn that the Corinthian church had begun to divide into various camps. People were taking sides. The congregation was in serious trouble. Paul called on the believers to base their relationships on solid Christian values.

The troubles at Corinth even extended into their religious meetings. Beginning with chapter 10, Paul discusses a variety of ways they could restore Christian decorum to those gatherings. He addresses acceptable hair styles, the use of spiritual gifts, speaking in tongues, and the orderly function of worship services. Paul's discussion of the Lord's Supper is part of this larger theme.

To introduce this discussion, Paul first writes about idolatry. He begins by drawing on the symbolism of the food and drink of the Christian Passover as typified in the wilderness experience of Israel:

> For I do not want you to be ignorant of the fact, brothers, that our forefathers were all under the cloud and that they all passed through the sea. They were all baptized into Moses in the cloud and in the sea. They all ate the same spiritual food and drank the same spiritual drink; for they drank from the spiritual rock that accompanied them, and that rock was Christ.[7]

Paul points out that Israel had communed with God. They had shared in a holy meal. Despite their personal, intimate feast with God, they turned away from him and degenerated into paganism. "The people sat down to eat and drink and got up to indulge in pagan revelry."[8]

Those who had once communed with God turned from him to commune with idols. Their immorality led to 23,000 deaths. Paul warned the church that they could be tempted in the same way. Yet no one should despair, for God would "provide a way out." Paul reminded the Corinthians that they, like Israel, also communed with God.

> Is not the cup of thanksgiving for which we give thanks a participation in [or communion with] the blood of Christ? And is not the bread that we break a participation in [or communion with] the body of Christ?[9]

When the Christians gathered to share bread and wine, the church participated in, or communed with, the body and blood of Jesus Christ. Christ was present — symbolically in the bread and wine, and literally through the Spirit.

However, Paul feared another type of communion that some at Corinth thought their Christian liberty permitted. Some wished to participate in the sacred meals of the pagan cults. They reasoned that since the idols were nothing, they could go into pagan temples and participate in the religious meals. Paul knew there was great harm in such practices.

To stop this practice, Paul contrasted Christ's sacrifice, represented in the bread and wine, with the altar in God's temple and also with the sacrifices of pagans. "The sacrifices of pagans are offered to demons, not to God, and I do not want you to be participants with [or commune with] demons."

Simply because the idols were nothing was no excuse. Demons were present at idolatrous feasts. The idols may have been nothing, but the demons were real. This was not simply a theoretical problem. Just as God was present when the Christians shared bread and wine, so demons were present at pagan feasts. A Christian had to decide with whom he or she was going to commune. Paul wrote, "You cannot have a part in both the Lord's table and the table of demons."

Paul then answered the question that naturally flows from the above discussion: Is it permissible to eat meats sacrificed to idols that are not a part of a temple meal? The communion took place only within the context of a religious meal. Therefore Paul judged that such meat is acceptable, as long as eating it troubles no one's conscience.

After having discussed these and other principles, Paul returned to the subject of Communion by addressing the specific practices within the Corinthian church.

> In the following directives I have no praise for you, for your meetings do more harm than good. In the first place, I hear that when you come together as a church, there are divisions among you, and to some extent I believe it. No doubt there have to be differences among you to show which of you have God's approval. When you come together, it is not the Lord's Supper you eat, for as you eat, each of you goes ahead without waiting for anybody else. One remains hungry, another gets drunk.... do you despise the church of God and humiliate those who have nothing? What shall I say to you? Shall I praise you for this: Certainly not![10]

Paul was disgusted that such practices existed within the church. Though they were drunken and gluttonous, the Corinthians' gravest sins lay in their callous disregard for one another, which resulted in the pollution of Christ's name. How could they commune with Christ when they despised his body, the church?

The origins of the Corinthian problem

How did such practices begin? Some believe that the Corinthians justified their practices as an imitation of Jesus, who ate a meal at his last Passover, when he instituted the symbols of bread and wine. But if that is what the Corinthians believed, why does Paul make no mention of that belief? Instead, his approach hinges on bringing Christ's example to their attention, an example they have forgotten, rather than correcting any false understanding of that example.

Paul begins his discussion of Communion with a warning about communion with demons, whose drunken, gluttonous festivals Christians were to avoid. The behavior of the Corinthians mimicked these practices much more than they did the example of Christ. It therefore appears that instead of justifying their approach with Christ's example, the Corinthians may have simply reflected the social values of their day:

> There was a Roman custom to serve different types of food to different categories of guests.... Given such a custom, it would have been normal behavior for the wealthier members not to have any qualms about eating their bountiful provisions and letting the poorer do the best they could.[11]

Since the church gathered for such meals in the homes of the rich, most likely the host was also the patron of the meal.... In a class-conscious society such as Roman Corinth would have been, it would be sociologically natural for the host to invite those of his/her own class to eat in the triclinium [the dining room], while the others would eat in the atrium [the courtyard].[12]

In the average well-to-do house of the Roman era, a dining room accommodated about nine people, the atrium thirty to forty. In any large Christian gatherings...some would have been in the dining room, others in the atrium outside. It would have been the natural procedure for the host's social equals to gather early in the dining room and for the lesser lights to find their places in the atrium.

Since the Corinthian church was composed of well-to-do...as well as slaves...the time of arrival would differ. The well-to-do could come early, while the slaves would arrive late. The latecomers would doubtless find no place to be besides the atrium of the house and would be entering hungrily a scene where others had already reached the point of satiety.[13]

Paul knew that if this situation continued, the congregation's spiritual life was jeopardized. Paul reminded the Christians of Jesus' own example and instruction:

For I received from the Lord what I also passed on to you: The Lord Jesus, on the night he was betrayed, took bread, and when he had given thanks, he broke it and said, "This is my body, which is for you; do this in remembrance of me."... For whenever you eat this bread and drink this cup, you proclaim the Lord's death until he comes. Therefore, whoever eats the bread or drinks the cup of the Lord in an unworthy manner will be guilty of sinning against the body and blood of the Lord.[14]

The Corinthians had forgotten the example of Jesus. Their selfishness, even if it had a social basis, was inexcusable. They were bringing shame and division to the Body of Christ and dishonoring the memory of their Lord.

Do you despise the church of God and humiliate those who have nothing? What shall I say to you? Shall I praise you for this? Certainly not![15]

Paul demanded changes in the Corinthians' Communion

The Corinthian Communion needed a completely new attitude and approach. Order and decorum would have to be restored to the service. Poorer members would have to be respected. Godly relationships within the church would have to be restored. Only then would the congregation's communion with Christ become secure.

It is in that context that 1 Corinthians 11:20 tells us, "When ye come together therefore into one place, this is not to eat the Lord's supper" (King James Version). If one reads Paul's charge "this is not to eat the Lord's supper" by itself, one might conclude that Paul commanded the church not to call Communion "The Lord's Supper." However, once Paul wrote about a problem, he never left the solution in doubt.

If Paul meant that they were not to call the gathering the Lord's Supper, then what were they to call it? Paul never said. Paul never even called the gathering a Passover. He was not writing about what to call the service. He had other more important matters in mind.

A small word is key to understanding

Let's look again at 1 Corinthians 11:21. The word translated into English as "for" is *gar,* which is a "conjunction used to express cause, inference, continuation, or to explain."[16] The word *for* in English can have that same meaning. Paul's own use of the word *gar* in this context shows that he intended his comments in verse 21 to explain his comments in verse 20.

What does Paul say is the reason for their not observing the Lord's Supper? Their ill-mannered, disrespectful and carnal approach to the whole evening — not the name they used. "It is not the Lord's Supper you eat, for as you eat, each of you goes ahead without waiting for anybody else. One remains hungry, another gets drunk…do you despise the church of God and humiliate those who have nothing?"

Put another way, what Paul said was this: Because you have so polluted Christ's memorial, it can no longer be said that you are observing the Lord's Supper. Yes, you should be observing the Lord's Supper. You think you are observing the Lord's Supper. But you are not. Repent. Correct the situation. Change your attitudes. Then you will again be observing the Lord's Supper.

Instead of condemning the term Lord's Supper, Paul implied that the term is acceptable when the participants' behavior is also acceptable. This term, just like "the Lord's table," is acceptable. Paul wanted them to observe the Lord's Supper. What a shame they were not!

The Lord's Supper is respectful

From Paul's letter we can conclude that the term Lord's Supper was used in the first-century church, at least at Corinth, and probably in other churches, too. The name is not derisive, but is an appropriately respectful term for the Christian ceremony. Its respectful character is proven by its etymology.

[Lord's Supper] is derived from the Greek collocation *kyriakon deipnon* in 1 Cor 11:20. *Kyriakos* means something like "belonging to the *kyrios* (lord)", "owned by the *kyrios*." In the papyri and inscriptions it designates Caesar's domain.... *Deipnon* was what the Greeks called the main meal of the day, eaten in the late afternoon or evening.... Moreover, *deipnon* also designated the festal meal or banquet (in the NT, e.g., Mark 6:21; Luke 14:16,17,24).[17]

John used *deipnon* in writing about both the Last Supper and for the future marriage supper of the Lamb.[18] Luke used *deipnon* to describe a great banquet in one of Jesus' parables. There *deipnon* is used as a type of God's kingdom.[19]

The fact that the Corinthian church debased the gathering is disappointing, but understandable. Their attitudes reflected the pagan Greco-Roman culture from which they had come and among which they still lived. Adherents of pagan mystery cults often communed with demons at their drunken gluttonous religious meals. Former pagans may have approached the Christian observance in the same way.

The word "supper" (*deipnon*) is common in Greek writers, and in papyri and inscriptions for cult meals of communion between gods and men. This circumstance may explain why the early church fathers seldom employed the term.[20]

We do not know why Christians began using the phrase "the Lord's Supper." Perhaps it arose from a need to distinguish the Christian ceremony from the Jewish Passover. In any event, the unfortunate association of a religious "supper" with hedonistic pagan celebrations made an otherwise perfectly acceptable name unpopular among early Christian writers. Having distanced themselves from the Jewish practice, they later needed to distance themselves from paganism. They then began to use another term, the Eucharist.

Eucharist replaces Lord's Supper and Passover

Among the early Christian writings outside of the NT the Didache, the letters of Ignatius of Antioch, and Justin Martyr's *Apology* deserve to be studied as witnesses to the Lord's Supper. In these writings the technical term for the Lord's Supper is *eucharistia*...a word which took the lead in Christian tradition for a long time and which is still, as in the past, dominant in Catholic circles.[21]

It may surprise some that the name Eucharist has a biblical basis. Eucharist comes from the Greek word for thanksgiving, *eucharistia,* a word used for the prayers of thanks offered at meals. Matthew and Mark chose *eucharisteo* as their word for Christ's prayer over the symbolic wine of the Last Supper.[22] When someone observes Eucharist, they are expressing thanks for Christ's shed blood.

The New International Version says that Paul, in 1 Corinthians 10:16, called the Communion cup "the cup of thanksgiving for which we give thanks." However, the word translated here as "thanksgiving" is not *eucharistia,* but *eulogias.* Other translations render this word as "blessing." The King James Version speaks of "the cup of blessing which we bless." This translation creates a problem in that it can be understood to mean that the church is the one that blesses the cup. It would be more accurate to say that God blesses the cup in response to our prayers.

"Blessing according to Jewish custom is bestowed by prayer."[23] And prayers for blessings should always have a profound sense of thanksgiving, of *eucharisteo.* The term Eucharist springs from this concept and this passage in 1 Corinthians.

In gathering to memorialize Christ's death, Christians remember Jesus is their Passover Lamb, slain from the foundation of the earth. Filled with thankfulness, their memorial is also a Eucharist, a thanksgiving for God's mercy, love, and selfless sacrifice. In consuming the sacred symbols of the Lord's Supper, their observance becomes a communion with the blood and body of Christ. In communing with Christ, they commune with Christians everywhere.

At the Last Supper, the apostles ate bread broken from a single loaf and drank from a single cup passed to them by Jesus. "Jesus took bread, gave thanks and broke it, and give it to his disciples.... Then he took the cup, gave thanks and offered it to them, and they all drank from it" (Mark 14:23). In passing the bread and that cup among themselves, they symbolically expressed their unity with one another and with Christ.

Paul implies in 1 Corinthians that this use of one communal loaf and one cup passed from one person to another continued to be practiced. He wrote:

> After supper he [Jesus] took the cup, saying, 'This cup is the new covenant in my blood; do this in remembrance of me.' For whenever you eat this bread and drink this cup, you proclaim the Lord's death

until he comes. Therefore, whoever eats the bread or drinks the cup of the Lord in an unworthy manner will be guilty of sinning against the body and blood of the Lord. A man out to examine himself before he eats of the bread and drinks of the cup (verses 25-28).

The sharing of a single cup heightened their sense of sharing in Christ and of belonging to his one body. Passed from hand to hand, this single cup, drunk from by all, emphasized the oneness of the faith. As the church grew, this practice changed, but the belief in Christian unity through communion with Christ remained.

Summary

Let's summarize some points we've discussed and the conclusions we can draw from them.

- Passover is the name the Gospels give to the Last Supper at which Jesus instituted the symbols of bread and wine.

- When Christians eat those symbols, they commune with Christ. The name Communion expresses that truth.

- Paul did not condemn the name Lord's Supper or suggest a substitute. This suggests that he found the name perfectly acceptable.

- The etymology of Lord's Supper shows it to be a respectful and reverent name. Using it reminds believers of whose "supper" they are eating.

- The Corinthians should have been observing the Lord's Supper but were not, because they were abusing their fellow Christians and thereby heaping shame upon Christ's name.

- Eucharist comes from a word meaning thanksgiving. Christ and the church gave thanks over the wine symbolizing Jesus' shed blood, the blood of the new covenant. Eucharist can then be an expression of the believers' thanks for what God has done for them.

Therefore, the names Passover, Communion, Lord's Supper and Eucharist all have a biblical basis. Each name expresses different aspects of either Christ's sacrifice or of church custom. The acceptance or use of these names does not imply the acceptance of any doctrinal error, immorality, or superstitious ritual associated with them. The fact that others may have misused these names is unfortunate. These names should be used with the respect due them. Immorality or doctrinal error in association with these names does not mean that the church should avoid their use. Avoidance of these terms may lead Christians to forget certain aspects of the ordinance. "Out of sight, out of mind."

Does the church now keep the Lord's Supper? The answer is yes; the church has always kept the Lord's Supper, though we have not always called it by that name.

Endnotes

[1] Ralph Orr. "Has God's Church Always Kept the Passover?" *Reviews You Can Use,* March-April, 1993, p. 32.

[2] Herbert Armstrong's copy of his letter to Katie Gilstrap, 3 May 1928. The Herbert Armstrong personal papers collection, Grace Communion International, Item 3690, Box 10.

[3] Did the Gilstraps influence Mr. Armstrong to keep the Holy Days? The Gilstraps had observed both Passover and Unleavened Bread since 1893. In 1907 they contacted the Church of God. Despite the church's differences with the Gilstraps over the Holy Days (the church did not keep them) they recognized J.G. Gilstrap as a Church of God minister well into the 1920s (Richard Nickels, *A History of the Seventh Day Church of God,* private printing, 1973, pp. 240-241, 146, 177, 197).

Katie Gilstrap wrote at least one article discussing how the spring Holy Days meshed with the arrest and crucifixion of Jesus Christ. Herbert Armstrong's 1928 letter to Katie was in response to that article.

Perhaps as a result of her influence, Herbert Armstrong started in the spring of 1928 an intense personal Bible study of the Holy Days. The record of this study has been preserved in his personal papers. His study apparently led him to start observing Unleavened Bread by the spring of 1929.

Into the middle 1930s Mr. Armstrong still referred to Communion both as the Lord's Supper and as Passover. By 1940, Passover had become the preferred name.

[4] "The 'Communion,' which is instituted by New Testament Bible authority, is a memorial of the death of Christ" (Herbert Armstrong, *The Plain Truth About Christmas,* 1987 and earlier editions, p. 3).

[5] The closest thing to an official statement on the verse is found in only two pieces of literature, "How to Observe God's Festivals," published in 1959 and 1974, and a revision of the same entitled "Observing the Spring Festivals," in the March 24, 1986 *Worldwide News.* Both articles read, "No leavened product is to be used with the Passover service — which is improperly termed 'Lord's Supper' (I Corinthians 11:20)." The article did not originate but instead repeated our oral tradition.

[6] Matthew 26:17-20; Mark 14:12-26; Luke 22:7-19. John's account of that

evening differs markedly from that of the Synoptics. In John's Gospel the Last Supper is simply called an evening meal (John 13:1-3).

Despite the fact that Jesus called his Last Supper a Passover, he evidently did not mean that it was a Passover in the traditional sense. This is evident from its timing (at the beginning of the Passover day as opposed to the beginning of the Feast of Unleavened Bread), and the absence of most traditional elements associated with the Jewish festival. "Everything that is typical of a Passover is missing: the paschal lamb, the stewed fruit, the bitter herbs, and the Passover haggadah" (Klauck, "Lord's Supper," *The Anchor Bible Dictionary*, vol. 4, p. 365). Yet the Synoptics teach that the Last Supper was a Passover, no matter how nontraditional it may have been.

[7] 1 Corinthians 10:1-3.

[8] 1 Corinthians 10:7.

[9] 1 Corinthians 10:16.

[10] 1 Corinthians 11:17-22.

[11] Charles H. Talbert. *Reading Corinthians: A Literary and Theological Commentary on 1 and 2 Corinthians*. New York: Crossroad, 1989. pp. 74-75.

[12] Gordon D. Fee. *The First Epistle to the Corinthians*. The New International Commentary on the New Testament, F.F. Bruce, editor. Grand Rapids: Eerdmans, 1991, p. 533.

[13] Talbert, p. 75.

[14] 1 Corinthians 11:23-27.

[15] 1 Corinthians 11:22.

[16] Bauer, Arndt and Gingrich. *A Greek-English Lexicon of the New Testament and Other Early Christian Literature*. University of Chicago Press, 1952, p. 151.

[17] Hans-Josef Klauck. "Lord's Supper," translated by David Ewert. *The Anchor Bible Dictionary*, vol 4. New York: Doubleday, 1992. pp. 362-363.

[18] John 12:2; 13:2, 4; 21:20; Revelation 19:9, 17.

[19] Luke 14:12, 16-17, 24.

[20] M.H. Shepherd, Jr. "Lord's Supper." *Interpreter's Dictionary of the Bible*, Abingdon, 1962.

[21] Klauck, p. 363.

[22] Matthew 26:27; Mark 14:23-24.

[23] Klauck, p. 364.

[24] *Which Day is the Christian Sabbath?* 1991 revision. pp. 68-69; *The Truth About Easter.* 1992. pp. 5, 19, 21.

Ralph Orr

79. QUESTION & ANSWERS
ABOUT THE LORD'S SUPPER

What is the meaning of the Lord's Supper?

The Lord's Supper is a reminder of what Jesus did in the past, a symbol of our present relationship with him and a promise of what he will do in the future. Let's examine these three aspects.

The bread and wine are memorials of Jesus' death on the cross (Luke 22:19-20; 1 Corinthians 11:26). In the Lord's Supper, we each eat a piece of bread in remembrance of Jesus. When we drink the "fruit of the vine," we remember that Jesus' blood was shed for us, and that it signifies the new covenant. The Lord's Supper looks back to the death of Jesus Christ on the cross.

Jesus' death shows how much God loves us — so much that he sent his Son to die for us, so that our sins may be forgiven and we may live forever with him. This is good news! Although we may be saddened by the enormous price that had to be paid for us, we are happy that it was paid. When we remember Jesus' death, we also remember that Jesus was dead for only a short time. We rejoice that Jesus has conquered death, and has set free all who were enslaved by a fear of death (Hebrews 2:14-15). Our mourning has turned to joy (John 16:20).

Christians look back to the crucifixion and resurrection of Jesus as the defining moment in our history. This is how we escape death and the slavery of sin, and this is how we are freed to serve the Lord. The Lord's Supper is a memorial of this defining moment in our history.

The Lord's Supper also pictures our present relationship with Jesus Christ. The crucifixion has a continuing significance to all who have taken up a cross to follow Jesus. We continue to participate in his death (Romans 6:4; Galatians 2:20; Colossians 2:20) because we participate in his life (Galatians 2:20; Ephesians 2:6; Colossians 2:13; 3:1).

Paul wrote, "Is not the cup of thanksgiving for which we give thanks a participation in the blood of Christ? And is not the bread that we break a participation in the body of Christ?" (1 Corinthians 10:16). With the Lord's Supper, we show that we share in Jesus Christ. We participate with him, commune with him, become united in him. The Lord's Supper helps us look upward, to Christ.

In John 6, Jesus used bread and wine to illustrate our need to be spiritually nourished by him: "Unless you eat the flesh of the Son of Man and drink his blood, you have no life in you.... Whoever eats my flesh and drinks my blood remains in me, and I in him" (verses 53-56). The Lord's Supper reminds us that real life is found only in Jesus Christ, with him living in us.

When we are aware that Jesus lives in us, we also pause to think what kind of home we are giving him. We allow him to change our lives so that we live the way he wants us to. Paul wrote that we ought to examine ourselves before we eat of the bread and drink of the cup (1 Corinthians 11:28). The Lord's Supper helps us look inward, to examine ourselves because of the great meaning in this ceremony.

As we examine ourselves, we need to look around, to other people, to see whether we are treating one another in the way that Jesus commanded. If you are united with Christ and I am united with Christ, then we are united to each other, too. The Lord's Supper, by picturing our participation in Christ, also pictures our participation (other translations may say communion or sharing or fellowship) with each other (1 John 1:3, 7).

Paul wrote in 1 Corinthians 10:17, "Because there is one loaf, we, who are many, are one body, for we all partake of the one loaf." The Lord's Supper pictures the fact that we are one body in Christ, one with each other, with responsibilities toward one another.

Third, the Lord's Supper also reminds us of the future, of Jesus' return. Jesus said he would not drink the fruit of the vine again until he came in the fullness of the kingdom (Matthew 26:29; Luke 22:18; Mark 14:25). Whenever we participate, we are reminded of Jesus' promise. Paul wrote that "For whenever you eat this bread and drink this cup, you proclaim the Lord's death *until he comes*" (1 Corinthians 11:26). The Lord's Supper helps us look forward.

The Lord's Supper is rich in meaning. That is why it has been an important part of the Christian tradition throughout the centuries. Sometimes it has become a lifeless ritual, done more out of habit than with meaning. Some people overreact by stopping the ritual entirely. The better response is to restore the meaning.

Is it wrong to use the term "Lord's Supper"?

Some say that the ceremony of bread and wine should not be called the Lord's Supper. Two reasons are given for this. First, that the ceremony should be called by its old covenant name, Passover. And the second idea was that 1 Corinthians 11:20 says that the Corinthians Christians were not eating the Lord's Supper.

The bread and wine is not a Passover. At Jesus' Last Supper, the meal was a Passover meal; the sharing of bread and wine was done *after* the supper, and Scripture does not call it a Passover.

What does Scripture call it? It does not give a formal name. In 1 Corinthians 10:16, Paul calls it a "cup of thanksgiving." In verse 21, he calls it "the cup of the Lord" and "the Lord's table." Since Scripture does not require a particular name, Christians are free to use any term that helps them understand that they are talking about the sharing of bread and wine in commemoration of Jesus' death. Historically, three terms have been most common:

- Eucharist. This comes from *eucharisteo,* the Greek word for giving thanks (1 Corinthians 11:24).

- Communion. This word is used in the King James translation of 1 Corinthians 10:16; it means sharing or participation.

- Lord's Supper. Since Paul calls the memorial "the Lord's Table," it is not much different to call it "the Lord's Supper." It would be picky to say that "table" is OK, but "supper" is forbidden. The Bible doesn't require us to use any certain term, and doesn't forbid us to use any term.

Why then does Paul tell the Corinthians that "When you come together, it is not the Lord's Supper you eat"? (1 Corinthians 11:20). He explains what he means in the next verse: "for [or "because"] as you eat, each of you goes ahead without waiting for anybody else. One remains hungry, another gets drunk." They were not eating the Lord's Supper, not because that was the wrong term, but because they were not participating in the right spirit. They were not sharing. Paul was commenting on the manner of their observance, not giving rules about names.

For a more detailed answer, see "The Name of the Lord's Supper."

What kind of bread and wine?

Since Jesus began the Lord's Supper after having told his disciples to prepare for the Passover, it is likely that he used unleavened bread. From the historical situation, we can also conclude that the bread Jesus used was made from grain harvested the year before, as required by old covenant law (Leviticus 23:10-14). However, neither the Scriptures nor the symbolism requires us to imitate these particular details.

The Bible does not attach any significance or importance to the age of the flour, nor whether it was leavened. Similarly, it does not specify whether the bread was made with wheat or barley. Scriptures about the last supper do not use the word for unleavened — the Bible simply says that it was bread. It used the common word for a common food.

When Jesus said, "I am the bread of life" (John 6:51), he did not specify whether he was wheat or barley, leavened or unleavened. The point he was making does not rest on such details. He was simply comparing himself to food in general, the most common staple of the diet. Just as bread is the basis of physical life, Jesus is the basis of eternal life.

When Jesus called himself bread, he was referring to its value in the common people's diet, not to any specifics of shape or density. If he had lived and ministered in southeastern Asia, he might have compared himself to rice as the staff of life. His point did not depend on the specific grain being used — just that it was a common part of the diet. Jesus is the staple of our spiritual nourishment.

The wine that Jesus used was probably red, fermented wine from the previous year. That was what was available. It was probably mixed with water, as wine usually was in ancient times. Scripture does not mention these specifics. It simply says "fruit of the vine."

When Jesus instituted the symbols, he did not make detailed requirements for the food or drink. He used words that were commonly used for ordinary food and drink. This made it easier for the disciples to do "this" in his remembrance. Whenever the original disciples shared a meal, they could remember what Jesus had done at the Last Supper.

The significance of the bread is not the type of grain it is made from, its texture, or whether it has fermented. Its significance is that it is food, and that we share it. Scripture simply says it is "bread," without specifying "unleavened." That is why the church teaches that members may use any type of bread whenever they observe communion.

Similarly, the significance of the wine is not its fermentation. The significance is that it is liquid, thus allowing it to represent Jesus' blood of the new covenant, and that we drink it, symbolizing our taking the new covenant into ourselves. Jesus called it by a general term: "the fruit of the vine." Therefore we allow either wine or juice to be used for communion.

Some people avoid wine because of allergies. Others avoid it because their body reacts with alcohol in undesirable ways. Some Christians in less-developed nations find it very difficult to find wine. Substitutes are permissible. The effectiveness of the ceremony does not depend on chemistry, but on our relationship with God.

Who should partake of the Lord's Supper?

Is it permissible for people to participate in the Lord's Supper or Communion before they are baptized?

The Lord's Supper is for people who have faith in Jesus Christ as Lord and Savior, even if they have not been baptized yet. The bread and wine are for those who have faith in Christ. People must make their own decision as to whether to partake. We do not believe it is appropriate to refuse to let people partake if they want to do so. God knows those who are his.

The Lord's Supper is for people who have faith in Jesus Christ as their Savior and Lord. However, we can't, nor do we wish to, police everybody's heart as to whether their faith is real. Some people may actually become convicted and come to faith during the course of the Lord's Supper service, and it would be right for them to partake.

Question: May people observe without participating?

Answer: Yes. Anyone is welcome to observe the service.

Do we want the Lord's Supper to be part of a formal church service, or something done privately in individual homes?

Question: Does the service have to be led by an ordained elder?

Answer: We have always made arrangements for members to take the elements (bread and wine) in their own homes when they were unable to participate with the congregation. Although an elder would officiate in such situations when one was available, we permitted a member to lead when an elder was not available.

The New Testament never even hints at the idea that administering at the Lord's Supper is a function restricted to ordained leaders. For example, Paul did not mention anything about ordained leaders when he addressed the Corinthian church about the Lord's Supper. No verse connects the Lord's Supper with leadership offices.

As far as we can tell from the New Testament, Christians were able to observe the Lord's Supper as often as they wanted, without any need for elders, whenever two or three or more were gathered in his name. If an elder is present, it is traditional, though not required, that the elder lead the communion.

Members may partake of the Lord's Supper at any time in small groups. We are pleased that groups commemorate our Lord's death, and see their own existence in that context, knowing that our unity comes because of our participation in him.

Question: May communion be led by a woman?

Answer: Yes. This function is not restricted to pastors, elders, or other church leaders, and may be done by anyone who has faith in Christ. Just as women sing prayers in church, they may also pray at a communion service that God will bless the elements for our commemoration of the Lord's death and our participation by faith in our Lord.

Question: As an ordinance of the church, what degree of standardization does the church wish to suggest regarding the service format for communion?

Answer: We want our service to follow a general standard, including prayer, a basic explanation of and blessing on the bread and wine, and worshipful music. Other Communion services can follow any dignified and respectful format that brings glory to God and does not bring reproach on the name of Christ. It must not be done flippantly, but with meaning. It should be a dignified occasion, yet at the same time, a joyous occasion—thereby appropriate for coming into the presence of God.

What is our position on transubstantiation?

Jesus said, "This is my body." Some churches take this statement literally, and teach that the bread becomes the body of Jesus Christ. However, other churches take this statement to be symbolic. It is possible that what Jesus said, and what he meant, was something symbolic or metaphorical. Jesus often used figurative language. For example, when Jesus said, I am the bread that came down from heaven, he did not mean that he was literally bread. He meant it figuratively.

At the Last Supper, when Jesus said the words, he was with the disciples, holding some bread, telling his disciples, This is my body. The disciples could see his body; they could see that the bread was not his body. In the original setting, the disciples would have understood Jesus' words in some figurative way.

Jesus also said that the cup was the new covenant in his blood. That's figurative language. He was not concerned about the actual cup. He used the word "cup" to refer to the wine inside the cup. It was a figure of speech. The wine wasn't the new covenant, either. Jesus was speaking figuratively. He did not say that the wine was his blood.

The pattern is consistent: Jesus was speaking figuratively. The bread symbolized the body of Jesus. However, this does not mean that the bread is "only" a symbol — as if symbols are not important. Symbols are important. The bread represents the body of Jesus, and that's an extremely important representation. Moreover, Jesus is present in the ceremony, as well as in the physical bread and wine, in some spiritual way. By partaking of the bread and wine, we participate in our Lord (1 Corinthians 10:16).

80. YOUR PART IN THE LORD'S TABLE

Places in the Heart, Robert Benton's Academy Award-winning film about the Depression-era U.S. South, ends on a mystical note. The last scene finds an odd collection of parishioners sharing pews in a church.

Here sits a white peace officer who, in a tragic accident, had been shot to death by a drunken black youth. By him is his young widow, who had been left to rear two children on a broken-down cotton farm. Nearby sits a black beggar-thief-farmer whom Ku Klux Klan terrorists ran out of town. There's a blind man who eked out a living by caning chairs. Plus a traveling minstrel whose simple, haunting tunes punctuated this poor world.

The group also includes town leaders who, at night, donned sheets to lead racist attacks. Over here is an elderly woman who died in a tornado. And there's an adulterous husband and his long-suffering but forgiving wife. And, finally, we see the black youth who was killed by vengeful whites after he had accidentally shot the lawman.

In a compelling benediction, Benton metaphorically unites these characters by having them eat and drink communion wafers and wine, symbols of the broken body and shed blood of Jesus Christ. Thus this disparate tableau of fellow humans, who never would have come together in any other way, finally shares the peace of God.

How many become one

Christians come from all backgrounds, all races, all economic levels, and all nations. Yet they all find unity in the Body of Jesus Christ, through the sacrifice of the Savior of the world. The bread and wine of the Lord's Supper, also called Communion and the Eucharist, are the memorials of that sacrifice.

"Is not the cup of thanksgiving for which we give thanks a participation in the blood of Christ? And is not the bread that we break a participation in the body of Christ?" asked the apostle Paul (1 Corinthians 10:16). "Because there is one loaf, we, who are many, are one body, for we all partake of the one loaf" (verse 17).

Jesus said: "Unless you eat the flesh of the Son of Man and drink his blood, you have no life in you. Whoever eats my flesh and drinks my blood has eternal life, and I will raise him up at the last day" (John 6:53-54).

Jesus' statement shocked the people of his day. God's law forbade the consumption of any blood, let alone human blood. Yet Jesus was not suggesting they eat human flesh and drink human blood. He was telling people that, if they wanted to receive eternal life, his life would have to become their own. They had to unite with him through his death and resurrection. They had to live as he required, relying on him to guide their every step.

When he ate the Last Supper with his disciples on the night before he was crucified, Jesus institutionalized these concepts for the New Testament church.

The Last Supper

For centuries, the Israelites had observed the Passover in memory of their Exodus from slavery in Egypt. Their ancestors killed lambs and smeared the blood on their doorposts so God would pass over their homes while striking down the Egyptian firstborn (Exodus 12:12-13). Because the Israelites left Egypt in haste, they ate unleavened, or flat, bread that had not had time to rise. The Passover lamb prefigured Jesus' sacrificial death. As the Lamb of God, he allowed his blood to be spilled to rescue humanity from sin — in symbol, the Egypt that is this God-rejecting world.

It was after a Passover meal that Jesus instituted the Lord's Supper: "When the hour came, Jesus and his apostles reclined at the table. And he said to them, 'I have eagerly desired to eat this Passover with you before I suffer. For I tell you, I will not eat it again until it finds fulfillment in the kingdom of God'" (Luke 22:14-16).

Jesus knew he was about to be slaughtered, just as innocent lambs would be killed for the Jews' Passover observance. "And he took bread, gave thanks and broke it, and gave it to them, saying, 'This is my body given for you; do this in remembrance of me.' In the same way, after the supper he took the cup, saying, 'This cup is the new covenant in my blood, which is poured out for you'" (verses 19-20).

In remembrance of him

Shortly after the Last Supper, Roman soldiers arrested Jesus. At the urging of the Jews, the Roman authorities tried, condemned and crucified him. Jesus bore our sins on the cross so we may be passed over and saved from the penalty of sin.

Christ's church continued to use bread and wine as a memorial of his death. Paul wrote:

> For I received from the Lord what I also passed on to you: The Lord Jesus, on the night he was betrayed, took bread, and when he had given thanks, he broke it and said, "This is my body, which is for you; do this in remembrance of me." In the same way, after supper he took the cup, saying, "This cup is the new covenant in my blood; do

this, whenever you drink it, in remembrance of me." For whenever you eat this bread and drink this cup, you proclaim the Lord's death until he comes" (1 Corinthians 11:23-26).

The Lord's Supper is not an Old Testament observance. It reminds us of a rescue far better that Israel escaping Egypt. Jesus, through his life, death, resurrection and his ongoing work as our High Priest, has delivered us, the Israel of God, from sin and eternal death. He has united all Christian believers, from all backgrounds, in his Body.

Paul tells us about our salvation in Christ:

> God was pleased to have all his fullness dwell in him, and through him to reconcile to himself all things, whether things on earth or things in heaven, by making peace through his blood, shed on the cross. Once you were alienated from God and were enemies in your minds because of your evil behavior. But now he has reconciled you by Christ's physical body through death to present you holy in his sight, without blemish and free from accusation. (Colossians 1:19-22)

"Christ is the mediator of a new covenant," Hebrews 9:15 tells us, "that those who are called may receive the promised eternal inheritance — now that he has died as a ransom to set them free."

For Christians — those who live by faith in Christ — the Lord's Supper service combines spiritual reflection with joyful appreciation and worship. By participating in Christ's death, we are united with all fellow Christians. We share our exaltation of the Savior of the world. We embrace the forgiveness we have through Jesus' shed blood. We celebrate at the Lord's Table as one spiritual Body in the peace of God.

Norman Shoaf

81. THE BREAD OF HEAVEN

Jesus said to them, "I tell you the truth, it is not Moses who has given you the bread from heaven, but it is my Father who gives you the true bread from heaven. For the bread of God is he who comes down from heaven and gives life to the world.... This is the bread that came down from heaven. Your forefathers ate manna and died, but he who feeds on this bread will live forever" (John 6:32-33, 58)

Bread, the staff of life, has been a staple food for thousands of years. Whether made from wheat, rye, barley, millet, rice or even potato flour, it has been the basic diet of common people. Bread has been synonymous with food for ordinary working people of many cultures.

As the common food of the average Israelite, it featured frequently in the spiritual consciousness and the ceremonial and sacrificial worship of ancient Israel.

The bread and wine that Abraham shared with Melchizedek king of Salem were a customary expression of peace and fellowship. To break bread with someone was an act of communion (Gen. 14:18). The unleavened bread of the Exodus reminded them of the haste and eagerness with which they had left their life of bondage in Egypt, on their way to a life of liberty as a new nation in their own land (Ex. 12:39). They remembered the manna in the wilderness—bread from heaven that had preserved their lives during the journey from Egypt through the wilderness to their new home in Canaan (Ex. 16:2-4). The Bread of the Presence, or showbread, that was placed daily in the holy place of the Temple, reminded them that God was their provider and sustainer, and they lived constantly in his presence. (D. Freeman, article "Showbread," *New Bible Dictionary,* InterVarsity Press, 1996)

So when Jesus said, "I am the bread of heaven, the bread of God, the bread of life," he was tapping into a rich reservoir of religious symbolism, historical tradition and cultural associations. Bread had represented many things to the Jews in the past.

But now Jesus challenged them to see that these historical meanings had been wrapped up in, and were superseded by, one great new meaning. The true bread was not the unleavened bread of the Exodus, or the manna of the wilderness, or the bread of the presence in the Temple. The true bread is Jesus Christ!

Jesus had adopted an ancient and familiar symbol, and had given it a new

291

and fuller significance. The new significance was not totally unrelated to the ancient significances, but it went much further.

For Abraham, breaking bread with Melchizedek had been an act of communion on the human level. But when we Christians partake of Jesus, the bread of God, we have communion not just with one another, but with him and with the Father.

Israel's unleavened bread reminded them of fleeing Egypt to a new life in Canaan. But for Christians, that exodus was symbolic of our entrance into the new life in the kingdom of God. The manna from heaven preserved Israel's life during their journey through the wilderness. Christians rejoice that in Jesus, the bread of heaven, our lives are nourished and kept safe as we journey toward the fullness of eternal life.

The showbread reminded Israel that God was the provider and sustainer of their earthly lives. Christians know that in Jesus, the true bread, our lives are lifted up above the mundane, earthly level, and we live with him "in the heavenly realms" (Ephesians 2:6). Jesus showed that the meaning of ancient traditions can be superseded by a new and eternal revelation.

Don Mears

82. FOOTWASHING: A TRADITION OF SERVICE

On the evening he was betrayed, Jesus "poured water into a basin and began to wash his disciples' feet, drying them with the towel that was wrapped around him" (John 13:5).

"When he had finished washing their feet, he put on his clothes and returned to his place. 'Do you understand what I have done for you?' he asked them.... 'Now that I, your Lord and Teacher, have washed your feet, you also should wash one another's feet'" (verses 12, 14).

In the days of dusty roads and open-toed sandals, feet often became dirty, and it was the job of the lowest servants to wash the guests' feet. But Jesus set an example of service by doing this job himself, despite the protests from Peter.

What did Jesus teach?

Jesus said, "I have set you an example that you should do as I have done for you" (verse 15). We must ask, then, just what did Jesus do?

1. He got up from the meal,
2. took off his outer clothing,
3. wrapped a towel around his waist,
4. poured water into a basin,
5. washed the disciples' feet, and
6. dried them with his towel.

Christians generally skip most of what Jesus did. We do not wash feet during a meal, take off our suit jackets or wrap towels around our waists. We do not pour water into a basin, or dry feet with our own towel. Most Christians do not literally wash one another's feet. Some churches have an annual footwashing service, but if they do, people usually wash two feet that are already clean. Jesus washed 24 feet that really needed to be washed. Jesus performed a service that really needed to be done.

Did our Lord instruct his disciples to "wash one another's feet" (verse 14)? Yes. Then why don't we have any evidence that the apostles actually did it? They didn't do it the evening Jesus commanded it, and we see nothing about it in Matthew, Mark, Luke, Acts, the epistles or in early church history.

The closest thing we find to it in the New Testament is 1 Timothy 5:10, which is about the qualifications of widows who may be put on a list of widows working for and supported by the church (we don't do that anymore, do we?). One of the qualifications is that she must be "well known for her good deeds, such as...washing the feet of the saints." Here, footwashing is a notable act of service, not something that all Christian women are expected to do on an annual basis.

Apparently the apostles understood Jesus to be talking about real service, not a ritual. When Jesus said, wash one another's feet, he meant, serve one another. He used a specific example as a figure of speech representing all types of service. (The Gospel of John has many such figures of speech that should not be taken literally.) Jesus is saying that we should humble ourselves and be willing to do even menial tasks for one another.

Symbol of service

It is not wrong for Christians to wash one another's feet. But we do not turn the figure of speech into a literal requirement.

The Bible was written in a specific culture, and its instructions are sometimes phrased with specific customs. Paul tells us to greet one another with a holy kiss, and footwashing is even more tied to culture than kissing is. It is based on foot travel, dusty roads and open-toed sandals. In Jesus' day, footwashing was a normal part of a formal banquet. Now it is not. It is no longer part of customary formality, and it is no longer viewed as an honor or service.

We obey the intent of Paul's command not by kissing, but by greeting one another with affection. We obey the intent of Jesus' command not by washing our guests' feet, but by helping them in other ways. There is no need to insist on taking one command literally and adapting the other to modern customs. Both may be adapted so that we obey the intent.

When we serve one another throughout the year, helping one another with real needs, we are obeying the spirit of the law of Christ. We are "washing feet" when we give people rides to church, when we help them move furniture, when we bring a meal for the sick, when we clean house for the bereaved. We wash feet when we encourage the depressed, are patient with the angry, spend time with the lonely.

There are a thousand ways to "wash the feet of the saints." Sometimes it might even involve washing their feet — even cutting their toenails and helping them with cleanliness. Real service for genuine needs is far more important than a sanitized ritual. As Paul wrote: "You, my brothers, were called to be free. But do not use your freedom to indulge the sinful nature; rather, serve one another in love" (Galatians 5:13).

Joseph Tkach

83. HOW BAPTISM PICTURES THE GOSPEL

Rituals were a prominent part of Old Testament worship—there were annual rituals, monthly rituals and daily rituals. There were rituals for birth and rituals for death, rituals of sacrifice, rituals of cleansing, rituals of ordination. Faith was involved, but rituals were prominent.

The New Testament, in contrast, has two basic rituals: baptism and the Lord's Supper —and there are no detailed regulations for either observance. Why these two? In a religion in which faith is primary, why have any rituals at all?

The primary reason, I believe, is that both the Lord's Supper and baptism picture the gospel of Jesus Christ. They rehearse the fundamental elements of our faith. The Lord's Supper reminds us of the Lord's death, his life now, which we share in, and his promise to return. It is a reminder that our salvation is based on the life and death of Jesus Christ.

Pictures the gospel

How does baptism picture the central truths of the gospel? The apostle Paul wrote:

> Don't you know that all of us who were baptized into Christ Jesus were baptized into his death? We were therefore buried with him through baptism into death in order that, just as Christ was raised from the dead through the glory of the Father, we too may live a new life. If we have been united with him like this in his death, we will certainly also be united with him in his resurrection. (Romans 6:3-5)

Paul is saying that baptism pictures our union with Christ in his death, burial and resurrection. These are the primary points of the gospel (1 Corinthians 15:3-4). Our salvation depends on his life, death and resurrection. Our forgiveness—being cleansed of sin—depends on him; our Christian life and future depend on him.

Baptism symbolizes the death of the old self—the old person was crucified with Christ—died with Christ—buried with Christ in baptism (Romans 6:8; Galatians 2:20; 6:14; Colossians 2:12, 20). It pictures that we are identified with Jesus Christ—he united himself with humanity. We accept that his death was "for us," and "for our sins." We acknowledge that we have sinned, that we have a tendency to sin, that we are sinners who needed a Savior. We acknowledge our need to be cleansed, and that this cleansing came through the death of Jesus Christ.

Baptism is one of the ways that we confess Jesus Christ as our Lord and Savior. We are saved by what he did, not by the way we responded. Therefore, the emphasis in baptism should be on what Jesus did, not on our faith or acceptance. The only reason that we can show our response of faith is because he is already committed to us.

Raised with Christ

Baptism pictures wonderful news—we have been raised with Christ to live with him (Ephesians 2:5-6; Colossians 2:12-13; 3:1). In him, we have a new life, and are called to live a new way of life, with him as Lord leading and guiding us out of sinful ways and into righteous and loving ways. Baptism reminds us that faith involves a change in the way we live, and that we cannot make this change in ourselves—it is done by the power of the risen Christ living in us. Christ has united himself to us in his resurrection not just for the future, but for life right now. This is part of the symbolism.

Jesus did not invent the ritual of baptism. It developed within Judaism, and was used by John the Baptist as a ritual to show repentance, in which the water symbolized cleansing. Jesus continued this practice, and after his death and resurrection his disciples continued to use it, but with a more profound meaning. Baptism dramatizes the fact that Jesus has given us a new basis for life, and a new basis for our relationship with God.

Paul saw that since we are forgiven or cleansed through the death of Christ, baptism pictures his death and that we (even before we were alive) are participants in his death. Paul was also inspired to add the connection with Jesus' resurrection. As we rise from the baptismal waters, we picture Christ raising us to a new life — a life in Christ, with him in us.

Peter wrote that baptism saves us "by the resurrection of Jesus Christ" (1 Peter 3:21). However, baptism itself does not save us. We are saved by God's grace, through faith in Jesus Christ. Physical water removing physical dirt cannot save us, this verse reminds us. Baptism saves us only in the sense that it is "the pledge of a good conscience toward God." It is a visible representation of trusting in Christ, trusting that he has cleansed our conscience and forgiven us. We are saved by what he has done, not by what we do.

Into one body

We are baptized not only into Christ Jesus, but we are also baptized into his body, the church. "We were all baptized by one Spirit into one body" (1 Corinthians 12:13). That is why people cannot baptize themselves—it should be done within the context of the Christian community. There are no secret Christians, people who believe in Christ but no one knows about it. The biblical pattern is to confess Christ before other people, to make a public acknowledgment of Jesus as Lord, to become part of a community of believers.

Baptism is one of the ways in which Christ may be confessed, in which a person's friends may see that a commitment has been made: Christ's commitment to us in his death, and our commitment to him as a response. It may be a joyous occasion in which the congregation sings hymns and welcomes the person to the family. Or it may be a smaller ceremony in which an elder (or some other authorized representative of the congregation) welcomes the new believer, rehearses the significance of what is being done, and encourages them in their life in Christ.

Baptism recognizes that a person has already repented of sin, already accepted Christ as Savior, already begun to grow spiritually — is already a Christian. We are simply catching up to what Christ has already done for us. Baptism does not make a person a Christian—it recognizes that they already are a Christian. Baptism is usually done soon after a person has come to believe in Christ as Savior, but occasionally it may be done much later.

Teens and children

When a person has come to faith in Christ, he or she may be baptized. This may be when the person is old, or when young. A young person may explain faith differently than an older person does, but young people may have faith nonetheless. Teenagers and younger children may have genuine awareness of sin, genuine trust that Christ has paid for their sins, and awareness that their life is united with Christ, and they may be baptized.

Will some of them eventually change their minds and fall away? Perhaps, but that happens with adult professions of faith, too. Will some of those childhood conversions turn out to be mistaken? Perhaps, but that happens with adults, too. There are no guarantees about what humans will do — the guarantee comes in what Christ has already done for us. That is what we can celebrate with certainty.

If the person has faith in Christ, then the person may be baptized. It is not our practice, however, to baptize minors without the consent of their parent or legal guardian. If the minor's parent objects to baptism, then the child who has faith in Jesus is still a Christian, even if he or she has to wait until later to be baptized.

In our denomination, we generally baptize by immersion. That was most likely the practice in first-century Judaism and in the early church. Immersion pictures death and burial better than sprinkling does. Sprinkling pictures cleansing, but not death. Nevertheless, we might say that the old person died with Christ, whether or not the body was properly buried. The old life is dead, and the new life is here, and that is what is important.

We do not make the method of baptism an issue to divide Christians. The important thing is that we remember that Christ has done the real work of salvation, and we are simply responding to what he has done. We give up on our own self-centered approach to life and begin to let him guide us by his Spirit.

Salvation does not depend on the exact method of baptism (the Bible doesn't give us many details on procedure, anyway) nor on the exact words. Salvation depends on Christ, not on the depth of the water. If a person has faith in Christ, that person is a Christian, no matter what kind of baptism was done. A Christian who was baptized by sprinkling or pouring is still a Christian. If such a person wishes to become a member of our denomination, we do not require a new baptism. Christianity is based on faith, not on performance of a ritual.

Occasionally people baptized in infancy wish to become members of our fellowship. Is it necessary for us to re-baptize them? If they have only recently come to a point of faith and commitment, it may be appropriate to baptize them. In such cases, baptism would emphasize to them that the old self has died with Christ.

If people were baptized as infants and have been living as adult Christians for many years, with good fruit, then they do not need another baptism. If they request it, we may do it, but we do not need to quibble about ceremonies of decades ago when Christian fruit is already evident. We can simply praise the grace of God. The person is a Christian whether or not the ritual was done in the "right" way or "right" time.

Sharing the Lord's Supper

For similar reasons, it is permissible for us to share the Lord's Supper with people who have not been baptized in the manner we are accustomed to. If people have faith in Jesus Christ, they are united to him and have been baptized, one way or another, into his body, and they may share in the bread and wine, even if they do not agree with us on every point of doctrine.

We should not get sidetracked by arguments about detail. We have our beliefs and practices, and we love those who have other beliefs. We focus on the larger picture, provided by the apostle Paul: Baptism pictures our old self dying with Christ, our sins being washed away by what he did, and Christ raising us up to new life in him and in his church. Baptism is a reminder that we are saved by the death and life of Jesus Christ. It is the gospel in miniature drama — the central truths of the faith being portrayed in the actions.

Joseph Tkach

84. SHOULD BELIEVERS BE BAPTIZED?

Is baptism essential to the Christian life? Should people be baptized again if they change churches or denominations? Is it essential to be baptized in a specific way, such as sprinkling, pouring or immersion?

On the first Pentecost after Jesus' resurrection, Peter exhorted his listeners: "Repent and be baptized, every one of you, in the name of Jesus Christ for the forgiveness of your sins. And you will receive the gift of the Holy Spirit. The promise is for you and your children and for all who are far off — for all whom the Lord our God will call" (Acts 2:38-39). We are among those who are "far off," and we can share in the grace of God along with those who heard Peter speak almost 2,000 years ago.

Note how the people responded to Peter's call after he finished his sermon: About 3,000 accepted Christ that day, and were baptized (Acts 2:41). When people accepted Christ as the Messiah, baptism was the appropriate response. Baptism sends a message to ourselves, to others, and to God. By being baptized, we acknowledge that God is the source of our life and the reason we exist, and that Christ is our Lord and Savior.

Baptism pictures the drama of our "I do" decision for Jesus Christ—but it is possible only because Jesus has already said the "I do" for us. He has already made a commitment to us, and we are now acknowledging it. He has already given his life for us; we are now responding and giving our lives to him. Baptism is a symbolic act that says there is a life-long commitment between Christ and us, and he is our Savior. Baptism implies that we will follow him wherever he may lead us.

People who request baptism are saying they accept Jesus' offer. He wants to be associated with us, to live with us forever and ever. In baptism, we say that we agree to be associated with Jesus Christ in a personal and intimate way — to belong to Christ, to share in the benefits of his life and death. That's what it means to be baptized "in the name of Jesus Christ."

Believers share in the life of Christ. As Christ died, so do the believers. As they share in Jesus' death, they also have a part in his resurrection and eternal life. In baptism, believers dramatize that we are united with Christ in his death and in his life. The apostle Paul explained this to the Romans:

> All of us who were baptized into Christ Jesus were baptized into his death. We were therefore buried with him through baptism into death in order that, just as Christ was raised from the dead through the glory of the Father, we too may live a new life. If we have been

united with him like this in death, we will certainly also be united with him in his resurrection. (Romans 6:3-4)

Baptism symbolizes our death and resurrection with Christ, that our old self is a thing of the past, and that our real life is in Christ. Going down into the water pictures the death of the self, and rising up out of the water pictures the resurrection of the self to a new life now, and eternal life in the future.

Baptism is not magic. It does not automatically bring the Holy Spirit to us, nor does it cause our spiritual renewal and salvation. Rather, it is done after the Holy Spirit has led us to faith and we have responded. Baptism is a metaphor that symbolizes that on the cross, Christ has crucified our former life and has brought us into a new life in him.

We can see this in some examples in Scripture. First, an example where the Holy Spirit did not come immediately to individuals who had been baptized. We read about this in Acts 8:14-17. Many people in Samaria had believed the gospel and accepted Jesus as Savior. They had also been baptized, but they had not received the Spirit in any noticeable way. In this case, Peter and John had to place their hands on these individuals and pray for them to receive the Holy Spirit.

In the case of the centurion Cornelius and his family and friends, the Holy Spirit came before baptism (Acts 10:44-48). They were baptized after receiving the Spirit, but there was no laying on of hands. These examples teach us that while baptism is an important public statement, it is symbolic. (The repentant "thief on the cross" could not be baptized at all, yet was saved.)

This brings up the matter of the method of baptism. Different churches baptize in different ways. If we understand that baptism is primarily a symbolic public statement of being united with Christ in his death and resurrection, then we can see that the mode is not critical. The fact of our baptism is the meaningful act.

We follow what appears to be the biblical example of baptism by full immersion. Our church also uses the formula of Matthew 28:19, baptizing candidates into the trinitarian fellowship of God. The minister will conclude the baptism prayer with words to the candidate such as the following: "Having repented of your sins, and having accepted Jesus Christ as your Lord and Savior, I now baptize you — not into any denomination or church — but into the name of the Father and the Son and the Holy Spirit."

When individuals who were once baptized in another church enter our fellowship, they sometimes wonder if they should be rebaptized. If they only recently came to faith in Christ, then they may feel that their previous baptism was not valid, and they may wish to be baptized as an acknowledgement that Jesus is their Savior. On the other hand, if they have been a Christian for a long time, living in faith in Christ and being led by the Spirit, their life has already been a public testimony of their new life in Christ; there is no need to repeat a ceremony when the reality has long been evident in their lives.

Individuals can counsel with a pastor if they have any questions about baptism. Others who are interested in discussing baptism, or other spiritual matters, can write to the church office in their country or contact us at: Grace Communion International, 3120 Whitehall Park Dr., Charlotte, NC 28273. Those in the United States can also call our toll-free number for church and minister information: 1-800-423-4444. Or see our website.

85. BAPTISM: COMMEMORATING COMMITMENT

We gathered around a swimming pool anticipating the ceremony about to begin. One person stepped into the shallow end of the pool. She walked through the water toward the minister who was about to baptize her.

It was a momentous and memorable day for this young woman, and we all felt some of her excitement. She now understood God's aim in salvation – to save us from our blighted human condition, to make us at peace with him, to give the Holy Spirit as the promised "down payment" on eternal life – and most importantly, she understood that Jesus had done everything necessary to make God's gift a reality.

New life in God

Jesus Christ has a profound role in God's purpose for us. He was sent by God to be the Savior of humanity. By his perfect obedience and his atoning work on the cross, we are saved. Now, the young woman was about to make a public statement that Jesus had saved her. Jesus had made a commitment to her, and she was making one to him. She had accepted Jesus as her Savior, and had accepted his new life. She was saying "I do" to God; she was saying "yes" to his "yes."

The baptismal ceremony began. "Have you repented of your sins and accepted Jesus Christ as your personal Savior?" the minister asked. "Yes, I have," the young woman replied. "Since you have repented of your sins, and have accepted Jesus Christ as your personal Savior, I now baptize you into the name of the Father and the Son and the Holy Spirit," said the minister.

He concluded with an "Amen," and we all whispered the word in agreement. We watched as the minister briefly immersed the young woman under the water. A second later, he lifted her back up to her feet. It was a dramatic moment. The young woman emerged from the water as if she had been resurrected from death. The baptism symbolized the fact that she had become a new person—a born-again child of God.

The minister welcomed the smiling woman into the family of Jesus Christ, and wrapped a towel around her shoulders to help keep her warm. It was a wonderful experience for the young woman and the other people baptized that day. They will remember their baptism as a special event for the rest of their lives. Some might even think of their baptism as a special birthday. It is a public testimony of our new birth, our new life that was brought into existence by the death and resurrection of our Savior.

Baptism reinforces our decision to accept God's gracious offer of salvation. It is a statement made to ourselves, to the community and to our Creator that we have accepted Christ's commitment to us, and we are responding to him. We acknowledge that he is the source of our life and the reason we exist. In that sense, baptism is the most important landmark and turning point in our lives. It has much in common with another ceremony that marks a milestone in many people's lives—marriage.

We know how important a marriage ceremony is to the couple in love as well as to their families and their friends. But the ceremony is not the beginning of the relationship. The reason the couple is getting married is because they have *already* agreed to commit to each other. The bonding process began long before the couple actually walked down the aisle. That doesn't make the marriage ceremony less meaningful. The ceremony is an outward statement of a couple's intention to make a life together. Marriage is their public commitment to say "I do" to each other.

Symbol of commitment

Baptism pictures the drama of our "I do" decision for Jesus Christ and all that he represents in our salvation. It is a symbol that reminds us he is our Savior, and we are his beloved. People who ask for baptism are saying they want to be associated with Jesus Christ in a personal and intimate way—to belong to Christ. That desire is effective only because Christ already wants to be associated with us! That's what it means to be baptized "in the name of Jesus Christ."

Believers share in the life of Christ. As Christ died, so do the believers. The old self is dead; we are acknowledging that our life is not defined by our past – it is defined by our association with Jesus. As we share in Jesus' death, we also have a share in his resurrection and eternal life. We are stating that we, by God's grace, have a part in the greatest events of salvation history. This includes the life, death and resurrection of Jesus Christ. In being baptized, we publicly dramatize that Christ has included us in his life.

Baptism is not magic. It is a ritual, a metaphor that symbolizes that we have been given a new life in Christ. What better metaphor for the individual's inner change than through the cleansing of water?

Author and pastor William Willimon described it well when he said: "To receive the Spirit through Christ is likened to a birth bath in John 3:3-5 and Titus 3:5-7; to a funeral bath and burial in Romans 6:1-11; and to a bride's nuptial bath in Ephesians 5:26. These baths were consummated in anointing and arraying the body in clean, or new, clothing (Galatians 3:27)" (*Peculiar Speech: Preaching to the Baptized,* page 58).

Need information about baptism?

Sometimes people don't want to be baptized because they aren't interested in joining a church. That's understandable. We are not baptized into a church or denomination—but into the Body of Jesus Christ.

Perhaps you have questions about whether you should be baptized. If you want to contact a minister about baptism or to receive help in spiritual matters, please contact one of our pastors. In the U.S., you may call our toll-free number, 1-800-924-4644, to find out how to contact a pastor near you. In other nations, see https://www.gci.org/our-churches/ for an address near you – or feel free to contact the pastor of another Christian church.

Paul Kroll

86. REMEMBERING BAPTISM

I was baptized more than 30 years ago. Many things have happened in my life since then. There were times when I doubted my conversion, and there were times when I, like Jonah, sought to run from God's presence. But one thing could never be changed: I had stated in public that I accepted Jesus Christ as my Savior.

I knew what that meant. I took on responsibilities as a Christian, as well as the promises. I would enjoy the benefits of having a personal relationship with God and would receive the promises of eternal salvation given to me by Jesus. When I was placed under the water, I understood this portrayed the death of my old life and sinning self. When the minister lifted me out of the water, I was being symbolically resurrected to a new life now, the new life in Christ.

I can never forget that I came to understand God's purpose for my life. I can never say: "Well, that was so long ago. I didn't really understand God's message of salvation." Of course I didn't understand it then as well as I do now, but I understood enough: that God had given me salvation through Jesus Christ. The drama of my baptism ceremony reminds me that, yes, I did understand, and yes, I did declare that I belonged to Jesus. He had already made me his own.

If God is moving in our lives, a time comes when we see how much we need him. We learn that because of sin, we have alienated ourselves from him and the blessings of knowing him. But we also learn of God's grace given to us through Jesus Christ. He has already bridged the gap and reconciled us to himself. The Holy Spirit has enlightened us about these important truths. We accept God's promises and trust in Jesus Christ as Savior.

Christ has already shown his commitment to us. He has already pledged his love to us. We can portray our commitment and desire by saying "I do" to God. We can be plunged into the watery grave of baptism, and then rise out of the water to picture the new life Christ has given us.

87. APPRECIATING OUR BAPTISM

We watch spellbound as the magician, wrapped in chains and secured by padlocks, is lowered into a tall tank of water. The top is then closed and the magician's assistant stands on top, draping the tank with a shroud of cloth, which she lifts above her head. After only a moment or two, the shroud is dropped and to our surprise and delight, the magician stands on top of the tank with his assistant now inside, chains securing her. This sudden, mysterious "exchange" happens right before our eyes. We know it's an illusion, but how the seemingly impossible was accomplished is not revealed so that this act of "magic" can be repeated to the surprise and delight of other audiences.

Some Christians view baptism as if it is an act of magic—at the moment one goes under the water, sins are washed away and the person is made new. But the biblical truth about baptism is far more exciting. It's not the act of baptism itself that accomplishes salvation—Jesus does that as our representative and substitute. Nearly 2,000 years ago, he saved us through his life, death, resurrection and ascension.

It's not in the act of baptism that we trade places with Jesus—exchanging our filth and sinfulness for his righteousness. Jesus doesn't take on the sin of humanity each time a person is baptized. He did that once, for all, in his own baptism, life, death, resurrection and ascension. The glorious truth is that our baptism is a sharing, by the Spirit, in Jesus' baptism! We are baptized because Jesus, our representative and substitute, was baptized for us. Our baptism is a sign and pointer to his. We put our trust in Jesus' baptism, not our own.

It's important to realize that salvation is not about what we do. As the apostle Paul wrote, it's about Jesus—who he is and what he has done (and continues to do) on our behalf: "It is because of him that you are in Christ Jesus, who has become for us wisdom from God—that is, our righteousness, holiness and redemption. Therefore, as it is written: 'Let the one who boasts boast in the Lord'" (1 Corinthians 1:30-31).

Thoughts of celebrating my baptism have begun to stir. The baptism I have in mind is more than my own in the name of Christ many years ago—it's the baptism with which Jesus himself was baptized as the representative (vicarious) human. In his vicarious humanity, Jesus is the last Adam. As a human being like us, he was born, lived, died and was resurrected with a glorified human body and ascended into heaven. When we are baptized, we join Jesus in his baptism—his baptism applied to us by the Holy Spirit. In other words, when we are baptized, we are baptized into Jesus.

This baptism is fully Trinitarian. When Jesus was baptized by his cousin John the Baptist, the Trinity was present: "As soon as Jesus was baptized, he went up out of the water. At that moment heaven was opened, and he saw the Spirit of God descending like a dove and alighting on him. And a voice from heaven said, 'This is my Son, whom I love; with him I am well pleased'" (Matthew 3:16-17).

Jesus was baptized in his role as the one mediator between God and humanity. He was baptized on behalf of humanity, and our baptism signifies our participation in the full and vicarious humanity of the Son of God. Baptism has a basis in the hypostatic union through which God draws near to humanity and humanity draws near to God (*hypostatic union* is a theological term derived from the Greek word *hypostasis,* which describes the inseparable union of Christ's divinity and humanity—making Jesus fully God and fully human at the same time). As Christ is fully divine and fully human, by his nature he draws God near to us, and us near to God. Here is how T.F. Torrance explained it:

> For Jesus, baptism meant that he was consecrated as the Messiah, and that he, the Righteous One, became one with us, taking upon himself our unrighteousness, that his righteousness might become ours. For us, baptism means that we become one with him, sharing in his righteousness, and that we are sanctified in him as members of the messianic people of God, compacted together in one Body in Christ. There is one baptism and one Body through the one Spirit. Christ and his Church participate in the one baptism in different ways—Christ actively and vicariously as Redeemer, the Church passively and receptively as the redeemed Community.

When Christians think they are saved by the act of baptism, they are misunderstanding who Jesus is and what he has done as Messiah, mediator, reconciler and redeemer. I love the answer T.F. Torrance gave when asked *when* he was saved: "I was saved about 2,000 years ago in the death and resurrection of Jesus." His answer articulates the truth that salvation is not in the experience of baptism but in the work of God in Christ through the Holy Spirit. When we talk about our salvation, we are transported back in time to the moment in salvation history that had little to do with us, and everything to do with Jesus. It was the moment when the kingdom of heaven was inaugurated and God's original plan to elevate us was sparked in time and space.

Though I did not fully understand this four-dimensional reality concerning salvation when I was baptized, it is no less real, no less true. The sacraments of baptism and communion are about Jesus uniting himself to us and us to himself. These grace-filled expressions of worship are not about our timing, but about what occurred in God's timing. So whether we were baptized by sprinkling, pouring or immersion, the reality is what Jesus did for us all in his atoning sacrifice.

In GCI, for adult, we follow Jesus' example and typically baptize by full immersion. However, that is not always possible—most prisons, for example, do not allow baptism by immersion. Also, many infirmed people cannot be immersed, and it's appropriate that infants be sprinkled. Some humorously refer to Jesus' encounter with the thief on the cross as baptism by "dry cleaning."

Let me wrap this up with another quote from T.F. Torrance:

> All this helps to make it clear that while baptism is both the act of Christ and the act of the Church in his Name, it is to be understood finally not in terms of what the Church does but in terms of what God in Christ has done, does do and will do for us in his Spirit. Its meaning does not lie in the rite itself and its performance, nor in the attitude of the baptised and his obedience of faith—even the secondary reference of baptism, by its nature as a passive act, in which we receive baptism and do not administer it to ourselves, directs us to find its meaning in the living Christ who cannot be separated from his finished work and who makes himself present to us in the power of his own Reality (*Theology in Reconciliation,* p. 302).

I find myself thinking fondly of the day I was baptized by immersion and how much better and deeper I now appreciate Jesus' act of obedient faith on our behalf. My hope is that a better understanding that your baptism is a real joining with Jesus in his baptism will be a cause for celebration for you.

Joseph Tkach

88. INFANT BAPTISM

Though it was not the general tradition of GCI to perform infant baptisms, we have since 1999 accepted as members people who were baptized as infants in other churches. That decision was based on seeing the fruit of the Holy Spirit in their lives. Because they are already Christians, they don't need another baptism.

In the New Testament we find examples of whole households being baptized upon the conversion of the head of the household (Acts 16:15, 31-33; 1 Corinthians 1:16). It is likely that there were infants and children in these households, but these texts are not conclusive evidence that infants were baptized. For example, the fact that entire households believed (Acts 16:34; 18:8) suggests that the terminology is a generalization, and not meant to include every single person regardless of age.

A more persuasive text is Acts 2:39. In Peter's speech on the Day of Pentecost, he speaks of the covenantal promises of God given to believers and their children, verifying that believer's children are already included in the household of faith even before any personal profession of faith. First Corinthians 7:14 likewise indicates that the children of believers are in a different category than the children of unbelievers, although neither text specifies exactly what the difference is, or how it is to be denoted.

Incarnational Trinitarian theology affirms from the Scriptures that it is the faith of Jesus Christ, not our own faith, that saves us (Ephesians 2:8; Galatians 2:20 KJV). Christian baptism signifies what God, of his own initiative, has done for us, and it is upon the truth of this already accomplished fact that faith comes to rest. As Paul says, "...while we were yet powerless" Christ died for all humanity (Romans 5:6). Christ lived on behalf of all humanity, died for all humanity, and rose again for all humanity. Similarly, he was baptized on behalf of all humanity, and in that way all have already been baptized, whether or not we are old enough to understand it. Powerless and helpless humans (both adult and infant) are loved and affirmed by God in spite of their current inability to understand or respond.

When adults are baptized, they are able to give their response of faith to God's claim and call upon their lives. Those who are baptized as infants also come to a point in their lives when they can consciously give their allegiance to Christ. For those who are baptized as infants, a "confirmation ceremony" can provide an opportunity to give public acknowledgement of their faith.

James Torrance put it this way:

> In the practice of infant baptism, we believe that in faith we are doing something for the child, long before the child comes to faith, in acknowledgement of what Christ did for all of us nineteen hundred years before we were born. But in faith we pray that Christ in his

faithfulness, and in his own, time, will bring this child to personal faith. The efficacy of baptism is not in the rite or in the water, but in the faithfulness of Christ. (pp. 80-81)

In most churches, infants are welcomed into the community of faith and their special status before God is recognized either by a blessing or by baptism. Either way, the community of faith (parents, extended family, care givers, and all members of the local congregation) has the covenantal responsibility to work together to bring up the child "in the training and instruction of the Lord" (Ephesians 6:4).

Daniel Migliori says:

> While the practice of infant baptism is not absolutely necessary in the life of the church, it may be permissible. And whether it is permissible depends on whether it is being practiced as a routine social rite, or as a form of cheap, magical grace, or instead with the clear understanding that it proclaims the unconditional grace of God in Jesus Christ and calls both parents and community to responsibility for the care, nurture, and guidance of the baptized child in the life of faith, hope, and love" (*Faith Seeking Understanding,* 2nd ed., p. 286).[1]

When infant baptism is practiced responsibly by the community of faith, it can be viewed as a sign of God's gracious initiative and a powerful expression of the fact that God loves us even before we begin to respond. Infant baptism proclaims that God's love, grace, and salvation are purely his gift. Any human response to this is just a matter of time as to when it occurs.

Therefore, GCI elders may baptize an infant when requested to do so by the infant's parents or guardians. They are also free to explain these principles to parents or guardians and offer infant baptism as a scripturally permissible and spiritually blessed expression of God's unconditional grace and love. They are also free to explain the principles involved in infant blessing and believer's baptism.

In some GCI congregations, we already have children attending who were baptized as infants. As these children come to faith, it is not necessary to baptize them again. Rather, it will be helpful to have a confirmation ceremony in which they can publicly express their faith in Jesus, and provide a "rite of passage" that helps mark their conscious acceptance of the grace that has already been given to them.

Endnote

[1]Migliori's book has an excellent discussion of the permissibility of infant baptism from a Trinitarian theological perspective (including a critique of Karl Barth's negative position).

89. PENTECOST: THE BIRTH OF THE CHURCH

Editor's note: This begins a series of articles that was, for the most part, written by Paul Kroll as part of the "Church History Corner" column for *Christian Odyssey* magazine. We have added a few other articles about history to the series.

After his resurrection, Jesus appeared to his disciples and instructed them for 40 days, after which he ascended to heaven. While with them, he said: "Do not leave Jerusalem, but wait for the gift my Father promised, which you have heard me speak about. For John baptized with water, but in a few days you will be baptized with the Holy Spirit" (Acts 1:4-5). That baptism of the Spirit would be called the birthday of the church.

Jesus' words were fulfilled on the day of Pentecost. The disciples were filled with the Holy Spirit (Acts 2:4), and the apostle Peter preached his first sermon, urging the crowds to repent, to believe in Jesus Christ as their Messiah and to receive the gift of the Holy Spirit (verse 38). That very day, some 3,000 people were baptized as the people of God (verse 41). The church had begun.

The day called Pentecost is named after the Greek word *pentekostos,* which means 50th. It is the festival observed by Jews, Shavuoth, sometimes called in the Old Testament the Feast of Weeks (Exodus 34:22; Leviticus 23:15; Numbers 28:26; Deuteronomy 16:9-12). Other names for the day are the Feast of the Harvest and Day of First Fruits (Exodus 23:16; Numbers 28:26). Pentecost was to be observed in ancient Israel on the 50th day after the priest waved a selected sheaf of the first grain that had been harvested in the spring (Leviticus 23:15-21). Seven weeks elapsed between the day of the wave sheaf offering and the beginning of Pentecost, thus the name of the festival — the Feast of Weeks. This festival had come to signify for Jews the commemoration of the giving of the Law of Moses (the Torah) at Mount Sinai in the third month after the Exodus Passover (Exodus 20–24).

Perhaps the Holy Spirit came on the Jewish day of Shavuoth, or Pentecost, to signal that God had now moved to write the Law not on tables of stone, but in the hearts of his people through the Spirit (2 Corinthians 3). The indwelling Spirit, the Comforter or Advocate Jesus had sent, was replacing the external "schoolmaster" Law of Moses that had supervised ancient Israel's worship under the old covenant (Galatians 3:23-25).

"If I am lifted up," Jesus said, "I will draw all people to myself" (John 12:32). God had moved once and for all through his Son to rescue humanity from sin and death. The coming of the Spirit into human hearts and minds on that Day of Pentecost in the early 30s was God's sign that in Christ he was creating a new people — a new Israel — an Israel of the Spirit (Galatians 6:16) that included Jews and Gentiles alike.

Pentecost or Whitsunday

Many Christians celebrate the coming of the Holy Spirit in worship activities on Pentecost, or as it is sometimes called, Whitsunday. This name is said to arise from the ancient practice of newly baptized individuals wearing white robes during this time. In the Christian liturgical year, Pentecost is the seventh Sunday after Easter and closes the Easter season.

Paul Kroll

90. EASTER IN THE CHURCH

The death and resurrection of Jesus have been the central events of the church's faith confession since it was founded (1 Corinthians 15:1-4). It's not surprising that the Lord's crucifixion and rising to life should become the focal points of communal Christian worship and remembrance.

There is evidence that the apostolic church celebrated Jesus' Sunday morning resurrection in its worship gatherings on the first day of each week (Acts 20:7; 1 Corinthians 16:2). The Lord's death was remembered in the bread and wine communion that was probably part of Christian fellowship meals (Luke 22:19-20).

The "Easter" festival begins

At some point in the first two centuries, it became customary in the church to have a yearly celebration of the Lord's death and resurrection called "Pascha." It is the same word used for "Passover" in the Greek version of the Scriptures. Our Easter[1] season has grown out of the old Pascha celebration. In time, the Pascha became observed throughout the church.

The early church saw the symbolic continuity between the slaughtered lamb of the Passover and the crucified Lamb of God, Jesus Christ. When Paul speaks of Christ as "our Passover Lamb" (Greek, *pascha*) in 1 Corinthians 5:7, he is affirming that the God who acted mightily in ancient Israel's release from Egyptian bondage, typified by the Passover, is the same God who has acted in Christ to free us eternally from all spiritual prisons of sin and death.

Originally, the great Paschal celebration of the church was a unified commemoration of the suffering, death, resurrection, and ascension of the Lord. Only later were the events divided into separate commemorations, with the ascension observance being moved to the 40th day of the Easter season.

Gradually, in the early centuries of the church, with an increasing emphasis on Holy Week and Good Friday, Pascha took on its distinctive character as the Christian celebration of the resurrection. Good Friday commemorated Jesus' crucifixion and death. The feast of the resurrection, which completed the whole work of redemption, became gradually the most prominent part of the Christian Pascha, and identical with our Easter Sunday.

Since as early as the fourth century, Resurrection Sunday, or what we call "Easter Sunday" in the English language, has been the center of the Christian liturgical year and calendar.

When to observe Easter?

Before A.D. 325, Christian communities in different regions celebrated Easter on a variety of dates and on different days of the week, and not always on Sunday. However, the Christian Council of Nicea of that year issued the "Easter Rule." Nicea decided that the resurrection of Jesus should be celebrated by all churches throughout the world on the same Sunday.

The council standardized the Easter observance date so that Easter is the first Sunday following what is called the Paschal Full Moon for the year. This means that the date of Easter can range between March 22 and April 25, depending on the lunar cycle.

Eastern Orthodox churches use the same calculation, but base their Easter date on the old Julian calendar and use different Paschal Full Moon tables. The Orthodox Easter Sunday in most years follows the Western Easter by one or more weeks.

Discussions began in the last century in hopes of forging a possible worldwide agreement on a consistent date for Easter. Various proposals have been put forth by churches, Christian organizations and clergy of various denominations. One idea is to disregard the moon altogether in determining the date of Easter. None of the proposals has been adopted by any church up to now.

Even if the date for Easter changes in the future, it won't affect our worship. Christians do not worship days or "holy time." They use such days and seasons as opportunities to worship Christ. Easter is a time when we can reflect on and contemplate the meaning of the wondrous events of our common salvation — a pure gift of God in Christ.

----

[1] Some claim that the word "Easter" is "pagan" because it may have once been associated with ancient heathen gods. However, Christian churches were celebrating the resurrection of Jesus in spring long before the English word "Easter" was adopted by English-speaking Christians. The objection against "Easter" is irrelevant in other nations because a different word is used for the Christian spring festival. In most other languages of the world, the name for the festival is derived from *Pesach* or *Pesah*, the Hebrew name of the Jewish Passover. The holiday is called in French Paques, Italian Pasqua, Spanish Pascua, Scottish Pask, Dutch Paasch or Pashen, Danish Paaske, and Swedish Pask, to name a few.

Paul Kroll

91. IRENAEUS
AND THE SECOND-CENTURY CHURCH

Irenaeus has been called the most important Christian theologian between the apostles and the third century. He was a Greek born in Roman Proconsular Asia, today southwestern Turkey, probably between A.D. 130-140. Raised in a worshipful Christian home, as a youth he heard and knew the bishop of Smyrna, Polycarp (c. 70-155). Irenaeus explained how Polycarp spoke of his conversations "with John [the apostle] and with the others who had seen the Lord."[1]

When a young man, Irenaeus migrated to Lugdunum, Gaul (modern Lyons, in France). He became a missionary to the Celts and eventually an elder in the Lyons congregation. Later, Irenaeus was ordained the second bishop of Lyons, replacing Pothinus, age 90, who had been martyred.

Irenaeus died perhaps around the end of the second century. His last known appearance occurs when he writes a firm but respectful letter of protest to Victor, the bishop of Rome between 189-199. Victor wanted to excommunicate the Christians of Asia because they kept the church's traditional Paschal festival on Nisan 14.

Against the heretics

His widely-circulated theological work in five books was titled *On the Detection and Refutation of the Knowledge Falsely So Called*. Written about 175-185, it exposed the heresies of various Gnostic sects, especially the most sophisticated group, the Valentinians.

Irenaeus lived too late to personally hear the apostles and their disciples speak or teach. He relied on the succession of bishops in each major city to provide a theological and faith link between himself and the apostles. He gave special attention to the succession of bishops in the church at Rome as an example of the deposit of apostolic tradition that could be found in other churches. Irenaeus cites this succession as "a complete proof that the life-giving faith is one and the same, preserved and transmitted in truth in the church from the apostles up till now."[2]

Irenaeus also relied heavily on the teaching of the New Testament to refute the claims of the heretics. He explained that in the church's writings can be seen "the unfeigned preservation, coming down to us, of the scriptures, with a complete collection allowing for neither addition nor subtraction."

Irenaeus "is the first writer whose New Testament virtually corresponds to the canon that became accepted as traditional."[3] He quotes from most of its writings, though he doesn't cite Philemon, James, 2 Peter or 3 John. We can't say whether he knew of these letters, or if he did, what his view might have been of their authority for the church.

Irenaeus was the first Christian writer to list all four Gospels as authoritative for the church. He said that through them "the tradition of the apostles, manifest in the whole world, is present in every church to be perceived by all who wish to see the truth."

Trinitarian theology

Irenaeus testified to the church's Trinitarian understanding of God's nature long before the councils of Nicaea (325) and Constantinople (381) produced their traditional confessional creed. "In his various statements of faith there appear all the essentials of the Creed of Nicaea except its technical terms."[4]

Irenaeus explained that the church "received from the apostles and their disciples the faith in one God the Father Almighty…and in one Christ Jesus, the Son of God, incarnate for our salvation, and in the Holy Spirit." He also insisted that God's word witnesses to the Son of God in the Incarnation being fully God as well as true human. "All the prophets and apostles and the Spirit itself" testify to this, he said.

Irenaeus believed that Jesus' redemptive work in his Incarnation, perfect life, death and resurrection was a "Victory in Christ" over all of God's enemies. He wrote: "[Christ] fought and was victorious…for he bound the strong man, liberated the weak, and by destroying sin endowed his creation with salvation."

Irenaeus' legacy is his struggle to preserve and pass on the revelation of God that had been given to the apostles. It's no wonder both the Roman Catholic and Eastern Orthodox churches consider him among the special "saints" of the church. Catholics celebrate a day in his honor each June 28.

Endnotes

1. Eusebius, *The History of the Church from Christ to Constantine*, bk. 5.20.6.

2. Quotes of Irenaeus are from *On the Detection and Refutation of the Knowledge Falsely So Called*, translated by Robert M. Grant, in *Irenaeus of Lyons*.

3. Henry Chadwick, *The Early Church*, 81.

4. Cyril C. Richardson, editor, *Early Christian Fathers*, 350.

Paul Kroll

92. PERSECUTION, PENANCE AND "THE LAPSED"

For the first 300 years of the church's history, believers faced many local and empire-wide persecutions of varying intensity. One of the most terrifying struck in A.D. 250. This was the "Decian Persecution," named after the Roman Emperor Decius Trajan (249-251), who started it.

Decius, a pagan, believed that the gods were unfavorable to Rome because the empire's citizens were not suitably worshipping them. The survival of the empire was in the balance, in his way of thinking. He considered Christians — and anyone else — who didn't worship the gods to be atheists and guilty of high treason. Decius issued a decree commanding all people throughout the empire to sacrifice to the gods and to the emperor. Those complying would receive a *libelli,* a certificate attesting to this fact.

Decius didn't want to turn Christians into martyrs, so comparatively few were actually killed. The goal was to force them to recant their faith and return them to the pagan fold. Arrest, exile, confiscation of property, threats and even torture were employed to force Christians to abandon their faith. The bishops and officers of the church were hit especially hard, with a number of martyrdoms in their ranks.

Many Christians steadfastly refused to go along with Decius' demands and confessed Christ even under brutal torture. They were given the honorary title "Confessor" by the church. However, many Christians did sacrifice to the gods and the emperor. Some bribed authorities to obtain fraudulent certificates stating they had sacrificed, even though they had not. The Christians who complied with Decius' order were excommunicated from the church as apostates and called the *lapsi,* those who had lapsed from the faith.

The persecution under Decius was severe, but it did not last long. He died in battle just two years after attaining office.[1] A decade later, Gallienus (260-268) was on the emperor's throne. Under his reign the church began to enjoy about 40 years of freedom from persecution.[2] Many of the lapsed Christians then wanted to return to the church.

This situation created a great controversy. Should the lapsed be readmitted? Should they be required to do penance and "prove" their loyalty to Christ and the church? Should the lapsed be rebaptized before being readmitted? What about those who had renounced their faith, but then reaffirmed it even while the Decian persecution was in progress?

Enter Novatian (c. 200-258), a prominent Roman presbyter and theologian. He insisted that no lapsed person should be readmitted to the church. Novatian contended that the lapsed had forfeited grace through a denial of Christ. The group he formed posed another problem when certain of its members later wanted to be readmitted to the church.

Enter Cyprian (248-258), the respected bishop of Carthage. Cyprian and his supporters held that the lapsed should be received back into full fellowship and communion, but only after an interval of probation and penance. Cyprian also insisted that those individuals who had been baptized by priests of schismatic groups, like Novatian's, would have to be rebaptized by priests of the church.

Cyprian convened several North African church councils between the years 251 and 256 to decide the issues. In 256, the North African synod voted unanimously that any individuals baptized by heretical or schismatic groups would have to be rebaptized before being granted full fellowship with the church.

Enter the bishop of Rome, Stephen (254-257). He ordered that the lapsed or heretics should be accepted into the church *without* a second baptism. Cyprian resisted this order for some time, but finally yielded.

Such thorny and divisive questions of how to deal with the lapsed led to the establishment of "a rigorous and fixed system of penitential discipline," wrote Philip Schaff in his monumental *History of the Christian Church*, page 189. Persons who had been excommunicated because they had lapsed, and were now seeking re-entry, became "penitents." They had to undertake a series of acts of penance before being readmitted.

The controversy over how to handle the lapsed had long-lasting repercussions for the church. As church historian Justo González points out in *The Story of Christianity*, page 90, "It was out of that concern that the entire penitential system developed. Much later, the Protestant Reformation was in large measure a protest against that system."

Endnotes

1. Decius was succeeded as emperor by Gallus (251-253) and then Valerian (253-260). While there were changes in the level of persecution, and temporary easing at times, those were still years when it was not safe to be a Christian.

2. The 40 years of rest was followed by the last and most violent persecution, under Emperor Diocletian (284-305).

Paul Kroll

93. JESUS CHRIST OF 'ONE SUBSTANCE WITH THE FATHER'

— The Council of Nicea, May-August, A.D. 325

May 20, 325 was a watershed date in the history of the Christian church. The first international Christian council was convoked at Nicea, a city in what is today northwestern Turkey. The council dealt with a number of issues, such as the controversy concerning the date for celebrating Easter. However, the most important reason was to discuss the nature of Jesus Christ. Apostolic writers had not systematically described Jesus Christ's relationship to the Father in a theological or formal way.

The subject might not even have arisen were it not for the influence of Greek philosophy in the Roman Empire, and even on some Christian thought. To the Greeks, the perfect deity was unchangeable and could have nothing to do with a flawed humanity or our world of matter, which is changing and corruptible. Some Christians began to think of God in the same way as the philosophers, that is, that God was immutable, impassible and fixed in his being.

In the early 300s, a man named Arius was a popular presbyter in Alexandria, Egypt. He taught that the Logos or Word, who became incarnate as Jesus Christ, was a uniquely brought forth and highly exalted being. Arius' teaching began what was at first a local quarrel in the church at Alexandria between himself and his bishop, Alexander. But bishops outside Egypt soon began to side with Arius against Alexander. In the years 318 to 320 the contest between the two views broke out into the open.

While Arius included the Word in the created order, Alexander placed all of creation on one side and the Father and the eternal Word on the other. While the motto of the Arians regarding the Logos was "there was when he was not," Alexander taught that the Word existed eternally with the Father.

Emperor Constantine appealed for agreement, but the controversy continued to rage. The emperor sent letters to Christian bishops throughout the empire, urging that they come to Nicea to settle the issue. Among the most prominent at the council were Alexander of Alexandria, the main opponent of Arius' teachings, and Eusebius of Nicomedia, the chief spokesman for the Arian position. Among the attendees was a young deacon, Athanasius of Alexandria. While he was unable to participate, not being a bishop, the council formed the prelude to his central role in later articulating the Trinitarian confession of the church.

Most of the bishops were repelled by the idea that Jesus Christ could be thought of as what to them amounted to a created being. When they worshiped Christ, they did not worship a creature — they worshiped God. They were saved not by a created being, but by God. The bishops proceeded to craft a creedal statement of faith concerning what they believed about the Son of God. They wanted the statement to absolutely exclude the claims of Arius that the Logos was a product of the will of God rather than of the very essence of God.

The bishops wrote in their statements that Jesus Christ was "God of God, light of light, true God of true God, begotten, not made, of one substance with the Father." A key phrase was "of one substance," which translates the Greek *homoousios*. This means that what God is in his essence, Jesus Christ the Son of God is also. Eventually all the bishops except for two signed the creedal statement, believing that it contained the ancient faith of the apostolic church and that it was an accurate reflection of the truth of God's nature to which the New Testament points.

The deity of the Holy Spirit did not come up for discussion at Nicea. The two bishops who opposed the statement were deposed and exiled. Arius and his writings were also anathematized and he was exiled to Illyria. The controversy continued, however, until the council of Constantinople in 381, when the Nicene creed was expanded, and ratified once and for all.

The creedal statement at Nicea regarding Christ's divinity and co-eternal existence with the Father formed the basis of the Nicene Creed, which after 381 became the most universally accepted statement of the church's confession about the being and nature of God.

Paul Kroll

94. IS JESUS REALLY GOD?
A LOOK AT THE ARIAN CONTROVERSY

Few Christians are aware that two of the most fundamental doctrines of the Christian faith — the divinity of Jesus Christ and the Trinity — were not finally decided until some 350 years after the death of Jesus.

Both doctrines were forged in the fourth century out of the religious and political firestorm sparked by Arius, a popular presbyter of the church in Alexandria, Egypt. Arius had a simple formula for explaining how Jesus Christ could be divine — and therefore worthy of worship along with God the Father — even though there is only one God.

The simple formula taught by Arius was well received by the common believers in Alexandria, but not by Arius' supervisor, bishop Alexander. Each man lined up supporters and the battle lines were drawn for what history would call the Arian Controversy. This bitter ordeal for the Christian churches of the eastern and western Roman Empire began in A.D. 318, led to the Creed of Nicea in 325 and finally ended with the Nicene Creed established at the Council of Constantinople in 381.

Monarchianism

Church Fathers from as early as the late 100s had been writing that the Word of God, the *Logos* of John 1:1-2, was co-eternal with the Father — and therefore uncreated and without beginning. The presbyter Arius was not the first to dispute this. Similar challenges had already arisen by the late second and early third centuries in the form of Monarchianism.

Monarchians fell into two broad categories. The Adoptionist or Dynamic Monarchians held that Jesus was only a man in whom dwelled the power of the supreme God.[1] The Modalist Monarchians taught that God revealed himself in three modes — as Father, Son and Spirit — but never at the same time. This preserved the idea of the full divinity of the Son, but at the expense of any real distinction between the Son and the Father. Some Modalists believed that Jesus Christ was actually the Father in the flesh. All forms of Monarchianism were eventually branded as heresy and rejected by the Christian churches across the empire.

Arius

In one sense, Arius was simply the latest thinker to try to reconcile monotheism (belief in one God) with the Christian belief that Jesus Christ was divine. But there was a great difference between Arius' attempt and all previous efforts. No longer was Christianity an officially unsanctioned, often underground and persecuted religion. Now the Roman emperor Constantine had granted Christianity unprecedented legitimate status in the Empire, so that the question of who Jesus is could finally come before the whole Church to be settled.

Arius was a popular senior presbyter in charge of Baucalis, one of the twelve "parishes" of Alexandria in the early fourth century.[2] By A.D. 318, Arius had begun teaching his followers that the Son of God (who is also the *Logos* or Word of John 1:1-2) did not exist until the Father brought him into existence. To Arius, the Father first created the Word, and then the Word, as the Father's unique and supreme agent, created everything else.

Arius' idea seemed to preserve monotheism as well as uphold the divinity of the Son, even if it was a bestowed divinity as distinct from the inherent and eternal divinity of the Father. With the help of catchy rhymes and tunes, Arius' ideas quickly caught on among the common converts of Alexandria.

Alexander

Alexander, the bishop of Alexandria, and his assistant, a presbyter named Athanasius, saw great danger in Arius' teaching and took action to arrest it. Contrary to Arius' teaching that God was once without the Word, Alexander asserted that God *cannot* be without the Word, and that the Word is therefore without beginning and eternally generated by the Father.

Alexander sent letters to neighboring bishops requesting support and convened a council at Alexandria that excommunicated Arius and a dozen other clergy.[3] Arius also sought backing, however, and obtained the support of several leaders, including Eusebius, the bishop of Nicomedia. Eusebius enjoyed a close relationship with Emperor Constantine, which would play a major role in the unfolding of the controversy. Another supporter of Arius was the historian, Eusebius of Caesarea, whose history of the early Christian church is still available today.

Constantine steps in

The Emperor Constantine became aware of the developing problem, and saw a need to resolve it. As Emperor, Constantine's concern was not so much for the unity of the Church as for the unity of the empire itself. Theologically, he viewed it as a "trifle."[4] Constantine's first move was to send his religious advisor, Bishop Hosius of Cordova, Spain, to sort out the differences. Hosius was unsuccessful in bringing Arius and Alexander to peace, but he presided over a council in Antioch in early 325 that condemned Arianism and censured Eusebius of Caesarea.[5] But the division continued, so Constantine called a universal council of the Church to settle the dispute.

Ancyra had been the original choice of venue, but Constantine changed the location to Nicaea, a city closer to his Nicomedia headquarters. The emperor personally opened the council in June of 325 with about 300 bishops present (most from the east). Constantine was looking for mutual tolerance and compromise. Many of the bishops present were also apparently prepared to find compromise.

As the proceedings unfolded, however, thoughts of compromise quickly eroded. Once the tenets of the Arian position became clear, it did not take long for them to be rejected and condemned. The ideas that the Son of God is God only as a "courtesy title" and that the Son is of created status were vehemently denounced. Those who held such views were anathematized. The divinity of the Logos was upheld, and the Son was declared to be "true God" and co-eternal with the Father. The key phrase from the Creed established at Nicaea in 325 was "of the essence of the Father, God of God and Light of Light, very God of very God, begotten, not made, being of one substance with the Father."

Homoousios (of the same essence) was the key Greek word. It was intended to convey, against the Arians, that the Son is equally divine with the Father. This it did, but it also left unanswered the question of how the Son and the Father, if they are of the same essence, are in fact distinct. Consequently, though Arianism was condemned and Arius banished, the Council of Nicaea did not see an end to the controversy.

A little letter makes a big difference

Athanasius and most other eastern bishops said that the Son was *homoousias* with the Father, meaning "of the same essence." The Arian theologians disagreed, but suggested a compromise: they could accept the word with the addition of only one letter, the smallest Greek letter, the iota. They said that the Son was *homoiousias* with the Father — a Greek word meaning "similar essence."

But similarity is in the "i" of the beholder, and the Arians actually meant that Jesus was not the same kind of being as the Father. It would be like saying that he was "almost" divine. The orthodox theologians could not accept that, and would not accept a word that allowed such an unorthodox interpretation.

Imperial reversals

Eusebius of Nicomedia, who presented the Arian cause to the Council and was deposed and banished for it, enjoyed a close personal relationship with Emperor Constantine. In time, he was able to convince Constantine to ease the punishment on the Arians, and to order Arius himself recalled from exile. Eventually, after a council at Jerusalem formally acquitted him of the charge of heresy in 335, Arius was to have been received back into the fellowship of the church in Constantinople. Philip Schaff wrote:

> But on the evening before the intended procession from the imperial palace to the church of the Apostles, he suddenly died (A.D. 336), at the age of over eighty years, of an attack like cholera, while attending to a call of nature. This death was regarded by many as a divine judgment; by others, it was attributed to poisoning by enemies; by others, to the excessive joy of Arius in his triumph.[6]

Athanasius, meanwhile, had succeeded Alexander as bishop of Alexandria in 328 only to be condemned and deposed by two Arian councils, one at Tyre under the presidency of Eusebius of Caesarea, and the other at Constantinople in about 335. He was then banished by Constantine to Treves in Gaul in 336 as a disturber of the peace of the church.[7]

This turn of events was followed by the death of Constantine in 337 (who received the sacrament of baptism on his deathbed from the Arian Eusebius of Nicomedia). Constantine's three sons, Constantine II, Constans, and Constantius succeeded him. Constantine II, who ruled Gaul, Great Britain, Spain, and Morocco, recalled Athanasius from banishment in 338. In the east, however, matters were quite different. Constantius, who ruled the east, was firmly Arian. Eusebius of Nicomedia, the leader of the Arian party, was appointed Bishop of Constantinople in 338. Before long, war in the west between Constantine II and Constans gave Constantius a free hand to again exile Athanasius in 340.

When Constantine II died, however, and the western empire was united under Constans, Constantius had to follow a more moderate line with the Nicene party. The two emperors called a general council in Sardica in 343, presided over by Hosius, at which the Nicene doctrine was confirmed. Constans also compelled Constantius to restore Athanasius to his office in 346.[8]

Semi-Arianism

When Constans died in 350, the pendulum swung again. Constantius, now the sole emperor and still Arian, held councils supporting Arianism and banished bishops who opposed their edicts, including Hosius and Athanasius. By now, Arianism had itself become divided into two factions. One party had slightly modified its position to affirm *homoiousios*, or similarity of essence, rather than the original *heteroousios*, or difference of essence, still held by the strictest Arians.

This "compromise," sometimes called "semi-Arianism," still represented an unbridgeable chasm from the orthodox *homoousios*, or same essence. It only served to pit the Arians against one another. For Nicenes who still had difficulty with the apparent lack of distinction between the Father and the Son represented by *homoousios*, though, the semi-Arian *homoiousios* did, for a time, afford a reasonable compromise. In any case, by the time of the death of Constantius, the Church had become Arian, at least on the surface.

Imperial reversals

It was the death of Constantius in 361 that set the stage for the permanent triumph of Nicene faith. Julian the Apostate became emperor and implemented a policy of toleration for all the Christian parties. Though Julian's policy, at first glance, seems positive toward Christianity, his real hope was that the opposing factions would destroy one another. He recalled the exiled bishops, including Athanasius (though Athanasius was soon banished again as an "enemy of the gods" but was again recalled by Julian's successor Jovian).[9]

It was through the efforts of Athanasius that the concerns of the Nicenes and the semi-Arians about blurring the distinction between the Father and the Son were assuaged. Athanasius argued that *homoousios* could be interpreted in such a way as to affirm the same essence as long as the distinction between the Father and Son were not destroyed. In other words, he made it plain that "same essence" must retain the unity but never be allowed to destroy the distinctions in the Godhead. With this understanding, along with the compelling work of the Cappadocian bishops, Basil, Gregory of Nazianzus, and Gregory of Nyssa, the Nicene faith again began to gain ascendancy.

Julian died in 363, and was followed by Jovian, who was favorable toward Athanasius and the Nicene faith. His reign was short, though, ending in 364. He was succeeded by Valens, a fanatical Arian, whose intensity against both semi-Arians and Nicenes tended to bring those two parties together. In 375, he was followed by Gratian, who was of Nicene faith, and who recalled all the exiled orthodox bishops.

By the end of Gratian's reign, Arianism was greatly waning in intellectual defense and in morale. At last, it was the long reign of Theodosius I, who was educated in the Nicene faith, that finally ended the long controversy. He required all his subjects to confess the orthodox faith. He appointed a champion of Nicene faith, Gregory of Nazianzus, as patriarch of Constantinople in 380. In 381, Gregory presided over the Council of Constantinople.

The Council of Constantinople

The Council of Constantinople affirmed the Creed of Nicaea, altering it only slightly and in non-essential ways. It is the form of the Creed adopted at Constantinople that today bears the name Nicene Creed. The controversy was at last ended in the empire. However, Arianism would continue to impact the Church for the next two centuries in the form of the various peoples outside the empire who had become Christians according to the Arian faith (most of whom scarcely even knew the difference).

Athanasius, who had so diligently and unswervingly opposed the Arian heresy, did not live to see the conflict ended. He died in 373 in his native Alexandria. In the end, the unyielding Athanasius is a fair representation of the unyielding truth of the orthodox Christian faith. Fundamental to the validity of Christianity is the reality of redemption, made possible only by the work of no being less than true God, the Lord Jesus Christ.

Arius believed that a Christ designated as divine by virtue of his special creation could serve as true Redeemer and true Mediator between God and humanity. It took the dogged, relentless, unwavering faith of an Athanasius to hold fast to the truth that no being less than true God could in fact reconcile humanity to God.

The apostle Paul wrote to the church in Corinth: "No doubt there have to be differences among you to show which of you have God's approval" (1 Corinthians 11:19). Likewise, the Arian controversy became an essential waypoint on the journey of the church, for despite the trial and pain of controversy, the truth of the nature of the divine One who had come to redeem humanity had to be made plain.

Who was who?

- Arius (c. 250-336): Theologian in Alexandria, Egypt, a presbyter (an elder) of the church. He taught his followers that the Son of God did not exist until he was brought into existence by the Father.
- Alexander of Alexandria (d. 326): Bishop of Alexandria and Arius' supervisor. He strongly opposed Arianism.
- Athanasius (293-373): A presbyter of the church in Alexandria and assistant to Bishop Alexander. He later succeeded Alexander as Bishop of Alexandria and spearheaded the effort to oppose Arianism and establish the Nicene faith.
- Eusebius of Caesarea (c. 263-339): Bishop of Caesarea and author of several works chronicling the history of early Christianity, including *Ecclesiastical History*. He hoped for a compromise in the Arian controversy, and as a historian he recorded the proceedings

at the Council of Nicea.

- Eusebius of Nicomedia (d. 341): Bishop of Nicomedia. He supported Arius' ideas and presented the Arian side of the controversy at the Council of Nicea.

- Constantine the Great (272-337): Emperor of the Roman Empire who legalized Christianity in the Empire. He called the Council of Nicea in an effort to bring an end to the dispute among the churches that was threatening the security of the Empire.

- Hosius of Cordova (c. 256-358): Bishop of Cordova, Spain. He was sent to Alexandria by Constantine to mediate the Arian controversy.

----

1 Clyde Manschreck, "Monarchianism," in *Dictionary of Bible and Religion* (Nashville: Abingdon, 1986), 704.

2 David Wright, "Councils and Creeds," *The History of Christianity* (Herts, England: Lion Publishing, 1977), 156.

3 Wright, 157.

4 Wright, 159.

5 William Rusch, *The Trinitarian Controversy* (Philadelphia: Fortress, 1980), 19.

6 Philip Schaff, *History of the Christian Church* (Charles Scribner's Sons, 1910; reprinted by Eerdmans, 1987), vol. III, 663.

7 Schaff, 663.

8 Schaff, 635.

9 Schaff, 638.

J. Michael Feazell

95. THE NICENE CREED

Ancient Greeks believed in a wide variety of gods and goddesses – beings who fought one another, were immoral, dishonest and only partly powerful. But eventually Greek philosophers began to teach that there was a supreme God, a being who had all power, wisdom and perfection. Since there could be only one being who had all power, there was only one supreme God. Since perfection does not change, this God did not change. This God was above all other gods, not swayed by humanlike emotions, not affected by physical things that change.

This philosophy eventually affected Christianity. At first, it was a convenient tool for the gospel. Christians who were criticized for having an invisible God could point out that even sophisticated Greek philosophers believed in an invisible, omnipotent God. The Christians then claimed to teach more information about this God whom the Greeks knew only imperfectly.

But sometimes it worked the other way around. Some Christians began to assume that the Christian God was like the philosophers' God – he was perfect, unchangeable, totally unlike physical beings. Such a perfect God would have nothing to do with flawed human beings. Nor would an unchangeable spirit being have anything to do with the changing world of matter.

So some Christians began to speculate that the supreme God created angels, and that these angels were the ones who created the physical world and interacted with the physical world. They were intermediaries between physical humans and God. In this way of thinking, Jesus simply became an intermediary, more like an angel than like God.

The Arian heresy

One of the people who was affected by this philosophy was Arius, an elder in the Egyptian city of Alexandria. He taught that there was one Creator, who created the Logos, the Word or Wisdom of God, who in turn created everything else. This Logos became Jesus Christ.

According to Arius, Jesus was the Son of God because God had created him. Moreover, because he is the closest thing to God that we can relate to, he could also be called God even though strictly speaking, he was not God. He was a unique created being, created even before time itself was created. He was an intermediary between the perfect spiritual world and the ever-changing physical world.

But Alexander, the bishop of Alexandria, said that the Word was eternal, not created. "If asked to draw a line between God and creation, Arius would draw that line so as to include the Word in creation, while Alexander would draw it so as to separate all of creation on one side from the Father and the eternal Word on the other" (Justo Gonzalez, *The Story of Christianity*, vol. 1, p. 161).

Alexander tried to remove Arius from his position. However, Arius was a popular church leader. The people of Alexandria, as well as several other church leaders, greatly respected Arius for his strict morality, his self-discipline and his teaching abilities. The people took to the streets in public demonstrations, chanting slogans of Arius.

Christians had been debating theology and the nature of Christ for centuries. But now there was a new element in the debate: the Roman Emperor Constantine. Constantine had just finished a war to unite a divided empire. He did not want religious debates to divide the people again, so he ordered all the Christian bishops to meet together to decide the issue.

The emperor was not then a Christian, but he was favorably disposed toward Christianity, and he wanted this rapidly growing religion to support peace within the empire. Constantine thought that an official council could settle the matter once and for all. So he called a meeting in the year 325 at the city of Nicea, in Asia Minor near Constantinople.

About 300 bishops came, almost all from the Eastern Empire. The bishop of Rome could not come because of his age, but he sent some elders to represent Italy. "Most of the bishops from the Latin-speaking West had only a secondary interest in the debate, which appeared to them as a controversy among eastern followers of Origen" (Gonzalez, p. 164). Even many of the Eastern bishops were not too concerned about the controversy.

The Nicene Council

The bishops met to discuss the nature of God and Jesus Christ. They reviewed previous controversies and the new arguments of Arius and his supporters. Most of the bishops could not accept the idea that Jesus was a created being. When they worshiped Jesus, they did not worship a creature – they worshiped God. They were saved not by a created being, but by God. They were convinced that Scripture taught that Jesus Christ was God.

So the bishops wrote a statement of faith concerning what they believed about the Son of God. They wanted to make it clear that they believed Jesus Christ to be fully divine, not created. So they said he was "God of God, light of light, true God of true God, begotten, not made, of one substance with the Father." The last portion was particularly significant in the debate: "of one substance" is a translation of the Greek *homoousios*, which means of the same substance, same essence, or one being. What God is in his essence, the Son of God is, too.

Two bishops at the council could not agree with this statement, and the council deposed them. The controversy was seemingly resolved, Constantine was happy and everyone went home.

But one of the chief supporters of Arius happened to live near the emperor, and it was not long before he was able to convince Constantine to support the Arian idea. (Constantine wasn't a Christian and had no training in theology. He was more interested in political stability than in any particular doctrine.) With Constantine's support, some new bishops were appointed who supported the teachings of Arius.

Several smaller councils approved Arian statements of faith. Nicene supporters were thrown out of office, banished or killed. For several decades, theological and political intrigues swirled, opinions went back and forth, bishops were reinstated, deposed and reinstated again. The tides of opinion changed quickly as nine emperors fought for power over the next 50 years.

In time, more of the issues were given a fair hearing. Nicene supporters made it clear that they believed the Father and the Son to be distinct, even though of one substance. They supported their views from Scripture.

The Holy Spirit also came under discussion. The Nicene council had merely said that "we believe in the Holy Spirit," without saying anything about who or what the Spirit is. Arius had taught that the Holy Spirit was a created spirit being; bishops such as Athanasius of Alexandria made it clear that the Holy Spirit is divine in the same way that the Son is.

Council of Constantinople

Eventually, Theodosius became emperor, and the council of Constantinople was called in 381. Theodosius expelled the Arian supporters, and Nicene bishops were appointed. The council agreed that Jesus is fully divine, eternal, not created. They accepted the divinity of the Holy Spirit. They taught that the Father is God, the Son is God, and the Holy Spirit is God, yet there is only one God – one God in three *Persona*.[1] They did not explain how this is so – they just said that it *is* so. They felt compelled by Scripture to come to this conclusion.

The result is a creed, called the Niceno-Constantinopolitan Creed, more commonly known by the shorter and more pronounceable name Nicene Creed. It is based on the creed of Nicea, reportedly edited at the council of Constantinople, but first seen in its final form 70 years later. Notice in it some phrases from Nicea, quoted above, and some phrases similar to the Apostles' Creed:

We believe in one God the Father, the Almighty, creator of heaven and earth, and of all that is, seen and unseen.

We believe in one Lord, Jesus Christ, the only Son of God, eternally begotten of the Father, God from God, Light from Light, true God from true God, begotten, not made, of one being with the Father. Through him all things were made. For us men and for our salvation he came down from heaven; by the power of the Holy Spirit he became incarnate from the Virgin Mary, and was made man. For our sake he was crucified under Pontius Pilate; he suffered death and was buried. On the third day he rose again in accordance with the Scriptures; he ascended into heaven and is seated at the right hand of the Father. He will come again in glory to judge the living and the dead, and his kingdom will have no end.

We believe in the Holy Spirit, the Lord, the giver of life, who proceeds from the Father (and the Son).[2] With the Father and the Son he is worshipped and glorified. He has spoken through the Prophets.

We believe in one, holy, catholic[3] and apostolic Church. We acknowledge one baptism for the forgiveness of sins. We look for the resurrection of the dead, and the life of the world to come. Amen. (Translation by the International Consultation on English Texts, 1975, published in appendix A of Gerald Bray, *Creeds, Councils and Christ*, InterVarsity Press, 1984.)

The Nicene Creed is accepted by almost all Protestant, Catholic and Eastern Orthodox churches, and it offers a basis for unity. Unfortunately, however, it has also been at the center of a controversy between Western and Eastern churches (see note 2). The church has its flaws. Doctrinal controversies are not always resolved in a Christlike way. The Nicene Creed is testimony to that. And yet truth wins in the end. Scripture supports the teaching of the Nicene Creed.

[1] *Persona* is a Latin word that originally referred to masks worn by actors on a stage. Theologians adopted the term to indicate three ways of being, not to imply three separate beings. The Greek term is *hypostasis*.

[2] The words "and the Son" were not in the Greek text of the creed, but they were added later in the Latin. The Eastern churches objected to this addition because it had not been approved by the council.

[3] *catholic* (with a small c) means "universal" or "worldwide." In the creed, it is not a reference to the Roman church, which later claimed to be universal.

Paul Kroll

Nicene Myths	Truth
• The Roman Catholic Church called the Nicene Council to enforce Trinitarian teaching.	• Rome did not call the council and was poorly represented. • The council did not have a complete doctrine of the Trinity, and gave scant mention of the Holy Spirit.
• Constantine forced the council to accept a pagan doctrine. • Constantine forced all Christians to accept the Nicene Creed.	• Arius' idea of God was shaped by the ideas of pagan philosophers. • Constantine cared more about uniformity than doctrine, and he soon supported the Arians and tried to enforce Arianism.

96. THE NEED FOR "DEPTH PERCEPTION" IN CHURCH HISTORY

An important part of learning to drive is depth perception. Drivers need to know where they are in relation to the other vehicles around them. I think depth perception should also be a part of a Christian education. We are Christians in a certain moment in time. We need to understand our time in relation to what has gone before and what may come after.

Most of us have a rather hazy view of church history. We've probably heard of the Protestant Reformation, but have little idea what was "reformed" and why it needed to be. Our knowledge of the early church is even sketchier. You may have heard of such figures as Athanasius, Arius, Eusebius, Chrysostom, Constantine or Augustine. But what did they do, or say? Were they "good guys" or "bad guys"?

Early church history is sometimes presented as a struggle against a "great conspiracy," when, in a "lost century," the "faith once delivered" was undermined by "false prophets" who introduced "pagan" ideas.

That's an idea that seriously lacks historical "depth perception." The real story of the church is one of continual struggle, punctuated with moments of turmoil, as sincere but less-than-perfect men and women tried to respond to the challenges of their times. Even the earliest Christians — those who knew and were taught by Jesus personally — took a long time to grasp something we now take for granted: that Gentiles should be accepted as equal partners in the faith.

In the second and third centuries other issues arose. Some of these would also cause us to say, "Huh? *That* was a problem for them?" Like, for example, a question about the nature of Jesus. "Was he really God in the flesh?" Or was he a created being, endowed by God with very special powers? Ideas and doctrines we now accept without question were once hot issues, debated with passion, tension and — sometimes, even intrigue.

Church history is not just the province of scholars. Our faith today also faces some important questions—about abortion, homosexuality, the role of women, the plight of the poor, evolution and an appropriate Christian response to the environmental crisis, to name only a few. Passions run high on all sides, and the answers are not easy. Some will disagree with that, claiming that the answers are so obvious there is no room for discussion. Here some depth perception will help.

As C. S. Lewis wrote,

Nothing strikes me more when I read the controversies of past ages than the fact that both sides were usually assuming without question a good deal which we should now absolutely deny. They thought that they were as completely opposed as two sides could be, but in fact they were all the time secretly united — united with each other and against earlier and later ages — by a great mass of common assumptions. We may be sure that the characteristic blindness of the twentieth century — the blindness about which posterity will ask, "But how could they have thought that?" — lies where we have never suspected it.

Remember how just two centuries ago, sincere Christians vigorously defended slavery on biblical grounds? Within living memory, the Bible was invoked to support segregation and Apartheid? We should not be so sure we have grasped today's controversial issues correctly. What will future generations see as our "great mass of common assumptions"?

Jesus promised that the Holy Spirit would guide believers into all truth (John 16:13). But that guidance often comes by the Spirit working through fallible human beings. So politics, prejudice and intolerance compete with a genuine passion for the truth.

The story of the battle over the divinity of Jesus is instructive on many levels. A vital truth was preserved, but *how* it was preserved can leave us wincing. Let's learn from the past, not just to strive earnestly to maintain the integrity of the faith, but also to treat each other with the love, mercy and patience of Jesus while we are doing it.

John Halford

97. THE FIRST CHURCH CHRISTMAS

"Joy to the world!" Christians look forward to a joyous Christmas season each year. Yet, surprisingly, for the first 300 years of the church's life there was no Christmas celebration of Jesus' birth. Possible reasons include:

- The apostolic church had expected that Christ's coming in glory was just around the corner and its worship pointed to the future instead of the past.

- The church's primary focus was on Christ's death and resurrection and his presence through the Spirit, which were celebrated during Easter and Pentecost.

- Epiphany, or "manifestation," another early church festival, afforded a remembrance of Jesus' Incarnation and birth.

- There was no corresponding Old Testament festival from which Christmas could emerge, as there had been for Pasha or Easter (Jewish Passover) and the Christian Pentecost (Feast of Weeks).

- The date of Jesus' birthday was, perhaps, not known.

First Christmas at Rome

In A.D. 336 the church at Rome proclaimed December 25 as the *dies natalis Christi*, "the birthday of Christ." An entry in the Chronograph of A.D. 354 (also called Philocalian Calendar) records, "Our Lord Jesus Christ was born on the eighth before the calends of January," or December 25. It doesn't state that Christmas was being observed on that date, but it is likely that the observance began at Rome around this time.

A generation after the Chronograph was published, church father John Chrysostom (c. 347-407) wrote that Rome was celebrating a December 25th Christmas: "On this day also the birthday of Christ was lately fixed at Rome in order that while the heathen were busy with their profane ceremonies, the Christians might perform their sacred rites undisturbed."

The "profane ceremonies" referred to by Chrysostom centered around the birthday of the "Invincible Sun," or Sol, which was also celebrated on December 25, the day of the winter solstice in the old Roman calendar. The cult of the Sun was of grave concern to the church at Rome. It was introduced in A.D. 218 when Elagabalus (c. 203-222) became emperor of the Roman Empire. Elagabalus venerated the Sun god and introduced his cult into Rome under the title *deus Sol invictus,* that is, the invincible, undefeated or unconquered sun god.

Emperor Aurelian, Roman emperor from A.D. 270 to 275, decreed the

Unconquered Sun as supreme god of the Roman Empire. Mithra, a god of Persian origin, was part of the Sun cult worship. Mithra's birthday was also on December 25. The Roman Emperors Diocletian and Galerius, who ruled prior to Constantine the Great (306-337), venerated the Sol Mithras Deus invictus cult. Constantine, the first Christian emperor, was a devotee of the Sun cult before his conversion.

Struggle against sun worship

A December 25th birthday celebration for Christ served to compete with and counteract the festival of the pagan devotees of Sol-Mithra. The church was able to challenge the worshippers of Sol Invictus with Jesus Christ, whom they proclaimed as the true Son of God and the Sun of Righteousness (Malachi 4:2; Revelation 1:13, 16).

Christmas celebration was an effective evangelizing event for turning the hearts and minds of people to Christ and away from worship of Sol. It also provided church members with a safe, Christ-centered worship alternative to other heathen festivals, such as the late December Saturnalia. Simultaneously, the Roman church could promote prayerful and moral behavior, in sharp contrast to the licentiousness that accompanied the pagan festivals.

Celebration of Christmas (or Advent, a term referring to Christ's coming) also was effective in combating heresies about Jesus, pointing to his incarnation as a real human being.

It's not surprising that the December 25th Christmas celebration quickly spread from the congregations in Rome to churches throughout the empire. From the fourth century on, every Western calendar assigns Christmas to December 25. By the middle of the fifth century, most of the Eastern churches had adopted the Christmas festival, although on January 6, and by the time of Jerome (347-420) and Augustine (354-430), Christmas is everywhere established in Christendom.

Over the next thousand years, Christmas observance followed the expanding community of Christianity around the world. Today Advent/Christmas is one of the church's most important worship seasons. Have a joyful Christmas celebration and a blessed new year.

Paul Kroll

98. CHRISTMAS PAST AND PRESENT IN THE CHURCH

Have you ever wondered how Christmas came to be part of the annual Christian calendar? Here's the fascinating story, which we begin with a surprising observation. Neither Jesus nor the apostles commanded or even suggested that the church should have a Christmas festival — and no evidence of such a celebration is in the New Testament.

In the church of the second century, we see evidence of an annual celebration of Jesus' resurrection in the spring, but no celebration of his birth. (It's possible that the roots of the resurrection celebration go back to the apostolic church.) The church also added Pentecost and Epiphany to its yearly worship calendar in the second century. Epiphany, on Jan. 6, celebrated not the birth of Christ, but the manifestation of his divine sonship, his kingship and his divine power as displayed in his baptism, the visit of the Magi, and his miracle at the wedding feast in Cana. Pentecost commemorated the coming of the Holy Spirit.

Epiphany was the church's earliest annual celebration in connection with the Incarnation of Jesus. However, it was not until the fourth century that we have clear evidence of the birth of Jesus being celebrated on Dec. 25.

Why December 25?

One theory for the origin of Christmas is that it was intended to compete with or supplant the pagan celebration of the sun-god on that date. According to this hypothesis, accepted by most scholars today, the birth of Jesus was given near the date of the winter solstice. On this day, as the sun began its return to the northern skies, the pagan devotees of Mithra celebrated the birthday of the invincible sun. The cult was particularly strong at Rome when Christmas celebration arose.

The idea is that the church tried to counteract this pagan worship with its own celebration of Jesus' birth. That makes good sense, since the church was, in effect, providing its members with a Christian worship and fellowship opportunity while the pagans were cavorting and doing homage to their gods. It was also an opportunity for the church to preach the true gospel. If this reasoning is correct, what Christians did, then, was to redeem in Christ an understanding that he (not a pagan sun god) was the true Son and Sun of Righteousness (Malachi 4:2) — the true light that lights our path with his grace (John 8:12).

Another idea as to why Christmas celebration began and expanded throughout the church has to do with its need to combat a heresy about Christ's Person. The council of Nicea in 325 had condemned Arianism, which claimed that Jesus Christ was only an exalted creature and not true God of true God.

It was not long afterward that the Christmas festival first appeared in Rome, and then spread to the churches in other parts of the Roman Empire. In this view, the controversies of the fourth century about the incarnation and person of Christ impelled the church to create a festival that would celebrate the mystery of God becoming human, as a kind of teaching tool for the church.

Birthday of Jesus?

Why wasn't Jesus' birthday celebrated earlier than the fourth century? One reason might be that neither the day nor month of Jesus' birth is given in the Gospels or any other early Christian writings—and cannot be determined with any certainty. Despite this, it seems to have been the opinion of some church leaders in the first four centuries that Christ was actually born on Dec. 25.

Theologian John Chrysostom (347-407) appealed, in support of this view, to the date of the registration under Quirinus (Cyrenius). He apparently believed that the census and tax records of Jesus' family were preserved in the Roman archives. Justin Martyr (100-165) stated that Jesus was born at Bethlehem, saying such can be ascertained "from the registers of the taxing" (*Apology I*, 34).

Tertullian (160-250), spoke of "the census of Augustus — that most faithful witness of the Lord's nativity, kept in the archives of Rome" (*Against Marcion,* Book 4, 7). The early church father, Hippolytus (180-236), came up with a Dec. 25 date, which he attempted to calculate from information in the Gospel of Luke regarding the ministry of the priest Zechariah, John the Baptist's father (Luke 1:5, 8-10).

Whatever the facts might be about the date of Jesus' birth, it is clear that the church sensed the need to have a festival that commemorated the birth of our Savior. In the words of the church historian Philip Schaff, it was inevitable that the church would have "sooner or later called into existence a festival which forms the groundwork of all other annual festivals in honor of Christ" (*History of the Christian Church,* volume 3, "Nicene and Post-Nicene Christianity," page 395). Schaff points to Chrysostom's observation that "without the birth of Christ there would be no salvation history in Christ — no baptism, passion, resurrection, ascension or outpouring of the Holy Spirit. Hence, there would be no celebration of Epiphany, of Easter or of

Pentecost."

However meaningful Christian worship was during the Christmas season, we must also acknowledge that Christmas was often celebrated with the same sensual excesses as some pagan feasts had been among the general populace. Truly, at several times in the history of the church, it was needful to put Christ back into Christmas.

Puritans in Britain and America

"Puritans" was the name given in the 16th century to a group of Protestants that arose from within the Church of England. As part of their broad-based reform agenda, they demanded that the church should be purified of any liturgy, ceremony or practices that were not found in the Bible.

Since the Christmas celebration was not mentioned in Scripture, the Puritans concluded that it must be stopped. When the group came to political power in England under Oliver Cromwell (1599-1658), they outlawed Christmas. Cromwell and the Puritans even banned special church services, not just on Christmas but also on Easter and Pentecost. Christmas Day was a regular work day and shops remained open. Parliament was to sit as it usually did. Criers were sometimes sent through the streets, shouting, "No Christmas today, no Christmas today."

The year 1642 saw the first ordinance forbidding church services and civic festivities on Christmas day. These were issued regularly in the ensuing years. On June 8, 1645, the Puritan-dominated Parliament abolished the observance of Christmas, Easter, Whitsuntide and the Saints' days. But in 1660, things changed. The monarchy was re-established, and the Puritan clergy were expelled from the Church of England.

But the Puritans were already established in America. Many Puritans had migrated to New England beginning in the second decade of the 17th century. In Puritan New England, Christmas was a regular workday, and any violation of this was punishable by fine or dismissal. In 1659, the Massachusetts Puritans declared the observation of Christmas to be a criminal offense. Offenders had to pay five shillings as a fine. In Massachusetts, Dec. 25 did not become a legal holiday until 1856. It is hard to realize now that worship on Christmas was outlawed in New England until the second half of the 19th century.

Twelve Days of Christmas and Advent

"The Twelve Days of Christmas" is more than a secular, traditional Christmas song. At one time it was common for Christmas worship and celebration to last 12 days, from Dec. 25 until Jan. 5, the beginning of Epiphany. This tradition has almost disappeared.

Today, the season of Advent begins the yearly worship or liturgical calendar. Advent is celebrated on the four Sundays preceding Christmas. It is devoted to the commemoration of the coming of our Lord in the flesh as well as to his return at the final judgment. That's why they are called Advent Sundays, since "advent" means the coming or arrival, especially of something extremely important. (What event could be more important than the coming of the Son of God in human flesh — and then his coming again as King of kings and Lord of lords!)

Lawrence Stookey, in his book *Calendar: Christ's Time for the Church,* explains it this way:

> The primary focus of Advent is on what is popularly called "the second coming." Thus advent concerns the future of the Risen One, who will judge wickedness and prevail over every evil. Advent is the celebration of the promise that Christ will bring an end to all that is contrary to the ways of God; the resurrection of Jesus is the first sign of this destruction of the powers of death.... The beginning of the liturgical year takes our thinking to the very end of things. (pages 121-122)

Meaning of Christmas

For the church, the entire Christian year centers on the person and work of Jesus Christ. Christians do not "celebrate" or "keep" days as though holy in themselves, but rather worship Christ and recall the great events of our salvation, using those special times as opportunities for worship. The purpose of the annual worship year is to keep our minds focused on the story of salvation and to worship Jesus Christ in a way that ministers to his glory. Specifically, Christmas, Advent and Epiphany were meant as vehicles to celebrate Jesus Christ.

The yearly Christian festivals remind us of the leading events of the gospel history, and beckon us to participate in worship of Christ. In the words of Philip Schaff: "The church year is, so to speak, a chronological confession of faith; a moving panorama of the great events of salvation; a dramatic exhibition of the gospel for the Christian people" (*History of the Christian Church,* volume III, page 387).

Paul Kroll

99. ATHANASIUS LISTS
THE NEW TESTAMENT WRITINGS

The 27 books of the New Testament are the Scriptures of the church. They are understood to be written by the apostles or their close associates, such as Luke and Mark. Along with the Old Testament they comprise the official canon[1] of the church.

But in the early centuries of the church, before the New Testament canon had been established, there was a significant variety of opinion among Christian churches about what writings should be considered authoritative. Because of this, some Christian leaders were concerned that heretical writings might carry an undeserved authority. For example, a writing called the Gospel of Peter, which was a product of a Gnostic group that claimed to possess a secret knowledge of God, circulated in parts of the world in the early centuries.

Some leaders also doubted the apostolic authority of writings such as the book of Revelation and the second letter of Peter. The question about which writings should be considered authoritative for the whole church became more and more pressing as influential leaders began to form lists of their own to support their heretical teachings. Marcion, for example, teaching in the middle second century, rejected the Old Testament and most of what is today our New Testament, creating his own short version of just a few New Testament writings.

Other heretics wrote compositions that claimed to record the acts of apostolic figures. Since some claimed the status of sacred Scripture for these writings, it's not surprising that this created confusion in the church.

Athanasius, Bishop of Alexandria, addressed this problem on Jan. 7, A.D. 367, when he wrote his annual Easter letter to his churches.[2] It was a landmark letter because it contained the same list of 27 books of the New Testament that are found in our Bibles today. So far as we know, Athanasius was the first Christian leader to compile a list of New Testament books exactly as we know them today. Bruce Metzger, a New Testament scholar, wrote, "The year 367 marks, thus, the first time that the scope of the New Testament canon is declared to be exactly the twenty-seven books accepted today as canonical."[3]

Here are portions of Athanasius' letter, in which he lists the books of the Old and New Testaments that he considered authoritative. The English translation is the work of the late F.F. Bruce:

Inasmuch as some have taken in hand to draw up for themselves an arrangement of the so-called apocryphal books and to intersperse them with the divinely inspired scripture, concerning which we have been fully persuaded, even as those who from the beginning were eyewitnesses and ministers of the word delivered it to the fathers: it has seemed good to me also, having been stimulated thereto by true brethren, to set forth in order the books which are included in the canon and have been delivered to us with accreditation that they are divine.

Athanasius then gives his list of Old Testament books and lists the 27 New Testament books.

Let no one add to these or take anything from them.... No mention is to be made of the apocryphal works. They are the invention of heretics, who write according to their own will, and gratuitously assign and add to them dates so that, offering them as ancient writings, they may have an excuse for leading the simple astray.[4]

Athanasius' letter was important because he was the bishop of a prominent city, Alexandria. He was one of the most influential theologians and apologists of the church at the time. Athanasius had spent much of his life battling the infamous Arian heresy, which had denied the co-essential divine nature of Christ.

We shouldn't think of Athanasius as sifting through a stack of writings, and pronouncing this one as Scripture and the next one as unscriptural. He was merely recognizing and recording what amounted to the general but unofficial consensus of the churches.

Some of the books not listed among the 27 continued to be considered something like devotional writings, such as the *Shepherd of Hermas* and letters of Clement. But these also needed to be defined for what they were so they would not be confused as having the same authority as the writings of the apostles and their colleagues.

The first church councils to approve the New Testament canon met in A.D. 393 at the Synod of Hippo Regius and in A.D. 397 at Carthage, in North Africa, some 30 years after Athanasius published his list. The councils merely endorsed what had already become the consensus in the churches of the West and most of the East about the extent of the canonical books of Scripture.

Endnotes

1. The word *canon* comes from the Greek *kanon,* where it meant a straight

rod that could be used as a measuring stick. The word came to mean a standard, norm or, in a biblical context, an authoritative list of Scriptural writings.

2. The bishop of Alexandria was given the responsibility of informing his brother bishops well ahead of time each year about the date of the next Easter. Athanasius, in his long tenure as bishop of Alexandria (328-373) issued 45 such festal letters. In these letters, he gave an Easter homily and also took the opportunity to discuss some other matter of current importance to the church. In his 39th letter he dealt with the question of the canon of the Old and New Testaments.

3. *The Canon of the New Testament: Its Origin, Development and Significance*, 212.

4. *The Canon of Scripture*, 78, 209.

Paul Kroll

100. AUGUSTINE, "FATHER" OF THE WESTERN CHURCH

Augustine (354-430) has been called the most significant Christian theologian "since New Testament times."[1] He was born Augustinus Aurelius in the North African town of Tagaste, in today's Algeria. His pagan father, Patricius, was a Roman official and his mother, Monica, was a devout Christian. They sent their son to a prestigious school in Carthage at age 17, where he studied rhetoric. The teenage Augustine took a young woman as a concubine, whom he kept for 15 years. She bore a son, Adeodatus, "given by God."

Dabbling in philosophy

Augustine adopted Persian Manichaeism when he was 19. The philosophy failed to answer his nagging question about why evil exists, so he cast it aside after nine years. At age 29, Augustine decided to move to Rome. His mother, Monica, vexed by his lifestyle and interest in pagan philosophies, determined to chaperone him. He eluded her, sailing away secretly.

Augustine won a position as professor of rhetoric at Milan's imperial court. He dabbled in the skeptical philosophy of the Academics and then adopted Neoplatonism around age 32, which would infuse itself into his theology.[2]

Augustine's mother caught up with him at Milan, imploring him to attend the congregation of the illustrious Bishop Ambrose (340-397). Augustine agreed, because Ambrose was known as a good orator. Ambrose was able to decisively answer Augustine's objections about the Bible and the Christian faith. Augustine now began an ambivalent struggle against his fleshly pulls. This conflict is poignantly summarized in his plea to the Lord in his retrospective spiritual autobiography, *Confessions*, "Give me chastity and continency, only not yet."[3]

Conversion and baptism

Augustine's conversion occurred in the summer of 386. In his *Confessions* he describes his tearful prayer in a Milan garden setting, beseeching God to purify his unclean thoughts and habits:

> I was saying these things and weeping in the most bitter contrition of my heart, when suddenly I heard the voice of a boy or a girl — I know not which — coming from the neighboring house, chanting over and over again, "Pick it up, read it; pick it up, read it."[4]

Augustine ran to the bench, where he had left the book of Romans.

I snatched it up, opened it, and in silence read the paragraph on which my eye first fell: "Not in rioting and drunkenness, not in chambering and wantonness, not in strife and envying, but put on the Lord Jesus Christ, and make no provision for the flesh to fulfill the lusts thereof" (Romans 13:13).[5]

Augustine explains that when he read the passage "there was infused in my heart something like the light of full certainty and all the gloom of doubt vanished away."[6] After prebaptism study and counseling, the 33-year-old Augustine and his son were baptized by Bishop Ambrose on Easter evening, April 24, 387. He mentions this baptism in a meaningful sentence in his *Confessions*, "We were baptized, and anxiety for our past life vanished from us."[7] He progressively left his old life, his career in rhetoric and his concubine.[8]

Soon after his baptism, Augustine was struck with a double tragedy. His devoted mother died unexpectedly and so did his teen-age son, Adeodatus. After a period of deep grief, Augustine sailed for North Africa in August 388. He hoped to live an ascetic and contemplative life studying the Scriptures and writing theological expositions. His expectation was quickly dashed. While attending church at Hippo in 391, he was put on the spot by Bishop Valerius, who openly prayed that "someone" — think Augustine! — would come to shepherd the congregation.

Augustine was virtually drafted into the priesthood by bishop and laity and ordained in 391. Four years later, at age 42, he was ordained co-bishop of Hippo. The elderly Valerius soon passed away and Augustine became full bishop.

He would also continue to write extensively throughout his life. Augustine authored more than 100 major Christian treatises, 200 letters and 400 sermons, covering important areas of Western Christian theology. Luther, Calvin and Roman Catholic theologians each appealed to Augustine's writings during the Protestant Reformation, leading to his being thought of as the "forerunner of the Reformation."[9]

For more than four decades Augustine wrote, combated heresies and dealt with church and pastoral problems. He died on August 28, 430 as the Vandal siege of Hippo was in its third month.

Endnotes

1 Justo L. González, *The Story of Christianity*, vol. 1 (HarperCollins, 1984), 216, 212.

2 Some theologians, Karl Barth and Thomas Torrance in particular, believe the influence of Platonic dualism is a major structural fault in Augustine's theology. Torrance says he heard Barth go so far as to refer to his theology as *süses Gift!* — "sweet poison" in German! On the other hand, Torrance speaks of Augustine's *De Trinitate* as among a class of "supremely great" works of Christian theology. See *Karl Barth: Biblical and Evangelical Theologian*, Thomas F. Torrance, pages 4-7, 122, 138, 156, 172, 185, 189, 194, 197.

3 Augustine, *Confessions*, translated by E. B. Pusey.

4 William C. Placher, *Readings in the History of Christian Theology*, page 105, "The Confessions," book 8, chapter 12.29.

5 Ibid.

6 Ibid.

7 Augustine, *Confessions*, translated by E. B. Pusey.

8 At this time Augustine betrothed himself to a young girl at his mother's encouragement, but his affianced bride was too young for marriage. He then took another concubine for a short time.

9 Philip Schaff, *History of the Christian Church*, volume 3, pages 1017-18, 1020.

Paul Kroll

101. THE COUNCIL OF CHALCEDON AND THE "TWO NATURES" CONTROVERSY

In A.D. 381 the Council of Constantinople rejected the teaching of an elderly bishop from Syria, named Apollinaris. Apollinaris had theorized that Jesus Christ's divine nature displaced Jesus' human mind and will. To him, Jesus possessed only a divine nature, and therefore did not truly take on the fallen nature of humanity.

Controversy about the relationship between the divine and human natures of Jesus continued with Nestorius of Antioch, who was appointed bishop of Constantinople in 428. Nestorius concluded that Jesus had two separate natures and two wills, making him two persons— a double being — one divine and the other human, sharing one body. Nestorius' teaching was condemned by a church council at Ephesus in 431, but the controversy did not end.

In the 440s, a respected monk from Constantinople, Eutyches, denied that Jesus was truly human. He taught that Jesus did not exist in two natures because his human nature was absorbed or swallowed up by his divine nature. Flavian, bishop of Constantinople, convened a synod in 448, condemning Eutyches' position, but Eutyches appealed the decision. The fight took a nasty turn when Dioscorus, Patriarch of Alexandria, became determined to reinstate Eutyches and his views. Eastern emperor Theodosius II, also favoring Eutyches' position, called another church-wide council to meet at Ephesus in August 449. He appointed Dioscorus to chair the proceedings and to silence any dissent.

Leo I, bishop of Rome, sent delegates to the synod with his *Tome*, an exposition of how the two natures, divine and human, are joined in Christ. Dioscorus prevented the reading of Leo's letter and rejected his position. Eutyches' teaching was declared orthodox. Bishops who refused to accept the council's decision were deposed.

Council of Chalcedon

An unexpected event dramatically changed the situation. On July 28, 450, while out riding, Theodosius' horse bolted. The emperor fell, broke his neck and died. His sister Pulcheria became empress with her husband, Marcian, as co-emperor. They were opposed to Eutyches' teaching and eager to redress the wrongs perpetrated by Dioscorus.

Emperor Marcian called for a church council to meet at Chalcedon, on the outskirts of Constantinople. More than 500 bishops attended — the largest church council gathering to that time. All delegates were from the

Eastern Church, except the few representatives from Rome and two from Africa. Deliberations lasted from October 8 to November 1, 451.

Leo again sent representatives with his *Tome*, which was read and approved by the council. Chalcedon reversed the "Robbers' Council" decision and condemned Eutyches' teaching. It anathematized those who taught that Christ had only a single, divine nature and those "who imagine a mixture or confusion between the two natures of Christ."

Definition of Faith

Marcian urged the council to write a statement of faith to provide unity and understanding for the Church. In response, the council produced the "Chalcedonian Definition." The Definition affirms that Christ is "complete in Godhead and complete in humanness, truly God and truly human." He is "of one substance (*homoousios*) with the Father as regards his Godhead, and at the same time of one substance with us as regards his humanity."

Jesus Christ is to be "recognized in two natures, without confusion, without change, without division, without separation." The "distinction of natures" is "in no way annulled by the union." "The characteristics of each nature" are to be considered as "preserved and coming together to form one person and subsistence." They are not to be "separated into two persons."

In summary, the Definition confesses Jesus Christ is "*one* person, who is *both* divine *and* human." Though its wording has been criticized as inadequate, it has helped the church in "setting the limits beyond which error lies" in speaking of the human and divine union in Christ. The Definition confesses the gospel message that Jesus Christ assumed our fallen humanity in order to save us, for as Gregory of Nazianzus (329-389), said, "That which he [Christ] has not assumed he has not healed; but that which is united to his Godhead is also saved."

Paul Kroll

102.   THE APOSTLES' CREED

As the Christian church spread throughout the Roman world in the first century, and as the first leaders died out, there was a practical need for local churches to have a basic statement of beliefs. As false teachers began to bring in strange ideas, Christians needed to know "Just what is it that we believe?"

Some of these churches had a few books of the New Testament, perhaps some of Paul's letters or one of the four Gospels. But none of the churches had all the New Testament. They needed a standard to judge whether a teaching was truth, or heresy. The early Christians also realized that new people didn't have to know everything before they could be baptized and accepted as believers. How much should they know and accept before being admitted into the church? This was another reason that early churches wanted a brief statement of what they believed to be most essential.

Churches in different cities and regions made their own lists, which had many points in common, since all the churches had traditions tracing back to the apostles in one way or another. The small differences were eventually eliminated as church leaders discussed these things with one another. They shared not only the scriptures they had, but also their statements of faith.

When Christianity became a legal religion in the fourth century, this process became easier. Churches throughout the empire agreed on which books should form the New Testament, and they agreed on several basic statements of faith.

A summary of apostolic teaching

One of the doctrinal lists commonly used in the Western empire was called the Apostles' Creed. The word "creed" comes from the Latin word *credo,* meaning "I believe." It was called "Apostles" not because the apostles themselves wrote it (although some people may have thought this), but because the Creed was believed to be an accurate summary of what the apostles taught.

The Creed was useful in several ways:

- The Creed was a public statement of faith, a standardized way in which new people could confess their faith in Jesus Christ.

- The Creed anchored Christian faith to a tradition, to make it difficult for people or churches to be led astray by strange doctrines.

- The Creed was a preaching and teaching tool, giving an outline for further discipleship.

- The Creed was memorized through frequent repetition, which helped the many believers who could not read.

- The Creed provided a doctrinal basis for different churches to accept one another, and to reject those who did not accept the basic truths.

- The Bible itself contains brief creed-like statements (1 Corinthians 8:6; 15:3-4; 1 Timothy 3:16). The early church leaders also wrote short creeds, perhaps as baptism ceremonies. These eventually were recited by congregations in their worship services.

Writing in Greek somewhere around the year 200, Irenaeus describes a creed that has some similarities to the Apostles' Creed, and may have been a precursor. He presented his creed not as something new, but as something the church had been using for a long time. He lived in what is now France, but had grown up in Asia Minor, where he had been taught by Polycarp, a student of the apostle John.

An early Latin version of the Creed is in the writings of Tertullian, from North Africa, about the year 220. About a century later, Marcellus, from Asia Minor, had a similar creed. In A.D. 390, after study in Rome, Egypt and Judea, Rufinus had a similar creed in northern Italy.

Augustine, bishop in North Africa in 400, had a nearly identical creed, and it was apparently standard in Gaul in 650. The text accepted today is identical to what was written in 750 by Pirminius, who lived in what is now Switzerland.

This history shows that churches in many different regions were involved in the development of the Apostles' Creed. As churches in one part of the empire communicated with others, their short list of doctrines became standardized.

What does the Creed say?

Let us look at what the Creed says, and comment on some of its points. It is short, so we'll begin by quoting all of it.

I believe in God, the Father almighty, creator of heaven and earth;

I believe in Jesus Christ, his only Son, our Lord. He was conceived by the power of the Holy Spirit and born of the Virgin Mary. He suffered under Pontius Pilate, was crucified, died, and was buried. He descended to the dead. On the third day he rose again. He ascended into heaven, and is seated at the right hand of Father. He will come again to judge the living and the dead.

I believe in the Holy Spirit, the holy catholic Church, the communion of saints, the forgiveness of sins, the resurrection of the body, and the life everlasting. Amen. (translation by the International Consultation on English Texts)

The Creed, although having a Trinitarian structure, is not explicitly Trinitarian. The Creed began to be developed before the Trinitarian controversy arose, and the Creed (unlike the Nicene Creed) was not an attempt to correct a specific heresy.

Numerous scriptures could be mentioned as support for the various points of the Creed. The Creed was believed to be in full agreement with the apostolic writings, and the same churches accepted both the Creed and the Scriptures as authoritative, as faithful reports of what the apostles taught.

The Creed begins with a simple statement of faith in God, who has all power and is the originator of everything. This statement is a rejection of pagan mythologies, but it was acceptable to Jews and to some of the more educated Greeks.

Most of the Creed is about Jesus Christ, for he is the definitive doctrine of the faith. Beliefs about Jesus separate Christians from everyone else. Jesus was a specific person, born of a woman, executed under a specific Roman governor. Unlike mythological deities, he did not come from the distant and hazy past — he interacted with the real world. He had a real body that was born, crucified and buried, and yet he was divine, too — conceived by the Holy Spirit, resurrected, ascended into heaven at a position of supreme power. He is the unique Son of God, a unique Lord who is above all earthly lords, and he is the Judge who will return to earth to determine everyone's reward.

The early church knew about Jesus' earthly ministry and his miracles, but they did not feel that these were essential to the Christian faith. The Creed focuses more on his supernatural birth, his death and his supernatural power. These are of greatest theological significance, and were therefore included in the statement of faith.

'Descended to the dead'

The phrase "descended to the dead" is of special interest, in part because it used to be translated "descended into hell." Some medieval theologians came up with elaborate theories about what Jesus did in hell, but this misses the original purpose of the phrase.

Irenaeus and Tertullian do not have this phrase; it first appears in the writings of Rufinus, who said that it meant only that Jesus went to the grave, the "place" of the dead. This is in agreement with Scripture, which says that Jesus rose from "the dead" (a plural adjective used as a noun, meaning the situation that all dead people are in, as in Acts 4:10).

Peter applied the words of Psalm 16 to Jesus: "You will not abandon me to the grave" — to Hades, the realm of the dead. When Jesus was dead, he was in Hades. Some believe he was conscious, and others believe he was not, but either way, he was in Hades, the realm of the dead.

The phrase "descended to the dead" disappeared from the creed for more than 200 years. Augustine did not have it. It occurs again in the Gallic Creed of 650 and remained from then on.

Some are troubled by this phrase and its history in the Creed; others are troubled by ancient and modern misinterpretations of the phrase. Some would prefer it be eliminated, since it does not add anything essential to the Creed, and is a point of disagreement rather than agreement.

Wayne Grudem argues:

> Unlike every other phrase in the Creed, it represents not some major doctrine on which all Christians agree, but rather a statement about which most Christians seem to disagree. It is at best confusing and in most cases misleading for modern Christians. My own judgment is that there would be all gain and no loss if it were dropped from the Creed once for all. (*Systematic Theology,* Zondervan, 1994, 583-594).

Nevertheless, the words are in the Creed, and we cannot change the tradition. However, we can understand the words correctly so we can agree with them. Others may interpret these words differently, but we do not need to argue about that.

'The holy catholic church'

The Creed ends with a few brief statements. We can easily agree to a belief in the Holy Spirit, the forgiveness of sins, the resurrection and eternal life. (Some may question "resurrection of the body." First Corinthians 15 says that our body will be transformed to be spiritual rather than fleshly, but it will still be our body.)

Some people are also put off by the words "holy catholic church." The word catholic comes from the Greek words *kat' holos,* literally meaning "according to the whole," or in actual use, worldwide or universal. The word catholic became part of the Creed before "catholic" became associated with the Roman church, and many Protestant churches use the Creed with the word catholic. In the Creed, we do not express faith in a specific denomination, but in the church worldwide — that is, that there is one body, united by God's Spirit. The phrase "communion of saints" implies the same thing — that as we all commune or have unity with Christ through the Holy Spirit, we also commune with each other. We will be united to one another forever.

The Apostles' Creed has been part of the Western church tradition for many centuries. It has not been perfect, but it has been useful for Christian confession, doctrine and discipleship. We accept the creed as a valid statement of faith for Christians. For further comments on the Apostles' Creed, you may want to read Alister McGrath, *"I Believe": Exploring the Apostles' Creed* (InterVarsity, 1998). Several other authors have also written on this subject, including William Barclay, Stuart Briscoe and Michael Horton.

Michael Morrison

103. HOW RUSSIA BECAME CHRISTIAN

Each July 15, Eastern Orthodox, Roman Catholic and some Protestant Christians commemorate the baptism of Prince Vladimir (956-1015). He was ruler of Rus, an area stretching from northwestern Russia to southern Ukraine.

The principal account of this pagan king's baptism and the Christianization of his domain are found in the *Russian Primary Chronicle*, dating from the 11th century.[1] This book explains that Vladimir had listened to envoys from Islam, Judaism and the Greek and Roman Christian church seeking to convert him and evangelize his people. The wise men he sent to investigate these religions were especially impressed with the church of St. Sophia in Constantinople and the splendor of its religious services.

When Vladimir heard their account, he decided to adopt the form of Christianity practiced at the Byzantine court, the center of what is today the Eastern Orthodox faith.[2]

Prelude to baptism

Before choosing a faith, Vladimir besieged the Byzantine city of Kherson, north of the Crimea. The *Chronicle* tells the story: A man from Kherson, Anastasius, informed him he could take the city by cutting off the springs feeding its water supply. Vladimir followed his advice, forcing the city to surrender.

Next, Vladimir engaged in some hard-ball political bargaining. He promised to be baptized and bring Byzantine Christianity to his people only if emperors Basil and Constantine gave him their sister, Anna, in marriage. If they refused, he threatened to destroy Constantinople, their capital city, as he had Kherson.

Greatly anguished, the emperors persuaded their sister to agree to the marriage. One church historian cynically says that Vladimir "captured a Byzantine town in the Crimea and as a price of peace exacted the hand of a Byzantine princess to add to his collection of wives and concubines."[3]

Anna arrived in Kherson around 988 with priests to perform Vladimir's baptism. When she heard he was afflicted with a terrible eye disease, she urged him to be baptized immediately to be healed of the condition. According to the *Chronicle:*

> When Vladimir heard her message, he said, "If this proves true, then of a surety is the God of the Christians great," and gave order that he should be baptized. The Bishop of Kherson, together with the Princess's priests, after announcing the tidings, baptized Vladimir.

When the Bishop laid his hand upon him, he straightway received his sight. Upon experiencing this miraculous cure, Vladimir glorified God, saying, "I have now perceived the one true God."[4]

Let the baptisms begin

After his baptism, Vladimir married Anna and prepared his subjects for baptism. He ordered that at a given hour all the people of Kiev — men, women and children — should go to the Dnieper River and be baptized in a grand religious ceremony. The *Chronicle* describes the baptismal event and Vladimir's prayer of thanksgiving:

> When the people were baptized, they returned each to his own abode. Vladimir, rejoicing that he and his subjects now knew God himself, looked up to heaven and said, "O God, who has created heaven and earth, look down, I beseech thee, on this thy new people, and grant them, O Lord, to know thee as the true God, even as the other Christian nations have known thee."[5]

The eminent church historian Philip Schaff saw this act from a disparaging perspective: "Thus the Russian nation was converted in wholesale style to Christianity by despotic power."[6] Yet, the spread of Christianity during the 9th through 11th centuries generally worked this way. The peoples of Scandinavia, central Europe and the Balkans were Christianized through the conversion of rulers who supported, often by forceful means, the work of Christian missionaries among their people.

After the Eastern and Western church split in 1054, the rulers and people of the expanding Russian empire continued to follow the Orthodox faith. Under the Czars, Moscow became the religious rival of Latin Christianity, "the Third Rome," and the bishop of Moscow took the title of Patriarch. As leader of the Russian Orthodox Church, he became a "Russian Pope."

---

[1] Even skeptical historians believe the *Chronicle* provides a generally accurate account of these events.

[2] Several decades later, in 1054, a formal split between the church in the East and West occurred. See article "The Great Schism of the Church."

[3] Kenneth Scott Latourette, *A History of Christianity*, vol. 1, p. 392.

[4] *The Russian Primary Chronicle*, edited and translated by Samuel Hazzard Cross and Olgerd P. Sherbowitz-Wetzor.

[5] Ibid.

[6] Philip Schaff, *History of the Christian Church*, vol. 4, "Medieval Christianity," page 141.

Paul Kroll

104. THE GREAT SCHISM OF THE CHURCH

July 6, 1054 was rapidly approaching, and the Christian world was about to experience a major event on the road to a schism that continues to our day — the divide between the Western and Eastern Christian churches. The central actors in the looming conflict were Michael Cerularius, the patriarch of Constantinople,[1] and Leo IX, the bishop or pope in Rome.

In the months leading up to July 6, 1054, Cerularius had strongly condemned the Western church for some of its religious practices and beliefs.[2] As part of his attack, Cerularius excommunicated the bishops of Constantinople who followed certain rites of the Western church, and he closed down their churches.

In April, Leo sent a legation to Cerularius, headed by Cardinal Humbert, with his own set of demands and accusations against the patriarch. As it turned out, Leo died in the midst of the mission, but the group continued its task. The meetings between Cardinal Humbert and Patriarch Cerularius were angry and bitter. Mistrust and a desire to maintain ecclesiastical power ruled the day. No useful dialogue could occur in such a poisoned atmosphere.

Mutual excommunication

Finally, relations between Cerularius and Humbert were strained to the breaking point. The Roman legates marched into Constantinople's St. Sophia church and placed a papal decree on the altar, excommunicating Cerularius. Cerularius then convened his bishops and issued further accusations about the practices of the Western church. They condemned Humbert and the other representatives of the papacy. The possibility of healing and reconciliation became a shattered dream.

The mutual excommunications of 1054 were the dramatic climax of a centuries-long period of growing estrangement between the two areas of the church, East and West, despite the fact that in earlier centuries they had been solidly united against a number of heresies, including Arianism.[3]

The split between the Eastern and Western halves of the church also had much to do with the political and geographical reality of the Roman Empire. The political disunion in the Roman Empire was replicated in the church. The last Roman emperor to rule over a united empire was Theodosius the Great, who died in A.D. 395. The empire was divided into eastern and western halves, with each having its own emperor. The Western Roman Empire was torn apart by barbarian invasions in the fifth century, while the Eastern Roman Empire, or Byzantine Empire, continued, with its capital at

Constantinople, the modern Istanbul, Turkey.

The churches of Rome and Constantinople grew in power and became rivals more for their political status rather than for any spiritual or religious reasons. In earlier centuries, ecclesiastical authority in the church had become concentrated in five bishops in the main Christian centers of Alexandria, Antioch, Constantinople, Jerusalem and Rome. This had occurred as early as the fourth century A.D.

A growing reconciliation?

For hundreds of years after the tragic events of July 1054, the Eastern and Western churches essentially went their separate ways, though there were contacts between them and periodic attempts at reconciliation. Meanwhile, the Western church expanded into the Americas and experienced further splits, which created the Protestant Christian world. The Eastern church expanded northward, into the Balkans and in Russia.

A significant step toward reconciliation began in March 1991, when the Eastern Orthodox Church and the World Alliance of Reformed Churches reached a consensus on the Filioque Clause disagreement.[4] Theologian Thomas F. Torrance was instrumental in the dialogue.

Overtures have also been made by leaders in the Catholic and Eastern Orthodox churches. In 1965, Pope Paul VI and Orthodox Patriarch Athenagoras issued a joint text that mutually nullified the joint excommunications of 1054. The declaration was read simultaneously at a public meeting of the ecumenical council in Rome and at a ceremony in Istanbul. The declaration showed a desire for reconciliation between the two churches.

In 1995, Patriarch Bartholomew[5] met with Pope John Paul II in a series of meetings intended to pull the two churches closer together. The patriarch, along with other leaders of Eastern churches, attended the funeral of Pope John Paul II in 2005. This provided a hopeful symbol — an olive branch extended to the Roman Catholic Church for reconciliation. Benedict XVI has said that he, too, wants to find reconciliation and dialogue with other Christians.

Only time will tell whether full reconciliation will occur in the future and what shape it will take. Christians can only pray that the unifying love and Spirit of Christ will shine from all who desire his body, the church, to exhibit a genuine unity and oneness.

Endnotes

1. The city once called Byzantium was renamed Constantinople after the

Roman Emperor Constantine, who made the city his capital in A.D. 330.

2. Perhaps the most notable difference had to do with the issue of the procession of the Holy Spirit. The Western church added what's called the Filioque clause to the Nicene Creed, affirming the double procession of the Holy Spirit from the Father and the Son. This was rejected by the Eastern church, which taught that the Spirit proceeded solely from the Father.

3. In the later Patristic period (ended about A.D. 450) theologians in the eastern empire had an integral part in fighting heresies and in giving authentic expression to the New Testament understanding of God's nature through their theological leadership and participation in the first seven ecumenical councils. One of the biggest threats confronting the church had been the ideas of Arius, who claimed that Jesus Christ was not true God of true God, but a created being. Churchmen from the East were instrumental in combating this heresy. The Second Council of Nicea, in 787, was the seventh and last council accepted by both eastern and western churches.

4. As noted in the article about the Nicene Creed, the Latin version of the creed says that the Holy Spirit proceeds from the Father *and the Son* (Latin, *filioque*); the Greek version says only that the Spirit proceeds from the Father. Torrance's proposal was that the Spirit proceeds from the being of the Father.

5. Bartholomew, whose seat is in Istanbul, the former Constantinople, is given the honor of primacy in the broader Orthodox faith. Self-governing national Orthodox churches choose their own patriarchs.

Paul Kroll

105. WILLIAM TYNDALE AND THE BIRTH OF THE ENGLISH BIBLE

On October 6, 1536, Englishman William Tyndale (c.1494-1536) was strangled by the civil executioner in Belgium and his dead body was burned at the stake. His crime? Tyndale had translated the New Testament and major portions of the Old Testament from the original languages into English so that English-speaking Christians could read the Scriptures in their own tongue.

Persecution and Bible burning

In our time, we are privileged to have access to a wide variety of Bible translations in English. The idea that a Bible translator could be hunted down like a criminal and his Bible translation burned and destroyed seems shocking. Why did such a tragedy happen? Let's briefly explore the religious-political situation in England between 1380 and the 1530s for the answer.

We begin with the first English version of the Bible, translated and published in 1380 by John Wycliffe (c. 1330-1384).[1] An Oxford theologian, Wycliffe was a severe critic of what he believed was a corrupt church. He hoped that people could be called back to a more biblical faith, and for this to happen he was convinced that they needed to read the Bible in their own language.

By producing a translation, Wycliffe ran afoul of church authorities. The few Wycliffe Bible copies in existence were banned by a synod of clergy in Oxford in 1408. An edict was issued against any unauthorized translation of the Bible into English. Wycliffe was pronounced a heretic and was called "a son of the old serpent, forerunner and disciple of Antichrist" by the English Archbishop.[2] In 1415, the Church Council of Constance condemned Wycliffe's writings and ordered his bones to be dug out of the ground and to be burned.

We can now begin to understand why Tyndale and his Bible translation would not be appreciated. Church authorities seemed to take a dim view of Christian folk having the Bible in the language of the uneducated laity. In the words of Church historian Philip Schaff, "Down to the very end of its history, the Medieval Church gave no official encouragement to the circulation of the Bible among the laity. On the contrary, it uniformly set itself against it."[3]

Genesis 1:1–2, from the Tyndale Bible:

In the begynnynge God created heaven and erth. The erth was voyde and emptie, ad darcknesse was vpon the depe, an the spirite of god moved vpon the water …

The Protestant Reformation begins

Tyndale would be in danger of the church hierarchy solely on the basis of his producing an unauthorized English translation. However, Tyndale had two strikes against him, because he was also enmeshed in the Protestant Reformation, which was in full swing by the time he completed his New Testament in English in 1526. The first shot of the Reformation had been fired nine years earlier, when Martin Luther posted his 95 Theses to the door of the castle church in Wittenberg on October 31, 1517. (Luther translated the New Testament into German in 1522.)

Tyndale had thrown in his lot with the Reformers and was highly critical of the church structure in England. The established church in England had no real case for objecting to a Bible in English, except perhaps on the traditional view that it was unhealthy for people to read the Bible for themselves. However, church officials also objected to the critical commentary that Tyndale's New Testament contained. This gave the clergy the rationale to condemn Tyndale and seize copies of his translation.

A determined Tyndale

Tyndale was aware of the dangers of embarking on the translation project he was contemplating. However, he was convinced that the common people must be able to read the Bible in order to be called back to the biblical gospel. In one debate with a cleric, he vowed that if God spared his life, he would see to it that the plowboy would know more about Scripture than untutored priests.

Tyndale first approached Bishop Cuthbert Tunstall (or Tonstall) of London in 1523 to request permission to translate the Bible into English. He hoped that the bishop would both authorize his translation work and also provide him with a residential chaplaincy so he could support himself financially during his project. The bishop denied both requests and suggested Tyndale look for employment elsewhere.

The next year Tyndale decided to go to the Continent, where, with the support of a group of British merchants, he completed his translation of the New Testament. Tyndale found a printer in Cologne, but opponents raided the printing establishment. Escaping with the pages that were already printed, he headed to Worms, Germany, where his New Testament in English was printed in 1526. The first printing of 6,000 copies was then smuggled into England.

Church officials in England, especially in London, did everything they could to intercept copies of Tyndale's New Testament and destroy them. But copies kept appearing, to the chagrin of Bishop Tunstall. He hit upon the idea of buying up as many copies as possible. Once he accomplished his aim, the bishop held a public burning of these New Testament copies at St. Paul's cathedral.

Despite this campaign against Tyndale's New Testament, new copies kept appearing in England. Tunstall then conceived of a plan to buy up large numbers of copies on the Continent before they made their way to England and then destroy these as well. The bishop made an agreement with Augustine Packington, a merchant in Belgium to buy all of Tyndale's remaining printed New Testaments.

Tyndale was made aware of this plot and agreed to sell the copies. He would use the money he received to publish a new edition and have even more copies to distribute. The bishop's plot was foiled. In the words of Edward Halle, a chronicler of the times: "And so forward went the bargain: the bishop had the books, Packington had the thanks, and Tyndale had the money."[4]

More translation, opposition and Tyndale's death

Meanwhile, Tyndale traveled to Antwerp, Belgium, where he began translating the Old Testament into English. By 1530, he had completed and published the English translation from the Hebrew of the Pentateuch, the first five books of the Old Testament.

Tyndale is also considered to have translated the Old Testament books from Joshua to 2 Chronicles, though his translation did not appear while he was alive. As Tyndale was involved in the theological disputes of the day and because he was hounded by those seeking to capture him, he was unable to complete the translation of the entire Old Testament.

Tyndale's second edition of the New Testament was finished in 1534. It was his definitive work, and it is this edition that served as the basis of the 1611 King James Authorized Version.

As Tyndale worked in Antwerp, the agents of King Henry VIII and other opponents were scouring Europe, hoping to find and capture him. Tyndale was betrayed by a fellow Englishman, kidnapped and arrested on May 21, 1535. He was imprisoned in a Belgian fortress and eventually brought to trial for heresy and found guilty. The verdict condemning him to death came in August 1536. On October 6 of the same year he was executed at Vilvorde, Belgium.

Tyndale's final prayer, "Lord, open the King of England's eyes," is said to have been directed to English King Henry VIII (1491-1547). His prayer was a hope that the king would allow copies of the Bible in English to be circulated. Tyndale's prayer had already been answered. An English version of the Bible that drew on his translation work was in circulation before his death. Three years after Tyndale's death, Henry required every English parish church to make a copy of the English Bible available to parishioners.

In the biblical books that Tyndale translated, perhaps up to 90 percent of his wording is found in the King James Version. Where the 1611 King James Version departed from Tyndale's translation, later revisers of this version often returned to it. For his pioneering work of translation, William Tyndale is considered the "Father of the English Bible."

In the United States, National Bible Week is celebrated each year from Sunday to Sunday of Thanksgiving week.[5] This is a timely opportunity to recall the struggles of individuals such as Wycliffe and Tyndale, who suffered grave injustices to help make the Bible available to people in the English language and to reform the church. It is also an appropriate time to remember that many people around the world do not yet have a Bible in their own language.

----

[1] Wycliffe's translation was made before the invention of moveable type and the printing press. All copies of his Bible had to be copied by hand. His version was not a translation of the original languages in which the books of the Bible were first written.

[2] David Ewert, *A General Introduction to the Bible*, page 184.

[3] Philip Schaff, *History of the Christian Church*, vol. vi, page 722.

[4] From Halle's 1548 chronicle of England from Henry IV to Henry VIII in F. F. Bruce, *History of the English Bible*, page 38.

[5] The National Bible Week celebration is sponsored by the Laymen's National Bible Association. The week-long observance began in 1941, when President Franklin D. Roosevelt issued a message in support of the event.

Paul Kroll

106. WHEN ASTRONOMY BECAME A THEOLOGICAL FOOTBALL

Imagine a book on astronomy being condemned as heretical by a Christian church. This is precisely what happened to *De Revolutionibus Orbium Coelestium (On the Revolutions of the Heavenly Spheres),* published in March 1543. The publication was written by Polish astronomer-mathematician, Nicolaus Copernicus (1473-1543).

Copernicus proposed a heliocentric model of the universe, in which the earth revolves around the sun. He believed that the sun, not the earth, was at the center of the planetary system. However, the cosmological theory accepted in Copernicus' day by many European Christians placed the earth at the center of the universe. His contrary proposition, if true, meant that the earth was just one planet among others. This concept opposed the official view of Rome. It took the church 73 years to place the book on the Index of forbidden books. Why so long?

A Lutheran pastor at Nuremberg, Andreas Osiander (1498-1552), wrote a letter to the reader that was inserted in the book as an anonymous preface. Copernicus had no knowledge of it. The preface claimed that Copernicus thought the heliocentric theory described in his book was only an unproven hypothesis.

Ironically, Osiander's unauthorized preface probably saved the book from instant condemnation by the church. *De Revolutionibus* was not placed on the Index of forbidden books until 1616, some 73 years after its publication. The papal decision to censor Copernicus' work was based on a conclusion that a heliocentric claim was contrary to the literal meaning of Scripture. But because *De Revolutionibus* had contributed to calendrical reform, it was not prohibited entirely, but would require revision.

Enter Galileo. Galileo Galilei was born in 1564 at Pisa, 21 years after *De Revolutionibus* was published. By 1598, Galileo believed in the truth of the Copernican heliocentric theory, and was teaching it publicly. In 1615 Galileo went to Rome to argue the merits of the Copernican theory. But the next year *De Revolutionibus* was placed on the Index, and Galileo was warned not to promote its theory as reality. In 1633, Galileo was interrogated under threat of torture and made to recant the heliocentric proposition. He was sentenced to life imprisonment, which he spent in house arrest at his home in Arcetri. Galileo died in 1642.

It is a good lesson for us today. We have no need to condemn the work of science by looking for biblical passages to back up our views about how the creation functions. The Bible is God's self-revelation as Creator and Redeemer of all things, not a science text on how he designed the physical universe. For that sort of knowledge God gives us the joy of research and discovery.

Paul Kroll

107. FASTING AND REPENTANCE AFTER THE SALEM WITCH TRIALS

On Jan. 15, 1697, the town of Salem and the Massachusetts Bay Colony proclaimed a day of fasting and repentance because of the senseless witch trials and executions that had occurred five years earlier in the colony. More than 150 people were accused of being witches and were imprisoned, and 19 suspected witches were hanged.

The day of personal and public repentance was called "so all of God's people may offer up fervent supplications unto him, that all iniquity may be put away, which hath stirred God's holy jealousy against this land; that he would show us what we know not, and help us, wherein we have done amiss, to do so no more."

The witch-hunting hysteria had begun when two children claimed they were bewitched by certain townspeople. Later, during the trial, other children and young people made similar accusations. No real evidence of Satan worship, witchcraft or other paranormal activities was presented. Most of the accused were women, though it included George Burroughs, former minister of Salem Village, who was hanged on Aug. 19, 1692.

While the witch trials were an isolated unbiblical miscarriage of justice in a tiny community, they point out the fact that Christians must avoid having their faith high-jacked by hysteria, scapegoating or superstition. There have been other, more extensive miscarriages in Christian history, such as the Inquisition, which remind us that we need to always live in step with the Holy Spirit and to show the wisdom and love of Christ to others in all situations.

Paul Kroll

108. THE GREAT AWAKENING

In 1734, Northampton village in the colony of Massachusetts experienced a remarkable revival that became the catalyst for revivals throughout the Colonies and in England, Scotland and Germany. By the early 1740s, revival events dominated Colonial newspaper headlines from Boston to Charleston. They reported on itinerant preachers thundering out messages of eternal damnation and salvation to frightened, wailing and repentant crowds on city streets, in parks and at meetinghouses.

This series of revivals was later dubbed the "Great Awakening." Some considered it a "mighty work of God" equal to the Holy Spirit's outpouring at Pentecost and an echo of the Protestant Reformation.

Edwards and Whitefield

Northampton's pastor was Jonathan Edwards (1703-1758), one of Colonial America's best-known theologians. Deeply involved in the Great Awakening from beginning to end, he preached, promoted and defended revival events through his many writings and contacts with other evangelicals. In 1736 he wrote "A Faithful Narrative of the Surprising Work of God." This article soon became a popular book relating how hundreds of Northampton citizens and people in surrounding communities had been converted and saved. It became a script for spotting, staging and reporting revivals throughout Colonial America.

The young evangelical preacher George Whitefield (1714-1770), known as the "Great Itinerant," provided the Great Awakening with its strongest momentum. The most notable of his three evangelistic tours through the Colonies lasted between November 1739 and January 1741. During one month crowds of 8,000 or more heard Whitefield speak nearly every day. An estimated 20,000 listened to his sermons in Philadelphia and Boston. "That tour may have been the most sensational event in the history of American religion," observed Mark A. Noll, professor of history at Wheaton College.

Jonathan Edwards' July 8, 1741, sermon, "Sinners in the Hands of an Angry God," is a famous example of Great Awakening hell-fire and brimstone preaching. "The God that holds you over the pit of hell, much as one holds a spider, or some loathsome insect over the fire, abhors you, and is dreadfully provoked: his wrath towards you burns like fire; he looks upon you as worthy of nothing else, but to be cast into the fire," Edwards warned his frightened congregation.

Hell-fire message

He defended this kind of "scare tactic" as necessary to wake up unconverted people from their spiritual lethargy. Edwards' grandfather, Solomon Stoddard, in a 1713 sermon had said: "The misery of many Men is that they do not fear Hell…so they take a great liberty to Sin…. If they were afraid of Hell, they would be afraid of Sin."

Revival sermons caused people in the audience to weep and scream in a frenzy. This rampant emotionalism was at the heart of a bitter dispute between "Old Lights" and "New Lights." Charles Chauncy, pastor of the First Church in Boston, Massachusetts, was one of the revival's most ardent critics. His sermon "Enthusiasm Described and Cautioned Against" was an attack on the revivalists' manipulation of listeners' emotions.

To counter Antirevivalist arguments and to defend the authenticity of conversions, Edwards wrote "The Distinguishing Marks of a Work of the Spirit of God" in 1741. He sincerely believed that the Great Awakening was a "work of God" and had resulted in many genuine conversions. While admitting that excesses had occurred, he defended the Colonies-wide revival as a special outpouring of the Spirit.

As suddenly as it began, the Great Awakening began to weaken. In a December 12, 1743, letter, Jonathan Edwards complained to Thomas Prince that a "very lamentable decay of religious affections" was beginning to creep back into Colonial society. By 1749, the Church had returned to "its ordinary State." According to Gilbert Tennent, another revivalist, the Great Awakening was dead.

Paul Kroll

109. MARY JONES AND THE FIRST MAJOR WORLDWIDE BIBLE SOCIETY

Mary Jones was born Dec. 16, 1784 in the Welsh village of Llanfihangely Pennant. From an early age, Mary longed to have a Bible in her own language that she could read. Mary's dilemma was that it was well-nigh impossible for a Welsh child from a poor family to afford a Bible. Bibles were expensive in 18th century Wales. Nevertheless, over the years Mary scrimped and saved enough money from doing odd chores for neighbors to buy a Bible. Mary was now around 16 years old.

Mary's odyssey

She heard that a minister named Thomas Charles in the town of Bala had some Welsh Bibles for sale. Bala was some 25 miles (40 kilometers) from her home. She gathered her savings and trudged across the hills to Bala to find the minister. He gave Mary some bad news. Every copy of the Bible he had was already sold. He was moved by the diligence she had shown in seeking a Bible and handed her his last copy, which he had put away for another buyer.

Mary's goal of obtaining her own Bible and her meeting with Charles set in motion the creation of a truly international Bible society.[1] Charles presented the need for more copies of the Scriptures in Welsh at a meeting of the Religious Tract Society in December 1802. Though the Tract Society was sympathetic about the need, they were not in a position to meet the demand. But one member, Joseph Hughes, suggested that "a society might be formed for the purpose [of distributing Bibles]—and if for Wales, why not for the [United] Kingdom; why not for the whole world?"

On March 7, 1804, a meeting was conducted at the London Tavern in Bishopsgate, at which the British and Foreign Bible Society (BFBS) was formed. Some 300 citizens from several denominations formed the society.[2]

The Society's work

The BFBS would be non-sectarian, and its governing committee was interdenominational. The members set as their goal "the wider distribution of the Scriptures, without note or comment." The Society had no interest in fostering any particular interpretation of the Bible. Its sole purpose was to provide people with easier and less expensive (or free) access to the Scriptures.

The BFBS was concerned with translating and distributing Bibles in all languages throughout the world. One of its first international achievements was the production of the Gospel of John in the Mohawk language. The society provided missionaries with Bibles for people being evangelized. William Carey (1761-1834), missionary to India, was funded by the society in his translation work. The society helped Robert Morris, the first Protestant missionary to China, with a translation of the Bible into Chinese, and aided Henry Martyn, who was working on a Persian translation.

Satellites of the main society sprang up. In just 10 years, 60 other Bible organizations had formed. By 1907, the BFBS had distributed 204 million Bibles, New Testaments and portions of Scripture throughout the world. An international organization providing Bibles to people around the world had been inspired by the needs of one girl in Wales, Mary Jones.

The British and Foreign Bible Society is now more commonly known as The Bible Society. Its slogan is "Making the Bible heard." Its website is www.biblesociety.org.uk. The BFBS marked its 200th anniversary in 2004 as it launched its Revised New Welsh Bible, harking back to Charles offering his last Welsh Bible to Mary Jones. The Bible Society distributed 256,548 Bibles, 68,985 New Testaments and 43,029 portions of Scripture in that anniversary year.

The BFBS today works through a global alliance of more than 137 Bible Societies. These national Bible Societies are part of a worldwide fellowship called the United Bible Societies, formed in 1946.

[1.] Mary Jones died in 1864, in her 80s. The story of Mary Jones and her Bible is a traditional one. Mary did not write down her own account, so over the past two centuries the story has been recounted with some variations.

[2.] Various kinds of Christian organizations and societies made efforts to disseminate Bibles long before the British and Foreign Bible Society was organized, but these did not achieve the international scope and lasting impact of BFBS.

Paul Kroll

110. THE AFRICAN-AMERICAN CHURCH
IN AMERICA

"Eleven o'clock Sunday morning is the most segregated hour, and Sunday school is still the most segregated school of the week," is an oft-quoted statement from Martin Luther King Jr. (1929-1968). King was referring to the fact that during his lifetime most African-Americans worshiped in congregations and churches mainly or entirely composed of black people.

These African-American churches' roots go back to the North and South of the Revolutionary War period of the 1760s and 1770s. Like whites, blacks also began to come to Christ during the religious revivalism of the period.

African-Americans shared a common belief with European-American evangelicals that the biblical account of God's past dealings with the world offered clues to the meaning of life in America. But, there was a difference. White Protestants often likened America to the Promised Land — the New Israel — a "city set on a hill." Black worshipers were more likely to see America as Egypt — as the land of their captivity. They longed for their own emancipation, just as God had delivered ancient Israel in the Exodus.

This desire for emancipation eventually led to the African-American church movement. Blacks in the Methodist church took the lead in creating independent denominations.

In the Revolutionary period, the impetus for blacks to have their own churches owes much to the work of Richard Allen. He was a former slave and deacon-elder at the integrated St. George's Methodist Church in Philadelphia.

In 1787, Allen with Absalom Jones organized the Free African Society in Philadelphia. Allen founded the all-black Mother Bethel African Methodist Episcopal Church in 1791, after Jones and he left St. George's over its segregationist practice of relegating black members to the church balcony during worship services.

Over time, growing numbers of African-Americans formed their own congregations. In 1816, representatives of these congregations joined to form the African Methodist Episcopal Church (A.M.E. church), with Allen as the first bishop. The most significant growth of this church occurred during the Civil War and Reconstruction.

African-American churches took up what has been their historical mission to care for the spiritual and physical needs of black people, since they were neglected and discriminated against by white society. Yet, they did not forget the ultimate mission of the church — to make disciples in all nations and among all peoples. The A.M.E. church sees its mission in this way: "To minister to the spiritual, intellectual, physical, emotional and environmental needs of all people by spreading Christ's liberating gospel through word and deed…that is, to seek out and save the lost, and serve the needy."

African-American churches have been a bulwark in the black community — a refuge from the larger, cruel world. Richard Wright, in his book *12 Million Black Voices,* wrote: "It is only when we are within the walls of our churches that we are wholly ourselves, that we keep alive a sense of our personalities in relation to the total world in which we live."

The black church was also a sanctuary for praise and worship of Christ. Here members could express themselves freely and unite culturally in their beliefs and life practices. As worshipful communities, African-American Christians saw their relationship with Jesus as the bedrock of a faith that gave them hope for a better future.

By the late 1950s, a generation of African-Americans began to drift away from the church. The relevance of the church was dealt a serious blow, as many urban youths felt it no longer had anything to offer — that it did not speak to the reality of their lives.

However, the African-American church continues to be for many black people the place of worship and source of strength, though it is much more diverse than it once was.

The Sunday service may still be a time when people of different racial backgrounds to some degree are segregated, as Martin Luther King Jr. observed. However, today even most exclusively black churches have made connections to the larger Christian community and serve black people as well as people of all races in ministry and the gospel of Christ.

Paul Kroll

111. BLACK HISTORY MONTH:
AN INTERVIEW WITH CURTIS MAY

J. Michael Feazell interviewed Curtis May, director of the Office of Reconciliation Ministries, an outreach ministry of Grace Communion International, about Black History Month.

JMF: *What is Black History Month?*

CM: Black History Month began in 1926 as Negro History Week. It was established by Carter G. Woodson as a way to bring attention to the positive contributions of black people in American history. In 1976 Negro History Week became Black History Month.

JMF: *Who was Carter G. Woodson?*

CM: Dr. Woodson was a son of former slaves. He worked in the coalmines in Kentucky to put himself through high school. He graduated from Berea College in Kentucky in 1903, and then went on to Harvard for his Ph.D.

It bothered Woodson to find that blacks had hardly been written about in American history books, even though blacks had been part of American history from as far back as colonial times. And when blacks were mentioned, it was not in ways that reflected the positive contributions that they had made.

So he wanted to do something about that. In 1915, he established the Association for the Study of Negro Life and History (now called the Association for the Study of Afro-American Life and History) and then founded the *Journal of Negro History* and *Negro History Bulletin*. Then in 1926 he started promoting the second week of February as Negro History Week.

JMF: *Why February?*

CM: Woodson chose February because the birthdays of Abraham Lincoln and abolitionist Frederick Douglass were in that month. These were two men who had a great influence on black Americans.

In addition, several other important events took place in February. For example, the 15th Amendment, which said that the right to vote could not be denied on account of race, was ratified on Feb. 3, 1870.

W.E.B. DuBois, educator and writer, was born in February 1868. The first black U.S. senator, Hiram Revels, took his oath of office in February 1870. The founding of the NAACP in 1909 took place in February, as did the murder of Malcolm X in 1965, and the Greensboro, North Carolina, sit-in at the Woolworth's lunch counter in 1960.

JMF: *Why is Black History Month important today?*

CM: All young people need positive role models to inspire them and spur them on and to help them know that they, too, have the potential to achieve their dreams and accomplish worthwhile and important things.

Young blacks need to know about the many positive achievements of black men and women throughout history in every field of endeavor. Knowing what others have done inspires confidence in young people to know that they can do worthwhile things too.

Knowing about the achievements of black doctors, scientists, lawyers, economists and journalists provides encouragement and incentive to black young people to strive for excellence themselves. Without such knowledge and encouragement, young people can end up wasting precious time and energy blaming the system and feeling victimized.

JMF: *How would you describe the value of Black History Month for nonblack people?*

CM: Black history is not merely black history; it is American history. By better understanding the positive contributions of another ethnic group, all Americans benefit. When we understand one another better, we are that much closer to having positive relationships with one another.

Many nonblacks, even many blacks, have erroneous stereotypes in their minds about blacks and their history in the United States. These negative ideas and impressions create barriers to good relationships and to the true potential that all Americans have for working together toward our common goals for freedom, peace and achievement.

Black History Month provides a focus on the positive history, achievements and contributions to American ideals that blacks have made throughout history. And that helps to dispel the negative ideas and stereotypes that invariably spring up when the truth is not given the light of day.

The experience of black Americans in our history can be a further inspiration to all Americans that no matter how tough the struggle, no matter what the odds, when we don't give up, when we stand together firmly for the right and the truth, great things can happen. And there's nothing more truly American than that. It's our collective legacy and heritage.

JMF: *How can Christians benefit from Black History Month?*

CM: The civil rights movement was born in Christian faith and values. The early leaders of the movement were Christian ministers, black and white alike, who saw injustice and worked in nonviolent ways to bring the love of Jesus Christ to bear on a system that reflected neither the gospel itself nor the deepest values of the U.S. Constitution.

As Christians, when we rehearse that struggle and celebrate the positive achievements of Americans who excelled despite having been socially marginalized, we affirm the values and responsibilities of our faith.

JMF: *Can you give me one word that in your mind characterizes Black History Month?*

CM: Well, I think I'd have to say *hope*. It's all about promoting hope — hope for a better tomorrow that springs from the lessons, the tears and the joys of what has gone before. It's a hope that grows from understanding and from truth — and from the power of love.

And I thank Jesus Christ, because he takes all our meager efforts and turns them into a real and true hope that sees past all the challenges of the present and into a future where his love binds all people together, all people of all backgrounds and ethnicities and histories all bound together as one in him.

112. BLACK HISTORY MONTH

February is Black History month in the USA and Canada, in which we acknowledge the contribution that African-Americans have made (a similar observance occurs in the United Kingdom in October). For example, the movie *Red Tails* tells a little-known story of African-American aviators who were a part of "the Greatest Generation" and helped defeat the enemies of democratic freedom in the Second World War.

Some people in other parts of the world may wonder why America devotes a month to recognizing the achievements of just one segment of our population. However, the contribution of African-Americans to this nation has not always been acknowledged. It was quite the opposite for a long time.

Carter Woodson

We owe the celebration of Black History Month, and the study of black history, to Dr. Carter G. Woodson. Carter Woodson was born to parents who were former slaves. He spent his childhood working in the Kentucky coal mines and enrolled in high school at age 20. He later went on to earn a Ph.D. from Harvard. Dr. Woodson was disturbed to find that history books largely ignored the black American population. If they were acknowledged, it was generally in ways that portrayed their inferior social position. Woodson set out to set the record straight. Carter G. Woodson and The Association for the Study of Negro Life and History announced the second week of February to be Negro History Week. In 1970, this was expanded to Black History Month and President Gerald Ford formally acknowledged it in 1976.

The awful stain on our nation's history that was slavery is now in our past, but the effects linger on. It is only in my lifetime that some of the most glaring injustices have been addressed. One of my close friends and colleagues, Curtis May, spent his early years in Alabama. He experienced the prejudice, humiliation and indignity of segregation. Curtis now leads The Office of Reconciliation and Mediation. This ministry (http://atimetoreconcile.org/) has gained respect and recognition as it seeks to promote forgiveness and understanding wherever there is need of reconciliation and healing.

During Black History Month in the US, we acknowledge the contribution that African-Americans have made to our nation. They have held some of the highest offices in our government (including president) and have made their mark. Thousands of less recognizable African-Americans have and are making significant contributions to our national life in entertainment, sports, academia, science and the arts.

Ethnic prejudice worldwide

Black History Month also reminds us of the tragic record of misunderstanding, prejudice and cruelty that has been a part of U.S. history. Thankfully, things have improved. However, I shudder when I think that only a generation or so ago much of this country was still mired in outright segregation and blatant prejudice. It leaves me asking how a people who sing proudly about "The land of the free and the home of the brave," and who pledge allegiance to a republic that promises "liberty and justice for all," could have been so blind, prejudiced and stupid.

However, the problem of racism (and the related problem of ethnic prejudice) is not limited to one nation and is not just a black/white problem. Black History Month reminds us that people everywhere are capable of inhuman behavior. The genocide in Rwanda at the end of the last century was a clash of two tribes of the same race. The deadly Bosnian conflict was between peoples who share a common language, much common history and probably ancient ancestry. The cruelties of Nazi Germany and Stalinist Russia were perpetrated mainly by Europeans on Europeans. Imperialist Japan and Communist China committed atrocities against fellow Asians. Cambodians killed other Cambodians. In the long and sordid history of racial/nationalistic conflict, no people can plead "not guilty" to prejudice and discrimination. These are signs of the fallenness of all humanity.

The Bible condemns prejudice

Sadly, these atrocities are sometimes committed in the name of God. Advocates of slavery and segregation used the Bible to support their arguments. Could anything be more contrary to the "ministry of reconciliation" (2 Corinthians 5:18)? Surely, this is one of the greatest perversions of Scripture. Regrettably, such teaching continues and still affects the way some think about others and even about themselves. I have friends who grew up with segregation who tell me that the scars take a long time to heal.

There is nothing in the Scriptures to indicate that any people are inferior or are excluded from God's saving grace on the basis of ethnic origin or skin color. God is "not wanting anyone to perish" (2 Peter 3:9). The book of Revelation expresses great joy that heavenly worship involves those "from every tribe and language and people and nation" (Revelation 5:9; 7:9; 13:7; 14:6). Jesus paid the same price for everyone. No race, nation, tribe or people group are outside the embrace of his love. As the old song goes, "red and yellow, black and white, all are precious in his sight."

God created humanity in his image. There is, in actuality, only one race—

the human race. Within this human race, by God's design, there is great diversity in culture, language, skin color and other physical characteristics. It is interesting that the Human Genome project has discovered that every human being on the planet is 99.9% genetically identical. There is only one-tenth of one percent of DNA that differentiates us from one another, no matter our race.

Furthermore, Jesus has done everything to forgive and redeem us all. When the angels appeared to the shepherds to announce the birth of Jesus, they said it was good news for *all peoples* (Luke 2:10). Jesus taught that he would "draw all people" to himself (John 12:32) and from east and west, north and south (Luke 13:29). The apostle Paul declared that Jesus was the new Adam, the new head of all humanity (Romans 5:14; 1 Corinthians 15:45) and that, in Christ, there is one new humanity (Ephesians 2:15). We celebrate this truth and there is no one who should be appreciated any less than another.

As Acts 17:26 reminds us, "from one blood [God] made the whole world of humanity" (*The Original Aramaic New Testament in Plain English*). We are one people with a common need for forgiveness and salvation. Thank God that we have one Savior and, therefore, a common destiny. God values us all and Jesus paid the same price for each of us. That leaves no room for prejudice, segregation or discrimination of any kind.

Christianity and racism are incompatible. We must work to not just overcome racism, personally, but eventually to obliterate it through our message and example of love and reconciliation.

Making progress

When Carter Woodson created Black History Week, he hoped that racial prejudice would eventually be eliminated when black history became fundamental to American history. We have made progress, but we are not quite there yet. There are still many tragic examples of hatred and oppression in the world today. So we still need Black History Month. It reminds us of where we have been and where we need yet to go. The more we learn about the accomplishments of our brothers and sisters, the more we learn to appreciate the variety God has given his children.

Our own denomination has had to grow in this. In our fellowship, we owe a great debt to our pioneer African-American elders, like the late Harold Jackson and Stanley Bass, and also Abner Washington, Maceo Hampton, Leslie Schmedes and Franklin Guice who, though well up in years, continue to make substantial contributions to the life of our denomination. The patience, humility and courage of these men and their families, and many like them, have helped GCI grow in understanding of the evils of racism and ethnic prejudice. I am deeply grateful for the unique contribution my African-American brothers and sisters have made, and are making, to our denomination.

So, as we are reminded this month of the significant contributions and the unique sufferings of our African-American neighbors, let me encourage you to take some time getting to know more of that history. Let us pray for the eradication of the lingering injustices still found in our nations. Let us thank God for the ministry of reconciliation our Lord Jesus has given us. And let us look for opportunities to extend that ministry in the power of the Spirit to those within our fellowship and beyond.

GCI is multi-racial, multi-ethnic and multi-national. We may be a small denomination, but we are a rich tapestry of many peoples from many different backgrounds and nationalities, working together with the same purpose. Let's thank God for that.

Joseph Tkach

113. WILLIAM WILBERFORCE: CHRISTIAN ABOLITIONIST, REFORMER, STATESMAN

"God Almighty has set before me two great objects, the suppression of the slave trade and the reformation of manners," said William Wilberforce (1759-1833), the man who would be the driving force in the ultimate end of slavery in the British Empire. When Wilberforce was born, English sailors were raiding the African coast, capturing tens of thousands of Africans yearly and shipping them across the Atlantic into slavery. An estimated one in four died in route.

The economies of the British colonies depended on the slave trade. A promoter of the West Indies trade wrote, "The impossibility of doing without slaves in the West Indies will always prevent this traffic being dropped."

As a young man, Wilberforce wasn't aware of the horrors of the slave trade. After attending St. John's College, Cambridge, he decided on a political career. At age 21, he won a seat in the House of Commons from his hometown, Hull. Small and frail, Wilberforce suffered throughout his life from various ailments, sometimes being bedridden for weeks and on several occasions at death's door.

Conversion to Christ

In 1784, at age 25, Wilberforce became an evangelical Christian within the Anglican Church. He questioned whether he could pursue politics and remain a Christian. Wilberforce's spiritual mentor was evangelical minister John Newton (1725-1807), writer of "Amazing Grace," and former slave trader captain. He encouraged him to remain in politics, saying, "It is hoped and believed that the Lord has raised you up for the good of his church and the good of the nation."

Once Wilberforce learned of the evils of the slave trade, he devoted his life to its abolition. He wrote: "So enormous, so dreadful, so irremediable did the Trade's wickedness appear that my own mind was completely made up for abolition." In 1787, abolitionists Sir Charles and Lady Middleton persuaded Wilberforce to use his political influence as a Member of Parliament to legislate against the slave trade. He joined the Committee for the Abolition of the Slave Trade, allying himself with such abolitionists as Thomas Clarkson (1760-1846).

Wilberforce became associated with the "Clapham Sect" called "the Saints." Members were Christ-centered, Anglican evangelicals, influential in government and business. The group included such abolitionist luminaries as

Granville Sharp, Zachary Macaulay, Hannah More and Thomas Clarkson. Wilberforce became the parliamentary "lightning rod" and team-building leader of this group of Christian reformers. John Venn, rector of Clapham parish church, was their chaplain.

The struggle and victory

In May 1788, Wilberforce introduced a 12-point motion to Parliament to abolish the slave trade. The motion was defeated as planters, businessmen, ship owners, traditionalists, MPs and the Crown opposed him.

The abolitionists, having to decide whether to attack the slavery institution or the slave trade, chose the latter course. Wilberforce educated himself on its evils and gave his first parliamentary speech in May 1789, a three-and-a-half-hour marathon. "I have proved that, upon every ground, total abolition [of the trade] ought to take place," he told Parliament. But legislators were unswayed and buried his motion in committee for two years. Then, in 1791, the bill to abolish the slave trade was put to a vote in Commons and defeated by a landslide, 163 to 88.

Wilberforce now understood that the struggle would be long and bitter. He unsuccessfully reintroduced abolition bills regularly during the 1790s. The early years of the new century were also quite bleak for the abolitionists, as all legislation introduced in Parliament against the slave trade failed to win passage. Eventually, the tide turned.

On February 23, 1807, Parliament voted in favor of Wilberforce's Abolition of the Slave Trade Act. Passing overwhelmingly, first in Lords and then in Commons by nearly an 18 to 1 margin, the bill received Royal Assent and became law on March 25, 1807. Through the efforts of Wilberforce, members of the Clapham Sect and others, the slave trade was declared illegal in the British Empire. Wilberforce wept for joy. Eighteen years he had fought the good fight in Parliament.

The struggle was not over, however. Although the slave trade was illegal, it still flourished, and slavery itself remained in the British colonies. Some abolitionists argued that the only way to stop slavery was to make the institution illegal. Wilberforce was convinced of this, but also correctly understood there was little political will for emancipation at the time. He also feared that a sudden abolition of slavery would be disastrous for both slaves and society.

Wilberforce decided legislation was needed to plug holes in the anti-slave trade law. He pushed for a Slave Registration Bill with other abolitionists, arguing that if a slave was registered, authorities could prove whether the slave was recently transported from Africa. The measure was not executed or enforced.

Finally, Wilberforce joined the campaign to end the institution of slavery, but his health was deteriorating. Unable to campaign as vigorously as he had against the slave trade, in 1821 he offered leadership of the parliamentary anti-slavery crusade to Thomas Fowell Buxton (1786-1845), an MP, abolitionist, social reformer and fellow evangelical.

In March 1825, at age 66, failing health forced Wilberforce's retirement from Parliament. His last public appearance for the abolition cause was at a meeting of the Anti-Slavery Society in 1830. While Buxton, Clarkson and others were equally important to the abolitionist cause, Wilberforce had played the key role, as team builder and inspirational, visionary leader.

Near death, on July 26, 1833, Wilberforce received wonderful news. The Slavery Abolition Bill ending slavery throughout the British Empire had passed the Commons, with passage assured in Lords. All slaves throughout the Empire would be freed and plantation owners would be compensated. Wilberforce said, "Thank God that I have lived to witness a day in which England is willing to give twenty millions sterling for the abolition of slavery."

Three days later, Wilberforce died.

The Slavery Abolition Bill became law August 29, 1833, and came into force a year later, abolishing slavery throughout the British Empire. On July 31, 1834, one year after Wilberforce's death, 800,000 slaves, chiefly in the British West Indies, were "free at last."

A generation later, U.S. President Abraham Lincoln issued the Emancipation Proclamation freeing slaves in states that had rebelled against the Union. With the ratification of the Thirteenth Amendment on December 6, 1865, the institution of slavery in America came to an end.

Paul Kroll

114. THE GREAT DISAPPOINTMENT

On October 22, 1844, as many as 100,000 Christians gathered on hillsides, in meeting places and in meadows. They were breathlessly and joyously expecting the return of their Lord and Savior, Jesus Christ. The crowds had assembled because of the prophetic claim of an upstate New York farmer and Baptist layman named William Miller (1782-1849). He was certain from his studies of the Bible that Jesus Christ was going to return on that day.

The prophesied return date had arrived. The waiting crowds, gathered at various places, mainly throughout the Northeast United States, peered expectantly upward as the hours slipped away. Anxiety grew as nightfall descended. Then the midnight hour tolled and still Christ had not returned. People became ever more restless. Through the wee hours of darkness, the dejected and stunned crowds began to disperse. When the daylight of Oct. 23 arrived, it was clear that Christ was not going to return as expected.

Failed prophecy and its aftermath

This dashed hope came to be known as "The Great Disappointment." In his book *When Time Shall Be No More,* historian Paul Boyer offers an example of the deep despondency suffered by the Millerites. In the words of one tragically disappointed believer: "Our fondest hopes and expectations were blasted, and such a spirit of weeping came over us as I never experienced before…. We wept, and wept, till the day dawned" (page 81).

When Jesus did not return as expected, many who had hopefully waited for the return of their Savior threw off their faith completely. Some refused to give up their hope and eventually replaced one delusion with another. They would claim that Christ must have come invisibly in 1844, moving into the Holy of Holies in heaven to begin his "investigative judgment" of Christian lives.

Many simply returned to the churches out of which they had come, no doubt confused, distraught and embarrassed to have accepted something that was revealed to have been an empty fantasy. Miller, having renounced his prophecy studies after the Great Disappointment, died in 1849. Any remaining followers split up over differences of belief and doctrine. Ultimately, a variety of groups arose from the ashes of the Millerite camp, including the Jehovah's Witnesses and Seventh-day Adventists.

Actually, the October 1844 debacle was the *second* great disappointment for followers of Miller's chronology and prophecy blueprint. He had previously announced that the coming of Jesus Christ would occur in about the year 1843. The year came and went without Christ's return. Miller's prophetic claim had failed and disappointed many people.

Then someone pointed out that he had neglected to take into account the transition from B.C. to A.D., so that his calculations were one year off. Miller then moved the expected return of Jesus forward by one year, this time to Oct. 22, 1844. But the great disappointment happened once again to the thousands of followers who had given away their possessions and waited in expectant belief — for nothing.

William Miller, as all Christians do, yearned for the coming of God's kingdom. However, this yearning was translated by him into a misguided belief that Christ's return would occur in his time on a specific date. Miller thought he had discovered in the Bible certain prophecies, which if rationally studied, could provide him with a certain date for Jesus' return. His study and calculations of various prophecies, such as the 70 weeks prophecy of Daniel 9 and the 2300 days of chapter 8, brought him, he believed, to Oct. 22 as the date for Christ's return.

American prophetic streak

Prophetic beliefs such as Miller's are strongly entrenched among some Christians and in American popular religion. The Millerite movement of the 1830s and 1840s was not an isolated event. As Miller and other leaders of his movement crisscrossed the northern states, they found a ready audience of people who held to various prophetic ideas about how and when Jesus would return.

The Millerite phenomenon is not an isolated movement, but grew up in a Premillenialist culture popular with many Christians. Many tens of thousands of Christians living at the time — average people — were eager to follow Miller's belief or some other prophetic scheme. As Boyer observes, quoting from David Rowe, a commentator on the Millerite experience: "Millerites are not fascinating because they were so different from everyone else but because they were so like their neighbors" (*When Time Shall Be No More,* page 82).

The excitement in speculative prophecy that characterized the Millerites has continued through the 19th and 20th century, and into our time, especially under a different mode of interpretive prophecy identified as Dispensationalism. This movement began through the work of John Nelson Darby (1800-1882).

Though most prophecy buffs of a Dispensationalist persuasion have avoided setting exact dates for Jesus' return, they nonetheless continue to use Bible prophecy as a blueprint for their views of the end time. Usually, they maintain that his coming is imminent — in our generation. They claim the next dispensation of God's dealing with humanity will begin with the rapture — when the Christian saints are supposedly taken to heaven while the rest of humanity is left behind.

'Imminent return' the watch phrase

To Dispensationalists, the signs of the times are always with us. While date-setting is usually avoided, Christians are told that they must be ready because the rapture could occur at any moment. The time of the end is always right now, even though we may not know the precise date. Many fundamentalists, evangelicals — and other Christians — still believe that biblical prophecy is meant to be interpreted in such an apocalyptical and speculative way. If rightly interpreted, they believe, biblical prophecy can tell us what will happen in the near future — in our lifetime.

But as with William Miller's failed calculations, all this speculation about the end of the age is the invention of often brilliant, but confused minds. Christians would do well to remember the Great Disappointment of Oct. 22, 1844. Miller's prophecy construct seemed like a logical and biblically based creation, but proved to be nothing more than a mirage.

Paul Kroll

115. WILLIAM SEYMOUR AND THE RISE OF PENTECOSTALISM

April 2006 was the 100th anniversary of a momentous revolution in Christianity that began at 312 Azusa Street in a ramshackle part of downtown Los Angeles. A writer for a local newspaper captured the significance of the Azusa Street Revival when he noted that it is "now seen as the great awakening of the Pentecostal / Charismatic movement."[1]

The pastor at the Azusa Street church was William J. Seymour (1870-1922). Seymour, the son of former slaves, had been raised as a Baptist and later joined a radical Holiness church. There he came to believe in divine healing, the rapture of the saints and Premillennialism, justification by faith and "sanctification as a second work of grace."[2]

Seymour had also been a follower of a Holiness preacher named Charles Fox Parham (1873-1929). He attended Parham's Bible school in Houston, Texas, where he was taught the idea that tongues-speaking is the biblical evidence of being baptized in the Holy Spirit.

Seymour came to Los Angeles, where he was invited to minister to a house church on North Bonnie Brae Street. It was here that a defining event happened during a worship service on April 9, 1906. A member of the small group suddenly spoke in "tongues." Then, in a chain reaction, other members at Bonnie Brae also became tongues-speakers.

This led to much notoriety and a crush of new worshippers filling the small church. It forced Seymour to relocate his congregation to a larger building on Azusa Street in what is today the Little Tokyo section of Los Angeles. The new church was called the "Apostolic Faith Gospel Mission." Here the revival grew into a crescendo as more and more people began to speak in tongues.

The Apostolic Faith, the Azusa Street congregation's newspaper, trumpeted the group's growing belief that tongues-speaking was a sign that all the gifts of the Spirit had been restored to the church. A headline in the paper's first issue (September 1906) proclaimed: "Pentecost Has Come. Los Angeles Being Visited by a Revival of Bible Salvation and Pentecost as Recorded in the Book of Acts."[3]

The local revival sown on Azusa Street became the seed-bed of an international Christian movement. Over the next three years, hundreds of people worshipped there, many speaking in tongues, and revolutionized Christianity in several ways:

- During a time of rampant segregation and discrimination, the Azusa Street congregation was multiracial. African-Americans, Anglos,

Hispanics, and Christians of other ethnic backgrounds freely mingled, worshipped together and shared leadership.

- A missionary fervor characterized the Azusa Street worshippers and those who had joined with them. Many members of the Azusa group streamed out across America and into other lands to preach the gospel. This evangelistic fervor would lead to a worldwide explosion in Pentecostalism.

- The Azusa Street revivalists possessed a deep-seated belief that *all* the supernatural gifts of the Spirit had been dispensed to believers so they could preach Christ's gospel and build his church.

- Speaking in tongues, faith healing, fervent prayer, emotional, from-the-heart participatory worship and stress on evangelism became the hallmarks of the Azusa Street experience. These traits appealed to many Christians and seekers. Pentecostalism's influence began to be felt in non-Pentecostal churches and denominations. The Charismatic movement developed out of this worship and stress on the work of the Holy Spirit.

Today, the number of classical Pentecostals worldwide and those who are considered Pentecostal-like charismatics has exploded. Because of a fervent missionary zeal, it has become one of the fastest-growing Christian movements in South America and Africa. *The Dictionary of Christianity in America* cites Pentecostalism as being "perhaps the single-most-significant development in twentieth-century Christianity."[4]

For the most part, Pentecostalism has been considered a movement of the poor and marginalized people of the world, and that has been true up to a point. However, it has also made dramatic inroads into mainstream and mainline Western Christianity. Because of Pentecostalism and the Charismatic Movement, all Christians have had to consider more deeply the role of the Holy Spirit in the life of the Christian and in Christian mission around the world.

Endnotes

1 Andrew Moyle, "A Century of Faith: Event Celebrates 100th Anniversary of Azusa Street Revival," *Downtown News*, April 24, 2006, page 7.

2 Vinson Synan, "Introduction," in Frank Bartleman, *Azusa Street: The Roots of Modern-day Pentecost* (Plainfield, NJ: Logos International, 1980) page ix.

3 "The Apostolic Faith," vol. 1, no. 1, Sept. 1906.

4 Roger G. Robins, "Pentecostal Movement," in *Dictionary of Christianity in America* (Daniel G. Reid, ed.; Downers Grove, IL: InterVarsity Press, 1990), page 885.

Paul Kroll

116. KARL BARTH:
"PROPHET" TO THE CHURCH

Swiss theologian Karl Barth has been called "the most outstanding and consistently evangelical theologian that the world has seen in modern times." Pope Pius XII (1876-1958) called Barth the most important theologian since Thomas Aquinas. By any measure, Karl Barth has had a profound influence on modern Christian leaders and scholars across a wide variety of traditions.

Student days and faith crisis

Barth was born in 1886, at the height of liberal theology's influence in Europe. He was a student-disciple of Wilhelm Herrmann (1846-1922), a leading proponent of what was described as self-authenticating religious experience in German Protestant thought. Barth wrote of him, "Herrmann was *the* theological teacher of my student years." In these early years, Barth also followed the liberal teachings of German theologian Friedrich Schleiermacher (1768-1834). "I was inclined to believe him blindly," he wrote.

Barth served as pastor for the Reformed congregation of Safenwil, Switzerland, between 1911 and 1921. In August 1914 his liberal Christian belief system "was shaken to the foundations" by a manifesto signed by 93 German intellectuals in support of Kaiser Wilhelm II's military aspirations. The liberal theology professors Barth venerated were among the group. "I could not any longer follow either their ethics and dogmatics or their understanding of the Bible and of history," he said.

Barth believed his teachers had betrayed the Christian faith. "When the Christian gospel was changed into a statement, a religion, about Christian self-awareness, the God was lost sight of who in His sovereignty confronts man, calling him to account, and dealing with him as Lord."

Eduard Thurneysen (1888-1974), pastor from a nearby village and Barth's close friend from their student days, experienced a similar faith crisis. One day, Thurneysen whispered to Barth, "What we need for preaching, instruction and pastoral care is a 'wholly other' theological foundation."

Together they struggled to find a new basis for Christian theology. "We tried to learn our theological ABC all over again...by reading and interpreting the writing of the Old and New Testaments, more thoughtfully than before" and "they began to speak to us." A return to gospel basics was needed. "We must begin all over again with a new *inner* orientation," he concluded, "recognizing God once more as God."

Romans and Church Dogmatics

Barth's ground-breaking commentary, *The Epistle to the Romans,* first appeared in 1919 and was completely rewritten for a 1922 edition. His reworked *Romans* introduced a bold new theological system "concerned quite simply with *God* in his independent sovereignty over against man, and especially the religious man."

Barth found a "new world" in Paul's letter to the Romans and in other scriptures that spoke "not the right human thoughts about God but the right divine thoughts about men." He declared God as "the wholly other" — beyond our comprehension, hidden from us, alien to our sensibilities — knowable only in Christ. Barth said "God's very *deity,* rightly understood, includes his *humanity,*" and should be thought of as "a doctrine of God and man."

In 1921 Barth was appointed to the position of professor of Reformed theology at the University of Göttingen, where he taught until 1925. There he lectured on dogmatics, which he described as "reflection on the Word of God as revelation, holy scripture *and Christian preaching...*as it is actually given."

Barth became professor of dogmatics and New Testament exegesis at the University of Münster in July 1925 and five years later was appointed to the chair of systematic theology at Bonn, a position he held until 1935. In 1932, Barth published the first section of his *Church Dogmatics.* The new work grew year by year out of his class lectures.

The *Dogmatics* has four "volumes," each in two or more part-volumes or sections and consists of 13 separate books in English, in 8,000 pages and 6 million words. Barth planned five volumes, one for each of the major doctrines of the faith: Revelation or the Word of God (CD I), God (CD II), Creation (CD III), Reconciliation (CD IV), and Redemption (CD V). He was unable to complete the Reconciliation volume, and the Redemption volume remained unwritten at his death.

Thomas F. Torrance described Barth's *Dogmatics* as "far and away the most original and remarkable contribution to systematic theology that the modern age has seen." He called CD II, parts 1 and 2 "the high point of Barth's *Dogmatics,*" especially "his doctrine of God as *being-in-his-act and act-in-his-being.*" Torrance believed CD IV to be "the most powerful work on the doctrine of atoning reconciliation ever written."

Christ: elected one and elector

Barth challenged the full range of Christian doctrine, reinterpreting existing theology in the light of the Incarnation. He said: "My new task was to rethink everything that I had said before…as a theology of the grace of God in Jesus Christ." Barth sought to position Christian preaching as an activity that proclaims "the mighty acts of God" rather it being "a proclamation of the acts and words of man."

Christ is the center of the *Dogmatics* from beginning to end. "Karl Barth was a *Christian* theologian, one concerned above all with the *uniqueness and centrality of Christ and his Gospel*," according to Torrance. Barth said, "If one goes wrong here, one is wrong all along the line." This starting point in Christ kept him free from entrapment in "natural theology," the idea that man "has a legitimate authority of his own over the message and the form of the church."

Barth insisted that Christ is the revealing and reconciling address of God to man, and as Thomas Torrance explained, "the place where we know the *Father*." "God is known only through God," Barth would say. True talk about God exists "when it conforms to Jesus Christ." Barth insisted that "between God and man there stands the person of Jesus Christ, Himself God and Himself man, and so mediating between the two." For Barth, it is in Christ that "God reveals Himself to man. In Him man sees and knows God."

Barth declared "the divine predestination" to be "the election of Jesus Christ" with "a double reference — to the elector and to the elected." Jesus Christ is "the electing God" and "also elected man." Election, then, has to do wholly with Jesus Christ, in whose election we are elected by him to share. "In the light of the election of the man Jesus, all election can be described only as free grace," Barth concluded.

Before and after World War II

Barth's teaching years at Bonn coincided with Adolph Hitler's rise to national power. The Protestant church in Germany, the "German Christians," supported Hitler, believing the *Führer* was sent by God to rescue the nation. In April 1933 the "Evangelical Church of the German Nation" was created on the idea that the German ethos "about race, blood, soil, people, state" was a second basis and source of revelation for the church. In response, the Confessing Church was formed, utterly rejecting this nationalist, human-based ideology, with Barth as one of its leaders.

The church produced the May 1934 Barmen Declaration, mostly written by Barth and echoing his Christ-centered theology. The Declaration in six statements called on the church to give faithful allegiance to Jesus Christ rather than to human powers and authorities. As Barth would say, "There is no different source of church proclamation from this one Word of God."

Barth was suspended from teaching at Bonn in November 1934 for refusing to sign an unqualified oath of loyalty to Adolph Hitler. Formally dismissed from his position in June 1935, he was immediately offered the chair of theology at the University of Basel, Switzerland, a post he held until his retirement in 1962.

Barth was invited back to Bonn in post-war 1946, where he delivered a series of lectures published the following year as *Dogmatics in Outline*. The book, using the Apostles' Creed as a framework, discussed themes he had developed in his massive *Church Dogmatics*.

In 1962, Barth visited the USA, lecturing at Princeton Theological Seminary and the University of Chicago. According to church lore, during his trip he was asked to summarize the theological meaning of the millions of words in the *Church Dogmatics*. Barth thought for a moment and said: "Jesus loves me, this I know, for the Bible tells me so." Whether or not he actually said this, it is the way Barth would often answer a question. It undergirds his understanding that at its heart the gospel is a simple message pointing to Christ as our Savior who loves us with a perfect, godly love.

Barth did not consider his revolutionary *Dogmatics* as the last word in theology, but "as the opening of a new conversation." He mused about the ultimate importance of this work: "I shall be able to dump even the *Church Dogmatics*...on some heavenly floor as a pile of waste paper." He concluded in his last lectures that his theological insights would require rethinking in the future because the Church "is directed every day, indeed every hour, to begin again *at the beginning*." Karl Barth died in Basel on December 10, 1968 at the age of 82.

Sources used

Karl Barth, *The Humanity of God* (Westminster John Knox Press, 1960).

Karl Barth, *Church Dogmatics*, Vol. I.1, edited by G. W. Bromiley and T. F. Torrance (T&T Clark, 1975).

Eberhard Busch, *Karl Barth: His Life from Letters and Autobiographical Texts* (William B. Eerdmans, 1975).

Thomas F. Torrance, *Karl Barth: Biblical and Evangelical Theologian* (T&T Clark, 1991).

Paul Kroll

117. THE PROTESTANT CHURCH IN HITLER'S GERMANY AND THE BARMEN DECLARATION

On January 30, 1933, German President Paul von Hindenburg appointed Adolf Hitler Chancellor of Germany. Less than two months later, Hitler was the nation's dictator. Many German Christians at first openly welcomed Hitler's Nazi party to power as a historic moment of Christ's work on earth through and for the Aryan people. A leading Lutheran theologian wrote in 1934, "Our Protestant churches have welcomed the turning point of 1933 as a gift and miracle of God."

A "faith party" of "German Christians" began to develop and grow in influence. In their first national convention in April 1933, in Berlin, the delegates stated their goal to reorganize the 27 Protestant regional churches in Germany into a single, national church under the leadership of a national bishop.

The "German Christians" published a number of programmatic papers during 1932-1933 that give us an insight into their hopes and goals. They wanted a church rooted in German nationhood based on an Aryan model. "We want a vital national Church that will express all the spiritual forces of our people," stated one "German Christian" document from 1932.

On June 28, 1933, with Hitler's authorization, Ludwig Müller, a fervent Nazi, took over chairmanship of the council of the Federation of the 27 regional Protestant churches. A new constitution established a single "Protestant Reich Church." On September 27, 1933, Müller was elected national bishop by a synod dominated by "German Christians."

Restrictions were immediately placed on the clergy. They had to be "politically reliable" and accept the superiority of the Aryan race. Pressure was exerted to expel Jewish Christians from ministry. The Nazi "Führer Principle" was to be adopted by the churches, which was a claim that Hitler was "lord" over the German church and that its Christ and Christianity were uniquely Aryan.

Confessing church and Barmen

Some German Protestant pastors, led by Martin Niemöller (1892-1984), stood in opposition to the "German Christians." In September 1933, Niemöller sent a letter to all German pastors, inviting them to join a Pastors' Emergency League. Niemöller asked the pastors to pledge themselves to be bound to Christ as Lord, teach the gospel message of the Scriptures and the historic Confessions of the Church. Aryanism, a doctrine of racial superiority, was to be rejected as an anti-Christian teaching.

In April 1934, the League created the Confessing Church. It included ministers and churchmen from Reformed, Lutheran and United Churches, as well as other church groups. The Confessing Church took its name from the fact that its members had pledged themselves to affirm the great historic Confessions of the Church.

The leaders of the Confessing Church met on May 29-31, 1934, at Barmen. Here they issued the historic Barmen Declaration, drafted by Reformed theologian Karl Barth (1886-1968) and Lutheran theologian Hans Asmussen, with input from other Lutheran, Reformed and United Churches leaders.

The Declaration was written in direct opposition to the national church government — the "Faith Movement of the German Christians" — rather than against the Nazi regime itself. It challenged Christians who were attempting to bring the Protestant church into line with the nationalistic ideals and aspirations of Nazi rule. However, since the "German Christians" were a proxy for the Nazi state, the Declaration became also a condemnation of Hitler's totalitarian rule.

The Barmen Declaration asserts that Christ alone is the one Word of God — the source of all authority and truth — whom we must hear, trust and obey. It rejects the notion that other powers apart from Christ could be sources of God's revelation. It stands on the principle that Christ cannot be co-opted by, used in the service of, or be remade in the image of religious or political ideologies created by fallen human beings and structures in opposition to God. Barmen confesses the reality that God's grace for us cannot be reinterpreted or replaced by ideas and programs growing out of human creaturely self-interest and evil designs.

In these ways, Barmen speaks not only to the times and crisis of the church in Nazi Germany, but to Christians throughout the history of the church and in our time and place.

Paul Kroll

118. ONE 'MERE CHRISTIAN' IN CHURCH HISTORY: CLIVE STAPLES LEWIS

He was listed as one of the 10 most influential Christians of the 20th century by *Christian History* magazine, along with such people as Karl Barth, Pope John XXIII, Billy Graham and Martin Luther King Jr. The magazine called him "the atheist scholar who became an Anglican, an apologist, and a 'patron saint' of Christians everywhere."

He has also been described as "one of the best loved 20th century Christian apologists" and the "apostle to the skeptics" because he decisively answered common objections people throw up against accepting Christ as Savior. This individual was chosen for a 1947 *Time* magazine cover because he, having been perceived as a secular academic, was affirming publicly his Christian faith in his writings, on radio and in his relationships with others. By now, many of you know this person is Clive Staples Lewis (1898-1963), or C.S. Lewis, as he is popularly known.

His varied background

Lewis, called "Jack" by his friends and family, was a distinguished professor at Oxford and Cambridge universities, renowned literary critic, and highly acclaimed author of science fiction and children's literature. His best-known work in this genre is the children's adventure tale, the *Chronicles of Narnia,* which retells the story of the Creation, the Fall and redemption of humanity and contains other Christian themes in allegorical form. Lewis' 25 books on Christian topics include *Mere Christianity* (1952), *The Problem of Pain* (1940), *Miracles* (1947), *The Screwtape Letters* (1942), *Surprised by Joy* (1955) and *The Great Divorce* (1945). *The Pilgrim's Regress* (1933) was a thinly disguised story of his personal road to conversion.

Between 1942 and 1944, Lewis went on British radio at the request of the director of religious broadcasting for the British Broadcasting Corporation (BBC). Lewis gave a number of talks in those years on what he called "mere Christianity," the common or central beliefs of the faith. The popular weekly broadcasts reached a wide audience of receptive Brits in the dark years of World War II. The collection of radio talks were later brought together in one of Lewis' most influential books, *Mere Christianity.*

One of Lewis' most-often-quoted statements is from *Mere Christianity,* where he insists that people are confronted with three choices by Jesus' claims about himself. Thinking of Jesus as a profound moral teacher will not do, said Lewis. People must decide whether he is a liar, lunatic or the Lord, as he claims:

A man who was merely a man and said the sort of things Jesus said would not be a great moral teacher. He would either be a lunatic — on the level with a man who says he is a poached egg — or else he would be the devil of hell. You must make your choice. Either this man was, and is, the Son of God: or else a madman or something worse. You can shut him up for a fool, you can spit at him and kill him as a demon; or you can fall at his feet and call him Lord and God. But let us not come with any patronizing nonsense about his being a great human teacher. He has not left that open to us. He did not intend to.

Becoming a Christian

What is most fascinating about Lewis, especially to evangelical Christians, is the story of his own conversion. The history of the church is a history of human beings who in one way or another at various stages of their lives encountered the risen Lord and responded with a "Yes, Lord, I will" to his "Yes, come." The church is the sum total of men, women and children who have been enabled by the Father to be drawn to Jesus Christ through the Spirit (John 6:44, 65). Most of their names are unknown to us, and so are their conversion stories. But we are fortunate to know C.S. Lewis' testimony because he has told it to us in his writings, especially in *Surprised by Joy*.

God works in many and diverse ways to bring his children to Christ — and he draws people to himself from all walks of life, cultures, intelligence rankings, ages, races and social levels. The Lord came to C.S. Lewis over several ways in a "small, still voice," using various means — especially intellectual ones — to reach him. His conversion story is one example of how Christ has built his church over the centuries and continues to build it today.

C.S. Lewis was born into a Protestant family in Belfast, today Northern Ireland, on Nov. 29, 1898. He endured an unhappy and lonely childhood. He was especially crushed by the unexpected death of his mother from cancer when he was less than 10 years old. Her death left a hole in his heart and caused him to be disillusioned about God's nearness. He rejected any Christian beliefs he might have had, even as a youth, and became an avowed atheist. When asked at age 18 what his religious views were, he called the worship of Christ and the Christian faith "one mythology among many." By the time he had served in the British army on the front lines of France during World War I and began his studies at Oxford University as a student, now barely 20, he was a thorough-going materialist.

Lewis had been a voracious reader of what we would call good books. What he didn't know was that Christ was beckoning him through his reading, slowly drawing the young man to himself.

Lewis was greatly influenced by two writers, George MacDonald, the 19th century Scottish Presbyterian minister and novelist, and G.K. Chesterton, a Christian apologist and London journalist. "In reading Chesterton, as in reading MacDonald," he wrote in *Surprised by Joy,* "I did not know what I was letting myself in for. A young man who wishes to remain a sound Atheist cannot be too careful of his reading. There are traps everywhere…. God is, if I may say it, very unscrupulous."

Lewis' close friends also played a vital role in causing his heart to be open to Christ's love through their talks with him about Christianity and Christ. One was Owen Barfield, who had also trod the road from atheism to theism and finally to Christ. Another was Nevill Coghill, who Lewis was amazed to discover was a Christian. Two close friends on the English faculty at Oxford's Magdalen College, where Lewis also taught, Hugo Dyson and J.R.R. Tolkien, were also among a group of diverse people who witnessed the Lord to Lewis.

Finding God

In 1929 C.S. Lewis found himself challenged with God's existence. This important milestone in his conversion journey was reached suddenly. As he tells the story, on one occasion during this time he happened to take a bus ride. When he got on the bus he was an atheist. When he came to his stop, he got off the bus believing in God's existence. Not that Lewis was seeking God. He said he didn't really want to find him. The revelation about God's existence was something of a fright to him. He wrote in *Surprised by Joy:* "Amiable agnostics will talk cheerfully about 'man's search for God.' To me, as I then was, they might as well have talked about the mouse's search for the cat."

But God was seeking C.S. Lewis and he found him. His call was coming and Lewis could find no place to hide. As Jonah running from the Lord, Lewis had been confronted with his own great "whale," so to speak. It was God beckoning to him. The reluctant prodigal finally knew it was time to come home. In *Surprised by Joy,* Lewis tells us about his feelings when he could no longer deny God's existence to himself:

> You must picture me alone in that room in Magdalen, night after night, feeling, whenever my mind lifted even for a second from my work, the steady, unrelenting approach of Him whom I so earnestly desired not to meet. That which I greatly feared had at last come upon me. In the Trinity Term of 1929 I gave in, and admitted that God was God, and knelt and prayed: perhaps, that night, the most dejected and reluctant convert in all England…. But who can duly adore that Love

which will open the high gates to a prodigal who is brought in kicking, struggling, resentful, and darting his eyes in every direction for a chance to escape.

When God drew Lewis' heart to himself, he became conscious of the presence of his own sinfulness. "For the first time I examined myself with a seriously practical purpose," wrote Lewis. "And there I found what appalled me: a zoo of lusts, a bedlam of ambitions, a nursery of fears, a harem of fondled hatreds. My name is legion."

When Christ comes calling

Though Lewis was frightened by what he saw in himself, the Holy Spirit would open Lewis' heart and mind to Christ's forgiveness and love. It happened in September 1931 when Lewis was converted to the faith. He had engaged in a lengthy conversation about Christianity with J.R.R. Tolkien and Hugo Dyson that started with dinner on the 19th and continued into the early morning hours of the 20th. The discussion challenged Lewis' thinking and set the stage for what happened two days later.

It was on Sept. 22, 1931 that Lewis said yes to the Lord's offer of himself —according to his testimony, this was the exact day he became a Christian. It happened on a ride to the Whipsnade Zoo with his brother, Warren. Lewis tells about it in his book, *Surprised by Joy:* "I know very well when, but hardly how, the final step was taken. I was driven to Whipsnade one sunny morning. When we set out I did not believe that Jesus Christ is the Son of God, and when we reached the zoo I did. Yet I had not exactly spent the journey in thought. Nor in great emotion…. It was more like when a man, after long sleep, still lying motionless in bed, becomes aware that he is now awake."

One recalls the experience of the apostle Paul, who was also on a road trip, in his case from Jerusalem to Damascus. When Paul started out for Damascus, he did not know the Lord. As a rabbi, he had a strong belief in the God of Israel. But he had not yet been encountered by the living Christ. When he started his journey he did not know Christ, but when he arrived at his destination at Damascus, he was a converted disciple of the Lord (Acts 9:1-20).

Lewis was not struck down with blindness on the road to the zoo and didn't hear the risen Christ audibly speaking to him. Nevertheless, the still quiet voice of Jesus had been dramatically impacting his mind and heart for some time, bringing him to the opportunity to utter the final yes. In *Surprised by Joy,* Lewis described that final time before he put his faith in Christ as a period of free and enlightened choice:

The odd thing was that before God closed in on me, I was in fact offered what now appears a moment of wholly free choice.... I became aware that I was holding something at bay, or shutting something out.... I felt myself being, there and then, given a free choice. I could open the door or keep it shut; I could unbuckle the armor or keep it on. Neither choice was presented as a duty; no threat or promise was attached to either, though I knew that to open the door or to take off the corslet meant the incalculable.

On Christmas Day 1931, C.S. Lewis joined the Anglican Church and took communion. For the next three decades he devoted much of his time to writing and speaking about Christ and the Christian faith. He had truly become a disciple of Christ who makes disciples. After several months of ill health and intermittent recovery, Lewis died peacefully on Nov. 22, 1963 — on the same day that U.S. President John F. Kennedy was assassinated.

Paul Kroll

119. VATICAN II
AND THE FUTURE OF CHURCH UNITY

On October 11, 1962, twenty-four hundred Roman Catholic bishops marched phalanx-style in rows of six through St. Peter's Square. Behind them strode the College of Cardinals, followed by Pope John XXIII, seated in a massive chair and carried by attendants. The entourage went into the splendid basilica, and the prelates took their seats. Across the aisle sat observers from other Christian faiths, invited by the Pope to attend the proceedings. The Second Vatican Council — the 21st ecumenical council recognized by the Roman Catholic Church — was about to begin.

Vatican II was the largest council gathering in the church's history. The Council held 178 meetings in four successive years, adjourning Dec. 8, 1965. It produced 16 official documents. Several focused on ecumenism and unity with non-Catholic Christians. Pope John XXIII died in 1963, after the first session. The newly elected Pope Paul VI continued Vatican II with the same goals John had proclaimed.

Inside Vatican II

Vatican II transformed the church's internal life[1] and inaugurated a new era in its relationships with non-Catholics. For the first time, Protestants and Eastern Orthodox were regarded as "separated brethren."

The Council acknowledged in its Decree on Ecumenism that the Holy Spirit was active in non-Catholic Christian communities. It said all who have been baptized and justified by faith "are members of Christ's body, and have a right to be called Christian" and "brothers" by the Catholic Church.

The same decree devoted a section to the strong family relationship — as "sister Churches" — that the Catholic Church believes exists between itself and the Eastern Orthodox Churches.

Great and present divide

Catholics and other Christians have always been in general agreement on essential teachings of their common faith — God's Trinitarian nature, the divinity of Christ, the Incarnation, Resurrection and Second Coming, and reverence for God's word.

However, it cannot be denied that deep-seated differences — doctrinal, historical, cultural and emotional — continue to divide them. "We have no illusions that the centuries-long wounds of our divisions will be quickly or easily healed," wrote Charles Colson, a Protestant, and Richard John Neuhaus, a Catholic. Problematic Catholic beliefs, especially to Protestants, include:

- Papal authority and infallibility.
- Means of grace and role of the church's sacraments.
- Relationship between Scripture and Roman Catholic tradition.
- Purgatory and devotions to the saints.
- Devotion to the Virgin Mary, her immaculate conception and bodily assumption.
- The real presence of Christ in the Eucharist.
- Identity of the Church as perceived by Catholic dogma.

In 2007, Pope Benedict XVI released a document prepared by the Vatican's Congregation for the Doctrine of the Faith. The brief document in the form of five questions and answers reaffirmed "the full identity of the Church of Christ with the Catholic Church." Other churches were said to be "separated churches and Communities." The document stated that though "the Spirit of Christ has not refrained from using them as instruments of salvation," they "suffer from defects." The Orthodox ("oriental") churches are considered to be "separated from full communion with the Catholic Church." Nevertheless, they "have true sacraments" and "the apostolic succession," and are therefore considered "sister Churches."

Many Protestant leaders immediately roundly criticized the statement, with some claiming that ecumenism had been set back to a time before Vatican II. The document itself stated that the Vatican remained committed to ecumenical dialogue. There was little new in the 2007 document; Benedict had said much the same thing in a 2000 document, "Dominus Iesus."

Perhaps some Protestants were in denial of what the Catholic Church believes about itself. The Vatican II Council statements, as the recent document notes, "neither changed nor intended to change" the Catholic doctrine of the church. The Catholic Church has always understood itself to be the one church "Christ 'established here on earth'."

Vatican II altered Catholic Church life in many fundamental ways and opened up dialogue between Catholics, Protestants and Orthodox churches with a new openness. However, Benedict's recent reassertion of Roman Catholic primacy has created a sense of realism among Protestants. How much headway in dialogue and ecumenism can be made in the future is anyone's guess.

[1] One example was Vatican II's institution of common-language forms of the Latin mass. In 2007, Pope Benedict XVI authorized a wider use of the Latin version, which had been marginalized by the council's decision.

Paul Kroll

120. THE LIFE AND TIMES OF MARTIN LUTHER KING JR.
1929-1968

Martin Luther King Jr. was a major leader of the U.S. civil rights movement beginning in the mid-1950s. Americans celebrate his birthday as a national holiday each January, recalling the struggle to end racism and bigotry in America. King was an eloquent Baptist minister who advocated and participated in nonviolent means to achieve civil right for blacks and equality for all.

King received a bachelor of divinity degree from Crozier Theological Seminary in 1951 and earned a doctor of philosophy degree from Boston University in 1955. He came from a long line of Baptist ministers. His father was pastor of Atlanta's Ebenezer Baptist Church, and in 1960, King moved to the city to pastor his father's congregation. King was chosen as the first president of the Southern Christian Leadership Conference in 1957.

In 1963, he was jailed in Birmingham, Alabama, after a nonviolent protest that led to a confrontation with Public Safety Commissioner "Bull" Connor and municipal authorities. While in jail, King was criticized by a group of white clergymen who blamed him for inciting the violence and who voiced concerns about his civil rights strategy. It was then that he penned his "Letter From a Birmingham Jail." King ended his letter with these words:

> I hope this letter finds you strong in the faith. I also hope that circumstances will soon make it possible for me to meet each of you, not as an integrationist or a civil rights leader but as a fellow clergyman and a Christian brother. Let us all hope that the dark clouds of racial prejudice will soon pass away and the deep fog of misunderstanding will be lifted from our fear-drenched communities, and in some not too distant tomorrow the radiant stars of love and brotherhood will shine over our great nation with all their scintillating beauty.

King's most soaring and hopeful civil rights plea came in August 1963 on the steps of the Lincoln Memorial in Washington, D.C. Here he delivered his rallying "I Have a Dream" speech."

For his work to end segregation and discrimination, King was awarded the Nobel Peace Prize in 1964. King was only 35 years old when he accepted the prize on behalf of all who participated in the Civil Rights Movement, making him the youngest recipient of the award at the time.

But the seeds of human hatred and bitterness cut short King's life less than four years later. On April 4, 1968, while standing on the balcony of the Lorraine Motel in Memphis, Tennessee, he was shot to death by James Earl Ray. King was only 39 years old. Though he did not waver from his position and practice that nonviolence must remain the approach of the civil rights movement, he died a martyr's death from an assassin's bullet.

Paul Kroll

121. BILLY GRAHAM:
EVANGELIST TO THE WORLD

My one purpose in life is to help people find a personal relationship with God, which, I believe, comes through knowing Christ. —Billy Graham

Graham's evangelistic tours in America and around the world awakened many people to the need for a spiritual rebirth and a personal relationship with Jesus. It is estimated that some three million people responded to Graham's offer at the end of his campaign sermons to come forward and accept Christ. Graham reached countless other millions with the gospel of Christ through television specials, satellite crusades, radio ministries, motion pictures, a literature ministry, and the books he wrote. Training ministries and seminars have equipped thousands of grass-roots evangelists in large-scale and one-on-one evangelism.

Graham met with the pope, the queen, several prime ministers and kings and celebrities. He met every U.S. president from Dwight Eisenhower to Barack Obama. Graham has often been called on to serve as "America's pastor," helping to inaugurate or bury a president or otherwise lend a public voice of assurance in times of tragedy or crisis.

Early life and education

William Franklin ("Billy") Graham, Jr. was born November 7, 1918, near Charlotte, North Carolina, the eldest of four children. His parents regularly attended the Associate Reformed Presbyterian Church with the children. While attending revival meetings in Charlotte at age 16, Graham experienced conversion, committing his life to Christ. He changed his denominational affiliation to the Southern Baptist Convention in 1938 and was ordained the next year as a Baptist minister in the St. John's River Association.

From 1936 through 1943, Graham attended three different Christian colleges. He stayed at the ultraconservative Bob Jones College in Tennessee for only a few months, graduated from the Florida Bible Institute in 1940 with a Bachelor of Theology degree and from Wheaton College in Illinois in 1943 with a B.A. in anthropology.

At Wheaton he courted fellow student Ruth Bell. The couple married on August 13, 1943. After graduation, Graham served for a little over a year as the pastor of a Baptist church in the Chicago suburb of Western Springs.[1] In 1945 Graham became the field representative of a dynamic evangelistic movement, Youth for Christ International. For the next four years, Graham traveled throughout the United States, Canada and Europe speaking at rallies and organizing YFC chapters.

Evangelistic missions

Graham gained sudden national attention in 1949 with a seven-week tent revival campaign in downtown Los Angeles attended by 350,000. Graham said of the Los Angeles tent campaign: "Overnight we had gone from being a little evangelistic team...to what appeared to many to be the hope for national and international revival."[2]

In part, Graham gained national attention because newspaper magnate William Randolph Hearst instructed his newspapers across the country to "puff Graham." Other newspapers and the Associated Press also picked up the story of his evangelistic rally. Newsreels of the campaign began to appear in theaters.

Graham launched his worldwide ministry with his 1954 London campaign, supported by a thousand churches in the greater metropolitan area. More than two million people heard Graham speak during his three-month-long series of sermons, and thousands came to Christ. The outstanding success of the Greater London Crusade[3] helped establish the validity and scope of Graham's international ministry.

Graham's successful 1957 New York City evangelistic campaign established him as the acknowledged standard-bearer for evangelical Christianity. At the 16-week rally in New York City, almost 2.4 million people packed Madison Square Garden and other venues and events to hear the young preacher. It is estimated that 96 million people saw at least one of the Madison Square Garden meetings on television. "That experience showed us that God was opening the door to a new medium for the furtherance of the Gospel," said Graham.[4]

Those are but three examples of hundreds of evangelistic campaigns through the decades that Graham has organized and led. He has preached the gospel to more people in more nations and territories before live audiences than anyone else in history — more than 210 million people in over 185 nations.

Creating a sure footing for evangelism

As Graham's fame increased, so did criticism of his evangelistic style. Some branded him a real-life "Elmer Gantry" preacher, after the 1925 Sinclair Lewis novel and 1960 film about a salesman who teams up with a female evangelist to sell religion to America in the 1920s. To counter such complaints he knew were sure to come, early on in 1948, Graham and his associates created "The Modesto Manifesto." They determined to avoid behavior that failed to reflect Christian values and gave evangelists a bad name.

The Manifesto dealt with the problem of evangelists falling into the trap of seeking financial self-enrichment and indulging in sexual immorality. Adherence to strict ethical standards allowed Graham to remain untouched by the sensational financial and sexual scandals that embroiled prominent television preachers during the 1980s.

Fundamentalists would accuse Graham of corrupting the gospel message by accepting help and support from mainline Protestant denominations and liberal Christian clergy. Despite the criticism, he was determined to seek a broad base of ecumenical support for his evangelistic campaigns. Graham once said, "I intend to go anywhere, sponsored by anybody, to preach the gospel of Christ, if there are no strings attached to my message."[5]

To enable his ministry to run on an orderly, businesslike basis, Graham, his wife and a number of key people in his ministry incorporated as the Billy Graham Evangelistic Association (BGEA) in 1950.

The role of the BGEA

The heart of the BGEA program was the mass evangelistic mission events that Graham led with fellow evangelists and in partnership with churches around the world. They are now chiefly conducted by his son, William Franklin Graham III, who has stepped into his father's shoes as president of BGEA (since 2001).

Graham's evangelistic campaigns have always been meticulously planned and organized down to practical details such as recruiting choir members, ushers and counselors. The BGEA sends out teams of workers to assist communities planning to hold evangelistic meetings. The organization holds rallies only where they have been invited by a large number of local pastors and churches.

People coming forward to accept Christ at the evangelist's service-ending invitation meet with volunteer counselors, who refer them to participating pastors in their community. BGEA's follow-up programs have proved successful. According to surveys, 70-80 percent of those converted at evangelistic missions remain committed Christians.

In 1992 the BGEA announced that Graham had Parkinson's disease and would be less involved in mission activities. He described his goal: "Whatever strength I have, whatever time God lets me have, is going to be dedicated to doing the work of an evangelist, as long as I live."[6] He died in 2018.

The Billy Graham Library

The Billy Graham Library in Charlotte, North Carolina, was dedicated on May 31, 2007 on the grounds of the international headquarters of the Billy Graham Evangelistic Association (BGEA). Though ill and infirm, 88-year-old Billy Graham was on hand for the festivities and briefly addressed the 1,500 guests. Former presidents George H.W. Bush, Jimmy Carter and Bill Clinton also spoke at the opening of the $27 million dollar, 40,000-square-foot complex.

Graham's son, Franklin, explained the purpose of the Library, pointing out that his father didn't want "too much of Billy Graham in it." He wanted it to reflect the message of the gospel he had preached for 60 years. Graham, speaking from in front of the Library, repeated this hope in his address. "The building behind me is just a building," he said. "It's an instrument; it's a tool of the gospel."

The Library complex includes innovative multimedia exhibits, a theater, bookstore and rustic café. Visitors can take an inspiring tour through six decades of the evangelistic work of Billy Graham and the BGEA, bringing the gospel to people of all walks of life. The cavernous lobby of the structure is styled after a dairy barn to highlight Graham's upbringing on a farm only four miles away.

The Library is open to the public free of charge. For information about the library, please visit the website www.billygrahamlibrary.org/.

----

1 Graham and his wife, Ruth, had three daughters, two sons, 19 grandchildren and many great grandchildren.

2 Billy Graham, *Just As I Am* (HarperCollins, 1997), p. 158.

3 Graham's evangelistic rallies, called "crusades" for many years, are now referred to as "missions."

4 *Just As I Am*, p. 323.

5 "Billy Graham: Evangelist to Millions," http://www.christianitytoday.com/ch/131christians/evangelistsanda pologists/graham.html.

6 Ibid.

Paul Kroll

ABOUT THE AUTHORS...

Charles A. Calahan earned a doctorate in family life education and consultation at Kansas State University. He was pastor of a GCI church in Kansas when he wrote his articles.

Russell Duke earned his PhD at Union University in Ohio. He was the founding president of Grace Communion Seminary and is now an adjunct faculty member of GCS.

J. Michael Feazell has a D.Min. degree from Azusa Pacific Seminary. He was vice president of Grace Communion International.

Sheila Graham was a writer and editor for Grace Communion International. She is the author of one of our most popular articles, on the Proverbs 31 woman.

John Halford was the editor of *Christian Odyssey* magazine and the author of numerous articles. He died in 2014.

Bill Hall is a district superintendent in GCI Canada.

Ted Johnston works with GCI U.S. Church Administration and teaches at Grace Communion Seminary.

Paul Kroll is a now-retired journalist and researcher for Grace Communion International.

Michael Morrison received a PhD from Fuller Theological Seminary in 2006. He is now Dean of Faculty at Grace Communion Seminary, author of several books, numerous e-books, and is the editor of this book.

Ralph Orr was a pastor, research, and writer for Grace Communion International.

Rick Shallenberger is a pastor and district superintendent for Grace Communion International.

Norman Shoaf was the editor of *The Good News* magazine, published by the Worldwide Church of God.

Brenda Steffen wrote articles for *Christian Odyssey* magazine.

Keith Stump wrote for magazines and telecasts of the Worldwide Church of God.

Joseph Tkach has been, since 1995, the president of Grace Communion International. He earned a D.Min. degree from Azusa Pacific Seminary in 2000.

Greg Williams is the director of U.S. Church Administration & Development for Grace Communion International. He has a D.Min. degree from Drew University.

G. Albrecht, Randal Dick, Donald Jackson, Don Mears and **Ken Williams** were elders in Grace Communion International; their articles were originally printed in GCI publications. **Shane Bazer** was prayer ministry coordinator for a GCI church in North Carolina.

ABOUT THE PUBLISHER...

Grace Communion International is a Christian denomination with about 50,000 members, worshiping in about 900 congregations in almost 100 nations and territories. We began in 1934 and our main office is in North Carolina. In the United States, we are members of the National Association of Evangelicals and similar organizations in other nations. We welcome you to visit our website at www.gci.org.

If you want to know more about the gospel of Jesus Christ, we offer help. First, we offer weekly worship services in hundreds of congregations worldwide. Perhaps you'd like to visit us. A typical worship service includes songs of praise, a message based on the Bible, and opportunity to meet people who have found Jesus Christ to be the answer to their spiritual quest. We try to be friendly, but without putting you on the spot. We do not expect visitors to give offerings – there's no obligation. You are a guest.

To find a congregation, write to one of our offices, phone us or visit our website. If we do not have a congregation near you, we encourage you to find another Christian church that teaches the gospel of grace.

We also offer personal counsel. If you have questions about the Bible, salvation or Christian living, we are happy to talk. If you want to discuss faith, baptism or other matters, a pastor near you can discuss these on the phone or set up an appointment for a longer discussion. We are convinced that Jesus offers what people need most, and we are happy to share the good news of what he has done for all humanity. We like to help people find new life in Christ, and to grow in that life. Come and see why we believe it's the best news there could be!

Our work is funded by members of the church who donate part of their income to support the gospel. Jesus told his disciples to share the good news, and that is what we strive to do in our literature, in our worship services, and in our day-to-day lives.

If this book has helped you and you want to pay some expenses, all donations are gratefully welcomed, and in several nations, are tax-deductible. If you can't afford to give anything, don't worry about it. It is our gift to you. To donate online, go to www.gci.org/online-giving/.

Thank you for letting us share what we value most – Jesus Christ. The good news is too good to keep it to ourselves.

See our website for hundreds of articles, locations of our churches, addresses in various nations, audio and video messages, and much more.

www.gci.org
Grace Communion International
3120 Whitehall Park Dr.
Charlotte, NC 28273
800-423-4444

You're Included...

Dr. J. Michael Feazell talks to leading Trinitarian theologians about the good news that God loves you, wants you, and includes you in Jesus Christ. Most programs are about 28 minutes long. Our guests have included:

Cathy Deddo, Trinity Study Center
Gordon Fee, Regent College
C. Baxter Kruger, Perichoresis
Cherith Fee Nordling, Northern Seminary
Alan Torrance, University of St. Andrews
N.T. Wright, University of St. Andrews
William P. Young, author of *The Shack*

Programs are available free for viewing and downloading at www.youreincluded.org.

GRACE COMMUNION SEMINARY

Ministry based on the life and love of the Father, Son, and Spirit

Grace Communion Seminary serves the needs of people engaged in Christian service who want to grow deeper in relationship with our Triune God and to be able to more effectively serve in the church. We offer three degrees: Master of Pastoral Studies, Master of Theological Studies, and Master of Divinity.

Why study at Grace Communion Seminary?

- Worship: to love God with all your mind.
- Service: to help others apply truth to life.
- Practical: a balanced range of useful topics for ministry.
- Trinitarian theology: a survey of theology with the merits of a Trinitarian perspective. We begin with the question, "Who is God?" Then, "Who are we in relationship to God?" In this context, "How then do we serve?"
- Part-time study: designed to help people who are already serving in local congregations. There is no need to leave your current ministry. Full-time students are also welcome.
- Flexibility: your choice of master's level courses or pursuit of a degree.
- Affordable, accredited study: Everything can be done online.

For more information, go to www.gcs.edu.

Grace Communion Seminary is accredited by the Distance Education Accrediting Commission, www.deac.org. The Accrediting Commission is listed by the U.S. Department of Education as a nationally recognized accrediting agency.

AMBASSADOR COLLEGE
OF CHRISTIAN MINISTRY

Want to better understand God's Word? Want to know the Triune God more deeply? Want to share more joyously in the life of the Father, Son and Spirit? Want to be better equipped to serve others?

Among the many resources that Grace Communion International offers are the training and learning opportunities provided by ACCM. This quality, well-structured Christian Ministry curriculum has the advantage of being very practical and flexible. Students may study at their own pace, without having to leave home to undertake full-time study.

This denominationally recognized program is available for both credit and audit study. At minimum cost, this online Diploma program will help students gain important insights and training in effective ministry service. Students will also enjoy a rich resource for personal study that will enhance their understanding and relationship with the Triune God.

Diploma of Christian Ministry classes provide an excellent introductory course for new and lay pastors. Pastor General Dr. Joseph Tkach said, "We believe we have achieved the goal of designing Christian ministry training that is practical, accessible, interesting, and doctrinally and theologically mature and sound. This program provides an ideal foundation for effective Christian ministry."

For more information, go to www.ambascol.org

Made in the USA
Columbia, SC
14 March 2021